Participatory Rural Appraisal

Participatory Rural Appraisal

Principles, Methods and Application

N. Narayanasamy

Los Angeles • London • New Delhi • Singapore
www.sagepublications.com

First published in 2009 by

 SAGE Publications India Pvt Ltd
B1/I-1 Mohan Cooperative Industrial Area
Mathura Road, New Delhi 110 044, India
www.sagepub.in

SAGE Publications Inc
2455 Teller Road
Thousand Oaks, California 91320, USA

SAGE Publications Ltd
1 Oliver's Yard, 55 City Road
London EC1Y 1SP, United Kingdom

SAGE Publications Asia-Pacific Pte Ltd
33 Pekin Street
#02-01 Far East Square
Singapore 048763

Published by Vivek Mehra for SAGE Publications India Pvt Ltd, typeset in 10.5/12.5 pt Minion by Innovative Processors, New Delhi, and printed at Chaman Enterprises, New Delhi.

Library of Congress Cataloging-in-Publication Data Available

ISBN: 978-81-7829-885-6 (PB)

The SAGE Team: Elina Majumdar, Ankur Agarwal, Sanjeev Kumar Sharma and Trinankur Banerjee

To my Parents and Wife

Contents

List of Tables

List of Figures

List of Abbreviations

AD	Approach Development	FPR	Farmer Participatory Research
AE	Appreciative Enquiry	FSD	Farming System Diagnosis
AuE	Auto-evaluation	FSR	Farming System Research
AKRSP	Aga Khan Rural Support Programme	FYM	Farmyard Manure
		GRI	Gandhigram Rural Institute
APA	Appreciative Planning and Action	ICSSR	Indian Council for Social Sciences Research
ASSEFA	Association for Sarva Seva Farms		
BDO	Block Development Office	IDS	Institute of Development Studies
BE	Beneficiary Assessment	IFAD	International Funding for Agriculture Development
CAP	Community Action Planning		
CBOs	Community-based Organisations	IIED	International Institute for Environment and Development
CDP	Community Development Programme		
		IRDP	Integrated Rural Development Programme
CLF	Cluster-level Federation		
CM	Community Monitoring/Citizen Monitoring	KKF	Karl Kübel Foundation
		KVK	Krishi Vigyan Kendra
CPRs	Common Property Resources	LFA	Logical Framework Analysis
CSI	Civil Society Institution	MEP	Minimum Evaluation Procedure
CWDP	Comprehensive Watershed Development Programme	MLA	Member of Legislative Assembly
		MP	Member of Parliament
DANIDA	Danish International Development Agency	MPA	Methodology for Participatory Assessment
DRA	Demand Responsive Approach	MSSRF	M.S. Swaminathan Research Foundation
DRDA	District Rural Development Agency		
		MYRADA	Mysore Resettlement and Development Agency
FAO	Food and Agriculture Organization		
		NGOs	Non-governmental Organisations
FF	Farmers First	NSL	Now, Soon, Later
FFA	Force Field Analysis	PALM	Participatory Learning and Management
FGD	Focus Group Discussion		

PAME	Participatory Assessment, Monitoring and Evaluation		RAP	Rapid Assessment Procedure
PAR	Participatory Action Research		RDT	Rural Development Tourist
PARR	Participatory Action Reflection Research		REA	Rapid Ethnographic Assessment
PCM	Project Cycle Management		RRA	Rapid Rural Appraisal
PE	Participatory Evaluation		SA	Social Assessment
PHC	Primary Health Centre		SARAR	Self-esteem, Associative Strength, Resourcefulness, Action Planning and Responsibility
PI	Participatory Inquiry		SC/ST	Schedule Caste/Schedule Tribe
PIM	Participatory Impact Monitoring		SE	Self-evaluation
PLA	Participatory Learning and Action		SHGs	Self-help Groups
PM	Participatory Monitoring		SSI	Semi-structured Interview
PM&E	Participatory Monitoring and Evaluation		SWOT	Strengths, Weaknesses, Opportunities and Threats
PPA	Participatory Poverty Assessment		TD	Theatre for Development
PRA	Participatory Rural Appraisal		ToT	Transfer of Technology
PR&D	Participatory Research and Development		TWAD	Tamil Nadu Water and Drainage Board
Prom	Process Monitoring		VAO	Village Administrative Officer
PTD	Participatory Technology Development			

Preface

Community participation has become an indispensable and integral component of development initiatives at the grass roots. It has been conclusively proved that the effectiveness, success and sustainability of development initiatives largely depend on wholehearted participation of the stakeholders, particularly the primary ones. But the question remains about where we should introduce this critical element of participation in the development process. In order to help achieve the desired output and outcome, participation needs to be introduced right from the appraisal to the monitoring and evaluation stage. Participation at different stages of the development process makes the participants realise that they are a part and parcel of the development, which ultimately makes them 'own' the output and outcome of the development intervention.

Participation is a socio-psychological process. The urge to participate should come from within; it should not be forced from outside. However, it can be facilitated through indigenous processes, which are stimulated by internal motivation and guided by local organisations. Participatory rural appraisal (PRA), now known as participatory learning and action (PLA), with a repertoire of user-friendly, easy-to-follow methods, and with an emphasis on attitude and behaviour of the facilitators and development professionals, provides enough space and environment for people to actively participate at different stages of the development process. Practised initially by the NGOs in select spheres of activities, PRA has now spread rapidly. Due to the thrust given by the funding partners, it has now become not only a necessity but also a conditionality in many of the development projects. PRA is now practised by a galaxy of change agents, such as NGOs, universities, research institutions, training organisations, donor agencies, international aid agencies and government departments.

The Gandhigram Rural University (GRU) introduced PRA in the early 1990s. A team of staff at the university, well-trained in PRA, drawn from different disciplines, with rich hands-on experience in the field, has been consistently using PRA in its research, outreach and training programmes and development activities. Initially, PRA was used to appraise the socio-economic conditions of the people in the service villages where GRU rendered its services. Later, the team expanded its field of application to include agriculture, irrigation, animal husbandry, fisheries, education, environment, health, sanitation, water supply, livelihood analysis, AIDS/HIV, community-based organisations, tribal development, food and nutrition, micro-plan, micro-finance and monitoring and evaluation.

The team thus applied PRA in a multitude of settings. This experience largely helped them organise training sessions among a wide variety of clients using the principle of 'learning by doing'.

Much of this book is the outcome of collective efforts of the PRA team at GRU. This book is based on the field experience of the author and members of the PRA team at GRU. It has also drawn lessons from the experience of PRA practitioners in the Third World countries.

The book comprises twenty-two chapters. The first two chapters deal with the origin, concept and principles of PRA. Chapters 3–20 deal with the methods of PRA. Each method is described in detail, explaining the concept, the procedure to be adopted, the participants to be involved, its application, merits and limitations and the precautions to be taken. In order to quickly grasp the methods, plenty of field-based illustrations are given. These illustrations are drawn from a wide variety of fields in order to make the readers understand and grasp the varied fields of application of PRA. Chapter 21 describes the roles and responsibilities of the PRA team members. This is an important segment in the book, for the effective practice of PRA mostly depends on the attitude and behaviour of the PRA team members. The final chapter dwells upon the application of PRA methodology in select fields of development.

The book should be of immense use to those who believe in the institutionalisation of participation. Students, teachers, researchers, NGO workers, donors and aid agencies in the development field will find this book comprehensive, meaningful and productive. However, the book does not aim to replace field experience, since the latter is always more rewarding. The author welcomes comments and suggestions from the readers.

Acknowledgements

My association and interaction with my colleagues, students, development practitioners, NGOs, government departments, development consultants and villagers have benefited me immensely in writing this book.

I am deeply indebted to Gandhigram Rural University (GRU), where I have been working for the last thirty years. The university provides excellent opportunities to teachers and students for undertaking field-based research and outreach activities. This has helped me practise and experiment the participatory rural appraisal (PRA) methods among a wide spectrum of audience and settings. I have drawn significantly from this experience to write this book.

I extend my deep sense of gratitude to Sri D.K. Oza (former Vice-Chancellor, GRU), who was responsible for introducing Robert Chambers to the Gandhigram community and for ushering in what can be regarded as an era of PRA at this university. I had the opportunity of interacting with Robert Chambers in a ten-day international workshop on 'Attitude Behaviour Change for PRA' in Bangalore and, subsequently, in a couple of workshops at Madurai, which reinforced my conviction in PRA. His thought-provoking articles and books have inspired me a lot. Any book on PRA cannot be written without referring to him. In this book too, I have liberally quoted from his works.

I am also grateful to Dr N. Markandan (former Vice-Chancellor), who himself is an adept practitioner of PRA. He has provided guidance and support in practising and experimenting PRA methods in a number of service villages of GRU.

I also want to record here my deep sense of gratitude to the Ford Foundation for providing financial support which helped me gain exposure to the world of PRA and enabled me to offer training to a wide variety of audience from villages, community-based organisations (CBOs), colleges, universities, training institutions, research organisations, NGOs, government departments, donor agencies, banks, etc. I am indebted to Dr Ruth G. Alsop (Programme Officer, Ford Foundation), now with the World Bank (Washington), for her constant support, guidance and help in our PRA related works.

PRA is a team work and team experience. It is a way of life for some of us. I have heavily drawn from the knowledge and experience of the members of the PRA team at GRU. I express my sincere thanks to Dr M.P. Boraian, Professor in Extension Education, who has been consistently helping and supporting all my PRA endeavours. My sincere thanks are due to the members of the PRA team at GRU who include Dr B.R. Dwaraki, former Professor of Sociology; Dr S. Ponnuraj, Dean, Faculty of Rural Health and Sanitation; Dr T.T. Ranganathan, Professor of Agriculture; Dr. N.D. Mani, Professor of Rural Development; Dr P. Sumangala, former Professor of Economics; Dr. R. Ramesh, Research Fellow; Dr S. Manivel, Reader in Cooperation; Dr K. Manikandan, Lecturer in Economics; Sri B. Baskar, Lecturer in Cooperation; and Dr E. Perumal, Field Organiser.

I have been fortunate enough to get trained by John Devavaram and his dedicated team at Society for People's Education and Economic Change (SPEECH) who are mostly responsible for spreading the concept of PRA in Tamil Nadu. John Devavaram has also opened up a lot of opportunities for participating in reflection sessions (which he used to organise at periodic intervals).

I am grateful to J. Bernard, Visiting Fellow at the National Institute of Rural Development, Hyderabad, who helped us fine-tune our skills in practising PRA.

I am thankful to Philip Abraham, a development consultant (formerly DANIDA Advisor for the Comprehensive Watershed Development Programme), who provided me with an opportunity to work as a consultant for a project in the field of PRA and CBOs. The experience gained in the project has been incorporated in the book.

This book would not have been possible without the resources and knowledge from thousands of rural people from hundreds of villages spread across the southern states of India. I wholeheartedly thank them for the invaluable time they spent with me in appraisal and analysis.

The Institute of Development Studies (Sussex) and the International Institute for Environment Development (London) have been playing an excellent role in promoting PRA. I get myself updated by constantly reading the publications from these institutions, especially the notes on participatory learning and action. I have liberally used some illustrations from these notes in this book.

I thank Mr Rohan Savarimuthu (Research Scholar, Faculty of English and Foreign Languages, GRU) for going through the manuscript. I am indeed very thankful to Mr Ashok R. Chandran, Senior Commissioning Editor, and Ms Elina Majumdar, Associate Commissioning Editor, SAGE Publications, for their unstinted support in publishing this book. I am indeed grateful to R. Saravanan and P. Sellachamy for tirelessly typesetting the manuscript. Finally, I thank my wife Dr S. Vijayeswari, who is a constant source of inspiration in all my academic, research and outreach pursuits.

N. Narayanasamy

Evolution of Participatory Rural Appraisal

INTRODUCTION

Development intervention approaches in India over the past sixty years (until the late 1980s when we started pursuing participatory approach) have been very much a 'supply-oriented one-way traffic'. The interventionists, by and large, did not care to notice the 'development process' and the 'by-products'. All that they were interested in was 'the product' of development intervention at its best; and in merely making the input delivery, at its worst. We have operationalised quite a number of approaches and strategies to bring about development in India. Some of the major approaches adopted include Gandhian approaches, community development approach, sector approach, target approach, area approach, minimum needs approach and integrated approach. These approaches have tended, primarily, to material giving, input supplying, infrastructure development, technology transfer and the like.

The limitations of these approaches include

- a top-down strategy;
- being target-oriented;
- the non-involvement of people, leading to problems in selecting the right development strategy;
- vertically controlled sectoral approach without any horizontal coordination at the micro level;
- the dominant development thinking oriented towards greater inputs (supply) than what people demanded;
- poor percolation effect due to bureaucratic practices involved at all the stages of implementation;
- the mistaken notion that bank credit *per se* can do the magic of development;
- frequent announcements of interest concession and loan waivers by the government that have since spoiled the repayment ethics and choked the recycling of funds;
- the inevitability of leakages and wastages;
- near-total absence of self-confidence and even self-respect;

- complete dispossession of much of the community infrastructure;
- lack of appreciation and promotion of indigenous technical knowledge and resources; and
- the ever-growing recipient attitude.

All these limitations have today become impediments to the process of development.

THE MAIN CHALLENGE

The main challenge, therefore, before the development facilitators is to dislodge the strong dependency culture in Indian villages; help them regain their self-image and self-respect; create in them a strong sense of public consciousness to care about and to stand as the sentinel on the community infrastructure and common property resources, prepare and transform them to realise the need for community-led initiatives and build in them the confidence and fortitude essential in making decisions and taking actions.

Thus the basal logic for the success of any intervention in development work depends not merely on the number of schemes and projects pumped in, but also on the confidence built and the power given to people to decide and take community initiatives. Consensus is its key.

The process of building consensus and confidence for collective community action definitely takes a longer time before one could see the whole process of facilitative intervention. But it is certainly worth the effort because it eventually empowers and sustains the village community. The primary factor for promoting consensus and instilling confidence is participation.

Participation is rapidly becoming a catch-all concept, even a cliché (Cornwall and Jewkes 1995). It has been increasingly emphasised in all rural development projects. Today, there are practically no programmes or projects that do not emphasise the necessity of participation. The government too, after reviewing the seven five-year plans, finally recognised the significance of participation and stated in the eight five-year plan thus: 'People's initiative and participation should be made a key element in the process of development instead of people being passive observers' (Mukherjee 1995).

PARTICIPATION: MEANING

Participation is a process through which stakeholders influence and share control over development initiatives, decisions and resources that affect them. (World Bank 1996)

Participation is the people's involvement in decision-making process about what to be done and by whom; their involvement in implementing the programme, sharing benefits and monitoring and evaluating the programme. (Cohen and Uphoff 1977)

The core features of participation are (*i*) it is a voluntary involvement of people; (*ii*) the people who participate influence and share control over development initiatives, decisions and resources; (*iii*) it is a process of involvement of people at different stages of the project or programme; and (*iv*) the ultimate aim is to improve the well-being of the people who participate.

PARTICIPATORY DEVELOPMENT AND PARTICIPATION IN DEVELOPMENT

Wignaraja (1991) has observed that participatory development is essentially top-down participation while participation in development is bottom-up participation. The distinction between participatory development and participation in development is central to understanding the practice of participation (see Table 1.1).

Table 1.1
Participatory Development vs Participation in Development

Participatory Development	Participation in Development
It approaches conventional project practice in a more participatory and sensitive manner	It entails genuine efforts to engage in practices which openly and radically encourage people's participation
It is introduced within the predetermined project framework	It stems from the understanding that poverty is caused by standard factors. It attempts to alter some of these causes which lead to poverty
It is top-down participation in the sense that the management of the project defines where, when and how much the people can participate	It is bottom-up participation in the sense that the local people have full control over the processes and the project provides for necessary flexibility
It is the more prevalent practice. It is more dominant in terms of resources available	It is prevalent more with NGOs than with the governments

Source: Oakley (1991).

PARTICIPATION AS A MEANS AND AS AN END

There are two major alternative uses of participation. They are: (*i*) participation as an 'end' in itself; and (*ii*) participation as a 'means' to development. As an end, participation entails empowerment. As a means, it leads to efficiency in project management; that is, participation is a tool to implement development policies (see Table 1.2). Participation, as an end, represents 'transformational participation', and as a means, represents 'instrumental participation'. Transformational participation is when participation is viewed as an objective in and of itself, and as a means of achieving same higher objectives, such as self-help and/or sustainability (Mikkelsen 1995).

Table 1.2
Participation as Means and Ends

Participation as Means	Participation as Ends
It implies use of participation to achieve some predetermined goal or objective	Participation as an end attempts to empower people to participate in their own development more meaningfully
It is an attempt to utilise the existing resources in order to achieve the objective of programmes/project	The attempt is to ensure increased role of people in development initiative
The emphasis is on achieving the objective and not so much on the act of participation itself	The focus is on improving the ability of the people to participate rather than just achieving the predetermined objectives of the project
It is more common in government programmes where the main concern is to mobilize the community and involve them in improving the efficiency of the delivery system	This view hardly finds favour with the government agencies; NGOs in principle agree on this viewpoint
Participation is generally short-term	Participation as an end is viewed as a long-term process
Participation as a means appears to be a passive form of participation	Participation as an end is relatively more active and dynamic

Source: Oakley (1991).

WHY PARTICIPATION?

The major reasons for emphasising participation are as follows:

- Participation results in better decisions.
- People are more likely to implement the decisions that they made themselves rather than the decisions imposed on them from above.
- Motivation is frequently enhanced by setting up of goals during the participatory decision-making process.
- Participation improves communication and cooperation (Locke 1968).
- People may learn new skills through participation; leadership potential may be readily identified and developed (Heller et al. 1998).

Types of Participation

Categorisation of participation originated from the work done by Arnstcin in the 1960s (Arnstein 1969). In the 'Ladder of Citizen Participation', Sherry Arnstein defines eight broad levels of participation (see Figure 1.1).

The fundamental point is that participation without redistribution of power is an empty and frustrating process for the powerless. There is nothing new about that process, since those who have power normally want to hang on to it. Historically, it has had to be wrested by the powerless rather than proffered by the powerful. Expressed another way, it means that getting as high as possible up Arnstein's ladder on each issue is favouring participation. However, the level of attainment up the ladder will vary from issue to issue, and several different levels will coexist in the same locality on different issues.

Figure 1.1
Ladder of Citizen Participation

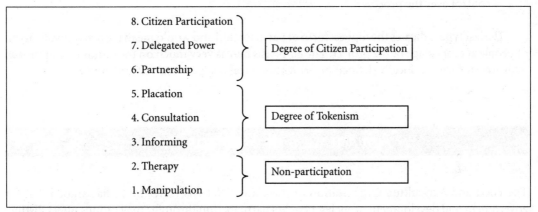

Source: Arnstein (1969).

There are many ways in which development organisations interpret and use the term participation. These range from passive participation, where people are involved merely by being told what is to happen, to self-mobilisation, where people take initiatives independent of external institutions. If the objective of intervention is to achieve sustainable development, then nothing less than functional participation will suffice.

Taking a cue from Arnstein, the World Bank defined (World Bank Development Research Group 2003) six 'levels' of participation in bank country work division, though later the Social Development Department of the World Bank adopted a more intuitive and mutually exclusive four-level classification, ranked in order from having least to most influence:

- Information sharing
- Consultation
- Collaboration
- Empowerment

Biggs (1989) has come out with more or less similar classification of participation. He has subsumed participation into four types:

- Contractual: where people contracted into the project of researchers/development agencies take part in their enquires or experiments
- Consultative: where people are asked for their opinion and consulted by researchers and development agencies before interventions are made
- Collaborative: where researchers and local people work together on a project designed, initiated and managed by researchers
- Collegiate: where researchers/development agencies and local people work together as colleagues with different skills to offer, in a process of mutual learning where people have control over the process

The last type indicates the highest form of participation and would mean the active involvement of people at every stage of the project. The emphasis here is very much on the bottom-up approach with a 'clear focus on locally defined priorities and local perspectives' (Chambers 1992).

ADVANTAGES OF PARTICIPATION

The Food and Agriculture Organization of the United Nations (FAO 1997) has argued that for government and development agencies, people's participation through small groups offers distinct advantages. These advantages are briefly stated here:

- Economics of scale: Participatory groups constitute a grass-roots 'receiving system' that allows development agencies to reduce the unit delivery or transaction cost of their services, thus broadening the scope of their impact.
- Higher productivity: Given access to resources and a guarantee that they will share fully the benefit of their efforts, the poor become more receptive to new techniques and services, and achieve higher levels of production and income.
- Reduced cost and increased efficiency: People's contribution to project planning and implementation represents savings that reduce the project cost.
- Effective utilisation of available resources: People and other agents work in tandem towards achieving their objectives. Local people take the responsibility of various activities. This improves the efficiency and makes the project cost-effective.

- Building of democratic organisation: A limited size and informality of small groups is suited to the poor man's scarce organisational experience and low literacy levels. Moreover, a small group environment is ideal for diffusion of collective decision-making and leadership skills which can be used in the subsequent development of inter-group federations.
- Sustainability: Participation leads to increased self-reliance among the poor and the establishment of a network of self-sustaining rural organisations.

LIMITATIONS OF PARTICIPATION

Participation has certain limitations. Oakley (1991) has listed certain limitations. They are stated below:

- Participation does not occur automatically. It is a process. It involves time. Hence, it may lead to delayed start of a project.
- In a bottom-up participation process, we have to move along the path decided by the local people. This entails an increased requirement of material as well as human resources.
- Participation leads to decentralisation of power. People at the top should be ready and willing to share power with the people. In practice, people at the top are reluctant to give up power.
- Participation sometimes generate dependency syndrome.
- Participation can result in shifting of the burden onto the poor. The government may relinquish the responsibility of promoting development with equity in the course of time.

PARTICIPATORY APPROACH—DOES IT HOLD THE KEY TO DEVELOPMENT?

How should one go about the task of enabling the people to participate in the process of shaping their own destiny without expecting outside support and assistance? Is this really a practicable and sensible proposition after all? Do the rural people have the capability and knowledge required to analyse situations and conditions, and take development initiatives upon themselves?

The answers to these questions mostly lie in an approach known as the 'participatory rural appraisal' (PRA). Although, by now, as an approach of interacting with rural people, it is well past the nascent stage, not only in India, but also in many of the other Asian and African countries, yet PRA cannot be claimed as a panacea for all the ills of rural communities. However, the experiences all over the world show and we have enough reasons to believe that the PRA way of dealing with people is found to be emancipating and empowering, and therefore considered a positive step in the right direction. Therefore, many governments of Third World countries and NGOs have quickly taken to participatory approach.

SOURCES OF PRA

PRA has borrowed methods and techniques from several sources and improvised upon them to suit the local conditions and situations (see Figure 1.2). The major sources of PRA are:

- (Biases of) Rural development tourism
- (Demerits of) Questionnaire survey
- Participatory action reflection research (PARR)
- Agro-eco system analysis
- Applied anthropology
- Informal survey
- Rapid rural appraisal

Robert Chambers (1997) labelled the first two as negative sources and the last five as positive sources. They are briefly described here.

Survey

The most common method of formal research is the survey method. A survey is a study utilised to find facts. It is a method of research involving collection of data directly from a population on a sample thereof at a particular time. The chief features of the survey are: (*i*) it is a field study and conducted in a natural setting; (*ii*) it seeks response directly from the respondents; (*iii*) it can cover a large population; and (*iv*) it covers a definite geographical area.

Merits

Following are some of the important merits of the survey method:

- The versatility of the survey method is its greatest strength. It is still the basic data-and information-gathering instrument used in socio-economic research (Krishnaswami 2002).
- The value of information depends on its trustworthiness. There are four tests of trustworthiness, namely, internal validity, external validity, reliability and objectivity. The survey method satisfies all the four tests.

Figure 1.2
Sources of PRA

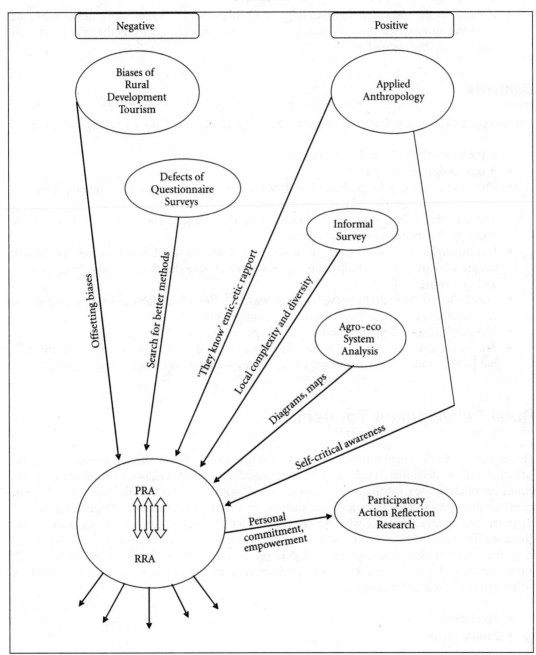

Source: Chambers (1997: 107).

- It is flexible to permit the use of various ways of data collection: observation, interviewing and mailing.
- It sensitises the researcher to unanticipated or unknown problems. The collection of data from the respondents through interviewing or mailing often uncovers the facts previously unknown to the researcher.

Demerits

The survey method suffers from certain limitations and drawbacks. They are briefly stated here:

- It is costly as it is a long-drawn process.
- It is investigator-oriented.
- The time consumed for gathering of data starting from the training of investigators way down to the preparation of reports turns out to be exhaustive.
- The direction of the interaction process is predetermined. The structure of the survey imposes rigidity on the interview process.
- It is hierarchical in nature as responsibilities are fixed for the different cadres. As a result, people who are in contact with the realities may not have the chance to interpret the data and vice versa.
- Data collected through the survey method may not always be reliable as there is limited and restricted scope to cross-check the data and information.
- The participation of the respondents in this process is low.
- Analysis of data is done only in the office. As a result, the interviewer or investigator does not have a chance to share findings of the survey with the respondents and the people.

Rural Development Tourism

The term 'rural development tourism' refers to the quick and brief visits often undertaken by 'core', 'urban-based', 'professional', 'important', 'distinguished', 'powerful' visitors to rural areas. These visitors, as observed by Chambers (1983), have three things in common: (*i*) they come from urban areas; (*ii*) they want to find out something and (*iii*) they have limited time. All these factors, either separately or together, influence what is perceived. A lack of required time drives out open-ended questions. Thus, meanings are imposed and cross-checking becomes impossible. Often, lies become facts. People get neglected and physical objects get attention. Rural development tourism thus introduces many biases that mask the perception of rural problems and rural realities. Chambers (1983) has described six types of biases:

- Spatial biases
- Project biases
- Person biases

- Dry season biases
- Diplomatic biases
- Professional biases

Spatial biases

There are two types of spatial biases, namely, (*i*) urban bias and (*ii*) tarmac and roadside biases. Urban bias concentrates on rural visits near towns and large administrative centres. However, the distribution of rural poor indicates that they are more concentrated in remote, obscure and inaccessible areas and are far from urban areas. The poor, by and large, remain unseen under this bias.

Tarmac and roadside biases direct attention towards those who are powerful and dominant. People who are living on the roadside are better placed in terms of transport, communication, electricity, health facilities, schools, market, education, etc. The rural development tourists (RDTs) normally visit only these roadside villages and not the interior and remote villages.

Project biases

RDTs tend to visit project villages. In other words, they visit villages where something is being done, some money is being spent, some staff is stationed, a project is in hand.

Person biases

Rural development tourism suffers from person biases too. Visitors do not meet all the people, just 'select' people. Chambers has listed four types of person biases, which include (*i*) elite biases; (*ii*) male biases; (*iii*) user and adopter biases and (*iv*) active, present and living biases.

(*i*) Elite biases: Elites comprise those rural people who are better off and more influential than the others. They are progressive farmers, village leaders of different types, traders, teachers and para-professionals. They are the main sources of information and voice the interests, wishes and aspirations of the village. Ultimately, their concerns emerge as the priorities of the village for development. RDTs tend to meet these people much more than the others.

(*ii*) Male biases: The RDTs tend to meet only men (most of the professional researchers and other rural visitors are men). They neglect women. Among women, the unseen and the most pitiable category is that of the rural single women, female-headed households and widows. These are totally neglected by the RDTs.

(*iii*) User and adopter biases: RDTs tend to see users of their services and the adopters of new practices rather than non-users and non-adopters.

(*iv*) Active, present and living biases: The active people are more visible than the weak, apathetic and miserable. The sick lie untended in their hut and the old people just confine themselves to their homes. RDTs usually meet the active ones.

Dry season biases

Seasons vary consistently and affect the life and livelihoods of the people deeply. Most of the poor rural people in the world live in areas which have marked wet and dry tropical seasons. The wet or rainy season is the most difficult season for those who depend on agriculture for their livelihood. It is during this season that people, especially the poor, experience food shortage, ill health, unemployment, low wages, hard work, silent hunger (malnutrition), indebtedness, etc. It is during this season that the poor are likely to become poorer by selling or mortgaging the little assets they possess. The wet season is the unseen season. The urban-based rural development professionals do not visit the rural areas during this season as they experience inconveniences such as floods, landslides, getting stuck, enduring discomfort.

Diplomatic biases

Urban-based professionals are hesitant to visit and listen to the rural poor as it is likely to offend the more influential. The powerful and influential who welcome and offer hospitality to the visitors may not like probing questions about the poor. Sometimes, the powerful in the village may not like the visitors walking into the poor section of the village, discussing with the women, interviewing the scheduled castes (SCs), and so on. The visitors under such circumstances are quite diplomatic. All these factors taken in together keep the tourists and the poor apart.

Professional biases

Professional training often tends to make one develop a weakness for looking at things within a restricted scope, thus blinding a person to what lies beyond. For instance, the agricultural extension staff trained to advise on cash crops or to prepare farm plans is drawn to the more 'progressive' farmers. Professionals are trained to look within just a limited area. In rural areas, they become even more single-minded; pursuing just their own tasks and looking for and finding only that which fits their ideas.

Participatory Action Reflection Research (PARR)

Participatory action reflection research (PARR), as the name suggests, is a comprehensive amalgamation of participation, action as well as reflection with research dimensions. These range from action science and reflection action—in which professionals act and reflect on what they do and how they learn—to approaches which use dialogue and participatory research to enhance the local people's awareness and confidence and to empower their action. Participatory action research (PAR) is a development strategy in which the community participates fully and, through its own critical analysis, gets to know the facts of its own situation, condition, strengths, weaknesses, resources, problems, etc. (Hari 1992). It is a collective effort by the participating community to pool its efforts and other resources in order to achieve the objectives that it has set for itself.

Basic features of PAR

- It believes in the fundamental intelligence of people, irrespective of whether they have had formal education or not, as they may be having immense experiential knowledge.
- It believes that everyone including the poorest has not only the right to make history but also the right to create knowledge and formulate theories.
- It believes that the marginalised/exploited poorest, with their experience and knowledge, could become resource-rich people.
- It believes that everyone is capable of learning.
- It believes that people learn best by doing.
- It believes that success helps in building confidence and makes people realise their self-worth.
- It believes in the strength of collective learning and in collective action.

PARR owes much to the work and inspiration of Paulo Freire, and to his book *Pedagogy of the Oppressed and Education for Critical Consciousness*.

Contributions of PAR to PRA

The major contributions of PAR to PRA are as follows:

- The professionals should reflect critically on their concept, values, behaviour and methods.
- Learning should take place through engagement and committed action.
- Professionals play the roles of conveners, catalysts and facilitators.
- The weak and the marginalised can and should be empowered.
- Instilling in the minds of the rural, especially the poverty-stricken, that they can and should involve in investigating and analysing their own problems as well as plan for solutions.

Agro-eco System Analysis

The agro-eco system can be defined as 'an ecological system' partly modified by man to produce food, fibre and other agricultural products which are useful to mankind (Conway et al. 1989).

The system permits both for experimental and applied research for the purpose of its continued development and sustainability. Agro-eco system has four different but interconnected system properties: (*i*) productivity; (*ii*) stability; (*iii*) sustainability and (*iv*) equitability.

   (*i*) Productivity: It is defined as 'the net output of valued product per unit of resource input'. The product is measured as field or net income on food value, etc.
   (*ii*) Stability: It is the constancy of productivity in response to small disturbances or changes caused by the normal fluctuations of the surrounding physical, biological, social and economic environment.
   (*iii*) Sustainability: It is the ability of the farm ecological system to maintain productivity and stability in spite of major environment disturbances, such as stress and shock which can neither be predicted well in advance nor measured accurately.
   (*iv*) Equitability: It is the evenness of distribution of the production of the agro-eco system among the human beneficiaries.

Agro-eco system analysis, developed in Thailand in the late 1970s at the University of Chaiang Mai by Gordon R. Conway and his colleagues, spread first through Southeast Asia and then to the other parts of the world.

Contribution of agro-eco system analysis to PRA

Agro-eco system analysis makes use of several tools. Some of the major contributions of agro-eco system analysis to PRA are as follows:

- Transects (systematic walks and observation)
- Informal mapping (sketch maps drawn on sites)
- Diagramming (seasonal calendars, flow and causal diagrams, bar charts, Venn diagrams)
- Innovation assessment (scoring and ranking different actions)

Applied Anthropology

Traditionally, anthropology has dealt more with understanding the facts of human existence than dealing with the solutions to human problems. However, the 1970s and 1980s witnessed the establishment of anthropological approaches in a professionalised manner, sorting out the vicissitudes of social change in tribal and rural communities.

Social anthropologists have helped other development professionals to appreciate better the richness and validity of rural people's knowledge and to distinguish the etic (the outsider's mental frame, categories and world view) and the emic (those of the local insiders).

Contributions of social anthropology to PRA

The present repertoire of PRA owes a great deal to the insights gained from the field of applied anthropology (Chambers 1992). Some of these are as follows:

- Recognising that learning from the field involves the flexibility contained in arts more than the rigidity seen in a scientific endeavour
- The meaning and the value of learning from relaxed and unhurried interactions and observations with people in their natural settings
- Importance of establishing rapport with the people with the important role of the underlying attitudes and behaviour
- The emphatic emic–etic distinction
- Recognition of richness and validity of indigenous technical knowledge

Informal Survey or Sondeo

Agricultural research teams, after having seen the 'expensive, bulky and hard-to-process' questionnaire survey, now go for an informal survey. The informal survey is a data-gathering method which can produce at minimum cost a rich description of life in a farming community, an understanding of the local ecology, cropping systems and how farmers, merchants, extension workers and others perceive their conditions and make decisions (Rhoades 1985).

An informal survey can provide basic data and information on the feasibility of beginning a project in a region. This is effective especially when dealing with a farming system about which very little is known. It can be also used to quickly obtain some basic information, specifically for the design and execution of formal surveys or more in-depth investigations. The important purpose is to help focus a subsequent formal survey that will utilise random sampling and quantify critical aspects of rural life or the production system. The need is not simply to get a feel of the area, but to discover important, albeit tentative, organising concepts upon which to base future research.

Contributions of informal survey to PRA

- Observation: the researcher needs to keep eyes open for patterns in crop production, land use and farm behaviour
- Informal conversation: the researcher needs to talk to the people and listen to their concerns and views
- Inter-disciplinary team
- Recording: the researcher has to discretely write everything down (complete field notes are crucial in an informal survey)

Rapid Rural Appraisal

The PAR system and agro-eco system analysis were developed and experimented in the 1970s for the purpose of gathering data and information for quickly appraising the situation and conditions of the farmers and the agriculture, especially in the Third World countries. The methods adopted by the experts for the agro-eco system analysis did not, however, find their place in any field other than agriculture. But then the development efforts and strategies are not confined to agriculture alone. It has a wider perspective and covers a whole range of activities, which affect the life of people in a locality or a country. The development professionals felt that it is essential to have a better understanding of the overall situation of the local area to plan, execute and evaluate the development and welfare programmes. Therefore, they started using quick appraisal methods of the conditions for planning their programmes. This resulted in emergence of rapid rural appraisal (RRA) in the late 1970s.

RRA is a way of organising people for collecting and analysing information within a short time span. It is defined as 'any systematic process of investigation to acquire new information in order to draw and validate inferences, hypothesis, observation and conclusions in a limited period of time' (N. Mukherjee 1994b). It has the flexibility of adjusting to situations because it does not imply or recommend a standard set of methods to be applied in each case. The methods vary from situation to situation and are determined by local conditions, local problems and objectives at hand.

RRA, as Robert Chambers has put, had three main origins. The first was dissatisfaction with the biases, especially the anti-poverty biases of rural development tourism. Second was disillusion with the normal processes of questionnaire surveys and their results. And the third was the continuous search for most cost-effective methods of learning the rural conditions.

Main features of RRA

- Fairly quick, flexible and adaptable to rural situations
- Helps to learn what needs to be known
- Allows outsiders to learn from the local people
- Helps to get many points of view and different angles to each issue: goes beyond and get answers/responses which formal survey cannot get
- Challenges anti-poverty biases which are common in other approaches, especially in rural development tourism
- Makes the researcher go beyond the roadside and reach interior villages and remote places and work in the field
- Insists on a multi-disciplinary team
- Uses techniques and methods that are easy to understand and easy to communicate, helping local people explain their ideas better
- Avoids over-collection of data and insists on collection of only the necessary data
- Accepts a certain degree of inaccuracy

Limitations of RRA

- It was extractive in nature. The team that gathered the data and the information from outside owned the information. They did not share this information with the people.
- Appraisal was the core activity of RRA. After the appraisal, the team from outside failed to make the people the focus of the issue.
- This method emphasised more on methods and outputs rather than on the attitude and behaviour of the outsiders.
- It had little aspiration to empower poor people or to generate self-help community development initiatives.

EMERGENCE OF PRA

PRA started with RRA. During the mid-1980s, the term 'participatory' became associated with RRA. At the international conference on RRA at the Khon Kaen University (Thailand), a typology of RRA was developed. Participatory RRA was one of them and the others included exploratory RRAs, topical RRAs and monitoring RRAs.

In 1988, two parallel events, one in Kenya and the other in India, marked the evolution of PRA. In Kenya, the National Environmental Secretariat (NES), in collaboration with Clark University (USA), conducted an RRA which led to the development of a village resource management plan. This was described as participatory rural appraisal (PRA).

During the same year, the Aga Khan Rural Support Programme (AKRSP), India, with the support of International Institute for Environment and Development (IIED), London, carried out participatory RRA in two villages. This proved valuable in the overall development of PRA.

Table 1.3
Comparison of RRA and PRA

Nature of Process	RRA	PRA
Major development	Late 1970s, 1980s	Late 1980s, 1990s
Major innovators	Universities	NGOs
Main users	Aid agencies, universities	NGOs, government field organisations
Key resource earlier overlooked	Local people's knowledge	Local people's capabilities
Main innovation	Methods	Behaviour
Outsiders' mode	Eliciting	Facilitating
Objectives	Data collection	Empowerment
Main actors	Outsiders	Local people
Longer-term outcomes	Plans, projects, publications	Sustainable local action and institutions

Source: Chambers (1997).

PRA is not completely different from RRA. In fact, PRA is a continuum of RRA (see Table 1.3) or an improved version of RRA. There are many commonalities between RRA and PRA. Many of the methods, techniques and practices followed in both RRA and PRA overlap. But there is a distinction between RRA and PRA. RRA is intended for learning by outsiders where the outsider takes the role of an investigator; whereas PRA is intended to enable the local people to conduct their own analysis and often to plan and to take action, where the outsider performs the role of a facilitator (see Table 1.4).

Table 1.4
RRA and PRA Continuum

Nature of Process	RRA	PRA
Mode	Finding out: elicitive	Facilitating: empowering
Outsiders' role	Investigator	Facilitator
Information owned, analysed and used by	Outsiders	Local people
Methods mainly used	RRA methods	PRA methods

Source: Chambers (1997).

DEVELOPMENT AND SPREAD OF PRA: IMPORTANT PHASES

The development of PRA can be traced under three phases (see Figure 1.3):

• First phase: Late 1980s and early 1990s
• Second phase: Mid-1990s
• Third phase: Late 1990s to date

The First Phase (Late 1980s and Early 1990s)

This was a period of innovation; a new way of doing things; a new way of training, developing and promoting a whole new approach. The field practitioners and facilitators along with the local people, women and men, poor and rich, able or not able to read and write, experimented, discovered, rediscovered and innovated methods. This was the period when major participatory group visual methods emerged.

This was the period of intensive interaction between the PRA practitioners from the north and the south, and the emergence of an evolving and growing community of practice. It was a period of launching of RRA/PRA notes, to share the experience of field practitioners throughout the world. The period also witnessed a growing debate about PRA's purpose, practices and politics.

Figure 1.3
Core Phases of Development and Spread of PRA

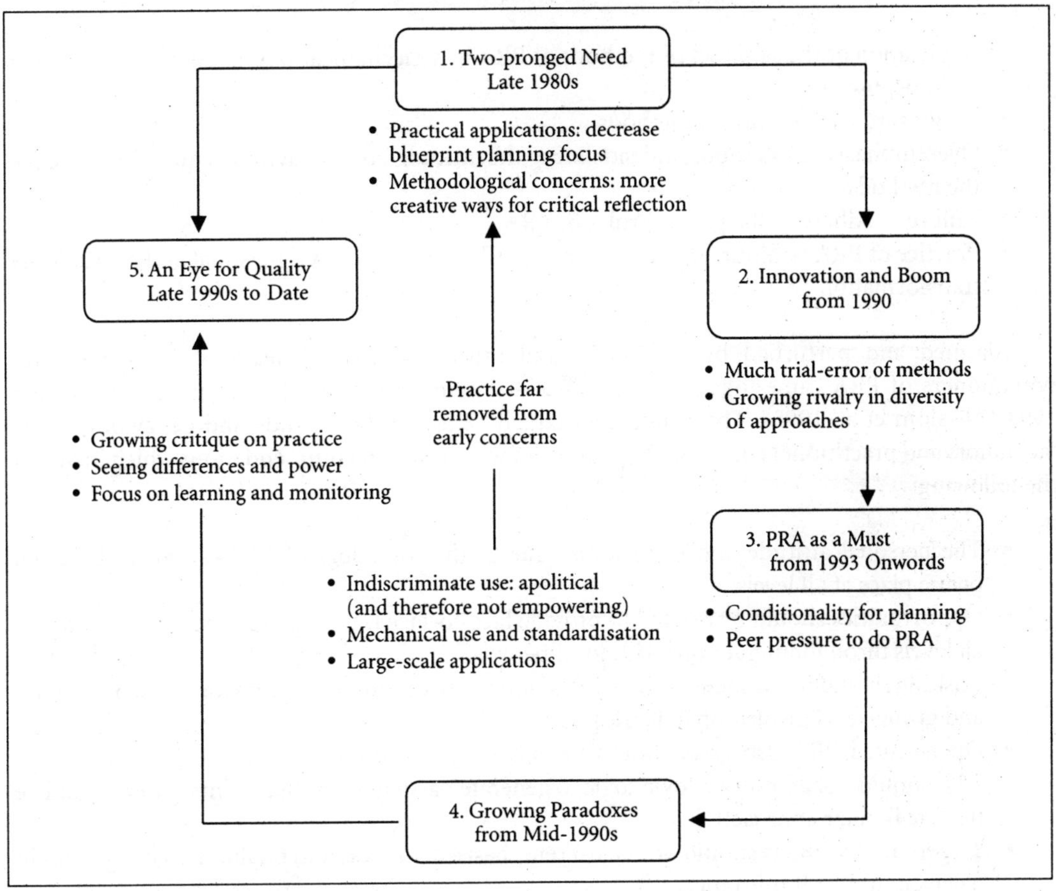

1. Two-pronged Need
Late 1980s

- Practical applications: decrease blueprint planning focus
- Methodological concerns: more creative ways for critical reflection

5. An Eye for Quality
Late 1990s to Date

2. Innovation and Boom
from 1990

- Much trial-error of methods
- Growing rivalry in diversity of approaches

Practice far removed from early concerns

- Growing critique on practice
- Seeing differences and power
- Focus on learning and monitoring

3. PRA as a Must
from 1993 Onwords

- Conditionality for planning
- Peer pressure to do PRA

- Indiscriminate use: apolitical (and therefore not empowering)
- Mechanical use and standardisation
- Large-scale applications

4. Growing Paradoxes
from Mid-1990s

Source: Cornwall and Guijt (2004).

The Second Phase (Mid-1990s)

The spirit of improvisation and innovation generated in the first phase continued to generate an astonishing range of methods and applications. With the passage of time, the centre of attention shifted to the extraordinary diversity of applications. What began with agriculture, natural resources and community planning, spread to various fields, and thus was applied in every major domain of human social activity. The tremendous growth and practice of PRA, and the fantastic innovations in carrying PRA into uncharted settings during this period could be attributed to open-ended encouragements given by Chambers, who shared PRA with countless others around the world.

With the quick growth and spread of PRA, reports of 'bad practice' and 'abuse' also began to trickle in. They included the following:

- Application of the same set of methods of PRA in a mechanical way, irrespective of context and purpose
- Haphazard use of random methods
- Overemphasis on methods and sidelining the attitude and behaviour required to practice the methods
- Failure to adhere to the ground rules of PRA
- Practice of PRA without adequate training and without required personal and professional transformation

Alarmed and perturbed by the 'abuse and misuse of PRA', a team of first-generation practitioners of PRA came together to produce a statement sharing their concerns in the year 1994 (Absalom et al. 1995). Their statement largely reflected the attitude and behaviour of the facilitators and practitioners of PRA. They came out with a set of recommendations which included the following:

- The personal attitude and behaviour—one of the three legs of PRA—need to be given prime place at all levels.
- Opportunities should be created to provide face-to-face learning experience for the staff at all levels through interactions with local people.
- Rushing should be avoided. Proper and adequate space should be given for local community and group-level institutional development.
- Open-ended PRA processes should be encouraged and continued. The practitioners of PRA should not allow top-down logic to generate participatory 'blueprints'. They should be flexible in their approach.
- Targets and products should not be overemphasised. Process and qualitative change should be given utmost importance.
- The institutions wanting to train their staff in PRA should encourage and engage such trainers who stress attitude and behaviour change and reject those who give importance only to methods.
- The PRA practitioners should work towards changing the culture, procedures and interactions in donor and government organisations and in NGOs.

The Third Phase (Late 1990s to Date)

The important developments during this period include the following:

- The practitioners of PRA started using PRA in a wide variety of fields in an intensive manner. A kind of depth and maturity could be noticed in their work.

- Methods and techniques were applied in policy research, participatory government and rights-based development work.
- Spread and application of PRA to a wide variety of fields led to a change in the nomenclature from 'participatory rural appraisal' to 'participatory learning and action'.
- Methods and techniques of PRA were used to monitor and evaluate the projects. It has been known as participatory monitoring and evaluation (PM&E).
- The idea of social learning gained currency during this phase. Under social learning, various stakeholders needed to come together and participate in the process of joint fact-finding, negotiation, planning, reassessing and refocusing.

MULTIPLE LABELS AND ACRONYMS

Starting from the 1970s, many participatory approaches have been applied and experimented in different fields. Many diverse names have been coined by individual practitioners and organisations for the participatory methods and activities in which they engage. Some of these are subject-specific. We will briefly present popular labels of participatory approaches.

- Appreciative planning and action (APA): APA provides a framework that helps empower groups as well as the community as a whole to take a positive action for their own development. It is built on the principles of searching for positive events, for success, for what works and for what gives energy to individuals and groups.
- Approach development (AD): It is a step-by-step method used to find out what to do practically when dealing with a concrete situation in a rural area. It is a field-oriented, action-based and participatory collection of experiences gained through implementation at selected sites.
- Appreciative enquiry (AE): AE asks us to pay special attention to 'the best of the past and present' in order to 'ignite the collective imagination of what might be'. Appreciative enquiry is about seeing what others may not see.
- Beneficiary assessment (BA): It involves the systematic consultation of project beneficiaries and other stakeholders. Its purpose is to undertake systematic listening, by giving the poor 'a voice' and to obtain feedback on activities.
- Community action planning (CAP): It is an action, intense community-based workshop, carried out over a period of two to five days, depending on the specific goals of the workshop. The output of the workshop is a development plan.
- Demand responsive approach (DRA): DRA provides information and allows user the choices to guide key investment decisions, thereby ensuring that services conform to what people want and are willing to pay for.
- Farmers first (FF): 'Farmers first' is a generic term coined by Chambers with an emphasis on farmers' knowledge and their participation in and ownership of research.

- Farmer participatory research (FPR): FPR is based on farmers' priorities, needs, interests and capabilities. It involves full participation of farmers right from problem identification through prioritisation, finding solutions, implementation to evaluation (MANAGE 1995).
- Farming system diagnosis (FSD): It is a process by which farmers draw out or diagram the interactions between bio-physical causes and socio-economic constraints to the farmers' problem.
- Farming system research (FSR): It involves a form of action research in which scientists work with the farmers in defining their problems and then seeking solutions with the aim of improving the benefits to the farmers in a sustainable way (Chambers et al. 1990).
- Participatory action research (PAR): Essentially, it is research which involves all relevant parties in actively examining together a current action (which they experience as problematic) in order to change and improve it.
- Methodology for participatory assessments (MPA): It builds on the earlier works on participation, demand responsiveness, gender, poverty and sustainability. The MPA mainstreams gender and poverty as part of the overall monitoring of sustainability in water supply and sanitation projects.
- Participatory technology development (PTD): It is an approach to learning and innovation. The approach involves collaboration between researchers and farmers in the analysis of agricultural problems and testing of alternative farming practices.
- Participatory poverty assessment (PPA): It is a process for including the views of poor people in the analysis of poverty and in the design of strategies to reduce it.
- Participatory research and development (PR&D): PR&D is described as a pool of concepts, practices, norms and attitudes that enable people to enhance their knowledge for sustainable agriculture and natural resource management.
- Project cycle management (PCM): It stands for participatory management approach when participation of the different actors and their respective roles and responsibilities are emphasised from the very start of a project.
- Participatory inquiry (PI): PI is a structural methodology centred on the principle that participation is a moral right, in which multiple perspectives are sought through a process of group inquiry (IIED 1994).
- Participatory monitoring and evaluation (PM&E): It is a process in which development interveners and local community jointly and continuously observe, document and critically reflect on the effects and changes caused by project intervention.
- Participatory action reflection research (PARR): It is used to encompass approaches and methods which have in various ways combined action, reflection, participation and research.
- Rapid ethnographic assessment (REA): It arose from a recognition that intensive techniques, such as observation, key informant interviews and group discussion, enable researchers to explore social issues in depth and to identify factors and relationships that may not be understood through qualitative survey.

- Rapid assessment procedure (RAP): It is described as methodologies that provide guidelines for health workers, social scientists in fields other than anthropology and anthropologists for conducting rapid assessments of health seeking behaviour.
- Social assessment (SA): It provides a comprehensive, participatory framework for deciding what issues hold priority for attention and how operationally useful information can be gathered and used.
- Self-esteem, associative strength, resourcefulness, action planning and responsibility (SARAR): SARAR is an education/training methodology for working with stakeholders at different levels to engage their creative capacity in planning, problem solving and evaluation.
- Theatre for development (TD): It means live performance or theatre used as a development tool.

Participatory approach, thus, has several labels and acronyms. Yet, there are common principles uniting most of them.

- All these approaches have a well-defined methodology.
- They take into account multiple perspectives of an issue, a problem or a situation.
- They adopt group inquiry.
- The methodology adopted is concerned with bringing about a change in the life of the people.
- All these approaches aim at sustained action.

It should be noted that some of the labels have come to stay; some have slowly waned and disappeared. But one label, namely, PRA, has stood the test of time. PRA is the best-known acronym for participatory methods (Mikkelsen 2005). It is being increasingly used, though it is currently known as participatory learning and action (PLA). We have used the acronym PRA throughout the book.

SUMMARY

Till the late 1980s, a top-down approach was followed in all our development programmes. They were mostly supply-driven. The approach, with its inherent limitations and shortcomings, could not bring about the desired results. Hence, alternative development approaches have been experimented and introduced with greater emphasis on grass-roots planning, implementation and evaluation. An important approach with its emphasis on participation and empowerment that emerged during the late 1980s was that of PRA. The basic logic for the introduction of PRA in development work is that the success of any development intervention depends on the confidence built and the power given to people to decide and to take community initiatives.

The crux of PRA is participation. It is the voluntary involvement of people in self-determined change. Participation is emphasised upon as it ensures better decisions and better execution.

PRA has borrowed methods and techniques from several sources. The major ones are: (*i*) (biases of) rural development tourism, (*ii*) (demerits of) questionnaire survey, (*iii*) PARR, (*iv*) agro-eco system analysis, (*v*) applied anthropology, (*vi*) informal survey and (*vii*) rapid rural appraisal.

PRA started with RRA. PRA is a continuum of RRA. It is an improved version of RRA. There are many commonalities as well as differences between PRA and RRA. The outsider in RRA is the investigator while in PRA he or she is a facilitator.

The development of PRA can be traced under three phases: (*i*) the first phase (late 1980s and early 1990s)—this was a period of innovation; (*ii*) the second phase (mid-1990s)—this was a period of wider application and critical reflection; (*iii*) the third phase (late 1990s)—this was the period that focused on social learning, participatory monitoring and evaluation.

There are more than twenty labels of participatory approaches. However, among all, PRA is being increasingly used as the best-known acronym.

2

The Concept and Principles of Participatory Rural Appraisal

INTRODUCTION

Participatory rural appraisal (PRA) emerged as a participatory tool of learning in the late 1980s. It is a continuum of rapid rural appraisal (RRA) and other field-based and people-oriented participatory approaches. Emerging primarily as an appraisal method, PRA has subsequently been applied in several activities of a project cycle, including planning, implementation, monitoring and evaluation. As a development tool, it cannot just stop with committing the people in appraising and analysing their problems, conditions and situations. Rather, it must go beyond that and extend into analysis, planning and action. Consequently, the concept of PRA has undergone several changes over a period of time. Even then, the crux of the PRA—'putting people first'—remains intact.

DEFINITION OF PRA

McCracken et al. (1988) define PRA as 'a semi-structured activity carried out in the field, by a multi-disciplinary team and designed to quickly acquire new information on, and new hypothesis about rural life'. Some of the important features that emerge from this definition are: (*i*) it is a field-based appraisal undertaken by a multi-disciplinary team; (*ii*) it is quick; (*iii*) it is mostly an information-gathering technique and (*iv*) it is exploratory in nature. An important limitation is that the precept of 'attitude and behaviour', which is very fundamental to PRA, is not considered.

According to Sam Joseph, 'PRA is both an attitude and a method. It helps an outsider to quickly understand the village system from the villagers' point of view.' The emphasis of this definition is on the personal behaviour of the practitioners of PRA. It has also stressed the concept of 'rapidity' and learning from the villagers. However, this definition has failed to explicitly pinpoint the purpose of understanding the village system.

Robert Chambers and Paramesh Shah describe PRA as a 'new approach and method in which rural people themselves do much of the investigation, presentation, analysis, planning and dissemination than has been normal in the past'. This definition has duly recognised the significance of the three pillars of PRA, namely, methods, attitudes and behaviour, and sharing (see Figure 2.1). However, it should be remembered that PRA is not only applied in appraisal and planning but also in implementing, monitoring and evaluation.

Figure 2.1
Three Pillars of PRA

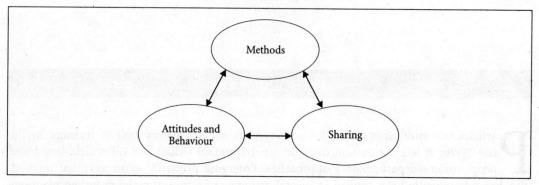

Source: Chambers (1997: 150).

A comprehensive definition incorporating all the essential aspects of PRA has been evolved by practitioners and researchers in an international workshop, South–South Workshop on PRA: Attitudes and Behaviour, held at Bangalore in 1996 (Kumar 1996). According to them, 'PRA is a growing family of approaches and methods to enable local people to share, enhance and analyse their knowledge of life and conditions, to plan, act, monitor, and evaluate.' According to this definition, people, the key and primary stakeholders in the development process, play a very significant role in deciding their future and destiny. PRA is now a philosophy and way of life that lays stress on self-critical awareness and commitment to the poor, the weak and the vulnerable.

FEATURES OF PRA

We may deduce certain characteristic features of PRA from these definitions. They are briefly stated in the following lines:

- PRA is predominantly a participatory process. It provides a vast scope and space for both people as well as outsiders to actively participate at every stage of the PRA process.

- A preset questionnaire is not used in PRA; rather a semi-structured interview technique is followed. This provides a lot of opportunities for the outsiders to explore and learn progressively.
- PRA is an interactive process. The ideas of outsiders and people interact and thus facilitate in mutual learning.
- PRA is enabling in nature. It enables the people to learn about their condition and situation. The PRA process also seeks to enable outsiders to learn; but through the sharing of information in a manner which enhances the analysis and knowledge of the people.
- PRA believes in flexibility in choosing methods. The practitioners of PRA are free to improvise the methods.
- The practitioners have the freedom to invent new methods of participatory learning and interaction and action.
- PRA seeks to empower. It empowers the weak, the powerless and the marginalised, by enabling them to analyse, discuss and deliberate on their condition. The output sought here is enhanced knowledge and competence and an ability to make demands and sustain action.
- PRA methods are adaptable. The practitioners are free to modify the methods to suit the local conditions and situations.

PRINCIPLES OF PRA

Principles are ground rules. A good practice of PRA presupposes the practice of all its essential features. All the principles are equally important as they are interrelated. They support and reinforce each other. All the principles of PRA have been enunciated based on field practice. As Chambers has rightly put it, 'these principles have been induced rather than deduced; they have been elicited by trying out practices, finding what works and what does not and then asking why'. They are experiential, not metaphysical. While listing the principles, different practitioners and authors have listed different principles underlying PRA and RRA. Chambers (1997) has listed two sets of principles, namely, (*i*) principles shared by RRA and PRA and (*ii*) additional principles stressed in PRA.

The principles shared by RRA and PRA are as follows:

- Reversal of learning
- Learning rapidly and progressively
- Offsetting biases
- Optimising trade-off
- Triangulating
- Seeking complexity and diversity

Additional principles stressed upon in PRA are as follows:

- Facilitating—they do it
- Self-critical awareness and responsibility
- Sharing

The principles shared by RRA and PRA are more conceptual and methodological in nature. The additional principles emphasised in PRA are behavioural in nature since they are applied in practice by the people who are involved in doing things. Thus, the emphasis in the case of PRA is more on attitude and behaviour.

To the principles listed in the preceding paragraphs we may add one more, namely, sequences or sequencing. PRA practitioners need to follow sequencing as a ground rule. Sequencing helps in adhering to the principles like learning rapidly and progressively. Further, sequencing helps in triangulating the data and information.

We will now examine the principles of PRA in detail.

Reversal of Learning

Reversal is used to describe a direction away from the normal practice and towards its opposite. PRA underscores the reversal of roles among the outsiders—researchers and professionals. The outsiders have so far been preaching, lecturing and teaching the rural people in the process of undertaking research and initiating development work. Any research or development work is a learning process. An outsider is ignorant of the local situation, local condition and local knowledge. Hence, they need to go to the rural areas as novices, as students and as learners. They need to cultivate the art of listening. The villagers, on the other hand, are aware of their conditions and lifestyle; besides long years of rich experience, they also possess local knowledge and a skill set and they therefore become the preceptors. The 'roles' to be performed by the outsiders and insiders in rural appraisal is given in Figure 2.2.

Figure 2.2
Role of Outsiders and Insiders in PRA

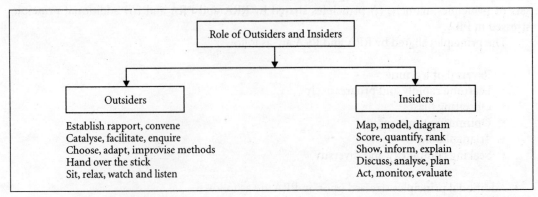

Chambers (1994a) has enunciated four clusters of reversals: (*i*) reversal of frames; (*ii*) reversal of modes; (*iii*) reversal of relation and (*iv*) reversal of power. He describes these as discourses of PRA, which are closely related to each other and are mutually supporting.

Reversal of frames

It is a reversal from the knowledge, categories and values of outsider professionals to those of the insider local people. Conventional investigations like questionnaire survey are preset. They are designed by outsiders and mostly reflect the outsiders' views, concerns and categories. PRA is more open. Its tool is a semi-structured checklist, providing a lot of scope for conversation, which in turn leads to greater freedom and equality. In PRA, there is greater autonomy for the insiders to change the agenda of discussion. The outsiders hand over the control and the insiders determine the agenda, categories and details. The shift is from preset and closed to participatory and open. Reversal of frame presupposes the 'putting the last first'. It means learning from the poorest.

Reversal of modes

Under PRA, the modes of interaction and analysis are reversed from their normal directions in three ways:

- *From individual to group*: The focus in PRA shifts from individual to group. Although interactions with individual do take place in PRA, yet a participatory analysis by groups is given much more emphasis. Group interaction and analysis have several advantages. The group has a collective knowledge and wisdom covering a wider field and spectrum. Groups often build up collective and creative enthusiasm, fill in gaps left by others, and add, cross-check and correct details. Groups do have disadvantages, such as dominance by a person or a local minority. However, this can be overcome through proper facilitation.
- *From verbal to visual*: This implies that the transfer of information takes place through visual media. These include social and census mapping, resource mapping and modelling, seasonal analysis, Venn diagramming, matrix ranking and scoring of options, etc. These methods are used as a means for the local people to express, share and analyse their knowledge. Diagrams then present an agenda for discussion. Visual diagramming is an equaliser between the literate and the illiterate, between the marginalised and the self-confident (see Table 2.1).
- *From measuring to comparing*: In the case of survey research, the tendency is to make absolute measurement. For identifying trends or changes, or for comparing conditions between households, measurements are made at different times, or of different things or in different places. Measurement, however, has a shortcoming. For instance, questions on sensitive subjects, such as income, assets and savings, can sow seeds of suspicion, even sabotage the rapport with people and ultimately generate misleading data.

Table 2.1
Verbal and Visual: A Comparison

Variable	Verbal	Visual
Mode and role of outsider	Investigator	Facilitator; catalyst
Mode and role of local persons	Reactive respondents	Creative analyst and preserver
Aim	Extraction of information	Generation of local analysis
Degree of eye contact	High	Low
Information flow	Sequential	Cumulative
Initiative for cross-checking	Outsiders	Insiders
Ownership of information	Appropriated by outsiders	Shared; can be owned by insiders
Medium and materials	Chosen by outsiders; outsiders mostly handle	Chosen by local people; insiders easily handle

Comparisons have certain merits: (*i*) they are easier and quicker to express than measurements; (*ii*) the trends and changes can be elicited without baseline data; (*iii*) they are less sensitive, for example, seasonal calendar, trend change and (*iv*) detailed and complex information can be elicited within a short time (e.g., matrix ranking and scoring).

Reversal of relation

This implies building a rapport, a good relationship with the community and also collecting information and data through fun. PRA stresses the process of building a rapport. Unlike the social anthropologists, PRA practitioners quickly gain rapport by showing respect, answering questions, being honest, being interested, ready to be taught and by learning through doing.

Reversal of power

This is also known as the reversal of dominance. The conventional as well as classical social anthropological investigations are extractive in nature. In the case of survey questionnaire, the power and initiation lie with the interviewers. The professional concern is less with the respondents and more with what they provide—the responses. The thrust of PRA is to reverse dominance. The objective is to gather less data, and the emphasis is on starting a process. The initiative is passed to the people; in other words, the stick is handed over. Instead of imposing and extracting, PRA is designed to empower.

Learning Rapidly and Progressively

PRA assists in quick learning. The methods used in a PRA largely facilitate both the insiders and the outsiders to learn about rural conditions in a rapid manner. However, rapid learning does not undermine the quality of PRA because PRA insists on progressive learning. Learning takes place with conscious enquiry and analysis. The PRA team with a checklist using semi-structured interview techniques consciously explores the different aspects of rural life. Jumping from one topic to another is deliberately avoided. Progressive learning also helps in cross-checking the data and information gathered, which ensures production of reliable and valid information.

Offsetting Biases

Conventional methods of data gathering, especially the hurried rural visits made by urban-based professionals to study rural poverty, have a lot of anti-poverty biases, such as spatial, project, personal, diplomatic and professional. These biases camouflage the various dimensions of poverty. As a result, any anti-poverty programme planned, designed and implemented has not yielded the desired results. PRA, therefore, emphasises that anti-poverty biases in all its forms should be stamped out. The process of neutralising or counteracting biases should start at the very stage of studying the root causes of poverty.

The spatial bias—urban, tarmac or roadside—should be countered by walking away from the road. Project biases can be offset by visiting non-project areas. Offsetting project biases would also mean that the PRA team interacts with non-users of services and non-adopters of technology.

Biases of personal contact are counterbalanced by meeting the poor people. Members of the PRA team should make it a point to see the women also. Women should never be neglected in any appraisal. Depending on the objective, the team should also visit and interact with the aged and the sick.

Dry season bias is offset by meeting people during the rains and during the worst time of the year, or at least by asking what is the worst time of the year. The professional bias is removed by having self-introspection to see the limitations of professional conditioning.

In short, the team should take all possible steps and initiations to see that the right people are met and interacted with at the right time to gather the right information and data without a tinge of bias.

Optimising Trade-off

This principle relates the cost of learning to the usefulness of the information with trade-off between quantity, relevance, accuracy and timeliness (Chambers 1997). There are two extremes among the conventional methods of appraisal. At one extreme is the survey method. Nobody can undervalue or underestimate the usefulness and merits of the survey. It is systematic, scientific and could ensure availability of accurate, reliable and valid data. However, carrying out extensive surveys is time-consuming and requires much administrative and logical support which ultimately makes the survey costlier. Chambers portrays survey as a 'long and dirty' method. The word 'long' denotes 'time-consuming' while the word 'dirty' indicates 'costly'. At the other extreme remains the rural development tourism. Appraisal of a situation or condition or a problem in a rural area under this method takes a very short period of time. Much vital information and data is likely to be left out. It has biases that would stand in the way of capturing a full and complete picture of a problem. Chambers characterises this method as a 'short and dirty' method. 'Short' implies 'less time consuming' and 'dirty' stands for the various biases associated with this method. PRA, to a certain extent, lies in the middle of the two extremes as it tries to trade off between the long and dirty method of data collection on one hand and the short and dirty method of information gathering on the other. PRA aims at the appraisal of a situation, or a condition or a problem, as quickly as possible, without sacrificing the basic prerequisites of the relaxed, non-dominating and non-imposing approach. It also endeavours to collect the data and information at as low a cost as possible and of course without forfeiting the quality of the data and information gathered. The relaxed rapid appraisal within a reasonable period at less cost is made possible mainly through team work, collective efforts of insiders and outsiders, employing people-friendly methods of data gathering, on-the-spot analysis of data and information and sharing.

PRA also attempts to trade off between excess data and information on one hand and too less data on the other. The survey method invariably results in over-collection of data, which has resulted in a chain or a succession of problems. In order to avoid such a problem, PRA advocates collection of optimum data. The team that gathers information and data constantly asks itself: What kind of information is required, for what purposes and how much information is required? This helps in gathering just the required data. This is known as principle of optimal ignorance. This implies that both the amount and the detail of information required to produce useful results in a limited period of time are regarded as expenses that are to be kept to a minimum. The aim is to arrive at an agreed sufficiency of knowledge relevant to the objectives of PRA and not to exceed this by investigating irrelevant aspects or being concerned with unnecessary detail (McCracken 1988). In other words, the PRA practitioners have to be optimally ignorant. The golden rule is to 'avoid collection of unnecessary detail'.

Yet another rule associated with the principle of optimising trade-off is that of appropriate imprecision. Data collected through PRA is quantitative as well as qualitative. A certain degree of inaccuracy is bound to exist in the qualitative data in spite of the in-built mechanism in PRA to cross-check and validate data through triangulation and sequencing. Although there is a need to give allowance for such inaccuracy, yet at the same time it should be seen that the inaccuracy of data does not affect the quality of the data. In other words, PRA practitioners need to be appropriately imprecise—not measuring what need not be measured or more accurately than needed, following the dictum 'it is better to be approximately right than precisely wrong'.

Triangulation

'Triangulation' or 'triangulating' is a form of cross-checking for validating the data and information collected. It is a test of validity. It means 'learning from several, quite often three, methods, disciplines, individuals or groups, locations, types of information, items and/or points in a discussion, to cross-check, compare, gain insights and successively approximate'. It is, thus, a multiple strategy to cross-check the data and information. It is done mostly through plural investigation. It is a method 'to overcome the problems that stem from studies relying upon a single theory, single method, single set of data and single investigator'. It is a process whereby findings may be judged, and validated when different and contrasting methods of data collection yield identical findings on the same research subjects—a case of replication within the same setting rather than replication across settings. In short, triangulation is a technique for validating the information and data by employing more than a method.

Triangulations are of many types. Mikkelsen (1995) has suggested five types of triangulation. They are:

- Data triangulation;
- Investigator triangulation;
- Discipline triangulation;
- Theoretical triangulation; and
- Methodological triangulation.

Data triangulation further comprises three categories, namely, time triangulation, space triangulation and personal triangulation. The influence of time on study design is considered in the case of time triangulation. Space triangulation is a typical form of comparative study. Personal triangulation deals with comparison of reactions at three levels of analysis: (*i*) individual, (*ii*) the interactive level among groups and (*iii*) collective level.

When more than one person examines the same situation, it is known as investigator triangulation. Discipline triangulation means that a problem is studied through different disciplines. Theoretical triangulation is one in which competing theories are used in any one situation. Methodological triangulation involves 'within-method' triangulation or 'between-method' triangulation. If the same method is used on different occasions, it is known as within-method triangulation, for instance, the use of mapping for collection of demographic data and wealth ranking. Between-method triangulation involves a combination of two or more different research strategies or methods in the study of the same empirical units.

These five forms or types of triangulation have been synthesised and presented in three forms. Under this, triangulation is done in relation to (*i*) composition of team, (*ii*) source of information and (*iii*) mix of techniques (see Figure 2.3).

The teams from the village as well as from outside which undertake rural appraisal are multidisciplinary in nature. They are of different age groups and sex and from various sections of the community. An appraisal of a situation or condition by such a well-balanced and well-represented team would naturally help to cross-check the gathered information.

PRA picks and chooses a variety of methods to appraise the situation. The appraisal invariably involves a combination of two or more methods. For instance, transect or group walk involves direct observation, semi-structured interviewing, transect and transect-based resource mapping. PRA emphasises on presenting the data and information in a visual form. With visual sharing of map, model, diagram, etc., all who are present can see, point to, discuss, manipulate and alter

Figure 2.3
Triangulation

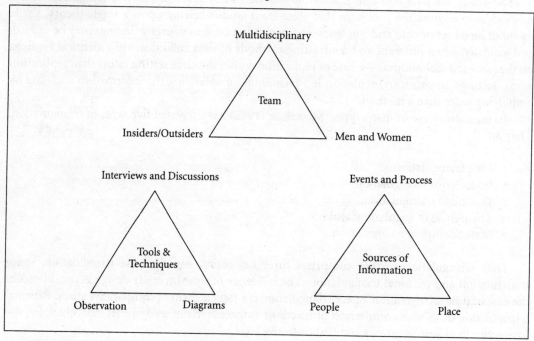

physical objects or representations. Triangulation takes place with people cross-checking and correcting each other.

The sources of information under PRA are more than one. Information flows from people, places, and events and processes. For instance, while sketching the timeline of a village, the oral testimony of the people is cross-checked by looking at places and also by recalling events and processes which occurred in the village at different periods of time.

Seeking Complexity and Diversity

The rural society is quite complex and diverse in nature. No two villages exhibit similarities in all aspects of life. Again, within the community also, there are obvious differences. The differences could be seen with reference to age, gender, ethnic or social group, poverty, education, livelihood strategy, types of assets, and so on. Outsiders normally do not look into these differences. Often, outside professionals treat the community as a homogeneous unit. They normally meet just middle-aged youth, males from dominant groups and economically better-off. And usually their criteria, preferences and priorities are taken as those of the whole community; but the community also includes those who are weaker and worse off—children, very old, females, social inferiors, subordinate groups, the disabled and those who are vulnerable and poor. Such a bias on the part of the outsiders results in the adoption of a blueprint rigid development strategy.

PRA takes into account the complex and diverse nature of the rural society. It recognises the differences between communities and within communities and their significance. Hence it seeks, enables the expression and analysis of complex and diverse information and judgement. This has been expressed in terms of seeking variability rather than averages (Beebe 1987) and has been described as the principle of maximum diversity, or maximising the diversity and richness of information (Dunn and McMillan 1991). This includes looking for learning from exceptions, oddities, dissenters and outliners in any distribution. This can also involve sampling in a non-statistical sense. It goes beyond cross-checking and triangulation. It deliberately looks for, notices and investigates contradictions, anomalies and differences. PRA thus recognises and supports diversity, complexity and multiple reality.

Sequencing

PRA is basically a relaxed and progressive method of learning about a rural situation or condition. It is a step-by-step learning process. To learn from the people, PRA employs a wide variety of people-friendly methods, for it believes that any one single method will not help in learning the different dimensions of a problem, an event, a condition or a situation. For instance, identification of the poor in a village begins with an analysis of the overall socio-economic conditions of the people through social mapping based on village transect. The completed social maps and the data and information gathered through these maps provide enough input and base for pursuing wealth or well-being ranking which facilitates in identifying the poor. To probe further on the prevalence of poverty among the poor, a focused group discussion may be attempted followed by a livelihood analysis. Thus, the use of participatory methods one after the other in a systematic manner to understand the different dimensions of a particular problem may be defined as sequences or sequencing (see Table 2.2).

Table 2.2
Sequencing

Problem under Study	Sequencing of Methods
Degraded forests	Participatory resource map—transect—root stock census of quadrats—identification of problems and opportunities—discussion—ranking options
Identification of micro-enterprises	Resource flow with demand map—card posting with focused group discussion—Enterprise matrix with priority ranking—consumers map with focused group discussion

Sequencing has several advantages. Chambers (1994b) calls it the 'power of sequences'. First, the commitment of the participant increases—the participants are likely to initiate further action; such actions are likely to be spontaneous and sustainable. Second, sequencing helps in cross-checking the information and data collected. It helps in detecting and locating the errors and mistakes committed earlier. Third, the different activities interact cumulatively. Each activity adds new dimensions and details which naturally enrich others. Fourth, both the insiders and outsiders learn through a process, by sharing what they know, through observation and analysis. Fifth, sequencing takes the process of PRA practice to the natural end. And the sixth, it helps the practitioner to do field work in a more systematic manner, which ultimately ensures the credibility of PRA findings and results.

Effective sequencing presupposes certain spadework which includes: (*i*) the group from outside must interact among themselves on the completion of each round of data collection and should discuss and decide on the data gap and the method to be adopted to fill in the gap, (*ii*) the process of each PRA sitting should be observed and be shared among the group members each day and (*iii*) the method selected may be improvised upon depending on the local condition and situation for better results (see Figure 2.4).

Figure 2.4
Building Understanding and Accumulating Knowledge through Sequencing of Methods

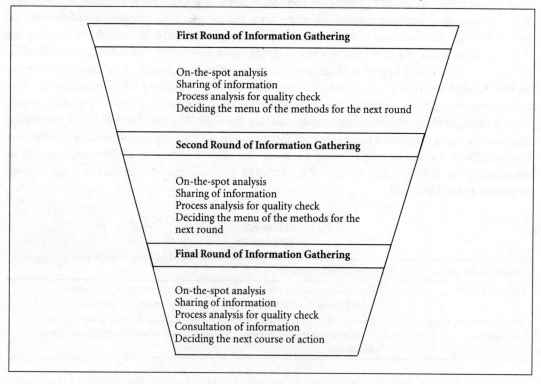

First Round of Information Gathering

On-the-spot analysis
Sharing of information
Process analysis for quality check
Deciding the menu of the methods for the next round

Second Round of Information Gathering

On-the-spot analysis
Sharing of information
Process analysis for quality check
Deciding the menu of the methods for the next round

Final Round of Information Gathering

On-the-spot analysis
Sharing of information
Process analysis for quality check
Consultation of information
Deciding the next course of action

They Do It

The people from the village play a significant role in PRA. They undertake the work of investigation, analysis and presentation of inferences. They own the outcome of all the exercises and in the process they learn about themselves and the conditions in which they live. This has been expressed as 'handing over the stick'. This would also mean that the outsiders' role should stop with the starting of the process. They have to then sit, watch, observe and listen to what the people say, show, explain, discuss, draw, analyse, and so on. The outsiders are not supposed to dominate. The outsider acts less as an extractor of data and information and more of a convenor, facilitator and analyst. The objective is less to gather data and much more to start a process. The initiative is passed on to the people who are the prime actors.

Self-critical Awareness

It is basically related to the attitude and behaviour of the PRA practitioners. It means that the PRA practitioners ought to examine their own behaviour continuously and critically. They must develop a spirit of self-criticism. Self-criticism or self-awareness is the ability of each person to accurately analyse his or her own work or his or her own behaviour or attitude in undertaking a work to distinguish good from bad in it. Such an analysis would help in acknowledging one's own errors and to discuss the causes and effect of these errors. Self-critical awareness is an act of frankness, courage, comradeship and an awareness of one's responsibilities. It is a proof of our will to accomplish and to accomplish properly. To criticise oneself is to reconstruct oneself from within in order to serve better (Hope and Timmel 1992). It demands personal insight and reflection.

Self-critical awareness results in self-doubt. Self-doubt would mean doubting various perceptions and realities, and being able to embrace and learn from error. It also opens up to the realities of others. It implies that others may know more or they may be right. Understanding that realities are multiple as well as the differences between one's own and others' realities helps in learning and doing better.

Self-critical awareness includes embracing the error. The practitioners need to welcome the error as an opportunity to learn. They have to face failure positively. Such an attitude helps the PRA practitioners to pursue the PRA exercise in the field with a sense of honesty and devotion. It also helps them to go nearer to the people and ultimately helps them to serve them better.

Self-critical awareness presupposes that PRA practitioners tend to take personal responsibility for what is done rather than relying on the authority of manuals or of a rigid set of rules. Using one's best judgement at all times has been a sort of meta-manual.

Sharing

Sharing is a cardinal principle of PRA and implies sharing of information and ideas. The culture of sharing takes place among the people, between the people and the outside facilitators and among different practitioners. Sharing has several advantages. First, everything is open—nothing is secret. Second, it results in a high degree of transparency in transactions. Third, it facilitates mutual learning and thus enhances the knowledge of every participant. Fourth, the outcome of a PRA exercise like map, model, diagram, and so forth is open to all who are present to participate. Different people add details, cross-check and correct each other. The information is visible and semi-permanent and can be checked, verified, amended, added to and owned by the participants. Thus, it enhances the quality of the outcome. Fifth, it brings the different actors of PRA closer. And sixth, it brings about an attitudinal and behavioural change in the minds of the participants.

Besides sharing of information and ideas, the practitioners sometimes share food also, which serves as a facilitating force for building up rapport among the participants.

BASIC GUIDELINES FOR PRACTISING PRA

The effective practice of PRA methods in the field depends on strict adherence to the principles of PRA which in turn rely on the adoption of certain dos and don'ts in the field. We present in this chapter certain dos and don'ts that are common to all the tools. Tool-specific dos and don'ts are presented in the chapters concerned.

Dos

- Stay in the village along with the villagers.
- Learn to unlearn by staying with the people, by more of listening and less of talking.
- Establish a rapport with the people.
- Organise 'do-it-yourself' to start the field work. This will involve the team in trying their hands at everyday local activities.
- Choose a place in consultation with the people where men, women and people from different sections of the community can gather and participate.
- Create an open and enabling atmosphere to encourage participation.
- Start and build up the interaction and dialogue gradually.
- Meet the people at their convenience.
- Ensure that the team from outside is multi-disciplinary in nature.
- Decide the role of each member of the team from outside.
- Cultivate the attitude of letting people set the agenda.

- Ask open-ended questions in an informal way. Resort to the six helpers of PRA: What? When? Where? Who? How? Why?
- Use locally available materials in all PRA exercises.
- Be humble in your approach, respect the local people, their culture, their customs and their way of life.
- Be flexible in your approach.
- Be an active participant in all the PRA deliberations.
- Be aware of the conflicts, if any; deal with them in a positive way.
- Be conscious of the silent and invisible people in the village.
- Be sensitive to the feelings of the people.
- Be careful about your body language.
- Think about the possible sequences of methods that can be used before leaving for the field.
- Share your knowledge with the people.
- Hand over the stick.

Don'ts

- Don't fail to listen closely.
- Don't ask leading questions.
- Don't ask insensitive questions.
- Don't fail to probe into issues.
- Don't fail to judge the responses.
- Don't interrupt.
- Don't dominate.
- Don't lecture.
- Don't personalise issues.
- Don't make false promises.
- Don't be arrogant and obsessive.
- Don't be judgemental.
- Don't use tricky language.
- Don't decide, rather facilitate the people to decide.

SUMMARY

PRA is an evolving discipline. Its strength lies in its practices in the field, field-based reflections and sharing the outcome of reflections with the different actors in the PRA process. The principles of PRA have been evolved and formulated based on field experiences and reflections. The outcome of PRA exercises, their validity and their reliability largely depend on strict adherence to the principles of PRA. There are two categories of principles. The first category of principles, common to RRA and PRA, provide certain broad guidelines and ground rules for practising PRA in the field. The second category of principles exclusively related to PRA speaks of attitudes and behaviour of the practitioners of PRA, such as openness, humility, curiosity, sensitivity, self-introspection, self-criticism, self-doubt, etc. The effective practice of the first category of principles hinges on the right attitude and behaviour of the PRA practitioners. The core of good PRA is therefore attitude and behaviour.

The principles of PRA are

- reversal of learning;
- learning rapidly and progressively;
- offsetting biases;
- optimising trade-off;
- triangulation;
- seeking complexity and diversity;
- sequencing;
- they (the people) do it;
- self-critical awareness;
- sharing.

The translation of principles into action depends on the adoption of certain dos and don'ts in the field.

3

Participatory Mapping

INTRODUCTION

Rural people are the natives of the area where they live. They have been living in these areas for many centuries and thus have a clear perception of the area. They possess the ability to represent their surroundings very accurately and diagrammatically, irrespective of their literacy status. Interacting continuously with the environment around them, they have a clear mental picture of their village and its environment. They can easily transfer the picture from their mind onto the ground in the form of a map. The participatory rural appraisal (PRA) facilitator can enable the people to map their village and facilitate an understanding of their situation and condition through the map. Maps can work magic. They are a very effective and immediate source of communication. They are vibrant and can be made a dynamic tool to aid communication. They can promote cross-generational communication and convey a sense of authority. They can also promote community cohesion and self-actualisation (Alcorn 2000).

MEANING OF MAPS

Mapping refers to maps made or drawn by the members of the community on paper or on the ground. It also entails building three-dimensional models on the ground. It is a process by which information is presented in a spatial form.

PURPOSE OF MAPS

Maps, in their simplest form, are employed to identify the comparative location and importance of different resources within an area (Institute of Development Studies 1995). There are several reasons for using maps in PRA. Some of these are

- to provide a framework for discussion over the relative location of resources;
- to highlight the resources of importance, using mapping as a spatial guide;
- to raise issues which are affected by these resources;
- to analyse the present status or condition of a location;
- to raise an awareness of the existing facilities or natural resources;
- to create a focus for interest in a discussion over the resources;
- to stimulate debate over the importance of specific resources;
- to develop a basis for comparing different perspectives;
- to create visual presentation which could be understood by everybody; and
- to create a baseline for assessing change, for use as a basis for impact analysis or for monitoring and evaluation (Mascarenhas et al. 1991).

TYPES OF MAPS

Maps are of different types. The range is quite extensive and types overlap. However, maps in PRA may be broadly categorised into two types: social map and resource map. Under each category there is a wide variety of topical maps.

SOCIAL MAP

Meaning

It is one of the commonly conducted mapping exercises. It is, by and large, used to present information on the village layout, infrastructure, population, social stratifications, chronic health cases, handicapped, malnourished children, family planning, vaccination, widows, destitute, and so on. Social maps can be used for analysis of the houses marked in the map. It can also act as the basis for identifying social issues such as female infanticide and untouchability.

Participants

In an exercise like mapping everyone cannot participate actively at one time. Some may participate in the form of 'gathering participants for mapping', some by 'gathering materials for the exercise', some by actually 'drawing the map on the ground', some by 'giving the information' and some are likely to participate by 'transferring the map from the ground to the papers'.

Regarding the composition of the participants, key informants from various sections of the community can be involved. Men and women of different age groups are to be involved for gathering different types of data and various household aspects of the community. There are certain benefits in working with mixed groups. However, mixed groups may affect people's willingness to participate where individuals feel more comfortable in smaller and more homogeneous groups.

With regard to the number of participants in the mapping exercise, no hard and fast rule can be stipuiated. It depends on the size of the group, cooperation of the participants and timing of the exercise. Although a small group of eight to ten would be ideal, yet in a visual exercise like mapping, a larger number of participants from the village are likely to participate. Even though there should be no restriction on the number, at the same time a large number should not affect the process.

Procedure for Drawing Social Map

- The participants for this exercise are the members of the community. Find the members of the community who know and who are willing to share their knowledge.
- Clarify the objective and purpose of the mapping exercise.
- Take a walk with the participants and establish compass directions at the boundaries on village areas. Observe the physical structure and interview the participants while you walk. Obtain a spatial overview through general exploration, a view from a high vantage point.
- Return to where you will be conducting the exercise. The venue for this activity should be a public place that is easily accessible and can accommodate a large group.
- Help the people get started; but let them draw maps by themselves.
- Facilitate the participants to prepare simple outline maps showing key features and landmarks. These include roads, lands, paths and homes, and major landmarks such as school, temples, churches, mosques, forests, hills, etc. Once they have started mapping and gained confidence, they could be asked to map other types of information too.
- The relevant features are introduced using local materials such as chalks, stones, *rangoli*, pebbles, seeds, goat drops, twigs, flowers and leaves for a map on the ground or as symbols for a map on the paper. Each different material (or its size) represents information such as location of homes and facilities, the relative importance of an individual or recent problems (such as a family which suffered an infant death in the previous year).
- Symbols used by the participants during the mapping exercise are of great importance and use. Normally, the participants discuss among themselves and decide the symbol to be used for each variable. The facilitator should provide adequate time for the participants from the village to decide the symbol to be used for each variable. For instance, the villagers

may choose a distinct symbol for each type of house; they may select a symbol for a vacant house; they may also choose a symbol for a migrant family. Similarly, the participants may also depict the household with electricity and TV with distinct symbols (see Figure 3.1).

- Observe and show interest in what they draw and depict.
- Facilitate the people to draw successive maps on the completion of the base map.
- Ask them to give numbers to the households; if possible, ask them to name the head of the household. This would be useful for gathering the data later and also for initiating a wealth/well-being exercise.
- Interview the map; the map in the visual form provides an excellent medium for probing the various aspects of life in the village.
- Transfer the map on the ground to paper after its completion. The map should have a title, name of the site/village and names of participants from the community.
- Triangulate the information with others in the locality.
- Thank the participants for their participation.

Figure 3.1
An Example of Symbols Used for Different Types of Households

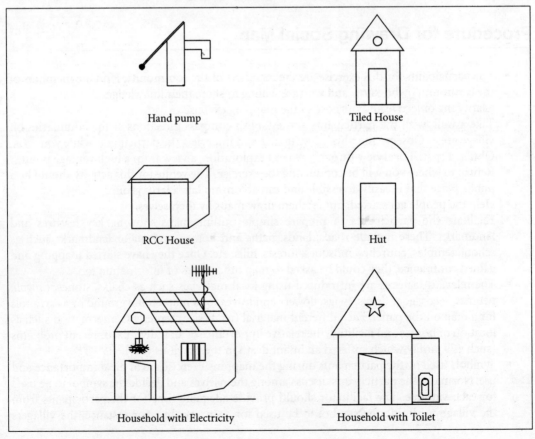

Dos

- Do spend time thinking about what information you are going to collect through map and why you need the information.
- Allow the villagers themselves to draw the map according to the way they perceive things and decide among themselves.
- Interview the map.

Don'ts

- Don't impose your way of drawing the map.
- Don't neglect the children.

Topical Social Maps

Filling up the social maps with a lot of information using different symbols and materials invariably causes confusion, especially while 'interviewing the map'. Hence, it is better to have a base map (see Figure 3.2), which provides the physical structure of the village. Using this map, a series of topical social maps can be drawn. A few types of topical social maps are discussed here.

Health map

The well-being of a household is often related to the physical health of household members. Various health-related aspects and variables can be effectively depicted on the health map. They include

- those suffering from chronic illness or disability;
- the sick classified by types of disease, location and social group;
- pregnant women and month of pregnancy;
- couples without children;
- family planning status;
- users and non-users of contraceptives;
- women with severe anaemia;
- deaths by category;
- children affected by polio;
- malnourished children;
- hazards, such as pollution, zones of defecation, places where mosquitoes breed, and so on;
- facilities like clinics, health post and medical shops;
- all those who use medical services and where they live.

Figure 3.2
Social Map: Kalkottai

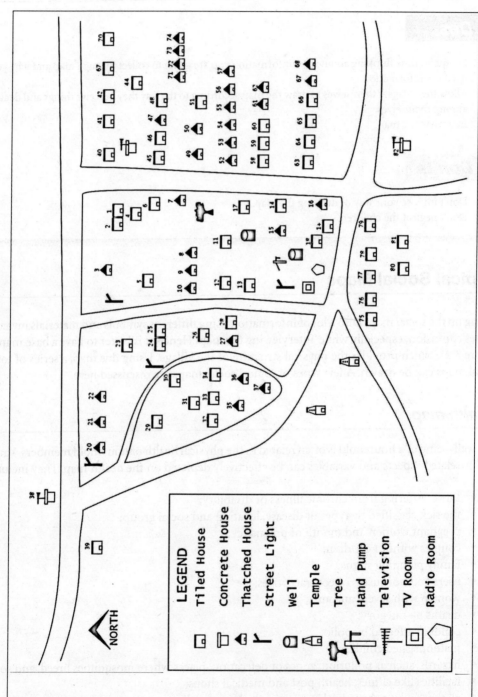

Source: PRA Unit, GRI (1997).

Water and sanitation map

This map can be drawn and used to learn about community's situation regarding all water supply and sanitation facilities, traditional as well as those provided by specific projects, and access of the poor, rich and middle-income households to them. The data and information that can be gathered include

- number, type and location of all water sources;
- distribution points;
- cut-off zones for water source use, classifying access of households to sources, particularly point sources;
- households that do not have easy access to any type of improved sources;
- number, type and location of sanitation facilities, both public and household, according to their installation;
- homes of community members with role in providing and maintaining water supply and sanitation services according to gender, involvement period, socio-economic level and function (including whether the service is paid or unpaid for);
- homes of community members who have received training for construction work or maintenance of services according to gender, class, involvement period and subject area.

Education map

This map can be drawn and used to discuss literacy levels and education (see Figure 3.3). The data and information that can be depicted on the map include the following:

- Literacy level among men and women
- Children who attend and do not attend school by category
- Drop-outs
- Men and women studying in colleges
- Men and women attending adult education centres
- Men and women undergoing vocational education programmes
- Men and women with technical qualifications
- Children who attend special schools.

Leadership map

This map can help in identifying the different types of leaders, both men and women, within the village. The leaders may be formal leaders such as the president and ward members of the local panchayat, presidents and boards of directors of cooperatives, office-bearers of self-help groups (SHGs), office bearers of farmers' associations, and informal leaders such as traditional leaders. The map can also be used to depict the local leaders of political parties (see Figure 3.4).

Figure 3.3
Map of Village Toot Ki Dhani (Balapura) Drawn Up during School Mapping

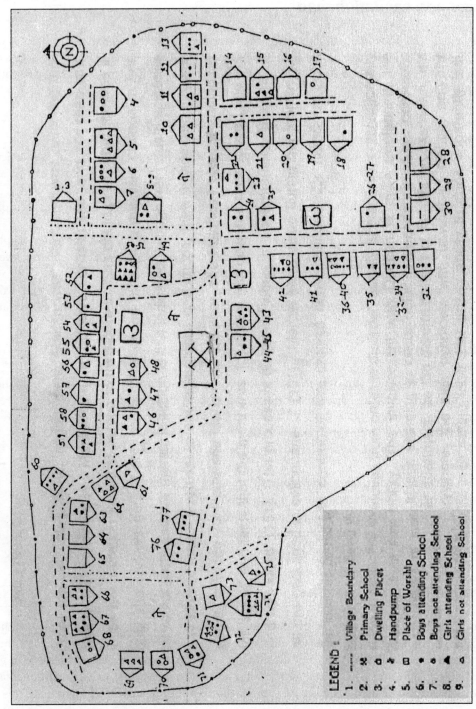

Source: PRA Unit, GRI (1997).

Figure 3.4
Leadership: Kurumpapatty Village

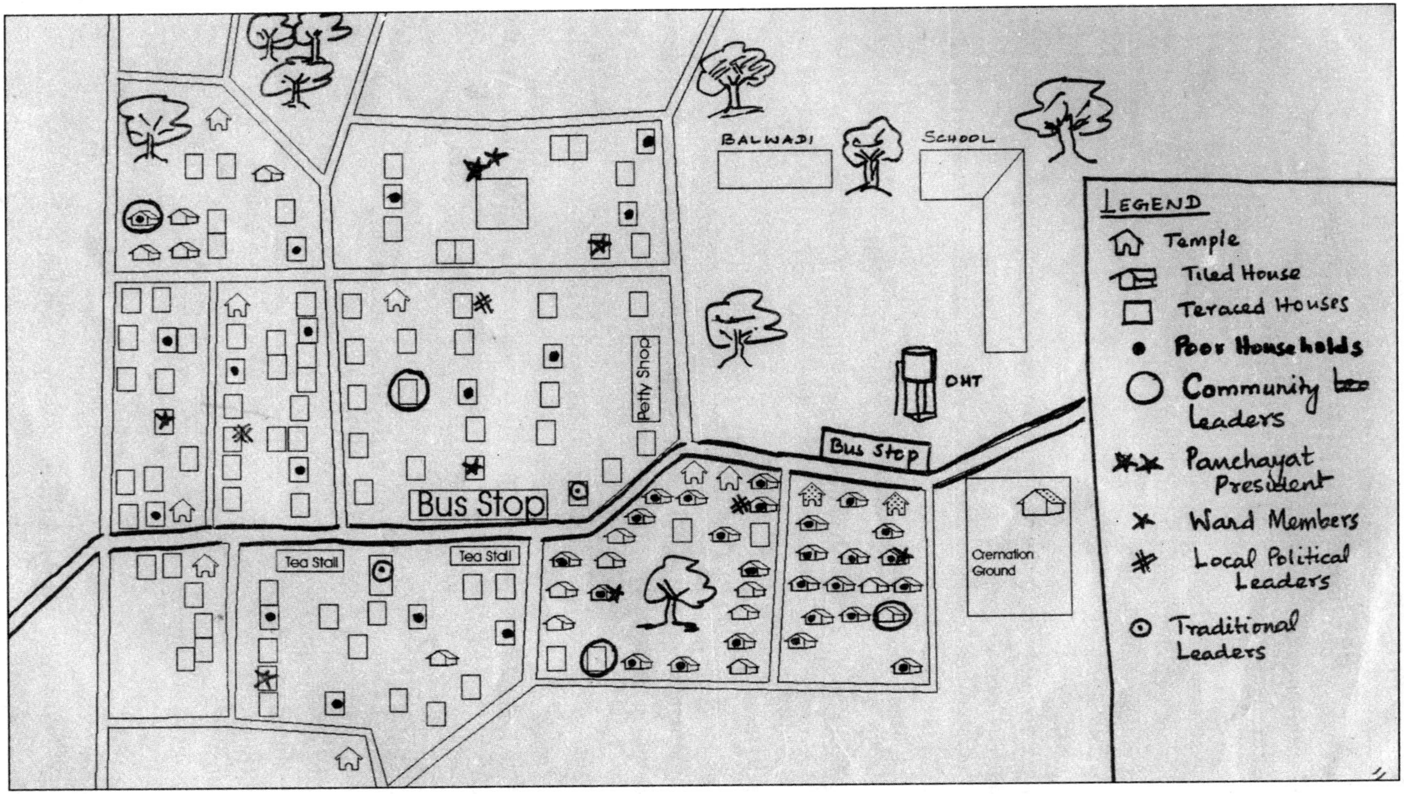

Source: PRA Unit, GRI (1995e).

Indigenous skill map

A topical skill analysis can also be created on a social map, identifying those who have skills which would be of importance in a veterinary or health programme. The people with indigenous skills may be in various fields, such as

- ethno-veterinary practitioners;
- farmers with excellent skills in cultural practices;
- traditional birth attendants;
- herbal collectors;
- herbalists;
- people who can forecast the weather through indigenous techniques;
- local therapists;
- local health practitioners;
- artists; and
- water diviners.

A full indigenous skills inventory may be taken through social mapping.

Vulnerability map

There are vulnerable groups of people in the community. They are the ones who are exposed to risks but are not able to cope up with these risks.

Vulnerability = exposed to risks + inability to cope

Any development project needs to include the vulnerable section of the people. A social map can be effectively used to identify the vulnerable people and their status. The vulnerable group includes

- families that cook only once a day and eat only once a day;
- those who have to go without food for days;
- those who lack a proper means of shelter;
- child labourers;
- street children;
- orphans;
- female-headed households;
- commercial sex workers;
- HIV/AIDS patients;
- the aged;
- families with a large number of non-earning dependants;
- wives and children of alcoholic men;

- discharged prisoners;
- pregnant women in poor families;
- widows;
- bonded labourers;
- malnourished children;
- children who grow up in a poor environment;
- children and women of migrant families;
- families living near pollution zones.

Applications

Social mapping has a wide range of applications. We would enumerate them likewise:

- It is an icebreaker. It helps to establish a closer rapport between the outsider and the community. Mapping creates a convivial atmosphere where the outsider and the people get closer and start interacting with each other as though they are long-time friends.
- Mapping along with the well-being ranking helps to identify the people in distress. Integration of the vulnerable and deprived section of the community in the development process is ensured if mapping is integrated in the planning process. The information could be used by the panchayat to cross-check the list of poor households that is identified by the government and sent to the panchayat.
- Mapping can be effectively used in educational activities too. The drop-outs could be quickly identified; their socio-economic background could be known from the social map. Steps may be taken to integrate them into the education system. An age-wise and sex-wise distribution of the children in the map would help identify the children who go to/do not go to school. This would help the school authorities take initiative to enrol all the children (see Figure 3.5).
- Social maps can help identify the equity issues in a village setting, especially in water supply. The PRA unit of Gandhigram Rural Institute (GRI) facilitated a social mapping exercise in a village called Pillaiarnatham. The water distribution system was shown in the map. It was found that Harijan Colony with forty households did not have even a single water tap, whereas each of the streets inhabited by higher-caste Hindus, with twenty-five to thirty-five households, had two or three water taps.
- Social mapping can help to identify the most vulnerable section of the community in a village. A case in point was an anaemic pregnant woman in a village. While facilitating a thematic social map on reproductive and child health, the women who were participating in the exercise identified a pregnant woman with severe anaemia. She was from a very poor household. If not treated, she was likely to die along with the baby. The team that facilitated the exercise took immediate steps to get the woman treated in a local hospital. Thus, at times, the map results not only in the identification of a problem but also in finding its solution.

Figure 3.5
Literacy Map: Krishna Rakshit Chak

Source: Neela Mukherjee (1994b).

Social mapping can also be used as a monitoring and evaluation tool. For instance, it can be used to monitor whether all the children in the community are vaccinated, provided we have baseline information on the map. Similarly, it can be ensured whether all the poor families have ration cards. Social mapping can also help to avoid welfare schemes being concentrated to just a few smart, poor families in a community. This would be done by depicting the reach of various welfare schemes being extended to various families.

The applications of social mapping given here are only indicative. Practitioners of PRA can use their ingenuity, improvise the method and apply it in their research and extension work accordingly.

Complementarity with Other Methods

Maps have been frequently used early-on in participatory exercise and provide a good jumping-off point for analysing a number of other issues that get raised during the mapping process.

With participatory mapping, the villages draw not just one but several maps, which become successively more detailed and useful, or which present new and complementary information. The map is then used as a reference for other planning purposes and is retained by the villagers for their own monitoring and evaluation.

Social mapping depicts people, social groups and other social characteristics. It further leads to an identification of the key informants, and then a discussion with them, resulting in analysing of the information by them.

Social mapping easily leads into well-being assessments or a more detailed analysis of a location, which in turn has been used to feed into institutional analysis and the discussion of power structures within an area.

Detailed household representation can be used to identify the target household for new programmes. It can also be used to look at the impact of projects in order to evaluate which households have been affected most.

Other methods can also precede social mapping. For instance, historical profile and transects can lead to social map.

Merits

- Social mapping helps participants to learn about a specific problem and to facilitate discussion with the group of community members.
- Participatory mapping on ground (see Table 3.1) forms an excellent and powerful tool for participatory assessment, planning and monitoring of rural development programmes, especially at the micro-level.

- Everyone can see what is being made and can chip in with their ideas, using familiar things to show what they mean.
- It is the most reliable and cost-effective way to collect, store and display information.
- It provides a highly reliable village-level database on quantitative as well as qualitative variables.
- The maps can provide a clear spatial structure for discussion.
- Specific issues or problems discussed at a later stage in the process can be referred back to the initial maps.
- The maps are interesting and enjoyable to create and engage participants in the process.
- They are generally easy to understand and construct, and participants feel comfortable starting with mapping, before getting on to make complex diagrams or treating more sensitive issues.

Table 3.1
Ground vs Paper

Criterion	Ground	Paper
Nature of participation	Participatory, inclusive and democratic	A few dominate
Type of participants	All sections of the community: the illiterate, the marginalised, the women and children	The literates
No. of participants	Quite a large number	Two or three participants
Role for participants	All have a role in the collection of material, drawing of map, providing information, copying the output	Only one will be active in drawing the map
Process	Creativity provides a scope for flexibility and innovation; encourages the use of familiar local materials	Creativity is restricted and limited
Time	Less time as work is divided	More time as one individual has to draw the map
Cost	Almost no cost	Incur expenses on paper, pencil, ball pens, eraser and symbols like stickers
Scope for triangulation	Very high and quick as a large number of participants keenly observe and point out omission and commission, if any	Limited as the medium is not familiar to many of the participants
Act of facilitation	Lively, interactive, fun	Mechanical and boring
Extent of information	Quite a great deal of information	Less information
Material	Locally available materials used; any type of material can be used	Paper, pen, pencil, etc.
Scope for modification	Quite large; can be altered or corrected easily	Quite less
Problem	Lack of permanency	Low participation, rigidity
Analysis of data	Quality gets enhanced as many participate	Fewer people watch and interact and therefore analysis may not be refreshing

Dangers and Limitations

- The participants from outside, at times, tend to overemphasise the product at the expense of the process and discussion.
- There are areas where land tenure and the rights on boundaries are uncertain. Asking the people to map these areas may bring the existing conflicts, if any, to the surface.
- The outsiders often have the tendency to intervene in the mapping process.
- The outsiders also have the tendency to include too much of information on one map.

Summary

Mapping, described as the mother of PRA methods, is widely used. It refers to a map drawn by the members of the community on the ground or on paper.

Maps can be of different types. They are classified into two categories: social map and resource map. Under each category, topical maps can be drawn depending on the objective and purpose of appraisal.

Regarding the participants, it is better to involve men and women of different age groups, including children from all sections of the community.

Social maps are drawn to depict information on location of village, village layout, infrastructure, population, social stratification, handicapped, etc. Topical social maps can be many. The most important among them include the well-being or ill-being map, health map, water and sanitation map, education map, leadership map, indigenous skills map and vulnerability map.

The major steps in facilitating the social mapping include the following: decide what sort of social map; find and convene the meeting of key informants; help choose a suitable place and medium; help people to get started; facilitate them to complete the exercise; encourage corrections and additions; and keep a permanent record, including the mappers' name.

The applications of a social map are varied and many. The major fields of application are appraisal, planning, monitoring and evaluation.

Social map can be effectively combined with other PRA methods such as transect, well-being analysis, livelihood analysis, focus group discussion, Venn diagram, impact diagram and historic profile.

The merits of the methods are as follows: (*i*) it is easy to create; (*ii*) it facilitates discussion; and (*iii*) it is a powerful tool for assessment, analysis and action. The limitations and dangers include (*i*) tendency to overemphasise the product rather than the process, (*ii*) tendency to intervene and interrupt and (*iii*) tendency to include too much information on the map.

PARTICIPATORY CENSUS

This method generates demographic and other data about a geographical area through a social map or card system with symbols and colours for different information (one card per household). There are two methods of conducting participatory census: (*i*) card method and (*ii*) social map method.

Card Method

The practice was first innovated by Anasuya and Perumalnaicker of Kethanaickenpatti village near Madurai in Tamil Nadu (Chambers 1997). They used a card for each household and marked details with symbols on the card. Details of each of the households were noted on the cards and compiled later on. The procedure adopted to collect census data using card method is as follows:

- Prepare a list of the households using social map. Give a number to each household in the social map.
- Prepare a card for each household. The size of the card may be 3 inch × 4 inch.
- Write the household number as found in the social map and the name of the head of the household at the top of the card in prominent letters.
- Discuss and decide with the representative group the type of data you would like to collect. You may also arrive at the symbols to be used in consultation with the participants and the way in which the information is to be recorded.
- Prepare a chart indicating the item of information to be placed and the symbols to be used for each item of information. Display the chart in a prominent place so as to facilitate the participants to refer to the chart and collect data/information.
- Start the exercise with an adequate number of participants.
- Distribute the cards to a small group of participants.
- Facilitate the participants to collect the information by 'households', using a card for each household.
- Ask them to display the cards on the ground, in a form perfectly resembling the way the village/locality is spatially organised.
- Ask the participants to have a look at the data and make changes wherever necessary.
- Record the data and tabulate it for further analysis.
- Thank the participants for their participation.

Social Map Method

Under this method, the demographic details or the individual households are shown on the map itself. The data on type of house, size of the family, age-wise distribution of the members in a family, sex-wise literacy status, differently abled people, caste, religion, occupation, assets, income, expenditure, etc., may be gathered.

The procedure to be adopted is as follows:

- Ask the participants to draw the social map. Let it be drawn very clearly on the ground with enough space in and around the house.
- Triangulate to see whether all the households are represented.
- Explain the participants the purpose of the exercise. Take a decision on the type of information to be collected, the symbols to be used and the process of collecting the data in consultation with the participants.
- Write down the data to be collected on a chart paper and also indicate the symbol. This would help as a reference to the participants and lead to doing the exercise without any problem.
- Take up any one item. You may be interested in knowing the total population of the village. Facilitate the participants to use different seeds. For example, the participants may use neem seeds to represent the male and tamarind seeds to represent the female. If the seeds are not available, locally available materials like stones, pebbles, flowers, twigs, sticks, or goat droppings may be used.
- Facilitate them to analyse the data collected.
- Encourage them to reflect on the inference drawn from the analysis.
- Details of the data on assets, liabilities, income, expenditure etc., are sensitive issues in a community. The collection of such data is likely to be influenced by people's expectations. Hence, cross-check the information using the principle of 'triangulation'.
- Analysis of data by the people may lead to discussion among the people. Listen carefully to such discussions.
- Record all the data carefully in a suitable form.
- Thank the participants.

Dos

- Keep the cards ready in an appropriate size if card method is going to be followed to collect census data.

Don'ts

- Don't try to collect more data than required.

Application

The data generated from participatory censuses can be used for various purposes. Some of the purposes as listed by Kumar (2003) are as follows:

- Data can help to identify the households with specific problems.
- Data can also enable estimation of the magnitude of the problems and the issues at the local and community level.
- Data provides a baseline for planning and subsequently monitoring of changes in the condition due to intervention.
- Data can be of much use in analysing problems and issues. This, in turn, can help design projects to improve the situation.
- Data can initiate a process of thinking and analysis among members of the local community about the problems and the possible solutions.
- Data can help identify the households which require immediate intervention and which fall under the target group.

Merits

- People undertake the responsibility of gathering, tabulating, analysing the data and drawing inferences from the analysis.
- People become aware of the existing situation and conditions.

Limitations

- The extent of information and data that can be displayed on the map/card is limited. Depiction of too much information may make the map clumsy. People may find it difficult to use, analyse and interpret.
- Practising PRA in a big village with a single team is likely to consume more time. If the practice of the exercise is stretched too far in terms of time, the interests of the participants are likely to wane.

Summary

Participatory census is a technique used under PRA to collect census data. There are two ways of collecting census under this method. They are: (*i*) card method and (*ii*) social map method. Under the card method, a list of households in a village is prepared using social map. The items of data to be collected are finalised. A card with appropriate size is used for each household. The data pertaining to each household is collected using various symbols decided by the participants from the village. The data thus collected is compiled, analysed and interpreted by the participants. Under the social map method, the census data are shown on the map itself using appropriate locally available materials and symbols.

The participatory census method helps to have a closer look at the individual household. It can help generate baseline information which can be used for planning, execution, monitoring and evaluation of the programme or the project. An important limitation of the method is that depicting too much information and data on the map may make the map clumsy.

RESOURCE MAP

Meaning

A resource map is mainly drawn to present information on land, water and tree resources, land used, land and soil types, cropping pattern, land and water management, productivity, watersheds, degraded lands, treatment plan, etc.

Purpose

A resource map can be used for many purposes: (*i*) it can be used to take stock of the existing resources including common property resources; (*ii*) it would help to ascertain the existing status of resources; (*iii*) it would enable gauging the extent of exploitation of resources; (*iv*) it would also ensure in assessing who holds control and access over resources; (*v*) it would help in locating the 'conflict zones' or 'trouble area' and (*vi*) it would provide a base for finding out ways and means for conserving and improving the existing resources by marking the treatment on the map, simultaneously.

Resource Map: An Illustration

A resource map of a small Harijan village of fifty-one households with a population of 186 is given in Figure 3.6. It is a general resource map drawn to understand the extent of land and land-use pattern. The information that is drawn from the map includes the extent of irrigation land, extent

Figure 3.6
Village Resource Map: Chellampatti

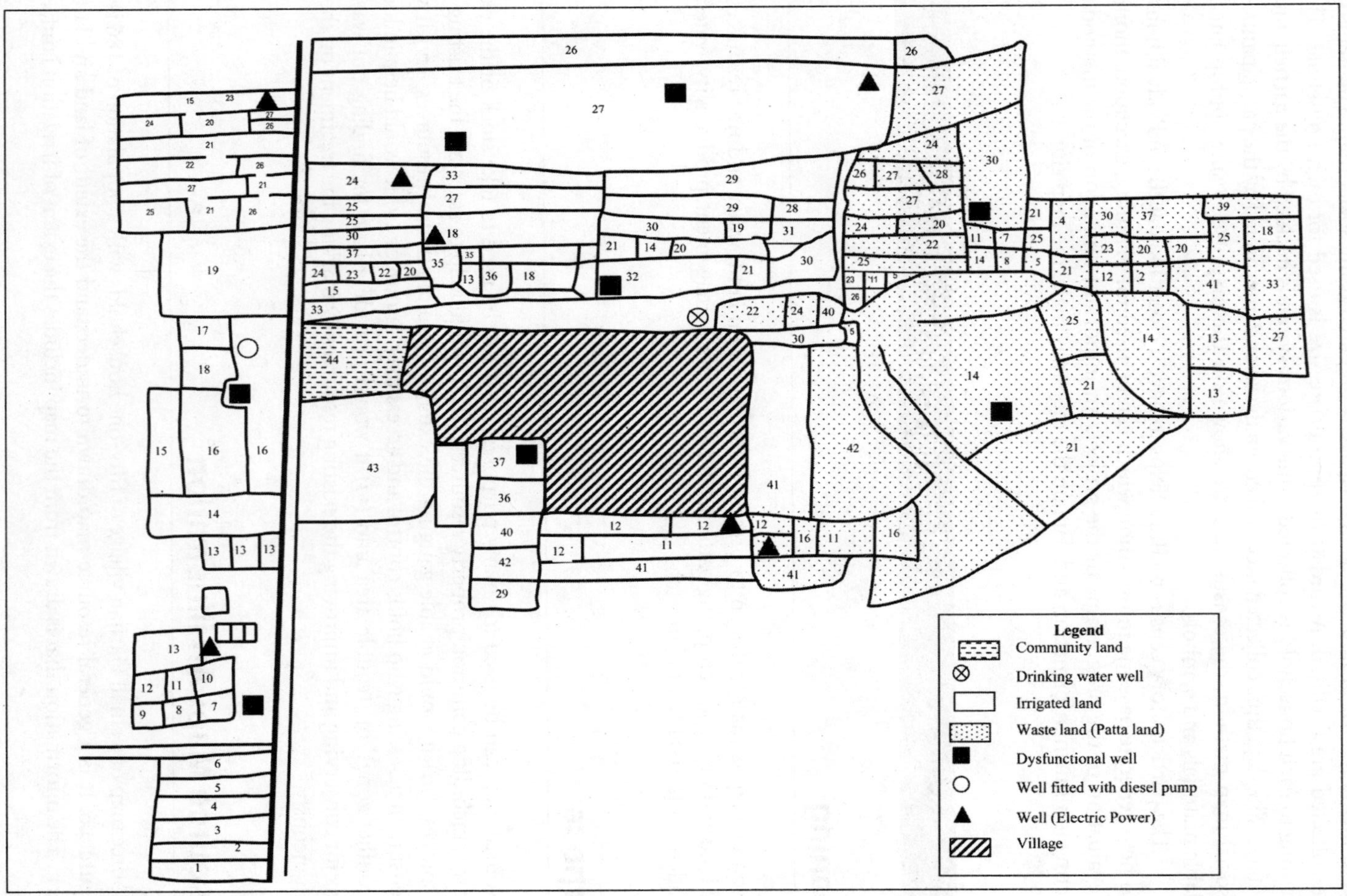

Legend

	Community land
⊗	Drinking water well
	Irrigated land
	Waste land (Patta land)
■	Dysfunctional well
○	Well fitted with diesel pump
▲	Well (Electric Power)
▨	Village

Source: PRA Unit, GRI (1996a).

of wasteland, extent of community land, source of irrigation, number of wells, wells which are in use, wells which are dysfunctional, wells with diesel pump sets and wells with electric power pump sets. The numbers indicate the owners of the specified land. This is a base map or a primary resource map based on which topical and thematic resource maps can be drawn.

The Participants

The participants for the exercise need to be carefully selected. Though there is no prescribed number of participants, we need to ensure that key informants, such as farmers of different types, landless agricultural labourers, shepherds, firewood collectors, woodcutters, herb collectors (if any), and people with indigenous knowledge and skill on various agriculture and agriculture-related activities, are in the team from the village. The number of participants during the transect may be ten to fifteen; it can be higher while drawing the resource map.

Procedure

- Establish rapport with the members of the community through visits, interactions and techniques like 'do it yourself'.
- Find out the key informants, the knowledgeable people who are willing to spend time and share information.
- Explain the purpose of the exercise and explain the methods that you are going to adopt.
- Ask the participants to choose a place preferably in the village where more people can join in. Let the chosen place be spacious with a flat surface. A threshing floor, for example, would be good enough to draw such maps. Keep the principle of equity in mind. Ensure the participation of all sections of the community.
- Facilitate the participants to draw the map on the floor/ground as it is user-friendly to the local people. Start with a basic resource map indicating boundaries, common property resources, etc. Gradually, you may ask the participants to depict more information related to the theme on the map.
- Facilitate the participants to use locally available materials to draw the map and to depict information on it.
- Facilitate the participants to complete the map; if time permits, make it colourful. *Rangoli* powder can be used for differentiating the area. It is always useful if people can describe the sources, process, status and problems in terms of colours and symbols.
- Ask one of the participants to explain the map. This would facilitate additions or omissions, if any. Allow them to change or modify.
- Keep the resource map as the base. Probe freely; use the helpers of PRA: what, when, where, which, why and how.

- The interviewing of the resource map may result in the emergence of sub-themes. This may lead to the creation of succession maps either on the ground or on paper.
- Copy the map on newsprint with the help of local participants. Try to copy it as it is drawn on the ground, giving the legend as depicted by the participants. Give credit to the participants by noting down their names on the newsprint.
- Thank participants for their participation and cooperation and part naturally.

Dos

- Facilitate the children to participate. It will help them to have a better understanding of the natural resources in the village and their status.
- Interview the map.

Don'ts

- Don't overload the map with information.
- Don't impose your ideas.

Thematic Resource Maps

Small thematic maps can be drawn on paper or on ground, focusing on a specific issue. These maps are generally an extension of the main map drawn on the ground. These maps generally include agriculture, water resources, local land-use classification, resource utilisation, cropping pattern, aquifer, forestry, historical and future maps. The nature and use of the resource maps are briefly stated here:

- **Agriculture:** This can be drawn to indicate various types of land and its use (such as dry, garden and wet), cropping patterns (both current and historical), soil type and fertility. The map can also indicate different treatments on different plots. It can also be used to find out the crop yields and their change over time.
- **Water sources:** These maps are drawn to show the various sources of irrigation, such as river, tank and wells, and their current status. Figure 3.7 indicates the sources of irrigation for the farmers of the village Ramachandrapuram. It shows the type of soil, depth of soil, areas irrigated through wells only, area irrigated through wells and tank, the type of well (round well, square well) and the active and dysfunctional wells.
- **Aquifers:** This map can be drawn with the participation of the farmers around the percolation or irrigation tank to show the impact of this tank. Key informants like indigenous water diviners, if any, would contribute a great deal in drawing such maps (see Figure 3.8).

Figure 3.7
Resource Map: Sources of Irrigation

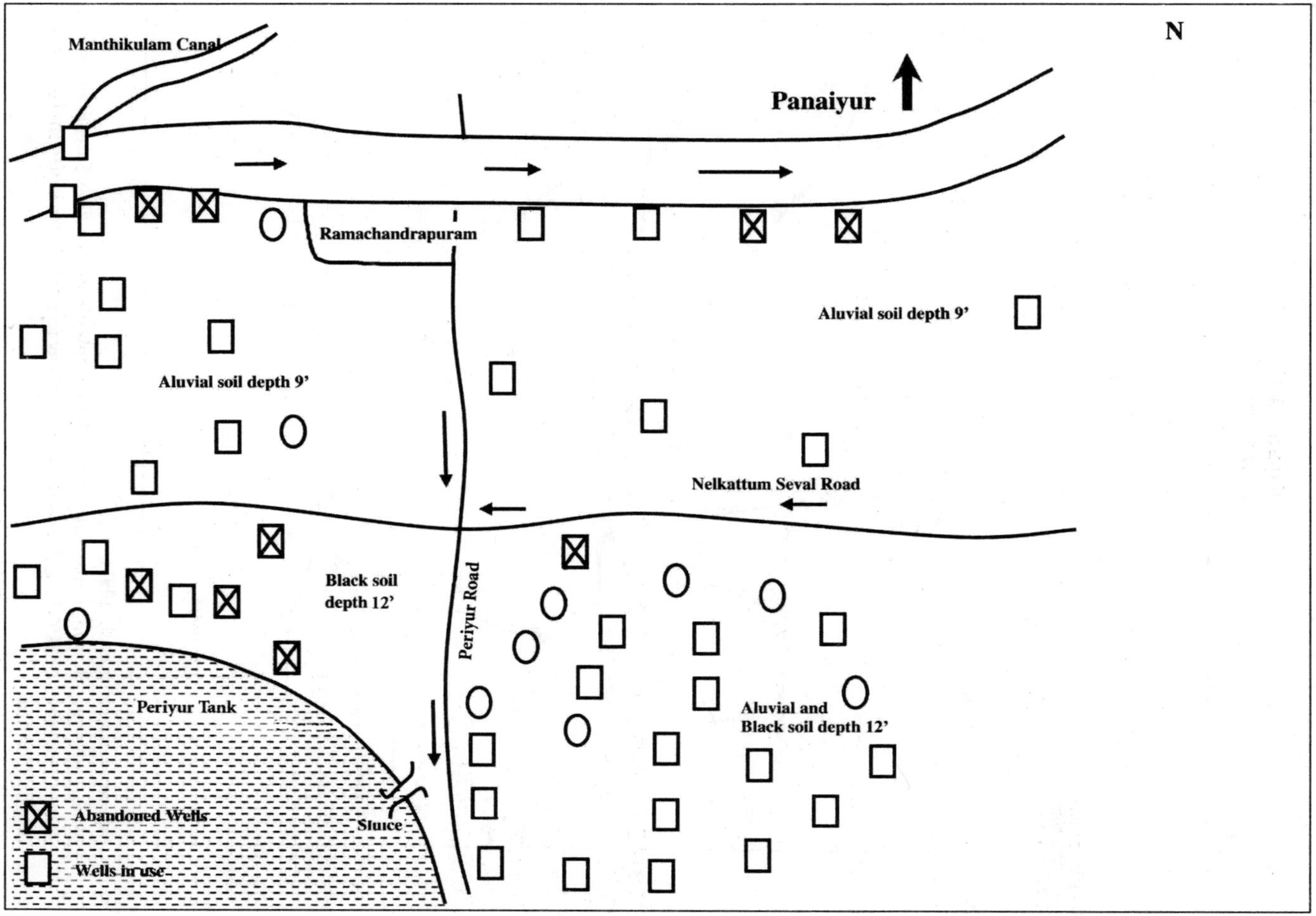

Source: Narayanasamy et al. (1998).

Figure 3.8
Aquifer Map

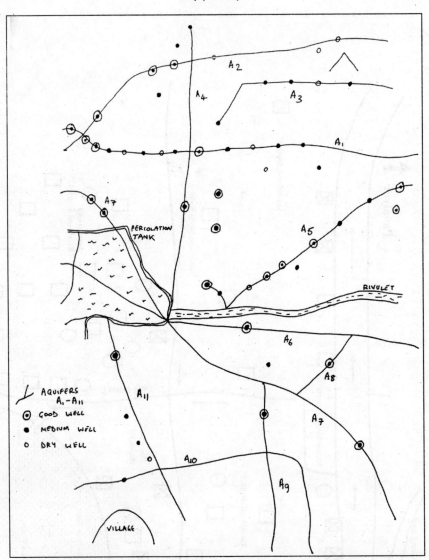

Source: Mascarenhas et al. (1991).
Note: Aquifer map showing impact area of percolation tank at Kansala village, Surendranagar district, November 1990. A1–A11 are aquifers identified by farmers. Original map shows names of all well owners.

- **Forestry:** The information that can be gathered through a forestry map includes access routes, collection areas for different minor forest products, degraded areas, fire zones, fishing areas and grazing zones (see Figure 3.9).
- **Mangrove forests:** This map can be used to identify the physical features of the mangrove wetland, such as open water, small tidal creeks and canals, sand dunes and mudflats. Besides, features such as healthy and degraded mangrove area, cattle grazing areas, shallow and deep water areas, location of oyster beds and clam beds, active fishing areas, areas where large quantities of fish are available and the ideal locations where various fishing methods are available can be located on such maps (see Figure 3.10).
- **Farm sketches and profile:** These involve mapping at a scale of farms per unit. This is important as it is often the basic unit of production and decision making. Figure 3.11 shows farm sketches of a few farmers. The details include extent of land, soil depth, wells, borewells and the duration of time for which it remained fallow.

Application

Resource mapping has several applications. We discuss here a few applications from the experiences of applying resource mapping techniques in field.

Project formulation

A resource map can be used to analyse the problem which may eventually result in the emergence of a project idea. PRA Unit, GRI, organised a workshop 'Priming PRA for Project Formulation' in a village called Chellampatti. An exploratory study revealed that the village had a vast stretch of wasteland and the villagers wanted to regenerate it. The PRA team employed a resource map (Figure 3.6) to ascertain the issues related to land-use pattern and wasteland, which ultimately led to the formulation of a project.

The main items of work proposed by the farmers include the following:

- Ploughing and contour bunding (raising bund to conserve water).
- Digging pits, manuring and planting seedlings; trees preferred by the people through tree preference ranking include mango, tamarind and neem. Mango would be a major tree crop; tamarind and neem would be planted only on the bunds and boundaries.
- Digging of three borewells in three different locations and fitting them with hand pumps and resurrecting the existing dysfunctional community well to irrigate the seedlings.
- Cultivation of short-term rain-fed crops for an initial period of three years.
- Renovation of the percolation pond.
- Live fencing.

The project idea mostly emanated from the local people, which could be mainly attributed to participatory resource mapping followed by focus group discussion.

Figure 3.9
Forest Resource Map: Tholthukki Village

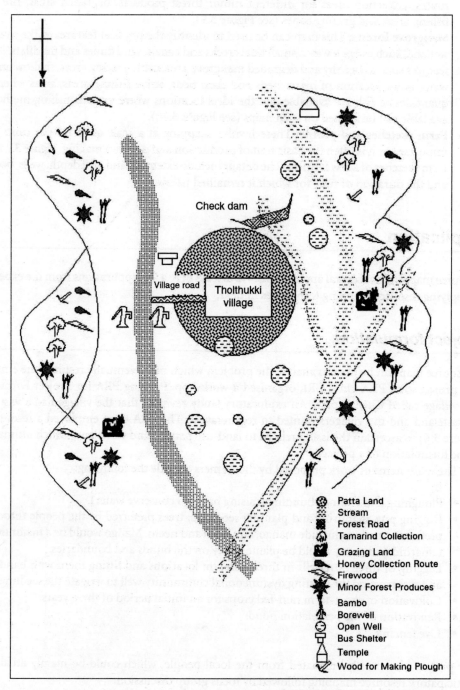

N

Check dam

Village road

Tholthukki village

Patta Land
Stream
Forest Road
Tamarind Collection
Grazing Land
Honey Collection Route
Firewood
Minor Forest Produces
Bambo
Borewell
Open Well
Bus Shelter
Temple
Wood for Making Plough

Figure 3.10

Resource Map of the Mangrove Wetland: Veerankoil Village

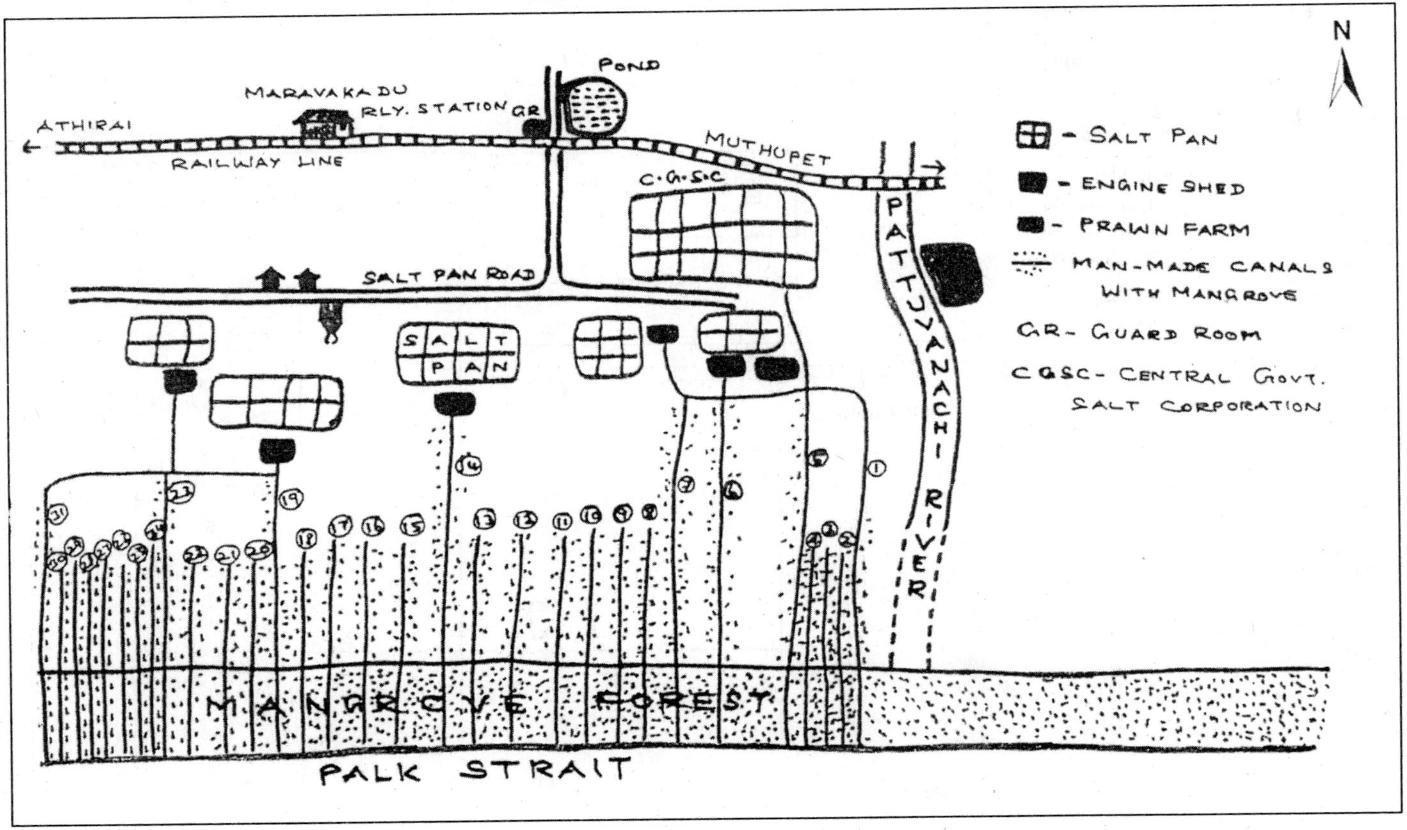

Source: Selvam et al. (2003).

Figure 3.11
Farm Sketches and Profile

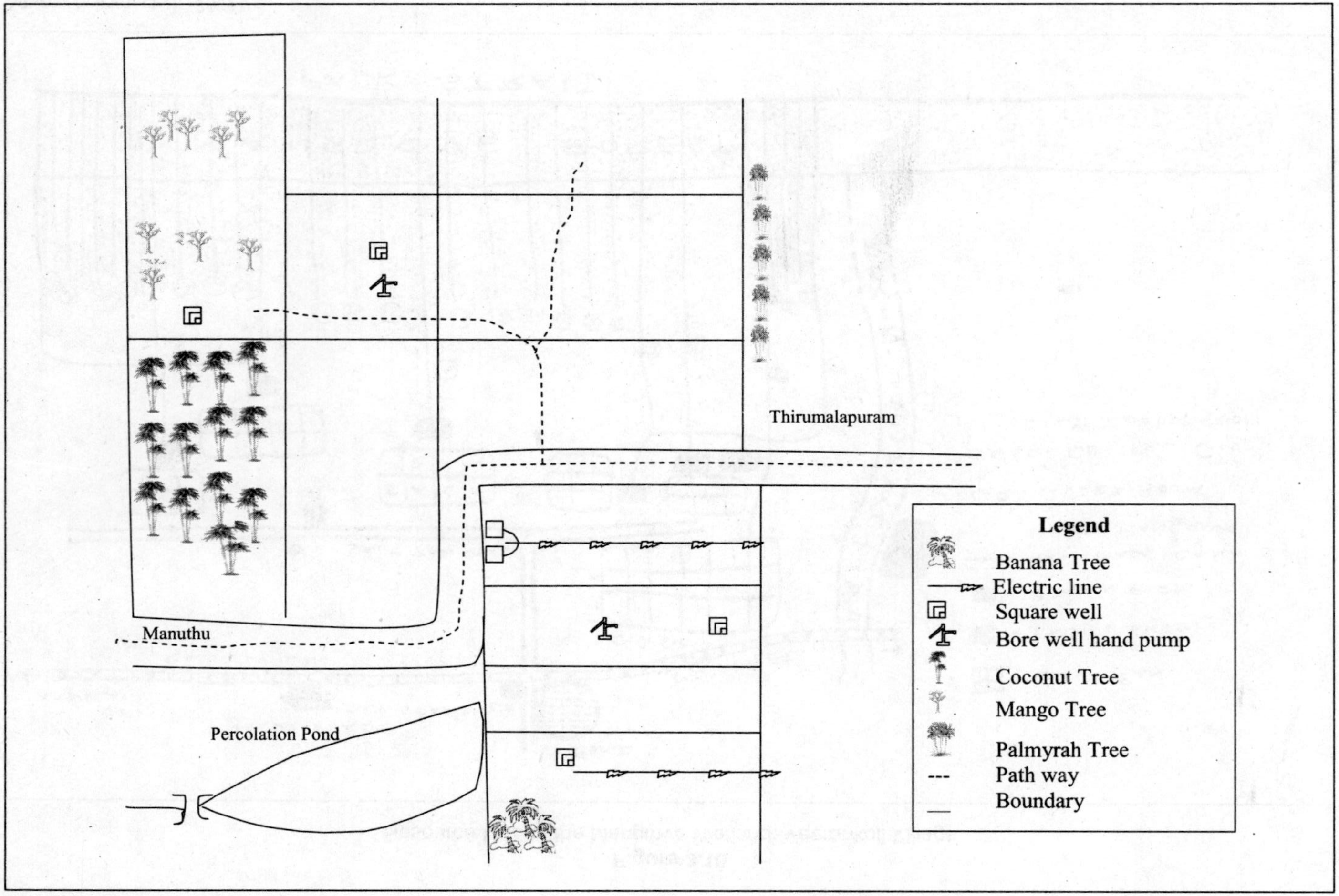

Thirumalapuram

Manuthu

Percolation Pond

Legend

Banana Tree	
Electric line	
Square well	
Bore well hand pump	
Coconut Tree	
Mango Tree	
Palmyrah Tree	
Path way	
Boundary	

Source: PRA Unit, GRI (1995d).

Problem identification

Resource mapping can be applied to study a long-standing problem that defies solution. We applied some of the techniques to study the effect of tannery effluents on farming practices. To start with, we asked people in one of the most seriously affected villages to draw resource maps depicting the irrigation wells which became dysfunctional due to effluents. The participants drew the map within an hour. The discussion that followed indicated that of the fifty-six wells located in the village, only sixteen (those near the river) were usable. Even these sixteen wells could not be used as a source of drinking water or for the animals. During the rainy season, farmers directed or pumped the river water into the wells situated on the banks of the river and used it for irrigation purposes. In non-rainy seasons, the water in those wells remained salty and saline and could not be used for irrigation (see Figure 3.12).

We subsequently went in for thematic maps on soil condition, cropping pattern and productivity, which clearly revealed that effluents had seeped into the arable lands of the surrounding areas, spoiling them to the core. This had resulted in the failure of agricultural operations.

Problem analysis

Resource mapping can also be used to analyse a problem. We used this technique to analyse the problems caused by shrimp farms in a village, Ariyankundru, on the Rameswaram island (Tamil Nadu). We undertook a detailed appraisal and analysis of the various problems faced by the people in order to come out with a micro-plan that would address their problems. A problem that repeatedly cropped up while practising exercises like problem inventory, timeline and trend analysis was the soil and water pollution caused by shrimp farms near the seashore. This was prioritised as the most serious problem in the village. Hence, in order to assess and analyse the nature and extent of damage caused by the shrimp farm, we resorted to the resource mapping technique.

A group of men and women from different sections of the community who were affected by the shrimp farms and who knew the genesis and effects of shrimp farms participated in the exercise. To start with, they drew the boundary within which their common and private natural resources lie. Further, they drew the location of the shrimp farms, the area under them, the area where the effluents from shrimp farms are let out, the area of land affected by shrimp farms, the water bodies affected by effluents from shrimp farms, etc. (see Figure 3.13). This was followed by an in-depth analysis of the problem caused by shrimp farms.

The outcome of the analysis is briefly stated here:

- Fifty acres of the promboke (common) pasture land was barren and unusable due to effluents released from the shrimp farms.
- Pollution of a local river (Panchakali River) had ultimately caused pollution of drinking water as well as irrigation sources.
- Decline of livestock population had occurred due to polluted pasture land.

Figure 3.12

Resource Map: Problem of Tannery Effluents (Kamatchipuram)

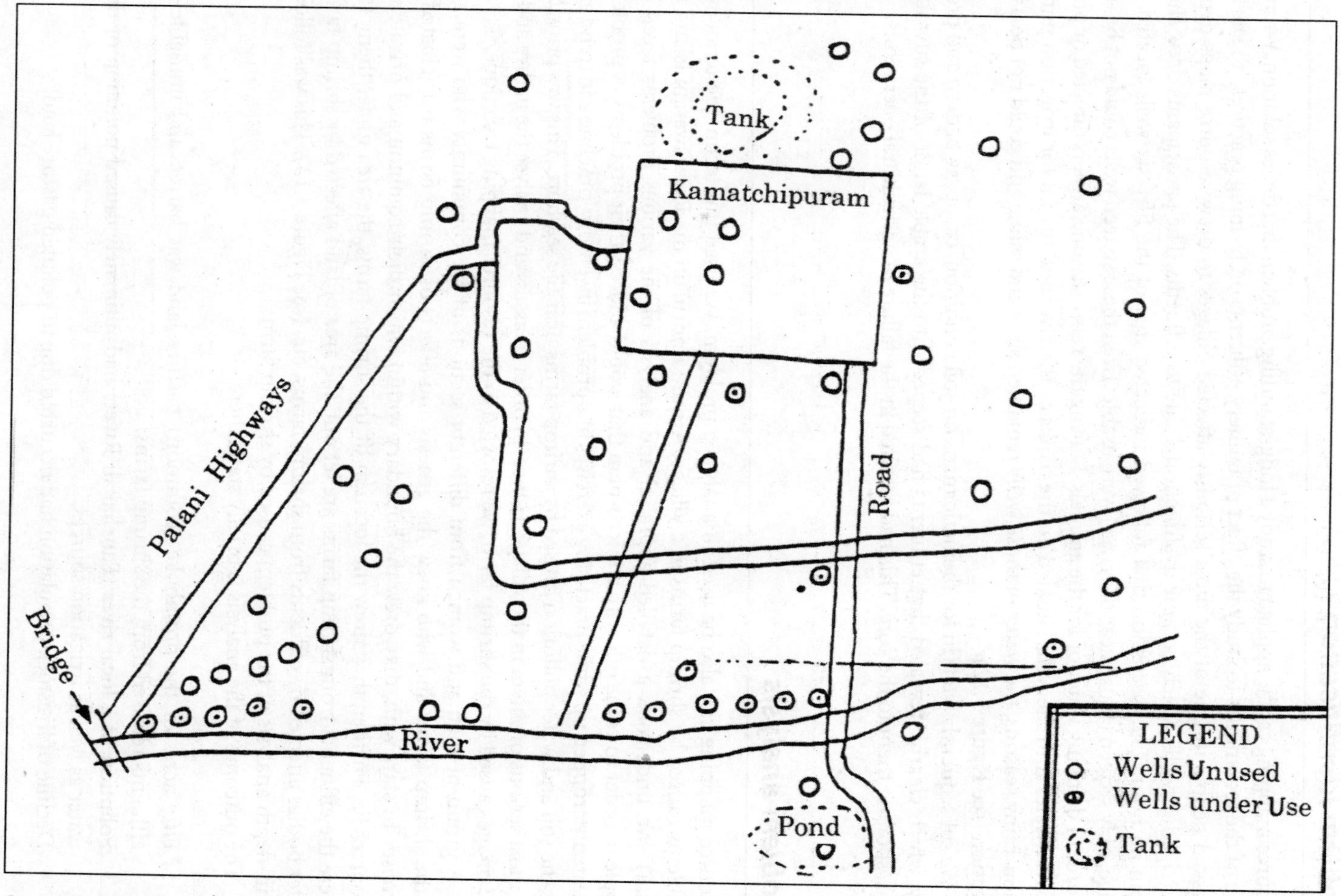

Source: Anbalagan et al. (1997).

Figure 3.13
Resource Map: Problem Identification (Ariyankundru Village)

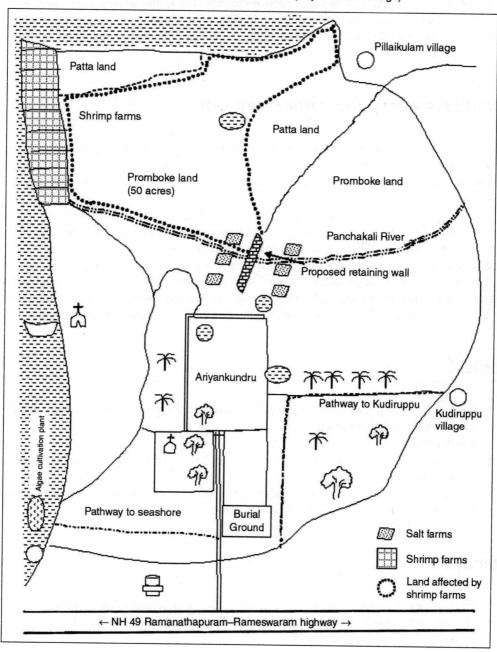

Source: Narayanasamy and Manivel (2002).

- Farmlands and trees, especially the coconut trees, had been severely affected.
- Fishing and related activities had been deeply affected as the shrimp farms were located quite close to the sea (hardly 10 m from the sea).
- Sometimes the effluents were let out to the sea, which had a negative impact on the flora and fauna of the sea.

Complementarity with Other Methods

Maps and transects can be used interchangeably to start the field work. Both provide an overview of the area and are good ways to start building a rapport with the local people. Transects largely facilitate in drawing the resource map. Similarly resource map sometimes facilitate fixing the transect routes.

Social maps in the case of forest-related issues would help in finding out the people who use forests for the collection of minor forest produce, firewood and thatching grass, grazing, fishing, etc. This information would help in identifying the key informants of the area, who in turn may be asked to participate in transect and resource mapping. These two exercises would help in assessing the area of operation of the people, the extent and type of resources they use, the extent of the pressure of population on the forest, etc. This may further lead to drawing up of a seasonal calendar which would help in assessing the season-wise utilisation of forest resource by the people.

Merits

- Resource mapping method can be improvised and used for many purposes in the field of natural resource management.
- It is flexible.
- It can be effectively combined with other methods like social map and transect and provide space for better sequencing.
- It opens up an excellent scope for using visuals, which in turn ensures active participation.
- It is an effective planning tool in natural resources management.

Limitations

- The facilitators sometime tend to emphasise on the output, neglecting the process.
- The exercise tends to create conflict, especially when sensitive issues like land tenure, encroached area, etc., are discussed.

Summary

Resource map is a visual method to identify and assess the existing natural resources and to ascertain the opportunities and problems associated with the resources. The method can also be used to ascertain the past status of the resources and of what the people expect the resources to be in future. It has thus emerged as a powerful tool of participatory planning. A resource map invariably leads to drawing of small thematic maps focusing on a specific issue.

The team can choose its own process of facilitating a resource map. It has to ensure that locally available material is used to enable all the participants to participate and interact. On completion of the map, 'interview the map' for in-depth interaction and analysis.

The method can be applied in problem identification, project formulation and impact evaluation. It can be very effectively used in combination with social map, transect, seasonal calendar and other PRA methods. It can supplement the other methods and be supplemented by other methods.

The merits are that (*i*) it can be improvised (*ii*) it is flexible (*iii*) it can be effectively combined with other PRA methods and (*iv*) it is an excellent planning tool. However, the methods need to be carefully used while dealing with sensitive issues like land tenure, land right and degraded areas.

4

Participatory Modelling

We have seen mapping, various types of maps and their applications. The maps we have studied are topographic maps, representing only two dimensions. Therefore, they are not always easy to use, especially if the map represents hilly and mountainous terrain. Modelling, an important method in participatory rural appraisal (PRA), is an advancement over mapping. It is a thing or a structure on a smaller scale. It shows in greater detail the features of an area. It relies less on writing materials like charts and colour pens and more on local materials. It allows the participants to express more freely and creatively. It brings a lot of fun for the villagers and outsiders. It provides a visual three-dimensional picture of a problem, a situation or a condition. As a result, it facilitates active participation of different age groups. The method has been used to analyse issues related to natural resources management.

MEANING

Participatory modelling is a three-dimensional visual model which captures and integrates people's knowledge and spatial information. It is a communication facilitation method conceived to support collaborative processes related mainly to resource use and tenure. It aims at facilitating grass-roots participation in problem analysis and decision making. Participatory models are constructed at the village level based on the merger of spatial information (elevation contours) and people's spatial knowledge (cognitive maps). In other words, it integrates participatory resource mapping and spatial information to produce a stand-alone relief model.

PARTICIPANTS

The participants may include groups of villagers—men and women, young and old (and children). Care should be taken to ensure that all participants are actively involved. Children, for example, may help in gathering locally available materials for constructing the model. Men and women may get involved in constructing the model. The participants may be more in number as the construction of a model involves creativity and fun. However, it should be remembered that only a few will remain actively engaged in modelling till the end. Such types of participants have to be identified and facilitated. Since the exercise takes time, the interests of the participants, therefore, need to be sustained till the completion of the exercise. The number of participants for this exercise may vary from five to fifteen.

PROCEDURE

The main function of modelling is to generate spatially defined, geo-referenced information. It requires thorough and careful preparation. The steps to be followed are briefly stated here:

- Have a fair idea about the terrain and features of the area that is going to be modelled. Define the area to be reproduced.
- Organise the logistics which include finding a spacious venue where the participants will be able to construct a model.
- Involve villagers in selection of the venue. The best places are flat with a good vantage view of the area being modelled. A fairly open and public place is likely to enhance discussion and participation. The team has to ensure that people from different sections of the community participate. The questions that could be raised at this stage are: How are you going to go about it? Whom do you want to involve? Why you need to do the exercise? What are you going to depict?
- Explain the purpose of the exercise. Discuss the method of construction of model with villagers. Ask them what they think is the best way to proceed. Allow them to construct the model themselves by using locally available materials. Supposing the model is on watershed; facilitate the people to use twigs of different species to show vegetation, pebbles and stones to show pavements and stone revetments, and so on. You may use colour powder (*rangoli* powder) to add colour and clarity to the model.

- Suppose you feel that certain things are left out, you may facilitate the participants to include such items by raising questions like, 'What about this …?' or 'What about that …?' See that you raise such questions only towards the end of the process. Do not interrupt in the middle.
- In course of the exercise, you may find participants engaged in discussion. Listen to what they discuss and say. Such discussions among the people are likely to provide valuable insights into how people arrive at decisions when interfaced with different perspectives and interests (Kumar 2003).
- Observe who are the active participants and whom do they represent? Try to involve participants from different sections of the community, consistently. Make special efforts to involve the women and marginalised groups to make the process and outcome of modelling more inclusive.
- Keeping the model as a base you may depict more information on the model depending on the context and purpose.
- On completion of the model (see Figure 4.1 for illustration), initiate the discussion on topics of interests like the current situation, problems, opportunities, causes of the problem and plan for improving the situation or condition.
- Thank the participants for their active participation and involvement.

Dos

- Try to make the exercise into a sort of game which everyone enjoys.
- Allow children to participate.
- Do have a fair-sized model, at least 5–6 ft in size, so that various features can be depicted.
- Try to involve local authorities.

Don'ts

- Don't take it for granted that the model will appear on its own. The exercise has to be properly facilitated.
- Don't overdo the planning part of the exercise. Sometimes, you may end up only planning, without any outcome.
- Don't be too rigid in the development of model in terms of fixing the venue, alignment or colour scheme. Let the participants decide and do.
- Don't overdo the detail. You are likely to neglect the main features.
- Don't make the model too small.
- Don't use sophisticated materials.

Figure 4.1
Participatory Modelling by Gender and Age

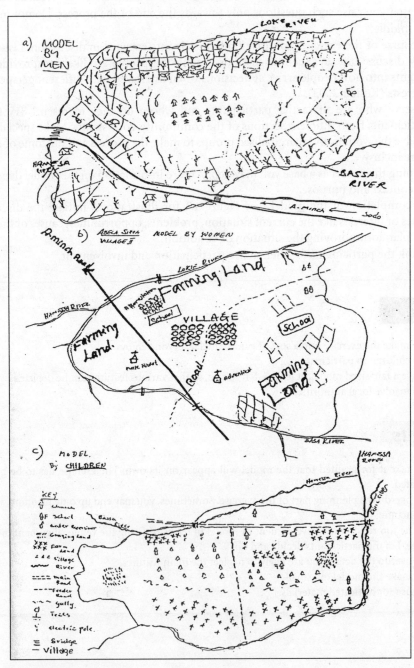

Source: Ejigu et al. (1991).

APPLICATION

Participatory modelling is, by and large, used in natural resource management. The application may range from raising awareness to conflict resolution. A few areas of application are briefly stated here.

- **Raising awareness and education:** The models produced generate a tremendous amount of data. The data and information generated through these models can be used for explaining the local geography and to enhance people's interests in conserving and restoring natural resources.
- **Preparation of plan:** Compared to the data appearing on a simple social or resource map, a model facilitates assimilation, interpretation and understanding. Participants, by and large, get an overview of their environment. This is likely to enhance their analytical skills, broaden their perspectives and help them deal with issues and conflicts associated with territory and resource use. The model also highlights the present points such as household concentration, converted forests, and access ways, making them visible and tangible to everyone. Models allow stakeholders to get a first-time factual perception of their location. All these facilitate the stakeholders to perceive the problem, ascertain different alternatives to overcome the problem and select the best alternative to solve the problem. Thus, the model provides a base for planning.
- **Local communication capacity:** A model makes information visible, eases communication, helps bridge the language barriers and increases the potential of all stakeholders to deal within their constituencies. Models and maps can be used as a part of the communication strategy to foster legal and policy reforms at the local level.
- **Protected area (PA) management:** Models can also be meaningfully applied in managing the protected areas. The areas of application include (*i*) involving communities in developing management, zoning and resource use plans, geo-referencing their priorities, aspirations, concerns, etc; (*ii*) monitoring the dynamics of settlements, infrastructure and access points, vis-à-vis protected area; and (*iii*) introducing visitors to the area.
- **Participatory monitoring and evaluation:** The model can be instrumental to conduct participatory monitoring and evaluation (PM&E). For this, we need to make the base model as a permanent model. This can be used as a baseline model. The data has to be updated at periodic intervals and the updated data has to be depicted on the model using different colours, symbols, etc. This would help us to compare what was at the beginning of the project with what is at present. This helps us to monitor and discuss the progress of the work and also in the final evaluation of the outcome of the project.
- **Conflict resolution:** Conflict resolution involves an area-based mechanism to prevent, mediate and resolve local conflicts and to strengthen communities in dealing with their management. Disputes over boundary issues, resource use and tenure are often contributory causes for conflicts. The strategies and processes leading to conflict resolution are complex and they need the backing of appropriate institutional and legal mechanisms. Participatory

model can be effectively used at the grass-roots level in settling boundary disputes through the visualisation of landscape-associated land uses and settlement pattern.

COMPLEMENTARITY WITH OTHER METHODS

Participatory modelling can be effectively used with other PRA methods. Resource maps and social maps can provide data and information that can be meaningfully depicted on the model. The model can provide a base for focus group discussion on various issues related to resource use and management. Transect diagramming and plotting natural and other resources on a sketch map can supplement and complement the information gathered through the model. The method can also be used in combination with more sophisticated techniques like ariel photographs and geo-information system.

MERITS

Participatory modelling technique has many advantages. Important among them are the following:

- The models constructed provide the participants and local authorities with a medium for easing communication as well as the language barrier and create a common group discussion.
- It is considered as a mobilisation tool for organising the community because it helps gather the people to share information and concerns. A right mix of old and young, women and children is likely to result in old people sharing history with the young, passing on legends and religious beliefs, sacred rites and places, all so essential for conserving tradition.
- The process and output enhance the self-esteem of the participants and raise local awareness of the interlocked local ecosystem (Rambaldi and Callosa-Tarr 2000).
- Participatory modelling is a powerful tool to use as the basis for the local area and to assess the importance of issues (Hardcastle et al. 2004).

LIMITATIONS

The method does suffer from certain limitations:

- Construction of a model is a time-consuming process. As a result, the interests of the participants are likely to drop in the course of time. Facilitators, therefore, need to identify the participants who have enough time to spend and sustain their interests throughout the process.

- A few participants are likely to dominate. This can be overcome by dividing the participants based on gender and age and permit them to come out with the model of a situation, problem, etc.
- Participatory models are usually constructed with locally available materials. They are invariably copied on a sheet of paper for reference and use. The three-dimensional features of the models cannot be copied on paper. As such, the third dimension and the details associated with that may be lost.

SUMMARY

Participatory modelling is a three-dimensional presentation which shows the features of an area in greater detail. It aims at facilitating the people in problem analysis and planning. The participants of this exercise may comprise a mix of people from different sections of the community representing various age groups. Special care need to be taken to involve women in the exercise. The practice of this exercise requires careful planning. Facilitate the participants to develop the base model. Ask them to depict the data on the model using locally available materials. Use colour to add clarity to the model. On completion of the model, interview the participants based on the information and data depicted on the model.

Facilitate the participants to create a fairly big size (5 inch x 6 inch) model, so that various features can be easily depicted on it. Participatory modelling can be applied in various fields like appraisal of existing situation, planning of activities and monitoring and evaluation of various activities carried out under a project. It also helps in building up local communication capacity, protected area management, conflict resolution, etc. The method can be used in combination with other PRA methods, such as social mapping, transect and direct observation. It is also used in combination with the geo-information system. The merits are that (*i*) it eases communication and language barriers, (*ii*) it is a community mobilisation tool and (*iii*) it fuels self-esteem of the participants. The limitations are that (*i*) it is a time-consuming process; (*ii*) a few participants are likely to dominate, and (*iii*) the models are not permanent in nature.

5
Transects

INTRODUCTION

An understanding of the life and livelihoods of people as well as the resources of different kinds that support and sustain the livelihoods demands a direct observation of the livelihood opportunities and resources. The outsiders cannot have a better, deeper and more comprehensive analysis of the resources by just sitting and interacting with a group of people in a village. They need to leisurely walk in and around the village, walk through the fields, spend a great deal of time in directly observing the resources of various types, interact with people on the basis of observation and learn gradually from the people. Transect or group walk, a method of participatory rural appraisal (PRA), provides opportunities for such an appraisal and analysis. Transects serve to help the outsiders see at close range several items of interest and relevance which they would otherwise miss. Through transects one gets insights and information into the nature and complexity of the existing scenario in a way that the traditional approaches do not provide. This largely offsets the biases of rural development tourism, particularly where visits to the rural areas are restricted to villages that are larger or situated on the roadside, and discussions are restricted to a few farmers who are available and observations just to nearby fields.

Transects are used to explain the spatial dimensions of people's realities. They are an effective way to learn about rural life and development, particularly about the complex interaction between man and his environment, of natural resources and their management, of farm-based livelihoods, about local vegetation and much more (Mascarenhas 1992).

A transect is different from a resource map. The resource map provides a bird's-eye view of the locality with a focus on natural resources. A transect, however, depicts a cross-sectional view of the different agro-ecological zones and provides a comparative assessment of these zones on different parameters. Transects differ from historical transects. The focus of transects is geographical while that of historical transects is on trends or changes on aspects related to natural resources over a span of time (Kumar 2003).

MEANING

Transects are observatory walks or treks across the countryside and fields to study natural resources, topography, indigenous technology, soils and vegetation, farming practices, problems and opportunities that are cross-tallied with resource mapping and modelling. These are done by walking through the area with a group of villagers—either following a particular course, cross-country or covering the area in a combing or sweeping motion. It is a systematic walk taken along with a few key informants through a particular area with a purpose. The focus of any transect is mostly natural resources. However, social aspects could also be depicted through transects. A village transect would help depict the social aspects, infrastructure and other resources available in the village.

PURPOSE

The purpose of the transect is to have a very clear understanding of the locality by identifying different zones, observing, asking, listening, discussing local technologies and problems, seeking solutions and opportunities and mapping and diagramming the resources and findings. It is to have a first-hand understanding of the physical resources and existing problems of their management with the opportunities available and to serve as a reference for resource management plan.

TYPES OF TRANSECTS

There are broadly three categories of transects: (*i*) village transects, (*ii*) resource transects and (*iii*) cultural transects (Mascarenhas 1992).

Village Transects

It is an observatory walk through the residential area of a village, observing and making notes of the layout of the village, housing, drainage, backyards, infrastructure, etc. It helps to locate map and analyse various aspects of the residential area of the village that normally go unnoticed. A village transect is different from the other transects as it has a greater focus on the dwelling zone of the village. Apart from the physical features of the village, it gives greater insights into the 'social' aspects of village life, for example, segregation of housing colonies according to community/caste. A walk through a village also brings into focus household and economic activities, such as livestock management, grain storage, rural trades and crafts. It throws up a number of aspects of rural life that would probably otherwise go unnoticed.

Resource Transects

They include the following:

- **Straight transects:** It is an ecologist's tool of coming to a quick understanding of a particular agro-climatic zone by analysing a cross section of the area. This is done by traversing the area in a straight path, usually starting from an upper reach and moving downwards towards the village (and/or beyond) or vice versa. This exercise is undertaken by a group of outsiders and is normally used to give participants an exposure into various aspects of the local situation that are related to natural resources and their management. These include soils, vegetation, crops, hydrology and topography. Some observations, though not detailed, can also be made about the problems and opportunities relating to resource management. During the transect, observations are made at different locations, such as the highlands, midlands and lowlands.
- **Zigzag transects:** As the name itself indicates, these transects are done by the group walking not in a straight line, but in a zigzag fashion over the ground to be covered. This method gives a greater coverage than the straight transect. Information is however collected in a similar manner and diagrammatically represented. There is also a chance to observe more.
- **Looping transects:** These can further be subdivided into two categories, namely, single loop and multiple loop.
  - ♦ **Single loop:** Only a single transect party (composed usually of a group of outsiders and villagers) covers the area to be studied in a looping movement from point A to B (usually from a low point to a high point, if available).
  - ♦ **Multiple loop:** This is a variation of the single-loop transect. In this, several loops, by several groups, are initiated. Each group starts from a fixed point and follows a selected path. The groups then meet at a given point (again preferably at a higher location) and exchange and compare information and discuss observations. This is more comprehensive than single-loop or zigzag transects. Multiple-loop transects are more practically oriented, in the sense that they are aimed at collecting information required for planning purposes.
- **Nullah transects:** They are performed by the group (or groups) moving systematically up or down a watercourse (nullah). Observations are taken on either side of the nullah.

Nullah transects help throw light on an important aspect of watershed by bringing out several opportunities and ideas. They are extremely useful in understanding how farmers manage soil and water in the watershed and the diversity and variation that exist at different locations of the watershed.

- **Sweeping transects:** These transects are carried out in combination with or as a follow-up to other transects. Sweeping transects are an important component of the planning of any resource development and management projects, such as forestry, agro-forestry, lift irrigation and watershed development. In sweeping transects, several groups 'comb' predetermined areas or sections of areas. They examine in detail problems and opportunities on a site-specific basis, sometimes even doing it plot by plot. These observations are discussed with the farmers who are accompanying the group. Thus, a deeper understanding of the entire area is arrived at, including site-specific problems and the treatments or solutions recommended for these problems. This information forms the basis of the master plan which is to be prepared for a watershed development, forestry or lift irrigation project. Also, during the course of this exercise, additional data such as the requirement of materials (length of pipes, cement) and labour (*mandays*) are worked out for different works (for example, bund formation, check dams, diversion drains and lift irrigation schemes, forestry, trenching). This is done jointly by outsiders and village people and is cross-verified once more during the group presentations which take place at the end of the exercise.

Cultural Transects

This is an interesting variation on the theme. It enables the participants to traverse through the 'life' of a person, a subsect of the village or the village itself over a period of time (it may be a day, or a week or more). It involves attaching oneself to a person, subsect or village and following on a journey of observations and discussions to discover the patterns of daily life. Some examples are a day in the life of a woman, a week in the company of migrant shepherds, a day spent with minor forest produce gatherers, and so on.

PARTICIPANTS

This is a group exercise. An important feature of transect is that the group doing this exercise consists of a combination of outsiders and local farmers. We should see that participants from the village consist of men and women farmers, landless labourers, shepherds, etc. The number of participants depends on the type of transect that we decide upon and undertake (see Table 5.1).

Table 5.1
Number of Participants Required for Transects

Type of Transect	Number of Participants
Straight	Six to nine key informants from the village. The team from outside may consist of three to five members.
Looping	It is a circular transect. It requires two sub-teams. Each sub-team may have a facilitator and three to five key informants from the village.
Combing	It is a slow and very systematic group walk. We may have two or three sub-teams. Each sub-team may have a facilitator and four or five key informants from the village.
Sweeping	We may have two or three sub-teams. Each team, as in the case of combing transect, should have a facilitator and four or five key informants.
Nullah	A small team with two or three key informants would be enough.
Village	A small team of three to four key informants along with the facilitator can do justice to the exercise.
Cultural	A team of six to eight persons can do the exercise.

PROCEDURE

Practice of this exercise requires decisions on certain preliminary arrangements. The team needs to take a decision on the transect route, number of transects, the type of transects and the transect group to be formed from the village. The resource map drawn on the ground may form the basis for deciding the transect route, number of transects and the type of transect. Participants of the resource map can be consulted to decide on these factors. For example, the people may decide on a transect based on soil classification, which would provide the most effective picture representative of the diversity of natural resources and the people affected by them. Regarding the participants for the transect exercise, the people may be asked to nominate key informants for the group. Similarly, timing can also be decided in consultation with the people. Ensure that the timing is convenient for all the key informants, including the women to participate.

Having decided the transect route, number of transects, the team from the village, the type of transect and the time of transect, explain the purpose of the transects. Prepare a checklist of data and information to be gathered during the transects.

- Go along with the people for the transects as decided. While walking, observe physical characteristics such as erosion, water logging, soil depth, soil type and people's perception of these issues. This can be done by walking through various resources like public lands, private lands, forest land, rivulets, nullahs, gullies, brooks, local land use and soil types. Encourage the people to talk about their own land and the problems as they affect them.

- Observe the crops or any other biomass. Ask the people about the relationship between productivity and the characteristic of their land and other resources. You may even ask the farmers to make a sketch map of their own field on the ground, showing the problems and constraints in the map.
- While on transects, you may come across a variety of 'chance encounters', such as shepherds, woodcutters, herb collectors, landless labourers, and so on. Do not avoid them. Speak to them, interact with them on issues related to the problems or issues under study.
- Facilitate the key informants from the village to draw up a number of small thematic maps like water resource map, local land-use classification map, resource utilisation map, cropping pattern map and aquifer map. These are generally an extension of the ground map and are very useful to understand the resources and problems associated with productive management and utilisation of these resources. It is very common to find a source of local expertise on a thematic issue like water diviner or a local soil expert who is able to contribute towards inventorying these resources and identifying critical areas requiring intervention. Encourage the participants to draw symbols to illustrate various aspects of the diversity, characteristics, problems and solutions. People are creative in drawing diagrams. It is always helpful if people can describe the resources, process, status and problems in terms of symbols and colours.
- Ask people about the problems and constraints in effective utilisation of resources. Utmost care should be taken in asking questions. Don't ask leading questions. Questions like 'What other problems and constraints have you faced?' should be asked. It is important at this stage to ask people to suggest solutions which they have tried earlier, which have worked and which have not worked (and why). It would also be appropriate to ask why they have not been able to try some solutions. Such a question is critical in order to ensure that the insiders and outsiders, while deciding their priorities, appraise their feasibility. All possible problems and solutions should be identified.
- Lead them to draw the transect diagram which is prepared by the local people in the form of opportunity identification matrices. These matrices show all natural resources, local land-use classification, existing state of resources, constraints and problems in productive deployment of these resources, social solutions tried out by the people and options identified by the people for solving the problems and development of each resource (see Figures 5.1 and 5.2).
- Copy the various map drawn on the large sheet of paper.
- Thank the participants.

Figure 5.1
Transect: Tirumalapuram Village

Variables / Farmers	Chinnakalai Brothers	Veluchamy Brothers	Paramiah	Veerakumar	Madasamy	Murugan	Puram Pokku	Percolation Pond
Slope	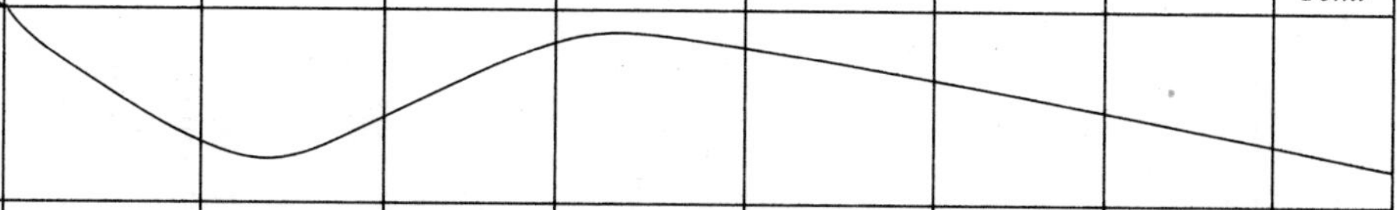							
Ownership	Private	Private	Private	Private	Private	Private	Public	Public
Soil Type	Sandy loam	Sandy loam	Sandy loam	Sandy loam	Sandy loam	Sandy loam	Sandy loam	Clay
Depth of soil	3 m	3 m	3 m	3 m	3 m	3.5 m	4 m	–
Crops (i) Standing	Gingili Horsegram	Gingili Horsegram Other pulses	Paddy Other grains	–	Chillies Onion Brinjal			
(ii) Raised	Do	–	Paddy Other grains	Gingili Horsegram	Paddy Grains Tomato	Cotton Castor grains Groundnut		
Trees	Palm Poovarasu	Palm Neem	Coconut Vagai Poovarasu Tamarind Palm	Palm Tamarind Neem Vagai	Coconut Palm Teak	Poovarasu Palm Coconut		
Cattle	–	–	Two	–	Shed	–		
Sources of irrigation	Rain-fed	Rain-fed	Rain-fed	Rain-fed	Rain-fed and open well (energised)	Rain-fed and open well (energised)		
Water level	NA	NA	–	–	3 ft	3ft		1 ft
Problems	Water scarcity, poor rain, scarce resources	Water scarcity, poor rain, scarce resources	Water scarcity, poor rain, scarce resources	Water scarcity, poor rain, scarce resources	Water scarcity, poor rain, scarce resources	Water scarcity, poor rain, scarce resources		
Opportunities	Willing to accept the department scheme and cooperate	Willing to accept and cooperate	Willing to accept and cooperate	Willing to accept and cooperate	Willing to accept and cooperate	Willing to accept and cooperate		

Source: PRA Unit, GRI (1995b).

Figure 5.2
Transect-based Resource Map: Uchikulam

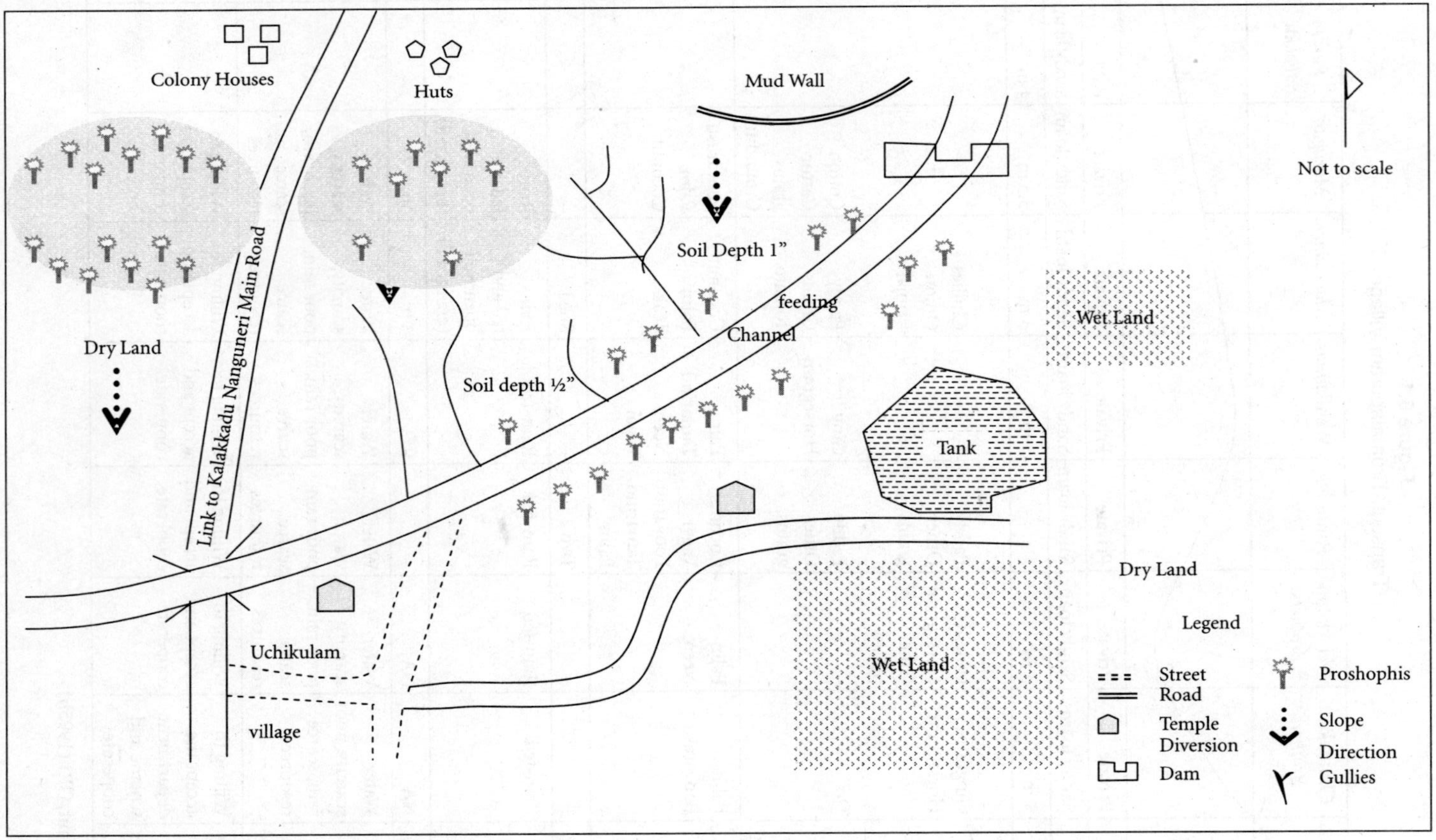

Not to scale

Mud Wall

Soil Depth 1"

feeding

Channel

Soil depth ½"

Huts

Colony Houses

Dry Land

Link to Kalakkadu Nanguneri Main Road

Uchikulam

village

Tank

Wet Land

Wet Land

Dry Land

Legend

:::	Street
‖	Road
⬠	Temple
	Diversion
⊔	Dam

Proshophis

Slope Direction

Gullies

Source: PRA Unit, GRI (1995b).

Dos

- Give some thought to the type of transect you want to pursue.
- Try to start at a low point and move towards a high point.
- Walk slowly, observe keenly, ask and listen.
- Record the observation in the form of a map.
- Take notes in detail on what you have observed, seen and heard.

Don'ts

- Don't do the transect in a haphazard manner.
- Don't miss an opportunity to talk to the 'chance-encounters'.
- Don't walk too fast; you may miss important things.

APPLICATION

A transect is used mostly in natural resource management. Following are some of the areas of application:

- Appraisal of watershed area
- Land-use pattern/classification
- Soil erosion
- Soil classification
- Irrigation system
- Cropping pattern
- Appraisal of the condition of tank
- Assessing the impact of the desilted tank
- Appraisal of common property resources
- Grazing-related issues
- The effect of reservoir on people (resettlement and rehabilitation)
- Indigenous farming practices and conservation measures
- Local farm management system
- Coping strategies of farmers towards declining groundwater
- Social forestry and community forestry
- Biotic pressure on forests, pressure of wild animals on people
- Census of wildlife
- Watershed management

- Water and sanitation
- Monitoring and evaluation

Appraisal of the Condition of Mangrove Wetland

A transect can be used to appraise the condition of mangrove forests. The M.S. Swaminathan Research Foundation (MSSRF) has extensively used this technique in its study on mangrove conservation and management. The aims of the exercise are to

- identify various resource systems used by the residents of the community, resources available in each system and its ownership;
- identify the perception of the villagers about the resource systems, strengths and problems in utilising the resource opportunities for development;
- cross-check information provided during mangrove wetland resource mapping.

The results of the transect-based matrix indicated that the backwater fishing resources associated with the mangroves are the villagers' major sources of livelihood. They look upon this resource system as their main life support system. However, their fishing methods like groping for prawns and bunding method entail a great deal of drudgery. They had to continue with unconventional methods of fishing since they lack the capital to buy crafts and gears which will increase fish catches and reduce drudgery. They also discussed strengths and opportunities available in various zones (see Figure 5.3).

Evaluation of Agro-forestry

Transects can be used to evaluate the watershed development programme. The Government of Tamil Nadu implemented a comprehensive watershed development programme in the two southern districts of Tirunelveli and Tuticorin. An important component of the programme is agro-forestry. Evaluation of agro-forestry was done using transects and transect map. A team consisting of technical experts along with the farmers decided on the transect route, transect types and the time to be taken up by transects and went in for a systematic transect exercise of the farms (mostly dry land) where the agro-forestry crop was being raised. Its status was assessed based on the growth parameters of trees planted under the project, such as plant height, girth and survival percentage. These parameters have been jointly decided by the technical team and the participant farmers. The team walked through different farms, observed the conditions of the trees, randomly measured the height and girth of the trees and enquired about the survival percentage of the trees. Later, the technical team facilitated the farmers/key informants to draw the transect map on the ground with details, such as the extent of land, name of the landowner and location of borewells.

After the completion of transect map, the farmers were asked to evaluate the status of the agro-forestry crop based on the criteria evolved using scoring technique. The scoring system used was as follows:

Very good : 4
Good : 3
Satisfactory : 2
Poor : 1

Figure 5.3
Transect-based Matrix

Resource systems	Hamlet and private land nearby	Mangrove forest and associated water bodies	Sea
Resources	Small piece of land around each house; palm trees in the private land	Fish, prawns, crabs, oysters, green mussel—in the water; wild cats, two tubers—in the sand dune associated with mangrove wetlands	Fish, prawn
Activities	Net mending & repairing; no farming; no rearing of livestock	Fishing in the mangrove waters mainly for prawn, hunting wild cats and gathering of tubers in drought season by a few; no firewood collection	Fishing by traditional fishers
Problems	No caste certificate; flooding during rain; saline groundwater; no fuel resource	No legal rights for fishing; fishing at the mercy of traditional fishers; lack of boats and nets; exploitation by traditional fishers	No boats and nets for sea fishing
Strengths or opportunities for the future	Traditional institutional mechanisms exist	Support from traditional fishers; community interest in mangrove conservation	Irular community gradually taking to sea fishing
Perceptions	Unsuitable living conditions	Mangroves are the only source of livelihood at present; must be conserved	Future source of livelihood

Source: Selvam et al. (2003).

The team evaluated the agro-forestry crop raised by ninety-six farmers and the final analysis indicated that agro-forestry in fifteen farms was rated as very good, in twenty-two farms as good, in thirty-three farms as satisfactory and in twenty-six farms as poor (see Figure 5.4).

The team then discussed the reasons for successful crop of agro-forestry and poor status of agro-forestry based on the transect map. The entire process of transect, mapping, drawing inferences, analysis and discussion took four hours. Everything was done in the field.

Figure 5.4
Evaluation of Agro-forestry

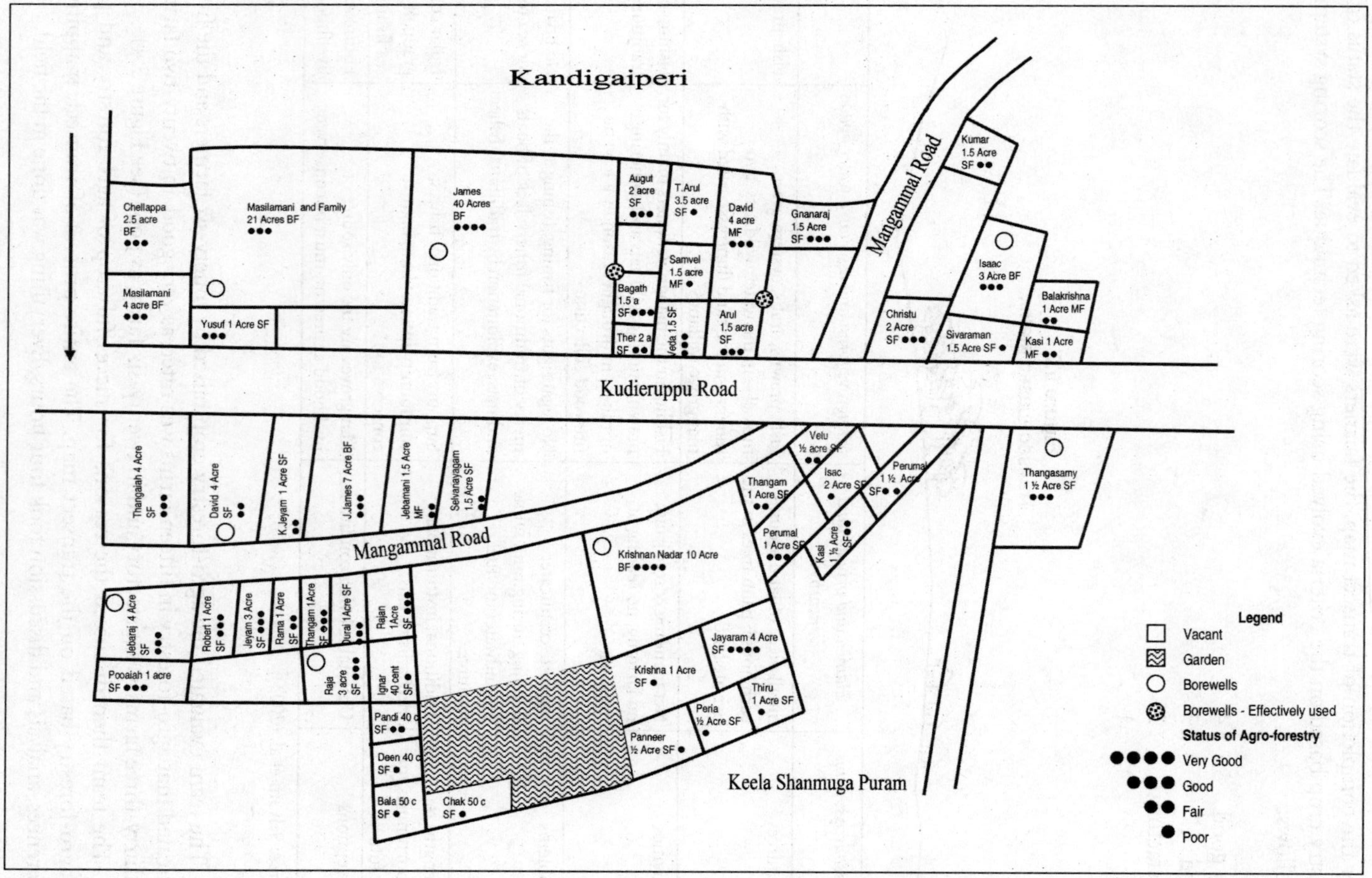

Kandigaiperi

Keela Shanmuga Puram

Mangammal Road

Kudieruppu Road

Mangammal Road

Legend

Vacant
Garden
Borewells
Borewells - Effectively used

Status of Agro-forestry

Very Good
Good
Fair
Poor

COMPLEMENTARITY WITH OTHER METHODS

A transect provides excellent opportunities to combine various methods of PRAs and make the outcome of the exercise more rich and meaningful.

Resource mapping helps in locating transect route, transect type and transect team members. Transect itself results in the creation of a series of site maps, such as farm sketch, soil classification map, cropping pattern, problem zone and water sources map. It also leads to interaction with 'chance encounters' which may sometimes help to build up case studies. Transects may also help in discussing issues that require further probing into and thus result in designing the methodology for a further investigation.

The group that walks the transect simultaneously uses methods such as direct participant observation, semi-structured interview technique and mapping, case study and do-it-yourself.

MERITS

- Transect is a multi-purpose tool. It can be used as an appraisal, planning and monitoring and evaluation tool. It can also be effectively used as a rapport-building tool.
- It opens up a huge number of opportunities for combining different methods of PRA and using them simultaneously. This helps in triangulating the data and makes the outcome of the exercise trustworthy.
- It helps in quickly understanding the different geographical areas in the region or locality and also issues and problems in each zone.
- The group from outside that walks the transect is to follow the rules of PRA, such as observation, listening, looking for oddities, non-domination, role reversal, relaxed appraisal and creating non-threatening situation, which in turn have a tremendous impact on the attitude and behaviour of the outsiders. The process of unlearning begins. The insiders slowly take the role of teachers, and the outsiders that of the learners. It is not a sort of talking down, but a development of partnership in learning.
- The local people gain confidence through their continued interaction.
- A transect helps in knowing the indigenous technical knowledge, especially the cultivation practices, soil conservation measures, irrigation management, livestock management, storage system, etc.

LIMITATIONS

- A transect requires very careful planning. Sidelining the planning aspect is likely to affect the quality of the transect.
- The richness of the transects lies in a slow and relaxed walk, team observation, interaction with 'chance encounters', seeking diversity, looking for oddities, and so on. There is a tendency to rush through the transects, which is likely to seriously undermine the quality of the outcome.
- Transects take time and are more demanding than other methods. It is difficult to sustain the interests of the local people for long in a transect exercise.
- Men dominate and women members normally do not participate in a large number.

SUMMARY

A transect is a group walk initiated to observe and study the natural resources. It is a systematic walk along with a few key informants through an area. The aim of the transects is to gain a good understanding of a region or locality by identifying different zones, observing, asking, listening, discussing local technologies and problems, seeking solutions and opportunities and mapping and diagramming the resources and findings.

There are different types of transects, such as straight or vertical transects, looping transects, multiple looping transects, combing transects, sweeping transects, nullah transects, tank transects and village transects. The number of participants for transects depends upon the type of transects. The number may vary from three to nine.

Resource map is the base for deciding the transect type, transect route and the number of transects. Walk the transects with a group of local people by following the ground rules of PRA. Facilitate the local people to draw small thematic maps like water resource map, local land-use classification map, resource mobilisation map and cropping pattern map. Study the problems, constraints and opportunities in utilising the resources. Lead them to draw a transect map in the form of an opportunity identification map.

A transect is a versatile tool which can be effectively used in combination with methods like resource map, social map, direct observation and matrix ranking. It can complement and supplement other methods of PRA.

The merits of the method are that (*i*) it is a multi-purpose tool and (*ii*) it helps in identifying the local technical knowledge and indigenous cultivation practices.

The limitations are that (*i*) a tendency to rush is likely to undermine the quality of the outcome, (*ii*) it takes time and (*iii*) the interest of the team is likely to wane soon.

6

Mobility Map

Villages are neither self-sufficient nor self-contained. All the services, facilities and livelihood opportunities are not available within the village. The location of services and facilities in a village depends on factors such as size of the village, population, need and demand for such services within the village, their technical feasibility and economic viability and initiatives taken by the village. It also depends upon the political clout and the leadership in the village. In spite of the prevalence of all the aforementioned factors, villagers may not have all the facilities and services they require. Hence, they need to move from their place of domicile to other places, either to avail services and facilities or to seek livelihood opportunities. Where do people go? Why do they go? What is the purpose of their visit or migration? What is the distance? What is the frequency? How do they go? Or what is the mode of transport? Are the places of visit easily accessible? A mobility map provides answer to these questions.

MEANING

A mobility map is a map drawn by the people to explore the movement pattern of an individual, a group or a community.

PURPOSE

Mobility maps can serve the following purposes:

- To understand the movement pattern of different sections of a community
- To ascertain the problems, if any, in travelling the distance

- To compare the mobility patterns of men and women and to ascertain the variations, if any
- To plan for the placement of services and facilities
- To assess the impact of an intervention on the mobility pattern of the people

PARTICIPANTS

A mobility map may be drawn by an individual, a group or a community. The nature and number of participants depend upon the objective of the mobility map. For example, if the purpose is to ascertain the mobility of school-going children, it is preferable to conduct the exercise among the school-going children and, of course, the parents of the children. Similarly, if the purpose is to assess the mobility pattern with regard to fetching of water, it is necessary to involve women in the exercise. With regard to facilities related to health, credit, agriculture, animal husbandry, public distribution system, and so forth, different sections of the community can be involved. The number of participants in the case of a group exercise can vary from fifteen to twenty. But then, the participants should be the key informants.

PROCEDURE

The procedure for facilitating the mobility map is described here:

- Decide the type of mobility map you want the people to draw. If the mobility map is general in nature, depicting movement pattern of all categories of people for varied purposes, select key informants from different sections of the community from different age groups. See that the women fairly represent the group. If the mobility map has a specific focus (e.g., the mobility pattern of landless labourers), the key informants should be from among the landless labourers.
- Explain the purpose and mode of doing the exercise. Make sure that the participants understand the purpose and procedure of doing the exercise.
- Initiate a discussion about the places they visit. Take down the names as they list them or you may ask one of the literate participants to take down the names.
- Ask the participants to write down the names of each place they visit in bold letters on a separate card. Ensure that all places they visit are written on the cards. Facilitate the participants to symbolically represent the places on the cards. This is possible because each place they visit may have some significance, which can be depicted by symbols. Leave it to their choice; do not impose your symbols.
- Facilitate the participants to draw a circle in the middle of the ground representing their village. Now ask the participants to place or locate each card with names of places they visit in correct direction.

- Ask the participants to link the place/locality with the places they visit by drawing lines.
- Facilitate them to follow the same procedure for all the places they visit one by one.
- Ask them to represent each aspect (credit, agriculture inputs, hospitals, etc.) with a symbol. Ask them to give the details such as

  - purpose of visit;
  - distance of place;
  - mode of transport;
  - importance of the place; and
  - frequency of visit.

- Ensure that all the participants actively take part in the exercise.
- Request one of the participants to explain the map; allow participants to add details or to make alterations in the diagram (see Figure 6.1).
- Interview the diagram; listen carefully to what they discuss and take down notes.
- Take a copy of the diagram on newsprint with necessary details.
- Thank the participants for their involvement.

Figure 6.1
Mobility Map: Kasturinaickenpatti

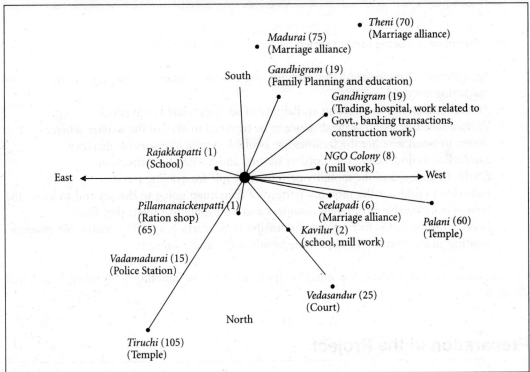

Source: PRA Unit, GRI (1993b).
Notes: Figures in brackets indicate distance from the village in km.
Not to scale.

Dos

- Decide whose mobility pattern you would like to appraise. Ensure the participation of each category of people.
- Facilitate the participants to use symbols for easy understanding and discussion.
- Allow them to depict the direction in the local language.

Don'ts

- Do not insist on exact and accurate distance.
- Do not depict too much of information on the mobility map.

APPLICATION

Mobility maps are being used in varied fields. They are listed here:

- Agriculture: to understand the mobility pattern of farmers for buying inputs and for marketing the produce
- Animal husbandry: to ascertain availability of services related to livestock
- Welfare schemes: to know the distance to be travelled to avail of the welfare schemes
- Water: to assess whether the facilities are available within a reasonable distance
- Sanitation: to understand the mobility of men and women for defecation
- Credit: to understand the mobility pattern of people for availing credit
- Fisheries: to find out the mobility pattern of fishermen going to the sea and to know the type of fish available at different distances and the problems/threats they face
- Location of facilities: to find out the feasibility of starting a facility centre, for example, locating an information kiosk, a mini-health centre and a *balwadi*.

We would now describe a few areas of application of the mobility map using field-based illustrations.

Preparation of the Project

The PRA Unit of the Gandhigram Rural Institute (GRI) organised a training workshop 'Project Formulation through PRA' in a village near Gandhigram. The purpose of the workshop was to enable the participants to formulate projects based on PRA. An important activity that was suggested by the community was dairying as a source of livelihood. The team used a combination of five methods to assess the feasibility of dairying. One of these methods was drawing a mobility map. It was used to ascertain facilities and services, such as grazing area, fodder, cattle market, veterinary hospital and market facilities. The mobility map drawn by the people indicated that the facilities and services are not available within the village. But then, they are available within a radius of 2 km from the village. Facilities available include grazing area, insemination centre, veterinary hospital and milk producers' cooperative society (see Figure 6.2).

Figure 6.2
Mobility Map: Sellampatti

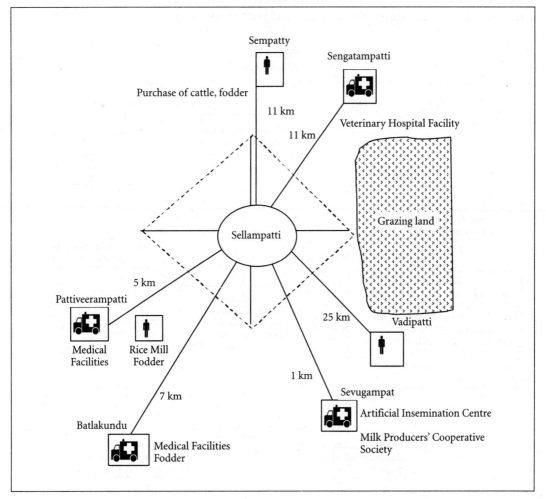

Source: PRA Unit, GRI (1996a).

Facilities, Services and Livelihood Opportunities

A general mobility map may be drawn to ascertain the pattern of mobility of the community. Such a map would give a fair idea about the location of different types of services, facilities and livelihood opportunities. The PRA Unit of the Gandhigram Rural Institute, for a PRA-based survey on project villages coming under the Comprehensive Watershed Development Project, extensively used the mobility map to ascertain the mobility pattern of the villagers. The information collected was mostly on the places they often visit, the purpose of the visit and the distance from the villages to the places of visit. The aim was to ascertain the problems in availing the services and to initiate action for the easy accessibility of services and facilities. Such a diagram was also helpful in establishing coordination among the various agencies and ensuring convergence of schemes and activities. It is quite an extensive list of places and purpose (see Figure 6.3).

Figure 6.3
Mobility Map: Uchikulam

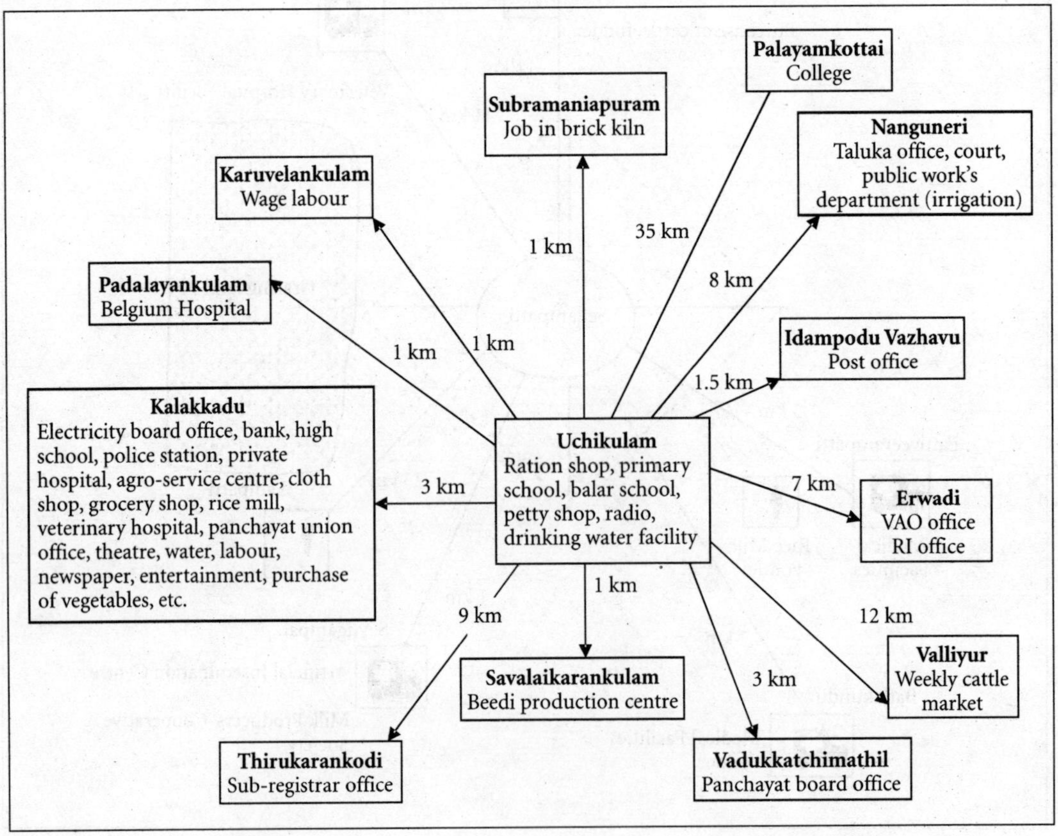

Source: PRA Unit, GRI (1995b).

Location of a Micro-enterprise

The mobility map can be very effectively used to assess the feasibility of starting a micro-enterprise. The PRA unit of GRI as part of their research study on 'Efficacy of participatory methods' has performed a case study on a 'self-help group' (SHG) which follows PRA methods to plan its activities. The group, known as Om Sakthi Mahalir Mandram (promoted by OUTREACH, an NGO in Bangalore), was regularly saving money and providing credit. However, the ultimate aim of the group was not mere savings and credit, but establishing micro-enterprises for promoting the economic conditions of women. The staff of OUTREACH, in one of the monthly meetings of the association, initiated a dialogue on the feasibility of starting an income generation project for the group. The members of the group discussed various options like running a ration shop, starting a provision shop or rice shop and establishing an agro-service centre.

They discussed the profitability and feasibility of different options and finally settled on starting an agro-service centre. However, they decided to probe further on the viability of an agro-service centre. The PRA technique adopted by them was the use of a mobility map as it was likely to help them find answers to key questions like: Where do farmers buy agro-inputs? What are the different types of agro-inputs they buy? How much distance do they need to travel? What is the transport cost? What are the difficulties? Where could the proposed centre be located? Who would be the clientele? Where are they? How many are there? Who are the competitors? Where are they? The mobility map helped them to know the location of the existing agro-service centres (private and cooperatives), the villages served by these centres, total households and farming households in these villages, presence of SHGs in those villages, distance between different villages, etc. (see Figure 6.4). This information helped them find out potential customers, feasibility of establishing link with other SHGs and the location of the proposed centre. They also discussed the advantages and limitations of establishing the centre at their village Nandimangalam.

Mobility Map of Fishermen Community

The mobility map can be used to assess the mobility pattern of people not only on land but also on sea. The PRA Unit of GRI in a project 'Preparation of Micro-plan' in a development block used 'mobility map' to assess the mobility pattern of the fishermen community. Situated near Rameswaram, the famous pilgrim centre in India, fishermen of the Kunjaravalasai village vividly portrayed their movement pattern both on land and sea. The mobility was mostly related to their work, livelihood security and accessibility to facilities and services (see Table 6.1 and Figure 6.5).

Figure 6.4
Resource Location through Mobility Map: Nandimangalam

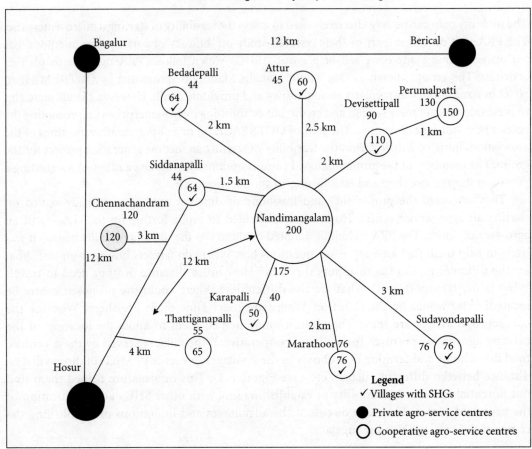

Source: Narayanasamy and Boraian (2005).

Notes: Figure within circle is total number of households in the village.
Figure outside the circle shows the number of farming households.
Big circle represents topmost usage by villagers.

Figure 6.5

Mobility Map of Fishermen Community: Kunjaravalasai

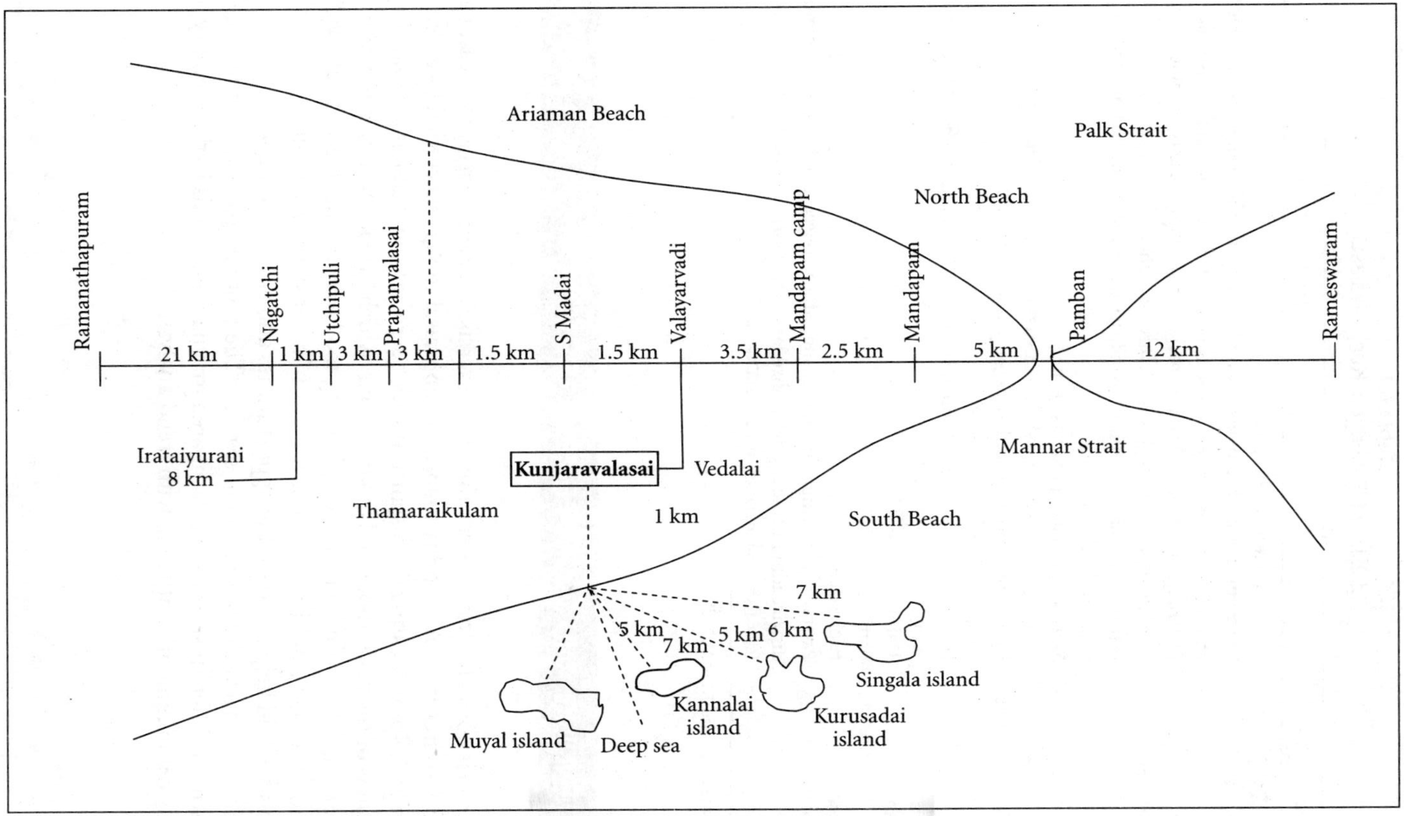

Source: Narayanasamy and Manivel (2002).

Table 6.1
Mobility of Fishermen: Kunjaravalasai

Place	Facilities
Valayarvadi	Bus stop, veterinary hospital
Vedalai	Government higher secondary school, panchayat office, ration shop, public telephone office, fishing, post office, electricity board, medical shop, siddha hospital
Mandapam camp	Electricity board, police station, marketing of palm products, training, village administrative office, high school, mechanic shop
Mandapam	Petrol pump, railway station, sawmill, ice plant, fishing, marketing of palm products, bank, hospital, fire service
Pamban	Marketing of palm products, fishing
Rameswaram	Temple, railway station, fishing, registration office, court, etc.
Sundaramudiyan (S. Madai)	Demo horticulture farm, Thillai Nachiamman Temple
Prapanvalasai	Temple
Utchipuli	Household items, hospital, job in shops, panchayat union office, banks, mechanic shop
Nagatchi	Temple
Thamaraikulam	Training centre
Rettaiyurani	Bank
Kadukkaivalasai	High school
Ramanathapuram	Passport office, employment exchange office, college, ITI, hospital, entertainment, district administrative office, tahsildar office, court, transport office
South Beach	Paar fish, prawn, singi, sura, seela, thirukkai

Source: Narayanasamy and Manivel (2002).

SEQUENCING AND COMPLEMENTARITY WITH OTHER METHODS

A mobility map is normally drawn after completing exercises like social mapping, seasonal calendar, transect and resource map. A mobility map, as an appraisal tool, is succeeded by a Venn diagram. A mobility map helps in locating the distance at which services and facilities are available. To assess the effectiveness of the institutions and organisations, which provide facilities and services, a Venn diagram is drawn. The mobility map, as a planning tool, may be succeeded by a SWOT analysis. While the mobility map would help analyse the feasibility of starting a facility or service centre, the SWOT analysis would help ascertain the opportunities and risks in doing so.

A mobility pattern varies in relation to seasons. The mobility pattern of individual or groups may be drawn for different seasons and compared for changes. Trends in the mobility pattern can be studied by combining mobility map with trend analysis.

MERITS

- It is easy to facilitate. All the participants irrespective of the age, sex, and literacy status can participate.
- It can be used as an appraisal planning and evaluation tool.
- It can facilitate the practice of exercises like Venn diagrams.
- It provides a vivid picture of the linkage of the group and the community with various institutions and organisations.
- It helps to assess the physical proximity of the facilities and services.

LIMITATIONS

- Too much of information may be located in the map, which sometimes makes the map too complicated, especially for the people to understand. A theme-wise mobility map may solve this problem.
- Failure to use visuals may distance the non-literate participants. It is always not possible to use visuals for all the variables.

SUMMARY

A mobility map is a visual depiction of the movement patterns of an individual, a group or a community. It is mainly drawn to find out the location of facilities, services and livelihood opportunities and the distance at which they are available.

A mobility map can be drawn with an individual or with the community. The number of participants depends on the purpose and objective of the exercise. In the case of group exercise, the number may vary from fifteen to twenty.

The procedure for facilitating the exercise is comparatively simple. The facilitator while facilitating the exercise has to see that information such as location, distance, mode of transport and frequency of visits is depicted in the diagram. He or she may also inquire into the problems in availing the facilities and services.

The method can be applied in varied fields. Some of the fields where this method is frequently applied are agriculture, animal husbandry, education, health, water and sanitation, fisheries and credit. The method can also be used to plan the location of a facility or service centre. It can also be used as a monitoring and evaluation tool.

The method can be effectively used in combination with other methods, such as Venn diagrams, seasonal calendars and trend analysis.

The principal merit of the method is that it can serve as an appraisal, planning and evaluation tool. The limitation is that it is not always possible to use visuals for all variables.

7

Venn Diagram or Chappati Diagram

Over a period of time, a network of different organisations has been established to serve the social, economic, political, religious, cultural and other interests of the people. The rural and urban communities are interlaced with a thickening web of organisations. These organisations are of different types: government and non-government; public and private; formal and informal; institutional and non-institutional; service-oriented and profit-oriented; sponsored and spontaneous; permanent and temporary; liberal and conventional; etc. While some organisations are created to promote the interests of all sections of the community, there are certain organisations specially created to cater to the needs of special categories of people or with a specific focus on certain sections of the community. For instance, the commercial banks function to promote the interests of all sections of the community, whereas the regional rural banks have an exclusive focus on small and marginal farmers and small entrepreneurs. Cooperatives have been promoted to protect the 'weak and the powerless'. What are the various types of organisations functioning in the rural areas to promote the interests of the people? What are their roles and responsibilities? Do they provide services to the people as expected of them? Are they able to put 'the rules of the game' into practice? What do people perceive about them in terms of importance and effectiveness? Venn diagram, popularly known as chappati diagram, provides answers to these questions.

MEANING

A Venn diagram or chappati diagram is a visual depiction of key institutions, organisations and individuals and their relationship with the local community or other groups. The key players in decision making are shown. Places of important social significance and interchange can also be included. Both formal and non-formal groups and their levels of cooperation can be discussed, highlighting the opportunities and problems. The institution analysed can be both local and internal to the community as well as external ones having a local influence.

Venn diagrams provide a basis for discussion of

- the roles and significance of various institutions for people in a locality;
- levels of communication between organisations;
- the role of project bodies and their intervention;
- improving the missing link between existing organisations;
- the potential for working through existing organisations;
- the potential roles for new organisations.

Local perceptions about the organisations are discussed. An analysis of different ideas within the locality is possible through the comparison of a number of diagrams with a range of groups.

PARTICIPANTS

This exercise can be carried out with groups or individuals or households. However, it is mostly a group exercise. A large number of participants ranging from fifteen to twenty can be involved. The composition of the groups depends on the topic. For instance, if it is a general analysis of the institutions affecting all aspects of the life of the community, a group consisting of representatives from different institutions would be an ideal mix. For a specific theme, say education, the children attending the school, their parents and the office-bearers of the parent–teacher associations should constitute the group. Mixed groups are better as they allow for a broader range of perspectives, including a spectrum of experiences. The facilitator has to ensure that the people who are aware of the functions of the organisation and who have availed services from such organisations are involved in the exercise. People who do not have any idea about the functioning of the organisation and who have not made use of the services may not be able to provide a correct and fair view of the organisation. Similarly, persons with bias towards an organisation due to their own fault (e.g., loan defaulters in cooperative organisations) may try to paint a bad picture of the organisation. Hence, it is better to obtain a great mix of opinions by working in larger groups. This also helps to depersonalise the discussion. Alternatively, groups divided along gender, age, well-being and caste lines can be compared.

Assessing the Effectiveness of Organisations

- Find the key informants and ask them to choose a place for doing the exercise. Let the key informants be from different sections of the community.
- Explain the purpose of the exercise.
- Make the procedure of doing the exercise clear; we are trying to assess the importance of the organisation as perceived by the community, their effectiveness in terms of the services extended and the reasons for effectiveness or ineffectiveness. Perceptions about the organisations and their effectiveness are ascertained through visual diagrams. Reasons for effectiveness or ineffectiveness are studied through a semi-structured interview technique. The diagramming part of the exercise needs to be clearly explained in order to ensure adherence to the principle of 'they do it'.
- Ask the participants to identify the organisations that are relevant, either in general or for a specific issue. It is desirable to select a field and ask them to list the organisations that cater to their needs. This would help them to systematically think and list the organisations (see Table 7.1). Note down the names of the organisations.

Table 7.1
Sample List of Relevant Organisations

Education	Health	Service	CSIs/CBOs	Credit	Others
Pre-primary school	Health sub-centre	Ration shop	NGOs	Cooperative credit society	Milk producers' society
Primary school	Government hospital	Veterinary sub-centre	SHGs	Commercial banks	Block development office
Middle school	Primary health centre	Agriculture department	Farmers' association	Regional rural banks	Taluka office
High school	.	Revenue department	Water users' association	Moneylenders	Area-specific organisations
Private school	Private hospital	Panchayat office	Village forest council	Friends and relatives	
Special school, if any	Indigenous health practitioners	Police station	Tree growers' association	Brokers	
Parent–teacher association		Other relevant departments	Youth clubs	Commission agents	
			Caste Association	SHGs	
			Temple committee	Other indigenous bankers	
			Panchayats (traditional and elected)		
			Other CSIs and CBOs		

- Prepare circles of two or three different sizes using newsprint. The size of the circle indicates the degree of importance attached to an organisation by the community. Big circle represents 'most important' organisation and smaller circle indicates 'less important' organisation as perceived by the participants. Cards for this purpose can be cut or torn to size.
- Facilitate the participants to draw a big circle or square which represents the group or village.
- Select an organisation from the list of organisations enumerated by the participants. Ask them whether they consider the organisation they have chosen to be 'more important' or 'less important'. If they say 'more important' ask them to select a big circle; and if they say less important, let them choose a smaller circle.
- Having chosen the circle, facilitate them to position the circle from the 'central circle', which represents the village. The distance between the central circle (the village) and the selected bigger or smaller circle indicates the effectiveness of the services rendered by the organisation. The longer the distance between the village and the chosen circle, the lesser is the effectiveness of the organisation. The lesser the distance, the greater is the effectiveness (see Figure 7.1). It should be noted, at this juncture, that the size of the circle can mean the importance while the distance can mean the accessibility.

Figure 7.1
Venn Diagram: Relations of Size and Distance

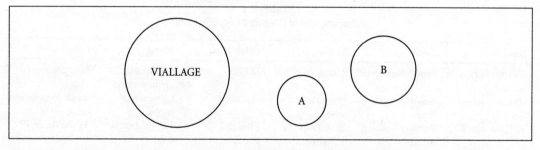

- It will be clear from the diagram that a large card placed far away from the village indicates that it is an important organisation but local people have little contact. In other words, it has failed to provide the services that they expected. The small circle next to the village indicates a less important but effective one with which they have frequent contact.
- Choose the next organisation and repeat the same for all the organisations. For each organisation, ask why they consider it more important or less important. Also ask what factors they have taken into account for rating an organisation as 'effective' or as 'less effective'. Do not jump; do not rush. Give the participants enough time to discuss, debate and come to a conclusion about an organisation. Do not suggest. At the same time try to see that each organisation is objectively assessed and reported.

- Ask the participants to draw the Venn diagram for each category, that is, organisation—like education, health and credit. Using one single diagram for all the organisations without classification would make the diagram clumsy and the participant may get confused. Category-wise presentation of the Venn diagram facilitates a better understanding and deeper discussion.
- Facilitate the exercise on the ground so that cards can be easily moved; more people participate; greater discussion is generated; proper triangulation results; and depersonalisation and more objectivity is brought about.
- On completion of the exercise, ask one of the participants to explain the exercise and the outcome to fellow participants and others who have gathered around.
- Repeat the exercise with another set of participants for cross-checking.
- Copy down the exercise with all the details.

Assessing the Relationship among the Organisations

Coordination among the organisations functioning in rural areas results in a provision of cost-effective services to the people on time and has a better impact on them. What is the extent of functional relationships among the organisations? If there is no relationship, why? What stands in the way of establishing a relationship? A Venn diagram with a slight improvisation would answer these questions. The procedure to be followed is briefly stated here:

- Ask the participants to identify key institutions and the individuals responsible for decision making in a community or organisation.
- Ask them to describe the degree of contact and overlap between them in terms of decision making. Overlap occurs if one organisation asks the other to do something or if they cooperate with each other in some activity (see Figure 7.2). It would be clear from the diagram that the SHG has more or less established some degree of contact with the panchayat, the NGO and the bank. The relationship between the NGO and the panchayat and that between the NGO and the bank is thin.
- Ask the participants to draw circles to represent each institution or individual, whereby the size of the circles indicates their importance or scope. Circles are arranged in such a way that separate circles represent no contact between organisations while touching circles indicate that there is coordination between organisations. A small overlap indicates some degree of cooperation while a large overlap reflects considerable coordination (see Figure 7.3).
- Triangulate the information with data from secondary sources.
- Discuss the outcome of the exercise and its implications for further activities.

Figure 7.2
Venn Diagram: Depicting the Relationship

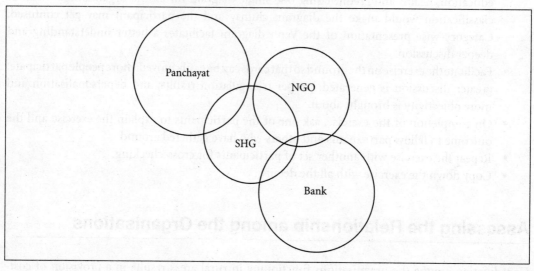

Figure 7.3
Venn Diagram: Depicting Coordination between Organisations

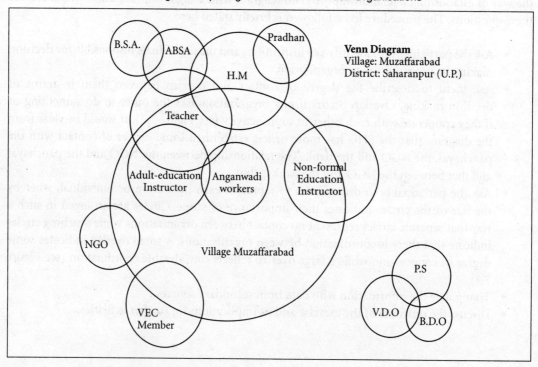

Dos

- Ensure that the methods are mutually understood.
- Ensure that the participants do know the mode of carrying out the exercise.
- Allow them to relocate the circles if they wish so, in the course of time.
- Probe the reasons for perceiving an organisation as 'important' or 'not important' and also for assessing an organisation as 'effective' or 'not effective'.

Don'ts

- Do not allow just a few participants to dominate.
- Do not be carried away by the emotional responses of a few participants.

APPLICATION

Venn diagrams have been used to explore a variety of linkages. Often the diagram is left open, with local people defining the organisations they feel are important to their lives in general terms. However, Venn diagrams can also be used to analyse the influence of organisation in relation to more specific issues:

- Examination of the role played by outside agencies
- Examination of the role played by village agencies
- Examination of the role played by informal groupings
- Relationship between individuals (family and community level)
- Local facility, local infrastructure and self-help system
- Institutional and individual support system
- Credit support system
- Health support system
- Forest management, agriculture, irrigation, fishing
- Livestock diseases and their linkages
- Income-generating institutions for women
- Links between government, NGOs, religious, individual and community organisations
- Institutional aspects of conflict and dispute resolution
- Aspects of policy, intervention and grant system
- Assessment of interventions, new structures, changes to old structures
- Perceptions of project and implementing agencies
- Importance of problems and their relationships to each other

We now discuss the application of Venn diagram in selected fields with illustrations.

Assessing the Effectiveness of Organisation

While attempting an overall appraisal of the existing condition and situation in a village or a community, the Venn diagram method can be applied to ascertain the effectiveness of various institutions functioning in the village and outside the village. A Venn diagram drawn by the women of a Harijan colony in a village revealed that they have transactions with nineteen organisations. They attached 'less importance' to organisations like cooperative bank, commercial bank, private moneylenders, youth club and post office. They considered ration shop, pre-school, primary school, SHGs, *mather sangh* (women's group), village administrative officer (VAO), veterinary sub-centre, primary health centre (PHC) as more important. Of the nineteen organisations identified, only nine organisations are perceived as more effective, six as moderately effective and the remaining four as least effective (see Figure 7.4).

Figure 7.4
Venn Diagram: Assessing the Effectiveness of the Organisations

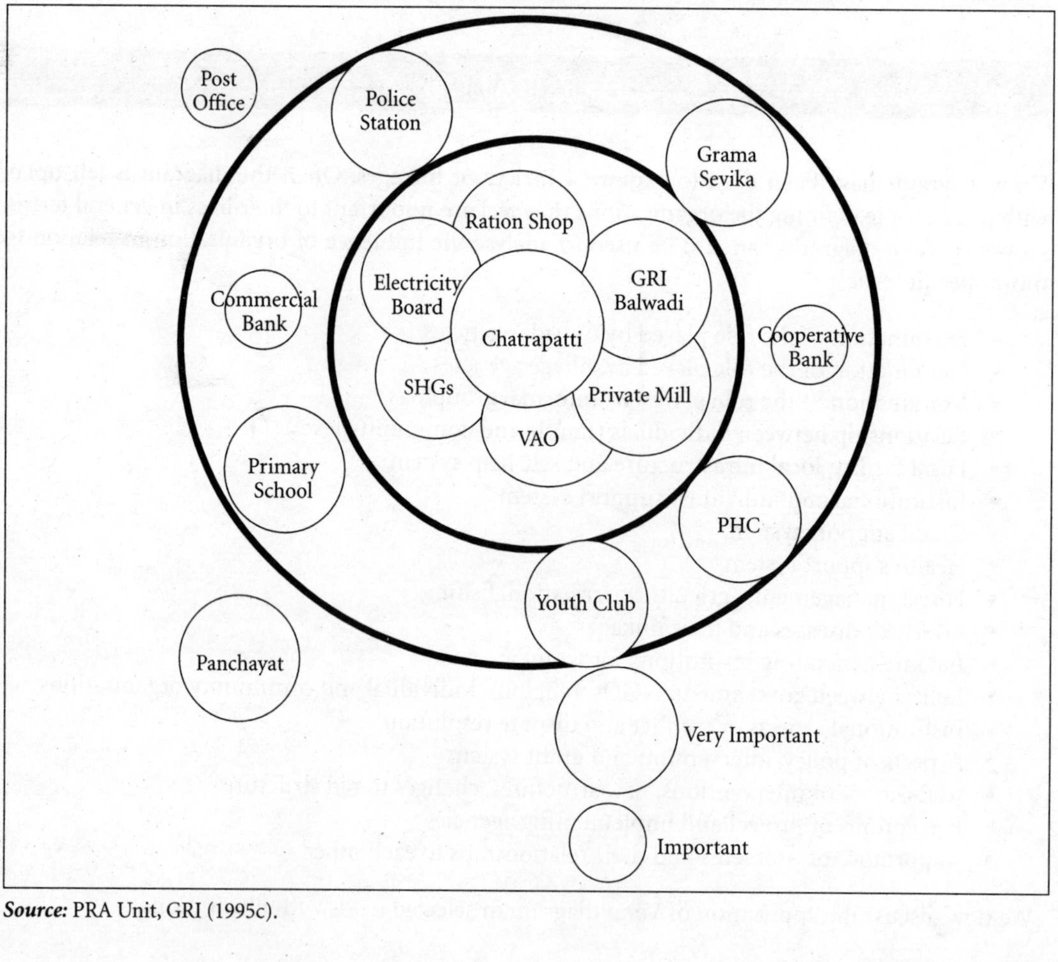

Source: PRA Unit, GRI (1995c).

Credit Sources

Venn diagrams can be used to find the quality and effectiveness of services rendered by various credit agencies, both formal and informal, operating in a village. A study on 'Credit delivery in practice' conducted by PRA unit of the Gandhigram Rural Institute (GRI) employed Venn diagrams to assess the effectiveness of various sources of credit. The villagers identified several sources of credit.

The villagers make use of different credit organisations inside and outside the village. The informal credit sources included affluent farmers, friends and relatives, traders cum moneylenders, commission agents, professional moneylenders, flower merchants, common village fund and local chit fund. The formal sources of credit that emerged were the Canara Bank, the State Bank of India and the primary cooperative bank. Having identified the different sources, the participants were then facilitated to locate the accessibility and effectiveness of services rendered by different agencies. The diagram as drawn by the people using cards (circles) indicates that the commission agents, local moneylenders and the State Bank of India have been located in the very important zone; professional moneylenders have been placed in 'moderately' important zone and the Canara Bank and cooperative banks have been placed in the unimportant zone. The agencies that provide effective and timely service and are easily accessible are in the very important zone. Agencies, which are in the least important zone, indicate that they are not easily accessible and their services have been found to be ineffective (see Figure 7.5).

Effectiveness of Leaders

Venn diagrams can also be used to depict how the villagers see their leaders. Such a diagram shows the importance attached to different kinds of leaders and their effectiveness as perceived by the villagers (see Figure 7.6).

The distances between the village and each of the circles represent the effectiveness of the leaders. If the distance is too far, it would mean that the leaders are not effective. If the distance is less or if the circles overlap with the village, it would mean that the leaders are effective. Based on the diagrams, the facilitator can have a detailed discussion with the people on

- why certain leaders are respected while others are not;
- how do women leaders function;
- what do the people feel about women leaders;
- the nature of relationship between women and men leaders;
- what types of decisions are taken and how.

Figure 7.5
Venn Diagram: Evaluating the Performance of Credit Sources

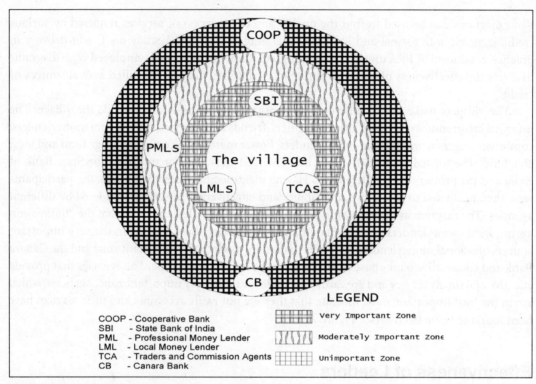

COOP - Cooperative Bank
SBI   - State Bank of India
PML   - Professional Money Lender
LML   - Local Money Lender
TCA   - Traders and Commission Agents
CB   - Canara Bank

LEGEND

Very Important Zone

Moderately Important Zone

Unimportant Zone

Source: Narayanasamy et al. (1998).

Impact Analysis

The biotic pressure on forests can be depicted through Venn diagrams. It is not possible to exactly quantify the pressure but it would definitely give an indication. People who are living either on the periphery of or within the forest make use of the forests for various purposes, which include (*i*) collection of minor forest produce; (*ii*) grazing of cattle; (*iii*) collection of firewood; (*iv*) cutting timber for household purposes; (*v*) collection of thatching grass; (*vi*) fishing and (*vii*) hunting. To assess the pressure of population on the forests with reference to different purposes, following steps can be followed: (*i*) Convene a meeting of the key informants and explain the purpose of the exercise. (*ii*) Cut newsprint into different size circles. The largest circle would mean most important and the smallest circle would mean least important; in between these two extremes there are different sizes of circles, indicating various degrees of importance. (*iii*) Ask the participants to draw a big semi-circle on the ground indicating the forest area. (*iv*) Ask the participants to list the

Figure 7.6
Venn Diagram: Effectiveness of Leaders

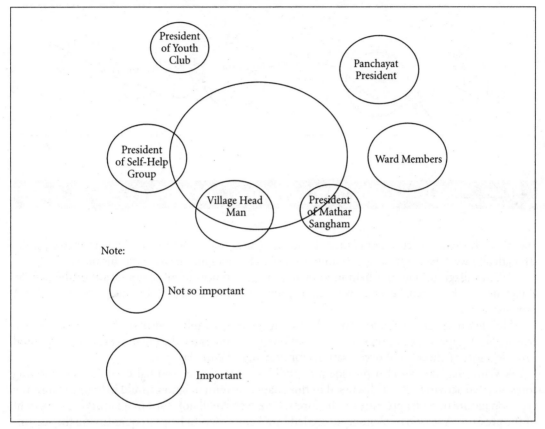

Source: PRA Unit, GRI (2001a).

purposes for which they make use of the forest. (*v*) Start discussing the purpose-wise utilisation of the forest. You may start with a collection of minor produce. If they attach much importance let them choose the bigger circle. (*vi*) Facilitate them to place the circle in the relevant area. If they make use of the forest for collection of minor produce quite often and the extent of the collection is considerable, the circle would have a more overlap; if the frequency and the extent of collection is less, the overlapping area would be less. (*vii*) Ask the participants to select the circle for each purpose and ask them to place it on the forest area depending on the extent of the use of forest for each purpose. (*viii*) Ask them to place the circle only after a thorough discussion and analysis. (*ix*) Repeat the exercise with another set of key informants for cross-checking and triangulation. The outcome of the exercise would provide a clear picture about the purpose-wise pressure of population on forests (see Figure 7.7).

Figure 7.7
Venn Diagram: Biotic Pressure on Forests

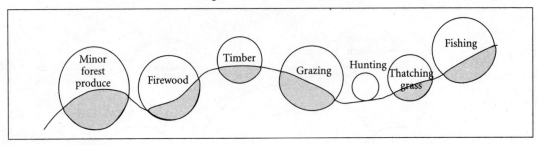

COMPLEMENTARITY WITH OTHER METHODS

Having analysed the effectiveness of organisations, the next step sometimes may be the analysis of the strength and weakness of the organisations. SWOT techniques may be used for this purpose.

A Venn diagram does not help in knowing the preferences of an organisation of the people. Preference ranking can be employed after Venn diagrams to ascertain the preference of the organisation.

Mobility maps are drawn to know whether the people are able to avail of the services within a reasonable distance. Various types of organisations get enumerated during the exercise. This would provide a sort of checklist of organisations for drawing a Venn diagram.

A Venn diagram can also provide a checklist for drawing a seasonal calendar for assessing forest-related activities. As we discussed in this chapter, a Venn diagram would help us to know the type and nature of biotic pressure on the forest. However, it will not assist in quantifying the extent of the pressure. A seasonal calendar succeeded by a Venn diagram helps in quantifying the season-wise exploitation of forest resources by the people.

Social mapping may help in identifying the key informants for drawing a Venn diagram. For instance, to assess the relationship between various types of institutions with different categories of community such as marginal farmers, members of SHGs and SC/ST households, a social map would provide a list of each household. Key informants can be drawn from such list to draw a Venn diagram.

MERITS

Formulation, initiation and implementation of any scheme, programme or project requires a detailed analysis of the existing organisations relevant to the programme or project. Venn diagram provides a clear picture of the existing organisations, their strengths and weaknesses. It helps us to know to what extent the existing organisations would assist in carrying out the activities proposed under the project. It also provides a broad guideline for plugging loopholes, if any, in the functioning of the organisation.

It leads to mutual learning. The participants, both the insiders and the outsiders, would have better insight into the functioning of the existing organisations. The outsiders in the course of the discussion may throw more light on the purpose of the organisations. Facilitated properly, the insiders would have a better understanding of the organisation and their roles and responsibilities therein. It may also ensure participation.

It is a flexible method. It can be improvised and can be used for many purposes, for example:

- assessing the effectiveness of existing organisations;
- understanding the relationship and coordination among the organisations;
- ascertaining the impact of the people on the forest;
- monitoring and evaluating a project.

LIMITATIONS

- The method is likely to take more time to make the participants understand. The ideas are too difficult to express, especially when one deals with illiterate men and women. It requires a lot of patience. The process of doing the exercise should be explained in the participants' own language in an understandable way. Facilitators are likely to lose patience and take over the exercise from the participants. Thus, it is liable for facilitator domination.
- An unpleasant experience of some of the participants with some organisation is likely to create a biased picture about that organisation. People normally do not own responsibilities and have a tendency to 'pass the buck'. Similarly, people without proper understanding of the 'rules of the game' may blame the organisation. The facilitators should not be carried away by emotions of the participants. The facilitator should guide the people to judge the functioning of the organisation in a rational way.
- A Venn diagram is silent on the discussion that created it.
- The realities of the weaker sections are likely to get submerged.
- There is the possibility of a highly individual opinion being identified as the collective representation of a particular group's reality.

SUMMARY

The Venn diagram is a PRA technique used to depict key organisations and individuals and their relationships with the local community and other groups. The Venn diagram provides a basis for discussion on the roles and significance of various organisations to the people in a locality and the levels of communication between such organisations.

The exercises can be practised with individual households or with the community, depending on the purpose. The number of participants can vary from fifteen to twenty. It can also be done in a small group of three to five participants.

The exercise needs to be facilitated on the ground for better participation and discussion. Two aspects have to be emphasised while practicing the exercise. First, the size of the 'circle' indicates the importance perceived. Second, the distance between the circle and the community indicates the effectiveness in rendering the service. The larger the distance the lesser is the effectiveness; shorter the distance, greater the effectiveness.

Venn diagrams can be used in different fields with a wide range of applications. They can be used along with various other PRA methods, such as a mobility map, social map, seasonal calendar, preference ranking and SWOT analysis.

The merits of the method are that (*i*) it helps in assessing the organisational effectiveness; (*ii*) it results in mutual learning; and (*iii*) it is flexible and provides scope for improvisation. The limitations are that (*i*) participants may take time to understand the method and (*ii*) the facilitator is likely to dominate by keeping the 'stick with him'.

8
Flow Diagrams

The PRA team, in course of their interaction with a group of participants, community, a family or individuals, may come across a problem, an issue, a situation or a phenomenon. These issues or problems may be broad or specific. They have to be studied in detail. The purpose here is to arrive at a solution. The team may also come across certain development interventions in the form of project, programme and schemes related to their study. They may like to ascertain the impact of these on the people. Further, a village is a dynamic system. It has various kinds of resources. Resources flow from the village to the outside world and from the outside into the village. What kind of resources flow outward and which flow inward? What are the problems related to the inflow and outflow of resources? What are the opportunities, problems and threats related to this inflow and outflow? A flow diagram, a dynamic tool in PRA, helps to assess the causes and effects of a problem or an issue, ascertain the impact of development interventions and study the flow of resources.

MEANING

Flow diagrams are used to analyse a wide range of issues in a systematic manner. It is possible to get a high level of details from these diagrams depending on the circumstances. These diagrams can be used to study broad and very detailed issues as well as specific issues. It is also possible to undertake a comparative analysis of the resource flow, for example, the resource flow from rich and poor households.

Flow diagrams aid in the examination of impacts, causes and effects, relationships and flow of resources. They can help in highlighting the gaps in understanding or can indicate the missing potential connections. They can also help in identifying a point at which the negative or vicious circle can be broken. They are sometimes used as planning and evaluation tools too.

A flow diagram consists of a central circle, which has the main issue written or symbolised in it with elements radiating from it. Secondary elements radiate from the main elements.

There are simple and complex flow diagrams consisting of a single sequential chain. They can, however, become more complex, with the build-up of complex webs. This includes both links and flows and illustrates the complexity of that system, whether they relate to the natural or human environments. Values, directions and other details can also be added to the diagram. However, such additions make the diagram more complex. Flows can be represented by lines in different thicknesses, indicating relative significance. In other cases, the flow can be represented by a thick or double line and secondary and tertiary interactions by progressively thin lines.

PURPOSE

The flow diagrams have several purposes. However, they are, by and large, used to

- appraise the existing situation or condition;
- monitor the ongoing programme, scheme or activity;
- assess the impact of a project, scheme or activity;
- design a suitable methodology for evaluation;
- examine significant changes over time, whether related to one specific event, such as a crisis situation or project intervention, or incremental change.

PARTICIPANTS

The nature of the participants depends upon the type of flow diagram that one employs in the field. The context of the diagram usually indicates whether this is an individual or group exercise. Flow diagrams on household systems or farm systems may be done with individual farmers or head of the household. For community issues, larger groups are preferred as the content of the diagram is important; thus all the related elements and interventions must be included. Discussion in groups leads to greater possibilities for triangulation. The impact diagram has to be conducted by involving all the stakeholders of the project, more particularly the primary stakeholders.

PROCEDURE

Flow diagrams are of different types. We discuss the procedure for drawing six types of diagrams:

- Causal diagram
- Cause and impact diagram

- Problem tree
- Resource flow diagram
- Impact diagram
- Systems diagram

Causal Diagram

A causal diagram is a flow diagram used to ascertain the causes for a problem. The procedure is very simple. Find out the major problem and facilitate the participants to depict the problem through a drawing or a symbol on the ground. Ask the participants 'What are the causes of the problem?' Write each cause on a card and put them around the problems. Draw arrows starting from the problem pointing towards the cause (see Figure 8.1). While drawing causal diagrams, there is a possibility that the symptoms and problems are confused with each other. The participant should be enabled to understand the difference between a problem and a symptom. A problem is a situation that causes difficulties. It is anything that is difficult to deal with or understand. It is a source of perplexity. A symptom is a sign of a problem. It is a sign that a problem exists. For example, diabetes is a problem. The symptoms are weight loss and fatigue.

Figure 8.1
Causal Diagram

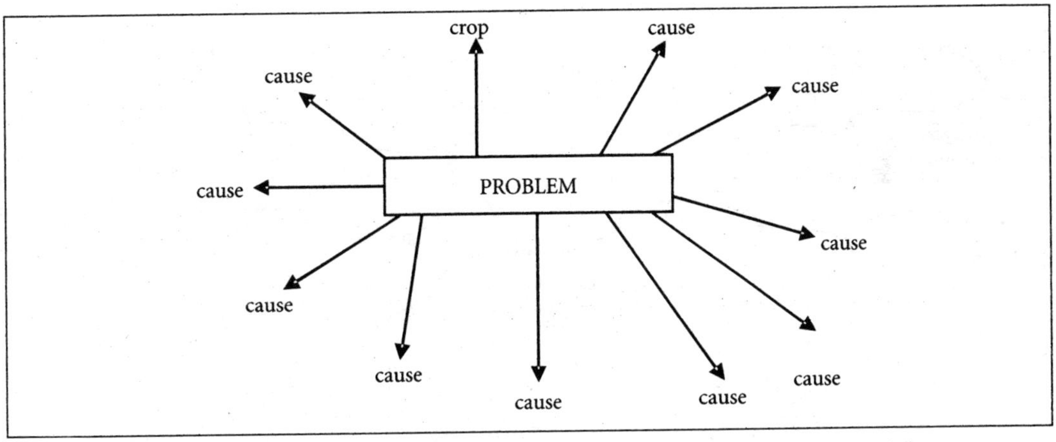

Cause and Impact Diagram

Cause and impact analysis is a form of flow diagram. It helps in understanding an issue in a complete form. It can be used to understand people's perception of causes and impact of a problem. This can be used to show the links between different causes and impacts of a problem as well as to show the flow of events. The same visual presentation can be meaningfully used to discuss possible solutions and the effects of the proposed solutions.

The steps that can be followed are listed below:

- Facilitate the participants to discuss about an identified core problem. Ask them to define the problem in precise terms. Ask one of them to write the problem on one card and ask him/her to place the card at the centre, preferably on the ground. Visual would be ideal.
- Ask the group to describe the causes of the problem. Once the discussion gets started, ask the participants to write each cause on a separate card.
- Place the cards for the causes on one side of the problem card.
- Keep asking the group what are the other causes of the problems and keep adding the cards.
- Similarly, ask the participants about the impact of the problem. For each impact use a separate card. Place these cards on the other side of the problem.
- Ask the participants whether there are any links between the different causes and impacts. Indicate the links by drawing arrows.
- Also ask the group if there are causes due to the problems and effects of the impact. Record the answer in each card, then place it on the ground.
- The diagram, when completed, looks like a web (see Figure 8.2).
- Once the diagram is ready, the facilitator can interview the diagram.

Figure 8.2
Cause–Impact Diagram

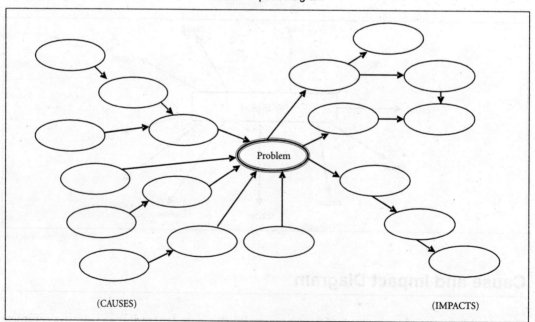

(CAUSES)   (IMPACTS)

Note: Arrows on the left-hand side of the diagram and pointing towards the problem circle indicate the causes. Arrows moving away from 'problem' circle and on the right-hand side of the diagram indicate the impacts.

Problem Tree

The problem tree is the variation of cause and effect diagram. The problem tree or the problem tree analysis identifies the negative aspects of an existing situation and establishes the 'cause and effect' relationship between the problems that prevail. Visualisation of the problems can be in the form of a diagram known as 'problem tree' or 'hierarchy of problems' to establish 'cause–effect' relationship. The analysis either in writing or in paper slips, presented in a diagram form, shows the effects of a problem on top and its causes underneath the 'core' problem. The analysis is aimed at identifying the real bottlenecks to which the stakeholders attach priority and which they seek to overcome.

The procedure to be followed is as follows:

- The first step is to identify the problem to be analysed.
- Have a fair idea about what the core problem is. Now, write a short summary statement on the core problem using a slip of paper and stick it either on the wall or on the ground. Explain to the participants the framework of the analysis.
- Second, ask the participants that what other problems and adverse circumstances are directly caused by the core problem. Write each of these negative consequences on slips of paper and stick these to the wall or ground above the core problem.
- Third, ask the participants that what further negative conditions are caused by the factors identified in the second stage. Record each of these on a slip of paper and stick them on the wall or upon the ground above their 'causes'. Try to continue to trace out these problem tree 'branches' as far as you think it is meaningful.
- Fourth, get back to the core problem and ask the participants that 'what factors or adverse conditions directly cause or contribute to the existence of the core problem'. Write each of the causes on a slip of paper and stick them on the wall or the ground below the core problem.
- Fifth, ask the participants what factors cause the problems that were identified in the fourth step. Record each of the causes and place them below the problems identified in the fourth step. Pursue these causal 'roots' as far as desired.
- Finally, ask the participants to go through the entire scheme and ask them to arrange all the individual elements to reflect the major causal links in the best way possible. You may, at this stage, facilitate the participants to add, delete and redraft items as needed to get an adequately complete and accurate picture. Then connect all items as appropriate, with links or arrows representing the important causal links (see Figures 8.3 and 8.4).
- The 'causes' are compared to the roots of a tree, the 'effects' are compared to the branches of the tree and the problem to the trunk of the tree. While analysing the cause of the problem step by step, use the helper question 'Why?' Similarly, while ascertaining the effects of the problem, use the helper question 'What?'
- It is important that all the participants remain to contribute until the completion of the analysis.

Figure 8.3
Problem Tree

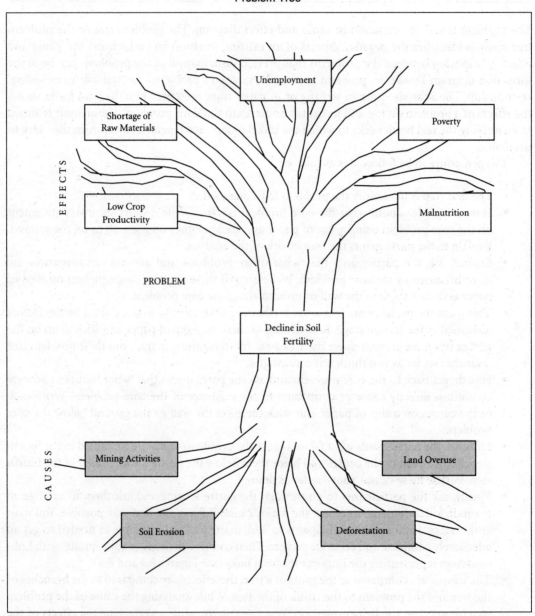

Source: Gubbels and Koss (2000).

Figure 8.4
Shrimp Farms: Problem Tree (Ariankunru)

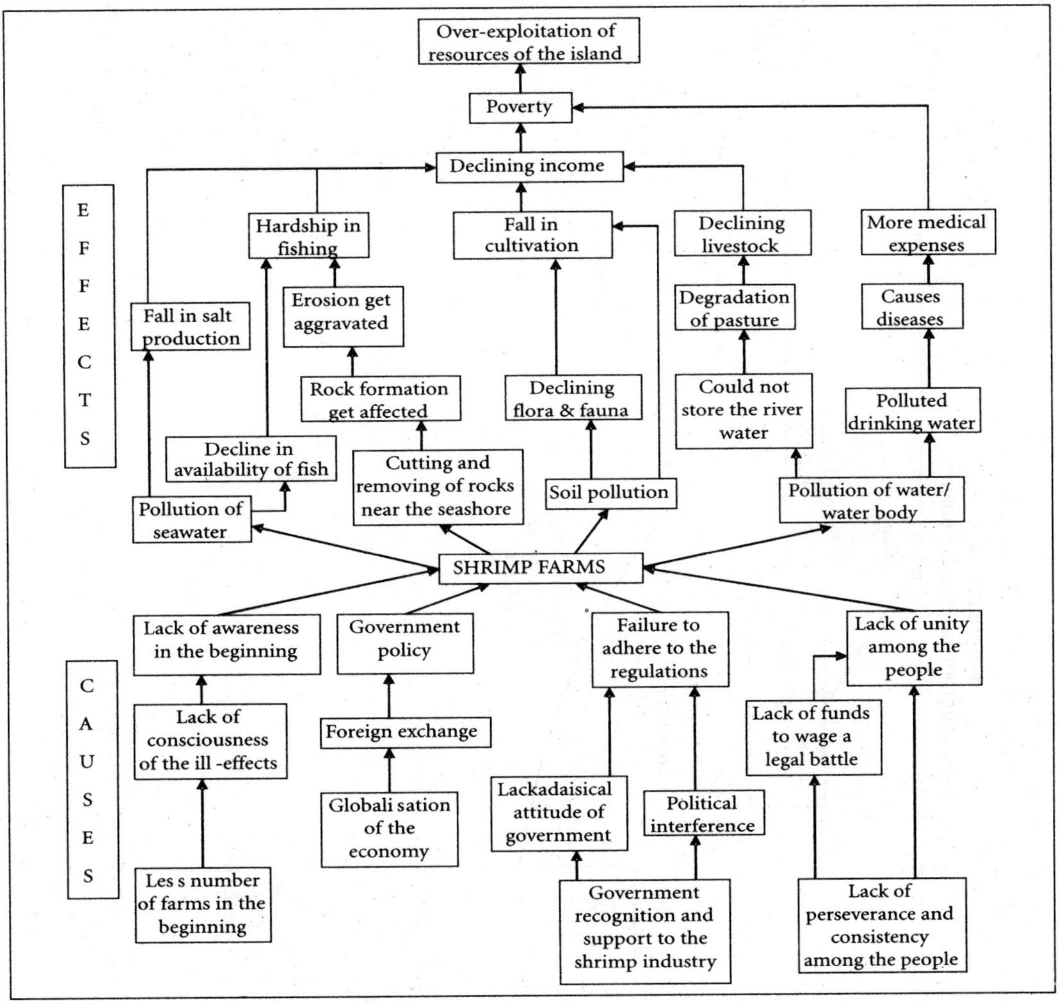

Source: Narayanasamy and Manivel (2002).

Impact Diagram

It is yet another flow diagram, which is used to identify the impact of an activity, event or intervention. It takes into account the changes planned and also the changes as perceived by the people. The impact can be qualitative and quantitative, positive and negative, planned and unplanned, perceived and unperceived, short-term and long-term, direct and indirect, etc. It can be used as an appraisal, planning and a monitoring and evaluation tool. It also helps in understanding the linkages, flow of effects and bottlenecks.

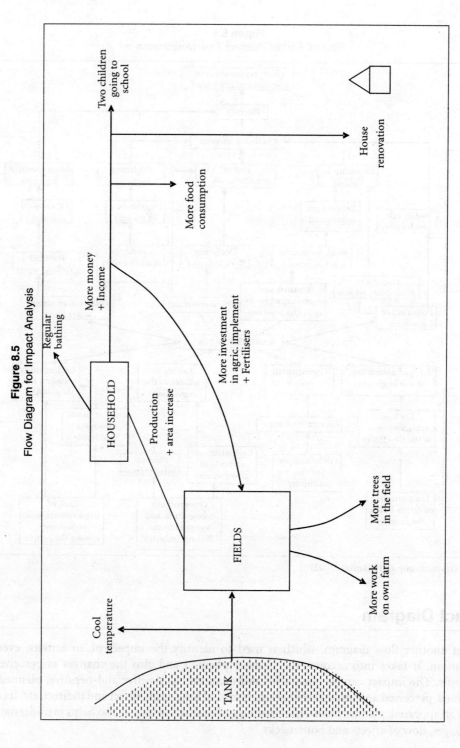

Figure 8.5
Flow Diagram for Impact Analysis

Two children going to school

House renovation

More food consumption

More money + Income

Regular bathing

More investment in agric. implement + Fertilisers

HOUSEHOLD

Production + area increase

More trees in the field

FIELDS

More work on own farm

Cool temperature

TANK

Source: Shah et al. (1991).

Impact diagrams have wider applications in areas such as agriculture, animal husbandry, forestry, irrigation, social issues, etc. For instance, the impact of an irrigation tank on the lives and livelihoods of the farmer(s) can be assessed using a flow diagram (see Figure 8.5).

The diagram can be used to assess the impact of an intervention. The procedure is as follows:

- Choose the theme or topic for the impact diagram.
- Identify and select the key informants.
- Explain the aim and purpose of the exercise.
- Ask the participants either to visually represent the topic or theme on the ground or write it on a card and place it at the centre.
- Ask them to concentrate on the topic and spell out the impact of that intervention.
- Facilitate them to define or state the impact in specific terms and ask them to record each impact. Use separate cards for each impact.
- Ask them to use cards of different colours for positive and negative impacts.
- Place all the impact cards around the topic card.
- Ask the participants to look at the cards and facilitate them to see whether there are any linkages. If so, ask the participants to link them with lines or arrows indicating their inter-linkages.
- Encourage them to add new cards if they come out with more impacts.
- Have a detailed discussion on the diagram to understand the impact.
- Copy the diagram on a sheet of paper for reference.
- Triangulate the diagram and findings by the following appropriate procedure.

Systems Diagram

The systems diagram was mostly used in agriculture in the early 1990s when PRA was slowly emerging as a participatory research and outreach methodology. It owes its origin to the systems approach. It is a detailed visual analysis of the flows of inputs and outputs of a system.

The systems diagram was used to discuss decisions made on the farm and the options open to the farmers. It can be used among either individual farmers or a group of farmers. It would be appropriate if the exercise is done after completing other exercises like social and resource mapping. The process is as follows:

- Select the key informants from among the participants (farmers) of the earlier exercise.
- Ask the farmer participant to draw his farm. Ask him to mention what he grows in the field or what is being grown in the field. The outcome would be in the form of a field map or farm sketch with various crops grown in the field.
- Switch over to specific questions, such as 'How many animals do you have?', 'Where are they located?' The farmer may draw the number of animals that he owns and their location.

- Slowly move to questions like 'What about manure?', 'Where does it go?', 'How it is being used?', 'Can you draw lines from cattle shed to where it is used?' Ask the participants to draw lines, which would help them ascertaining the movement of manure from cattle shed to different destinations where it is used for varied purposes.
- Then start exploring other components and flows—seeds, credit, fertiliser, pesticide, fodder, straw, water, money, vaccination and advice, market, etc. Facilitate them to use symbols. Do not suggest symbols. When symbols are suggested, it results in farmers depending on the outsiders. It does not encourage analysis by the farmers. Encourage the participants to use locally available materials, which would help in easy identification, recollection and analysis. This also makes the exercise quite lively and makes the participants the proud owners of the output and outcome.
- After completing the diagram, discuss the flows and constraints in the flows. Probe further by asking how this differs for different farms.
- When constraints and problems are linked, ask them about what do they do to overcome the problem and how do they adapt themselves to solve the problems or meet the challenges arising out of the problems.
- Copy the diagram on a sheet of paper with all details. Interview the diagram to gain more clarity on the subject (see Figures 8.6 and 8.7).
- The exercise can be repeated among different types of farmers based on the size of holding, mode of irrigation, ownership, crops grown, etc. This would provide a wealth of information on the system of farming.

Figure 8.6
Systems Diagram

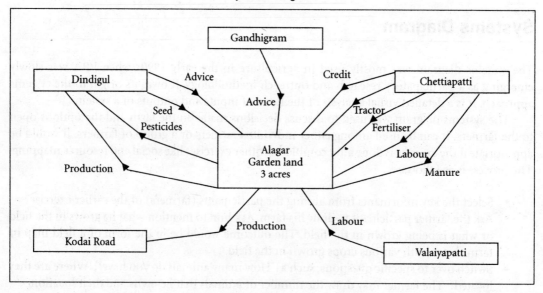

Figure 8.7
Systems Flow

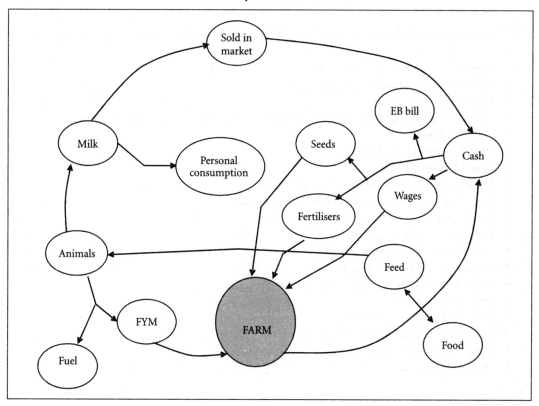

Dos

- Keep the diagram simple as far as possible.
- Use symbols and visuals for better understanding.
- Debate, discuss and have a dialogue.

Don'ts

- Don't be subjective.
- Don't be superficial.

APPLICATION

Flow diagrams have numerous applications. The specific areas of application are listed here:

- Household systems, farm systems
- Resource flows, income and expenditure
- Household energy flows
- Agricultural and other production systems, marketing systems or product flows
- Nutrient flows
- Credit system or credit flows
- Forest product flows
- Health, diseases, child death cause/effect flows
- Households/community-level enterprise systems
- Forest crops/forest management systems
- Indigenous knowledge systems
- Causal diagram for deforestation
- Causal diagram for river pollution
- Impact of introducing new crop varieties
- Impact of drought
- Impact of project intervention
- Effect of husband's/father's drinking
- Effect of male/female child births
- Problem/solution analysis

Production and Marketing of Crops

Flow diagrams can be meaningfully used to indicate the flow of inputs and steps in the production of various crops. The facilitator can, in consultation with the participants, select a particular crop. The participants can be asked to indicate the inputs needed to cultivate the chosen crop and the sources from which they obtained the inputs. The facilitator can slowly move on to the various operations related to the cultivation of crops and enquire about the inputs required for such operations and sources of procuring such inputs. Once the discussion on the production aspects of the selected crop is over, the facilitator may take up the processing and marketing aspects, ask the participants for the inputs and the sources of input for processing the crop and ask them to indicate the channels of marketing. The facilitator should also ask the participants to spell out the problems and issues at different stages of production and marketing. He can do this after completing the flow diagram (see Figure 8.8).

Figure 8.8
Flow Diagram of Rice Production and Marketing

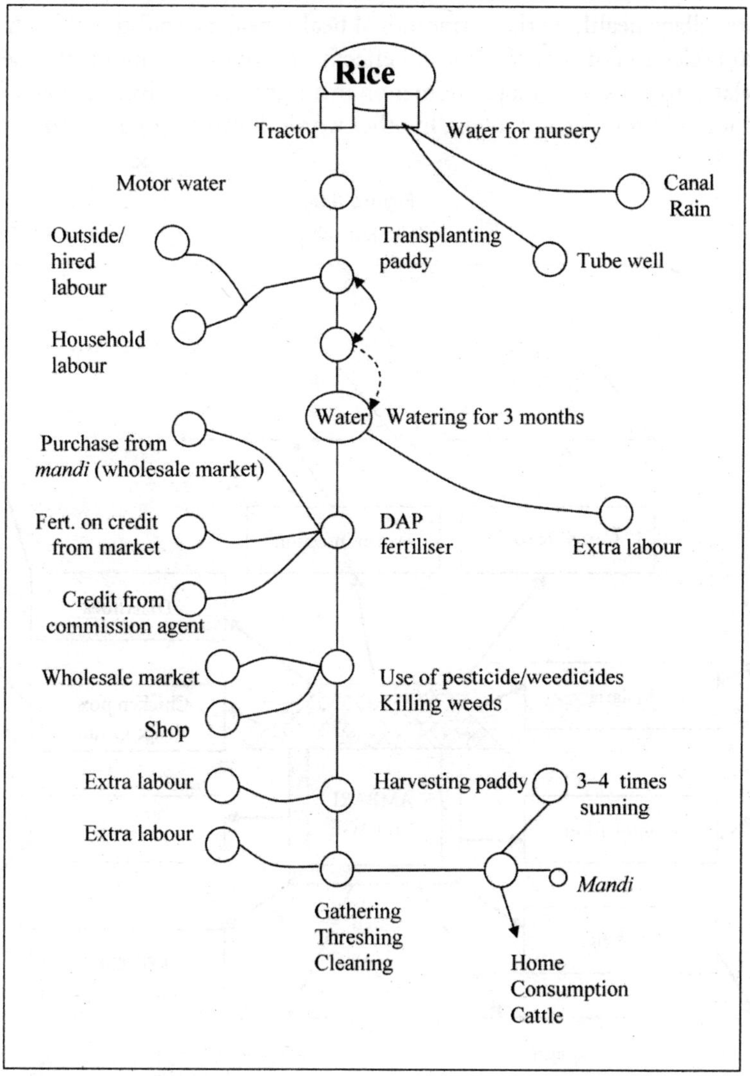

Source: Pretty and Guijt (1992).

Causes of Child Mortality

A causal diagram is widely used in health fields. It can be used to assess the causes of disease, child mortality, ineffective functioning of the health system, etc. Figure 8.9 shows various diseases prevalent among children, the diseases which have caused death among children and the number of deaths. It is a very quick way of assessing the causes for child mortality. The key informants for the exercise are village health workers, traditional health healers, traditional birth attendants and women. Careful selection of participants and effective facilitation would help assess the situation or problem related to a disease or a phenomenon in a right perspective. Such an analysis provides various possibilities in solving a problem. In other words, it can be used as a tool for planning.

Figure 8.9
Child Mortality

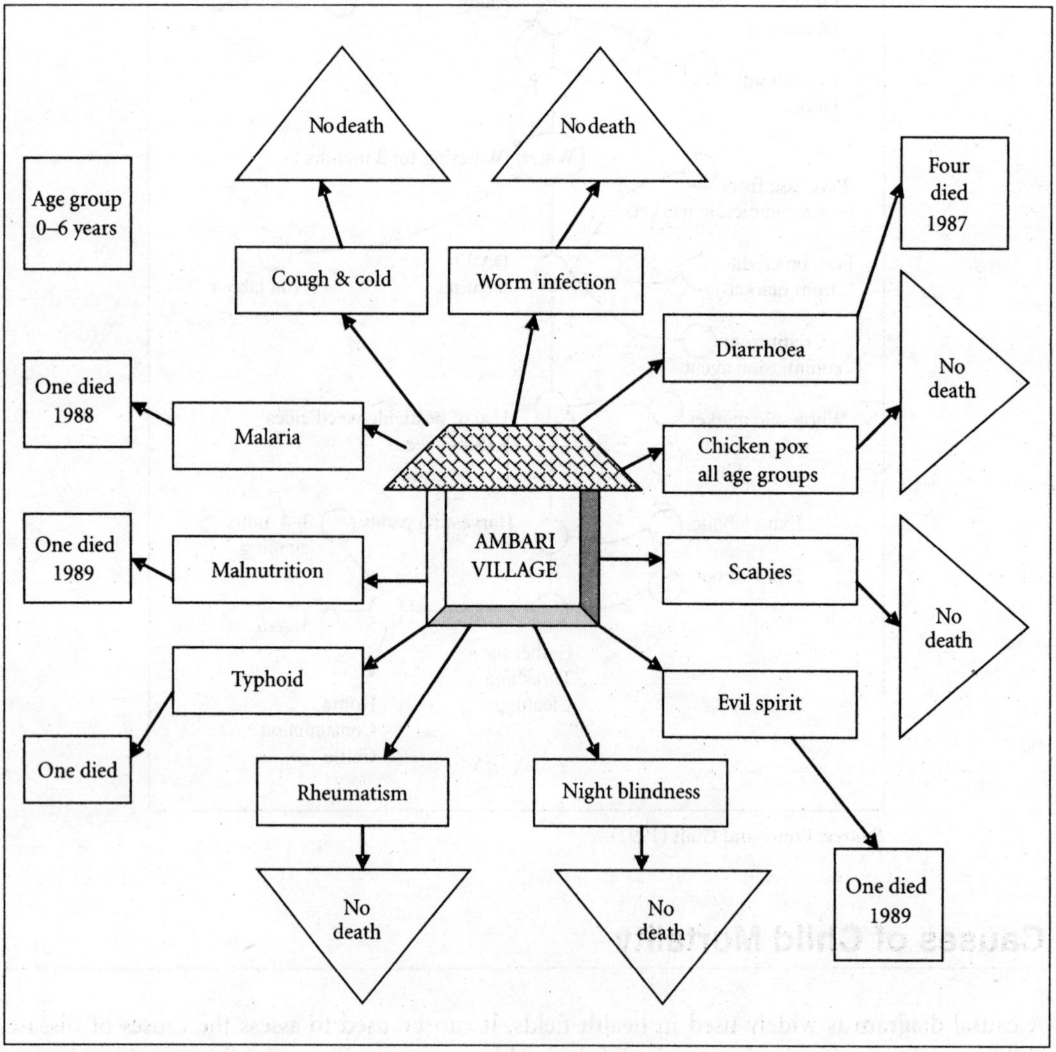

Source: Kumar (1992).

Impact of an Intervention

An impact diagram can be effectively used to assess the impact of a project or an intervention. A conventional type of impact assessment mostly attempts to quantify the output or outcome of an intervention in terms of return on investment or net profit margin. Even then, impact assessment under PRA using an impact diagram looks at the impact from different angles and identifies both the quantitative and the qualitative outcome of the project intervention. An illustration from the field would make things clearer. An NGO in Dindigul district (Tamil Nadu) had undertaken an action project 'Integrated Tribal Development', funded by Karl Kübel Foundation (KKF), Germany. A major intervention under the project was the provision of a pair of buffaloes to each of the selected 300 families. The PRA Unit of Gandhigram Rural Institute (GRI) was assigned the task of assessing the impact of the project. A combination of conventional as well as participatory methods was used to assess the impact. The impact diagram was used to assess the impact of buffaloes on the tribal households. An important finding was a reduction in dropout from schools. Buffaloes, it was reported, checked the migration of tribal families to far-off places in search of work. Provision of buffaloes forced the women members of the family to be at home, which in turn resulted in sending the children to school regularly. The impact diagram also helped in assessing various other outcomes besides increased income. The diagram also came out with problems and risks in rearing the buffaloes. After completing the diagram, the participants were asked to rank various outcomes of the provision of buffaloes and also the problems and risks involved (see Figure 8.10). The exercise, which took hardly an hour and a half, also helped in designing supplementary tools to probe further.

Problems in Cultivation of Crops

A flow diagram is used to ascertain problems related to the cultivation of crops. The exercise can be done with either a single farmer or a group of farmers. It would help in understanding the various issues and problems faced by the farmers. This, in turn, would help the field extension workers and staff to design an appropriate methodology to overcome the problem, of course, in consultation with the farmers. It would also help the farm scientists to identify the diseases that attack the crops and the preventive measures that need to be taken to prevent the disease. The flow diagram regarding the problem in the production of potatoes is presented in Figure 8.11. Conducted with a farmer in Pakistan, the flow diagram clearly brings out the various problems related to the production of potatoes.

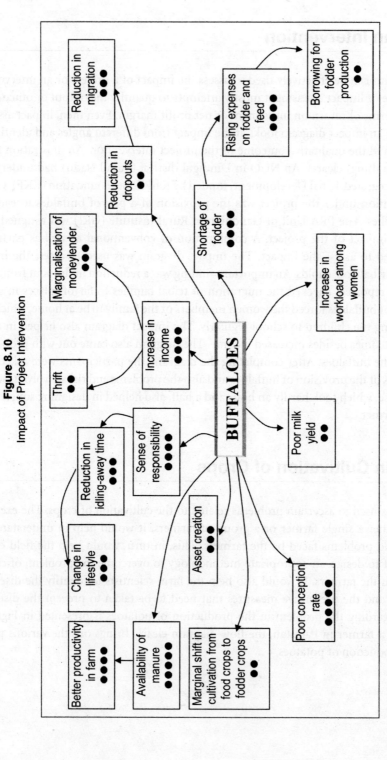

Figure 8.10
Impact of Project Intervention

Reduction in migration

Borrowing for fodder production

Rising expenses on fodder and feed

Reduction in dropouts

Shortage of fodder

Marginalisation of moneylender

Increase in workload among women

Increase in income

Thrift

BUFFALOES

Sense of responsibility

Reduction in idling-away time

Poor milk yield

Change in lifestyle

Asset creation

Better productivity in farm

Availability of manure

Marginal shift in cultivation from food crops to fodder crops

Poor conception rate

Source: PRA Unit, GRI (2002).

Note: The dots within a box indicate ranks assigned by the participants to each of the impact variables on a five-point scale.

Figure 8.11
Flow Diagram of Problems Related to Potato Production

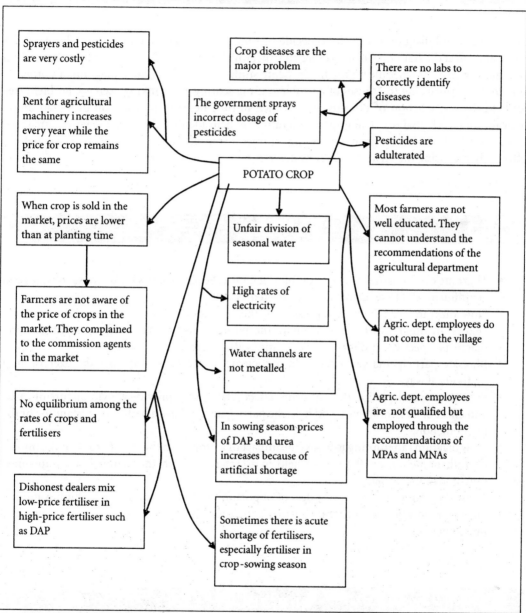

Source: Pretty and Guijt (1992).

COMPLEMENTARITY WITH OTHER METHODS

Drawing a causal diagram may help to decide major questions for a focused group discussion. A cause and effect diagram may help explore an issue, which may provide a base for the construction of a questionnaire or schedule for further in-depth study and analysis. Causal diagram of a problem may lead to prioritising the causes of a problem using scoring and ranking exercise. Problem tree leads to the construction of objective tree, which in turn helps in preparation of a plan under logical framework analysis. The impact diagram may help identify the broad areas of impact of a project, which in turn helps in identifying a project. Transect-based resource map may help in effectively practising the farm-related flow diagrams.

MERITS

- There are certain issues that are complex in nature. Several factors influence such issues and get influenced. These factors are interrelated as well.
- Flow diagrams can help in representing the connection between external and internal factors. In other words, they facilitate the participants to analyse micro-realities, think macro-perspectives and link micro-realities with macro-perspectives.
- Illiterate participants can effectively participate, if the facilitator does the exercise in a methodical way.
- Flow diagrams depicting the cause and effect relationship provide a vivid picture of cause and effect of a phenomenon and help the participants to have a better understanding of the phenomenon.
- Flow diagrams attempting to assess the impact of a project on the target group or the impact of a phenomenon on the people help in ascertaining both the planned and unplanned outcome of the project.
- These diagrams open up a great deal of opportunities for improvisation and innovation.
- Flow diagrams provide a base for further and deeper analysis as they explore a situation or phenomenon.

LIMITATIONS

- Confusions are likely to crop up if the diagram becomes too complex and complicated as the boxes become too numerous and interaction too detailed.

- There is a tendency among the facilitators to get satisfied with the diagram. Diagram is only the 'tip of the iceberg'. Several links and interlinks and deeper causes and effects can be ascertained and analysed only if the diagram is succeeded by in-depth probe and analysis.
- The exercise is likely to become facilitator-driven which needs to be carefully avoided.
- The exercise generates a lot of qualitative information. Subjectivity is likely to creep in.

Summary

Flow diagrams are the diagrams drawn by the people for examining causes and effects, impacts, relationships, flow of resources, etc. The purpose of the diagrams is to appraise the existing situation, places or action, and monitor and evaluate the impact of an action.

A flow diagram, depending on the purpose, can be presented among either individuals or groups. Larger groups are preferred for community issues.

Some of the important flow diagrams are (*i*) causal diagram, (*ii*) cause and impact diagram, (*iii*) problem tree, (*iv*) resource flow diagram, (*v*) impact diagram and (*vi*) systems diagram.

The procedure for facilitating the drawing of the diagram is simple. However, when complex issues are discussed, the linkage and inter-linkages need to be carefully studied and analysed.

The flow diagrams have a wide range of applications. They can be applied in agriculture, forestry, fisheries, health, environment and natural resource management. The methods used have a wide scope of applications both at the individual and the community level. They can also be used in assessing the impact of a project. Flow diagrams can complement other methods of PRA and conventional methods like surveys.

Some of the merits are that (*i*) they can facilitate even the illiterate participants to articulate and sort out complex issues, (*ii*) they have potential for improvisation and (*iii*) they provide a base for a further analysis and for designing methodology.

The limitations of the method are that (*i*) complicated and complex flow diagrams are likely to cause confusion among the participants, (*ii*) the exercise tends to become facilitator driven and (*iii*) subjectivity is likely to creep in, especially when qualitative information emerges during the exercise.

9

Timeline

INTRODUCTION

We have so far discussed some important participatory rural appraisal (PRA) methods that help to appraise the present situation and condition of the people. They do not deal with the past situation or condition. It should be noted that every village, every community, every organisation, every family and every individual has a history behind it. The past is full of events, incidents, happenings, processes, experiments, development initiatives and interventions, etc. The past carries a great deal of experience along with it. These experiences are varied in nature and may be good or bad, positive or negative. They need to be carefully studied and viewed in a proper perspective for understanding the present and shaping the future. This is so because the present and the future are the continuum of the past. The best prophet of the future is the past. Therefore, there is a need to study the past. Timeline, an important exercise in PRA, enables the people to have a peep into the past.

MEANING

A timeline is a list of key events, changes and landmarks in the past, presented in a chronological order. It is often a useful way of putting an individual's or a community's history into perspective by identifying the broad framework of events which shaped its past. It is a way of charting trends, showing how past events led to the present situation and illustrating recurring themes. A timeline is constructed by looking back over a given period and mapping critical events. This provides the opportunity to discuss with the people who were there at that time questions such as the following: What really happened and why? What were the factors that contributed to the events? Can the core trends be observed and what are they? Which of the core trends may be expected to continue into the future?

A timeline exercise is done to identify the important key events that occurred in the past. The events could be generic (timeline of a village) or specific (timeline of famine) in nature, depending on the objective of the timeline.

A group of people, including both those with the direct knowledge of the events conceived and those without the knowledge who can ask questions, construct a timeline perfectly. It discusses significant events and identifies changes. It is employed to (*i*) identify the sequence of significance of events and changes over time; (*ii*) identify coping strategies; (*iii*) monitor the impact of the identified changes and (*iv*) understand past interventions. It promotes discussion of events, consequences and associated issues in a historical context. It can also be a sort of visual biography tracing the life of a particular phenomenon. The phenomenon might be a famine or a drought, development of a kind of a technology, etc.

PURPOSE

Any problem, either at the individual, family or community level, has a historical perspective and dimension. Study of a problem in a historical perspective would help approach the problem with a clear perspective and the future course of action to solve the problems can be suitably designed. A timeline helps in putting the problem in a proper perspective by indicating the trends.

Development initiatives and interventions largely depend upon the self-initiative of the people. A timeline provides scope for assessing the self-initiative of people by indicating whether the people have made use of development opportunities at appropriate time.

PARTICIPANTS

Who should be the participants? What should be the number of participants? The answers to these questions depend on the purpose and objective of the exercise. Supposing the purpose is to trace the history and the important events of a village, the participants should consist of men and women of different age groups. While the old men and women would be able to trace the history of the village, the young adults would be able to provide authentic information on recent incidents and events. The number of participants may vary from fifteen to twenty though the ideal number is less than ten for effective interaction and participation.

Supposing the objective of the exercise is to trace the leadership pattern, the participants would necessarily be the past and present, formal and informal leaders. They are the key informants. Others can also be roped in. The number of participants can be less than ten. This has the advantage of discussion and triangulation, possibly increasing the reliability of information. This maximises the participation of individual members, and allows for a range of perspectives to be brought to light.

PROCEDURE

A timeline exercise can be done in a very relaxed manner. The procedure that may be followed in sketching the timeline of a village may be stated as follows:

- Convene a meeting of the key informants. Ensure that there are men and women of different age groups. Assure the presence of knowledgeable old people who know and could recall the history of the village and important events and could walk down the landmarks.
- After exchanging pleasantries, explain the purpose of drawing a timeline.
- Begin from general aspects. For example, ask 'How the village got its name?' Several interesting stories are likely to be told by the elders. Sometimes, elders in the group may come out with funny stories, which create a right climate to proceed further. Then ask who the first settlers were and when did they settle. The participants may find it difficult to answer the questions if the village is quite old. Still, they may be able to answer the questions based on oral history. Do not insist on the exact year. Dates do not need to be absolute. Follow the principle of 'appropriate imprecision'.
- Then ask about the various temples in the village and enquire when they were constructed. Probe further about the significance of each temple, festivals associated with the temples, ancestral stories about the temples. This would further reinforce the rapport between the participants and the team from outside.
- Ask about the events and trends that cause stress either regularly or intermittently. Also ask about historical occurrence of floods, drought, epidemics, local environmental trends and cycles. Use the helpers what, when, how and why.
- Ask about interventions in the form of projects, programmes, activities, new technology, etc., along with the year of intervention, and probe further by asking who was responsible.
- Ask about the creation of infrastructure over a period of time and the year in which it was created. Probe the status of the infrastructure created.
- Prompt and probe with short questions, which encourage participants to expand further in one direction. The questions that can be asked are: Could you tell me more about that? Could you explain how exactly the system worked?
- Use freely the props and mnemonics to inspire the participants to go down the memory lane and recall the past events. Physical objects such as old tools and equipments, buildings, lamp posts, photographs, traditional customs and artefacts can provide the focus for a detailed group discussion.
- Revisit the place and conduct an interview about the situation during a walk. This can relax the mind and allow someone to recall the past more easily. Such walks might include degraded watersheds to discuss environmental history and change; or abandoned wells, abandoned broken pumps, ponds, tanks, etc., to discuss irrigation techniques and land use.

- Ask them to narrate more such events that they would like to add.
- Ask the participants either to depict each event in a pictorial form or write it on a card with the year written on the left side of the event as and when the event or incident is narrated.
- Facilitate the participants to arrange the cards in a chronological order—earlier events first followed by later events.
- Participants always encounter problems in arriving at the exact year due to memory failure, use of different period, etc. This can be overcome to a certain extent by identifying the key events about which both the participants and the PRA team members know. This would help in synchronising the time frame. In other cases, the facilitator needs to use his best judgement to arrive at the years.
- Once the exercise is over, ask one of the participants to read out the events or the incidents in a chronological order. Additions, deletions and modifications suggested by the participants can be done at this stage.
- A subject-specific timeline can also be attempted, for example, agricultural practices, irrigation system, community-based organisations (CBOs), leadership, health practices, sanitation and food habits.
- Based on the timeline, an in-depth probing can be attempted in a more relaxed manner. Such a probe would provide valuable insights into the historical perspective and the perceptions of change that the local people have. The output from the timeline is not an end. It is the base on which more valuable information can be gathered and shared.
- Take a copy of the timeline presented. Give credit to the participants by noting down their names. Also, write details such as facilitator, location, dates and legends used.

Dos

- Decide in advance the type and nature of the timeline you want the people to construct.
- Encourage the participants to use symbols and visuals.
- Start from general observation. For example, you may ask the participants how the village got its name.
- Ensure the participation of the people from different age groups.
- Create an atmosphere where women can participate and talk.

Don'ts

- Don't insist on the participants to come out with exact date, month and year of occurrence of an event or an incident.

APPLICATION

Specific and diverse subjects could use timelines. The most common are village histories where significant events in the development of village are considered. This may include

- leadership or local activist changes and administrative/political events;
- changes in the natural resources—forests, land and agriculture;
- the development of infrastructure, such as roads, clinics and school;
- emergencies/crisis periods;
- introduction of the first TV, cycle, bike, tractor, etc.;
- who went to college first;
- who got the first government job;
- who was the first woman to go to college.

All this information forms part of the landmarks in the history of the village (see Table 9.1).

Table 9.1
Timeline: Somalingapuram

1940	A few families from the village adjacent to Karur came and settled here. The village is named after the local deity Somalingasamy. He is the presiding deity of the small temple situated at the foothill of Panrimalai.
1941	A few families bought land from the local farmers of Kannivadi—a big village near Somalingapuram.
1950	The first well was dug in the farm owned by a Rauthar.
1951	The panchayat union provided loan for digging a community well.
1960	Palanichamy, a resident of the village, joined as a supervisor in a cooperative society.
1968	Electricity was provided.
1969	More families settled down at farmhouses. Paramasivam was the first to complete schooling.
1970	Pump set was installed, tractor was used to plough the land. Chemical fertilisers and pesticides were used. Sprayer was used to apply pesticides. Cash crops like sugarcane, banana and coconut were cultivated.
1973	Women started using hospital for delivery.
1977	Family planning methods were adopted.
1985	Students started attending colleges.
1989	Road was laid.
1990	Farmers started using the van and lorry for transporting agricultural produce.
1992	Krishi Vigyan Kendra (KVK), GRI, started its work in the village.

Source: PRA Unit, GRI (1996b).

Timeline of Leadership

The exercise can be used to trace the development of leadership in general and women leadership in particular. This would help to understand the place of women in the village setting and to ascertain the factors responsible for women occupying leadership position (see Table 9.2).

Table 9.2
Timeline: Women Leadership

1975	Establishment of a *mather sangh* (women's group), organised by an NGO; activities were mostly related to meeting and discussing issues related to child care. The *sangh* was headed by a woman nominated by the NGO.
1978	The *sangh* became defunct as the NGO ceased to function in the village.
1980	A new NGO started interacting with the women through a woman administrator appointed in the village itself.
1981	Self-help group (SHG) was organised. Membership was open to all. Women from all communities were enrolled as members. The group functioned as an informal one.
1982	The women's group was registered as a society under Societies Registration Act. It opened account in a local bank. It started providing loan to members mainly for consumption purpose. Rules and regulations were framed.
1984	The SHG became a member of the Women's Collective—a network organisation established to protect and promote the interests of the women.
1985	The members of the group participated in a 5-day awareness programme organised by the Women's Collective at Chennai.
1986	Members of the group staged a *dharna* in front of the ration shop for better services.
1987	There were communal problems in the village. Members of the SHG played an active role in settling the problem.
1988	Another SHG was started at the initiative of the first group.
1989	The collector of the district visited the village and had an interaction with the members of the group.
1990	It received bank loan and also one-time grant from the Social Welfare Board.
1991	A Harijan woman was elected as president of the SHG.
1992	73rd Amendment.
1994	Tamil Nadu Panchayat Act was enacted.
1996	Election to the panchayat. The secretary of the SHG was elected as the unopposed president of the panchayat. Two of the members of the group were elected unopposed as members.

Source: PRA Unit, GRI (1998a).

Timeline of an Institution

A timeline can be employed to sketch history of local institutions like cooperatives. It would reveal the boom and recession period in the history of the organisation, the leadership and their impact on the functioning of the organisation, and the causes for the efficient functioning of the organisation. A personal interview with the leaders and a review of secondary sources of data would help in building up the history of the organisation (see Table 9.3).

Table 9.3
Timeline: Milk Producers' Cooperative Society

1960	DD 225 Pithalaipati Sri Krishna Milk Producers' Cooperative Society was registered. The society commenced its business in the same year.
1960–1962	The society was functioning well.
1962–1970	From mid-1962 to 1970 it was performing poorly. It was almost defunct, but without official declaration of dormancy.
1971	President Mr P. V. Naidu rejuvenated the society. The society had nearly 200 members. It was serving five villages, namely, Kuttiapatti, Royarpatti, Vannampatti, Vakkampatti and Pillayarnatham.
1971–1978	Excellent period. The society produced 450–500 litres of milk per day. Sometimes the society used to send milk to Madurai. The society gave bonus to members.
1978–1983	The society was performing moderately, with occasional delays in payment to the producers.
1984	President Mr Varadharajan took over from Mr Naidu (his father).
1985	Special Officer joined.
1985–1986	There was a gap between the members and the society. Irregularity in payment was very much prevalent.
1987	Pillayarnatham people started their own society. It functioned just 4 days or so, then became defunct.
1988	The people from Vakkampatti started their own society.
1988–1991	There was a decline in operations.
1992	From March to October it was defunct. Later, it was started again.
1993	It was defunct again.
1994	It was finally closed. The private people completely took over the milk procurement and marketing business from the cooperative.

Source: Narayanasamy et al. (1998).

Timeline of Common Property Resources

The exercise can be used to trace the history of common property resources like tanks, ponds, promboke lands (common land belonging to the government), wells, grazing lands, and so on. It would also help to assess the participation in maintaining and protecting resources, the efforts initiated by the people to get support from outside for protection and preservation of resources. The exercise would take us on a historical tour and would let us know the status of the resources at different periods (see Table 9.4).

Table 9.4
Timeline of Kovil Oorani: Michael Patinam

Year	Structure	Who was responsible	Current Status/Remarks
300 years ago	Oorani was dug (bowl type)	The people of the village	Used for drinking water purpose
50 years ago	A small well was dug within the Oorani on the eastern side	The people of the village	Was dug when the Oorani dried up in summer; water had high salinity and was not potable

(Table 9.4 Contd.)

(*Table 9.4 Contd.*)

Year	Structure	Who was responsible	Current Status/Remarks
45 years ago	Very small wells were dug within the Oorani on the western side	The people of the village	Potable water from this source helped in easing water problem in summer
30 years ago	A well was dug (with parapet wall) within Oorani on the south–west side	Block development office	Faulty construction; high salinity; not potable; closed after five years
25 years ago	A well with a depth of 30 ft with *pucca* parapet adjacent to Oorani on the western side was dug	The people of the village	Used for two years; later on dried up; not in use at present
15 years ago	A borewell was sunk within Oorani on the southern end	TWAD	Was in use for two years; salinity; hence abandoned and not in use at present
14 years ago	A borewell was dug adjacent to Oorani on the western side	TWAD	Being used even now despite salinity; mostly used for washing
8 years ago	A borewell was sunk adjacent to Oorani on the southern side	TWAD	Potable when the storage is high in Oorani; in summer, the water cannot be used for drinking purposes
4 years ago	A filter well was constructed within Oorani on the eastern end	TWAD	Functioned for one year; could not be maintained properly; filtering system failed; not used at present
3 years ago	Desilting, deepening and fencing	TWAD	Fencing is in good condition
2 years ago	Water inlet was constructed on the western side near the old inlet	DRDA under watershed development programme	In good condition
1 year ago	Retaining wall around half of the Oorani	DRDA under CWDP	In good condition

Source: PRA Unit, GRI (2000).

Note: The size of the Oorani in the beginning was very small. The water in the Oorani right from the beginning has been used for drinking purpose. The people of the village, once in two or three years, desilted, deepened and widened the tank. The tank bed has deposits of limestones. They were collected and used for constructing a building for parking Church's Chariot. The low-lying area in front of the church was filled with soil dug out from Oorani. The villagers, thus, have been mainly responsible for the maintenance of tank. The government help came only at a later stage.

Timeline of a Problem

A timeline can be effectively used to trace a specific problem over a period of time. This helps us to know how a problem gets accentuated with time. It also reveals the causes of the problem, its impact on the people, strategies adopted by the people to overcome the problem, etc. (see Table 9.5).

Table 9.5
Declining Groundwater—Historical Timeline

200 years ago	Check dam was constructed by the local *zamindar* across the river Nitchepanathi near Ramachandrapuram.
100 years ago	Kasi Thevar, the grandfather of Arumuga Thevar, dug the first well in the village. The implements used to dig the well are still found. The depth of the well was 25 ft. Mhote was used to lift the water.
75 years ago	More wells were dug on the land adjacent to the river.
50 years ago	The system of hiring professionals from outside the village to dig the wells came into existence. Water table was very high—20–25 ft. Mhote was used.
40 years ago	The Ministry of Food and Agriculture, Government of Madras renovated the check dam across the river. The exact year is 1953. The canal, which branches off just above the check dam, was also cleared. Water level was very high. The check dam was a boon and it recharged water in all the wells around.
35 years ago	Ramaiah Thevar energized the well by installing oil engine. Ayyappa Thevar and Ganapathy Thevar subsequently bought oil engines.
30 years ago	Many wells were energised with electric pump sets. Sugarcane started being cultivated. Water level in the wells was still 20–25 ft.
25 years ago	Shanmugasamy and brothers were the first in the village to dig their well up to a depth of 65 ft at one stroke (deepest well in the village). Drinking water scheme to Sankarankoil was commenced by diverting water from river Nitchepanathi.
22 years ago	Famine struck the village; 20 families migrated to Veermankudi in Thanjavur district. Stayed there for three months, worked in farms and came back. The wage rate was Rs 4 per day. Groundwater started declining.
20 years ago	Shortage of rainfall.
18 years ago	Check dam across the river was washed away by flood water. Sharp decline in groundwater.
10 years ago	Wells adjacent to the river were abandoned for want of water. Mhote almost disappeared. Water level in the well was around 15–20 ft in rainy seasons and 5–10 ft in summer. The bund of Periyur Tank was raised.
5 years ago	Railway Pillai (so named because he is a retired executive engineer from Indian Railways) came and settled in Panaiyur. He initiated steps to reconstruct check dam but failed in his efforts. Further decline in groundwater; water level in the wells was 12–15 ft in rainy season and 3–6 ft in summer.
3 years ago	RR masonry channel from Periyur Tank was laid through the fields of farmers.

Source: Narayanasamy et al. (1998).

Timeline of a Family

A timeline can be helpful in weaving the life story of a family. It can indicate the crises and shocks experienced by a family, a person or a woman and how they overcame the crisis, or how they absorbed the shock (see Table 9.6).

Table 9.6
Mudamma's Life Story

1935	Born in a poor family, Mudiyannur.
	Childhood: casual work/ on alms.
1950	Married to an equally poor person from Gundalpat.
1951	First son born.
1954	Lost her husband.
	Back to Mudiyannur with her son.
	For livelihood: casual work and missionaries' help.
	Migrated to Bangalore: working with nuns.
1960	Came back to the missionaries in Banakahally.
1961	Finds her new marriage partner, Bagyarathnam.
1962	Bagyarathnam excommunicated and returns to Mudiyannur.
1964	Life's struggle worsens: drought.
1965	Has a third son: unable to feed children.
	Sickness in the family; forced to seek alms.
	Has another son and a daughter in succession.
1970	Second and third sons placed in bondage in order to release the eldest and get him married.
1972	Worst drought; no drinking water: walks 5 km to Doddapurma for water.
1980	Eldest son releases one of his brothers and gets him married.
1982	Loses her husband.
1985	MYRADA's intervention in second son's development (Laurance); sericulture: cross-bred calf.
1986	Second son releases both brothers and gets the elder married.
1987	Moves to government-allotted house with Laurance's family; gets her daughter married.
1988	Participates in the development attempt of Laurance: IRDP loan; Bicycle shop.
1990	Narrates her life struggle.
	Looking forward …

Source: Mascarenhas (1991).

COMPLEMENTARITY WITH OTHER METHODS

Timeline complements the other methods very effectively. The information gathered through timeline would supplement the outcome of the trend analysis. Timeline may also help in fixing the reference year for doing trend analysis.

The timeline exercise can be followed by key probe and focus group discussion if there is a need to investigate further an issue, event or incident.

Although timeline is introduced as a first exercise, yet it would be more useful and appropriate if it is preceded by a transect-based resource map and social map. This is because the information gathered through resource map and social map would provide a sort of checklist for facilitating the timeline exercise.

MERITS

- The timeline exercise is employed in the initial stage of PRA. It is sort of an icebreaker. The participants, especially the older ones, become quite enthusiastic in narrating the history of their village. The young intensively listen. The participants as a whole are proud of their village and its history. The timeline thus takes the outsiders closer to the people.
- The timeline is a precursor to other time-related methods. Time, trends, transects and historical matrices have emerged from timelines.
- Timeline provides reference points for trend and change analysis. An important step in trend analysis is fixing the reference point. A discussion on the timeline would help the participants to suggest a reference point for analysis of the change or trend. For instance, the participants may suggest 'particular political party coming to power', 'fall of a government', 'introduction of crop variety', 'election to panchayat', 'advent of a technology', 'creation of an infrastructure' as reference periods.
- A timeline can be combined with illustration, and be related to other aspects of historical changes to provide a greater depth of analysis. It can be individual, cultural, environmental, agricultural, economic, political and social events.
- It is a simple exercise and one-dimensional.
- The outcome of the timeline exercise provides a historical backdrop for the analysis of the situation in the village.
- It helps the participants, both insiders and outsiders, to know whether the village has been able to get various infrastructure facilities like transport, electricity and communication on time by comparing introduction of such facilities in the neighbourhood villages. It also helps them to know whether they are 'leading' or 'lagging' with reference to 'development intervention', self-initiatives, infrastructure, and so on.
- It can also be a good way into a life story interview or focus group discussion and may provide the basis for interviewing maps.

LIMITATIONS

Timeline is a very popular exercise. It provides a great deal of insight into the past. Participation is also quite intense and lively as old people in the group narrate various events and incidents. Yet the method suffers from certain limitations.

- The older key informants may have a tendency to 'romanticise' the past. Unless the information flowing from the exercise is properly judged, checked and cross-checked, a certain degree of subjectivity is likely to creep in. For example, if an old informant mentions that in his childhood the village had a huge forest, it should be understood that the view is captured from a child's perspective where, say, the chances of taking thick vegetation for forest are high. Hence, the facilitators need to be careful in raising questions, judging answers and validating information.

- Sometimes, the exercise is dominated by written words, pen and paper. As a result, there is a potential for one individual to hijack the process. Further, there is a possibility of the process becoming facilitator-driven, especially where the literacy levels are low. Hence, the PRA team has to see that the exercise is conducted with symbols.
- The local people have a different concept of time from that of the facilitator. It poses a major problem to the facilitator in drawing parallels between the local system's and the facilitator's time frame. This, largely, leads to imposing the facilitator's understanding of time on the people, which is likely to undermine the process. The problem can be sorted out by identifying some key events which both the facilitator and local people know (e.g., flood and drought). This has to be taken care of while designing the process of timeline by the PRA team.
- Men, mostly old, dominate the exercise. Old women are not included. Even if they come, they are silent spectators. They listen to men and agree with what men say. Hence, the facilitator needs to see that women do actively participate in the exercise.

SUMMARY

A timeline—constructed by looking back over a given period and mapping critical events—is a list of key events, changes and landmarks in the past written up in a chronological order. It facilitates a discussion of events, consequences and associated issues in a historical context. It can be a visual biography of a particular phenomenon.

A timeline enables the positioning of the problem with a right perspective by indicating the trend. It also provides scope for assessing the development initiatives of the village and the individuals. The number of participants can be less than ten to ensure a meaningful interaction.

The timeline method is carried out by involving old people who would be eager to narrate the history of the village and the key events. Topic-specific and problem-specific timelines can also be constructed depending on the need. Visual presentation makes the exercise lively and ensures active participation.

Some of the applications of timeline are (*i*) sketching the history of the village; (*ii*) tracing the emergence of leadership; (*iii*) assessing the maintenance and status of common property resources over a given period of time; (*iv*) tracing important milestones and landmarks in the development of formal and informal institutions and (*v*) tracing the genesis of a problem.

Timeline complements other PRA methods such as trend analysis, key probe and focus group discussion. The merits of the method are that (*i*) it is an icebreaker, (*ii*) it is a precursor to time-related methods, (*iii*) it provides a reference year or landmark year for trend analysis, (*iv*) it is simple and (*v*) it is one-dimensional. An important limitation is that it is likely to be facilitator-driven.

10
Trend Analysis

Nothing is permanent in life but change. Change is inherent in nature. It is the law of nature. Change is a natural condition of physical, biological and social systems. Of late, more seems to be changing, and changing faster. Changes are more interrelated and interconnected. Rural areas are no exception. The villages have been witnessing tremendous changes. They are observed everywhere and in every field. There are changes in social structure, agriculture, livelihood systems, employment pattern, education, lifestyle, culture, etc. The changes in rural areas may not be rapid, but they are steady. These changes have a discernible impact on the people. The changes, the causes behind them and their effects are to be appraised and analysed. The purpose is to ascertain the positive and negative effects of changes and to plan what we should continue doing and what we should stop doing. Trend analysis, a time-related method in participatory rural appraisal (PRA), helps to analyse the changes and trends in the life of an individual, family, institution, systems, practices and community.

MEANING

Trend analysis attempts to study people's accounts of the past, of how things that were closer to them have changed at different points of time. It is used to explore temporal dimensions with a focus on change. The information sought through the technique of trend analysis gives insight on various facts such as ecological histories, changes in land-use and cropping patterns, changes in customs and practices, changes and trends in population, migration, fuels used, education, health, sanitation and credits. The causes of changes and trends could be ascertained using trend analysis method. Based on the past trend, future trends could also be forecasted, by facilitating the people to peep into the future.

PURPOSE

The exercise would help in finding answers to many questions that one may come across in situation appraisal. What are the changes that have taken place in the village? What is the direction of these changes? Are the changes happening in the village in tune with such changes occurring outside the village? Are the changes positive or negative in nature? What is the attitude of the people towards the changes? How do they perceive the changes? Are they comfortable with the changes? What is the impact of such changes on their lives and livelihoods? How do they cope up with the changes? Trend analysis, by providing answers to these questions, would help in assessing the current situation of the village against the backdrop of the past.

PARTICIPANTS

The number of participants may vary from ten to fifteen. The participants should be an ideal mix of different age groups, sex, caste, occupation, if the trend analysis is about the entire village. Topic-specific trend analysis requires specific type of participants. For example, if the topic of study is trend in health practices, the participants would then include men and women of different age groups, traditional health practitioners, birth attendants, therapists, village health workers, and so on.

PROCEDURE

- Convene the meeting of a group of participants from the village comprising men and women of different age groups. Ensure the participants of the timeline exercise to get involved in trend analysis, as these two exercises are related to each other. This would help in getting the right type of informants for the exercise and also in cross-checking the information.
- Explain the purpose of the exercise.
- Prepare a checklist of various aspects of the selected topics to be covered under the exercise. For instance, if the topic of study is trends in agriculture, prepare a checklist encompassing aspects such as preparation of land, ploughing, sowing, cropping pattern, irrigation practices, manuring, cultural practices, productivity, production, processing and marketing.
- Facilitate the participants to fix the landmark years. Adequate care has to be taken in fixing the landmark year as the outcome of the exercise depends on its careful selection. Two factors are to be kept in view while fixing the landmark year. First, the year chosen should be

relevant to the topic of study. For example, for a study on 'rise and fall of a milk producers' cooperative society', the participants from the village along with the facilitator fixed three landmark years, namely, period of the elected board, period of the special officer and period of private milk producers. These three periods were chosen as they had a considerable effect on the functioning of the society. Second, it should be easy for the people to relate to the years.

- Further, fixing the landmark years depends on the type of trend analysis we propose to pursue. If it is a general trend line with an objective of exploring aspects of rural life, the landmark year may be fixed with reference to certain key events, namely, flood, drought, famine, change in government, war, etc. If the trend analysis is topical in nature, the landmark year relevant to the topic has to be fixed. The facilitator should keep in mind that it is always better to spend an adequate time with the participants fixing the landmark years for better outcome of the exercise.
- Having fixed the landmark year, initiate a discussion on the present situation and then move on to the aspects you are interested in pursuing. This sets the tone for trend analysis.
- Though a checklist is prepared in advance, even then facilitate a discussion among the participants to decide the aspects of trend analysis. This would help in comparing the list prepared by us and the list suggested by them. Arrive at a common checklist in consultation with the participants.
- Facilitate the participants to depict the selected reference or landmark year on cards. Visuals and symbols are preferable. Ask them to put the cards on rows at the top from left to right. Various aspects of the topic under study may be written on cards from top to bottom. Ask the participants to make a matrix on the ground using chalk (see Figure 10.1).

Figure 10.1
Trend Analysis: An Illustration

Sources of Irrigation \ Period	1980	1990	2000
Source of Irrigation	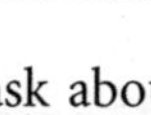	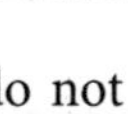	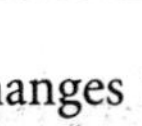
Number of wells	30	50	75
Water level in the well	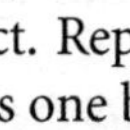	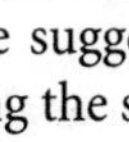	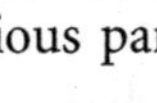
Mode of lifting water	Oil engine	Oil engine and electric motor	Electric motor only

- Take a particular aspect; ask about the changes; do not stop with the changes that have taken place. Probe the reasons for the changes and note down these reasons.
- Move on to the next aspect. Repeat the procedure suggested in the previous paragraph. Discuss all the other aspects one by one by following the same process.
- After the completion of the exercise, ask one of the participants to read aloud and explain

the outcome of the exercise. This is a sort of quick recapitulation of the process and the outcome of the exercise and a sort of cross-checking the information gathered.

- Interview the diagram. Raise questions to clarify your doubts and gain an insight into the trend.
- Ask them to reflect on the trends and the effects of trends and their well-being; ask them to suggest measures to overcome the problems, if any, faced by the people due to changes.
- Copy the diagram on a newsprint providing details such as village, date, names of participants from inside and outside, the legends used, the time taken to complete the exercise and the materials used.

Dos

- Spend an adequate amount of time in fixing the landmark year.
- Use the information from trend analysis to amplify and make a more precise local account of changes.
- Probe the causes and effects of changes.

Don'ts

- Do not jump from one topic to another.
- Do not trivialise the objective of the exercise.

APPLICATION

Trend analysis may be general in nature, highlighting the major trends in agriculture, demography, socio-economic conditions, health, education, sanitation, culture, customs, values and norms, etc. It can also be applied for an in-depth and focused analysis of a specific topic, such as ploughing, sowing, irrigation practices and harvesting. We will now present a few such areas of applications on trend analysis.

Understanding the Socio-economic Conditions

Trend analysis can be employed to analyse and understand the various facets of life in a chosen village. Table 10.1 indicates the various changes that have taken place in the village over a period of forty years. Notable among them are (*i*) decline of the joint family system and emergence of nuclear families, (*ii*) marked increase in the age at marriage, (*iii*) decrease in the size of the family, (*iv*) practice of family planning methods, (*v*) childbirth at hospital, (*vi*) increase in the literacy level, (*vii*) shift in cropping pattern, (*viii*) change in food habit and (*ix*) declining groundwater. This exercise provided an insight into the changes that have taken place over a period of forty years.

Table 10.1
Trend Analysis: Kathiranampatti

Details	*40 years ago*	*Now*
Number of houses	10	50
Types of houses		
(*i*) Tiled	3	35
(*ii*) Thatched	7	15
Size of the family	8–10	2–5
Nature of the family	Joint	Nuclear
Age at marriage		
(*i*) Male	19	25
(*ii*) Female	12	20
Dowry	Almost absent	Widely prevalent
Delivery	At home	At hospital
Family planning	Not practised	Largely adopted
Infant mortality	High	Low
Education	Low level of literacy; education of women not encouraged	Literacy level is high; women go to school in large number
Employment	Mainly in agriculture	In agriculture, government and mills
Agriculture		
(*i*) Rainfall	High	Low
(*ii*) Crops	Groundnut, millets and pulses (mostly food crops)	Millets, pulses, groundnut, paddy, vegetables, flowers, coconut (mostly commercial crops)
(*iii*) Ploughing	Plough bullocks were used	Tractors are used
(*iv*) Manure	Organic	Organic & inorganic
(*v*) Pesticides	Not used	Used heavily
(*vi*) Water level in wells	20–30 ft	120–150 ft
(*vii*) Mode of irrigation	Mhote	Pump set
(*viii*) Wage rate		
(a) men	Re 1	Rs 25
(b) women	Re 0.50	Rs 10
Mode of payment	Kind	Cash
(*ix*) Food habits	Bajra and jowar	Rice, bajra and jowar
(*x*) Drinking water	Well water (not protected)	Borewell (Protected)
(*xi*) Economic status	Normal	Some improvement

Source: PRA Unit, GRI (1993a).

Analysis of a Problem

Trend analysis is also being applied to analyse specific problems. OUTREACH, an NGO based at Bangalore, has identified 'soil erosion' as an important problem in one of the service villages. They decided to probe the problem further in all its dimensions with a historical perspective. They employed trend analysis. Two landmark years with an interval of ten years were fixed. Seeds were used to indicate the trend. The exercise revealed that (*i*) topsoil has been eroding over the period of twenty years, resulting in depletion of soil fertility; (*ii*) flooding has increased; (*iii*) tree coverage in the forest has gone down and (*iv*) extent of land available for agriculture has come down as the top soil has been eroded and the land has become rocky (see Table 10.2).

Table 10.2
Trend Analysis of a Problem

Variables	1978	1988	1998
Agriculture yield			
Ragi	●●●●● 5	●● 2	●● 2
Paddy	0	●●● 3	●●●●● 5
Soil depth	●●●●● ●●●●● 10	●●●●● 5	●●● 3
Flood (run-off)	●●●●● ●● 7	●●●●● 5	●●●●● ●●●●● 10
Tree species in the forest	●●●●● ●●●●● 10	●●●●● ● 6	0
Land availability for cultivation	●●●●● 5	●●●●● 5	●●● 3
Population	●●● 3	●●●● 4	●●●●● ●●● 8
Fertilisers			
Organic manure	●●●●● ●●●●● 10	●●●●● ●●● 8	●●●● 4
Chemical fertiliser	0	0	●●● 3
Livestock			
Cow/Buffalo	●●●●● ● 6	●●●●● ●●●●● 10	●●●●● 5
Goat	●●●●● ●●●●● 10	●●●●● 5	●●●●● 5
Sheep	0	0	●●●●● ●●●●● 10
Cattle diseases	●● 2	●● 2	●●●●● 5
Crop diseases	●● 2	●●●● 4	●●●●● 10
Literacy: Men	● 1	●● 2	●●●● 4
: Women	● 1	●●● 3	●●●● 4

Source: Narayanasamy and Boraian (2005).
Notes: (i) Stones have been used to study the trend.
(ii) Ten stones indicate the highest prevalence and one stone the lowest.

Status of Natural Resources

Trend analysis can be attempted to explain the perception of community members about the status of local natural resources. It also helps in determining the major trends affecting the natural resources and in identifying the principal causes of these identified trends (see Table 10.3). Based on the exercise, a further probe needs to be done on the signs of change, the most degraded natural resources, the natural resources that have improved, the causes for positive and negative trends, causes for certain natural resources changing quickly and the activities both inside and outside that are most responsible for the changes in natural resources.

Table 10.3
Status of Natural Resources

Resources	Today		10 years ago		20 years ago	
Food security	○○○○	4	○○○○○	5	○○○○○	
					○○○○○	10
Rainfall	○○○○	4	○○○○○		○○○○○	
			○	6	○○○○○	10
Crop production	○○○○		○○○○○		○○○○○	
		4	○○	7	○○○○○	10
Soil fertility	○○		○○○○○		○○○○○	
		2	○○○	8	○○○○	9
Water for animals	○○		○○○○○		○○○○○	
		2	○○	7	○○○○○	10
Drinking water	○○○		○○○○○		○○○○○	
		3	○○○	8	○○○○○	10
Pasture land	○		○○○○○		○○○○○	
		1	○○	7	○○○○○	10
Grass for roofing	○○		○○○○○		○○○○○	
		2	○○	7	○○○○○	10
Cattle	○○○○○		○○○○○		○○○○○	
	○○○○○	10	○○	7		5
Fruit tree	○○		○○○○		○○○○○	
		2		4	○○○○○	10
Firewood	○○		○○○○○		○○○○○	
		2	○	6	○○○○○	10
Trees for fencing	○○○○		○○○○○		○○○○○	
	○○○○	8	○○○○○	10	○	6

Source: Gubbels and Koss (2000).

Poverty Assessment

The World Bank has developed a participatory methodology guide to assess poverty, and trend analysis is an important method found in its guide. The use of this method is mainly to know about changes that have been taking place in the community and people's perception about the future. The group that suggested the methodology indicated that trend analysis should be done after completing the well-being analysis. The participating group from the community can be asked to discuss whether there have been any changes in the well-being of the community members over the last ten years. These changes should include changes in the number of categories (more or less of them now as compared to the past), the type of categories (whether the criteria have changed) and number of households in each of the categories (whether some people have become better off or worse off than before). The groups may also be asked whether they perceive any changes in the situation in future and what these changes could be (see Table 10.4).

Table 10.4
Trend Analysis: Assessment of Poverty

Well-being category	Proportion of households (scores out of a total of 100)		Remarks**
	Today	10 years ago	
1	3	–	
2	5	–	
3	8	6	
4	36	53	
5	40	41	
6	8	–	
Total	100	100	

Source: Poverty Reduction and Economic Management Network, World Bank (1999).
Note: ** The remarks include the details of changes and an explanation if the number or type of categories is different from the past. They also include changes, if any, in the criteria for categorisation.

Table 10.4 shows that there are now six well-being categories as compared to ten years ago, including two that are higher or better than the previous best category. An additional category has been added to show that there are some people in the community who are worse off than the lowest well-being category ten years ago. This analysis is very helpful to start a discussion about why some people have become worse off than before, how some people have moved up to new highs of well-being; and such discussions should lead to further ones on vulnerability, risk, security, etc.

Gender Analysis

PRA methods offer a wide scope for analysing a situation in relation to gender. Some of the PRA methods frequently used to assess the status of women are daily schedules, access and control, decision-making matrix and body mapping. Along with these methods, trend analysis could be used to understand and analyse the status of women and causes for such changes. Select variables, such as age at marriage, dowry, widow remarriage, employment, political power and decision making, have been used to assess the status of women through trend analysis. The results indicate that the women are not forced to marry early and they resist the demand for dowry. Women have started participating in various income generation activities. They have also gained political power by participating in the local bodies. They have a voice in making decisions that affect their life (see Figure 10.2).

Figure 10.2
Status of Women in Easanur Village

Details	Then	Now
Age at marriage	Before 18 years	After 22 years
Dowry		
Widow remarriage		
Antenatal care		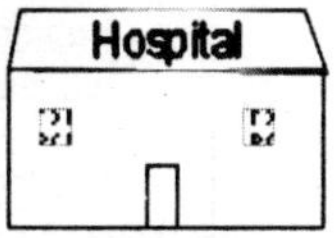
Political power and decision making		

Source: Narayanasamy and Boraian (2005).

Monitoring and Evaluation

Trend analysis is a useful tool for monitoring and evaluating a project. The participants from the village may be facilitated to list the criteria or variables for evaluating the project. Then they may be asked to narrate the situation before the project intervention and the situation after the intervention with reference to the selected variables. They may further be asked to say what/who is responsible for the changes, if any. The technique was used to assess the impact of an organisation known as Association for Sarva Seva Farms (ASSEFA) at a village in Sivaganga district. The impact was assessed with reference to select variables such as education, creation of public property, health status, community-based organisations, economic status, financial assistance, etc. The visually depicted trend analysis clearly indicates the impact of the organisation on the people (Figure 10.3). This diagram can be used as a base for further discussion and an in-depth analysis of the impact.

Figure 10.3
Evaluation of Project Intervention

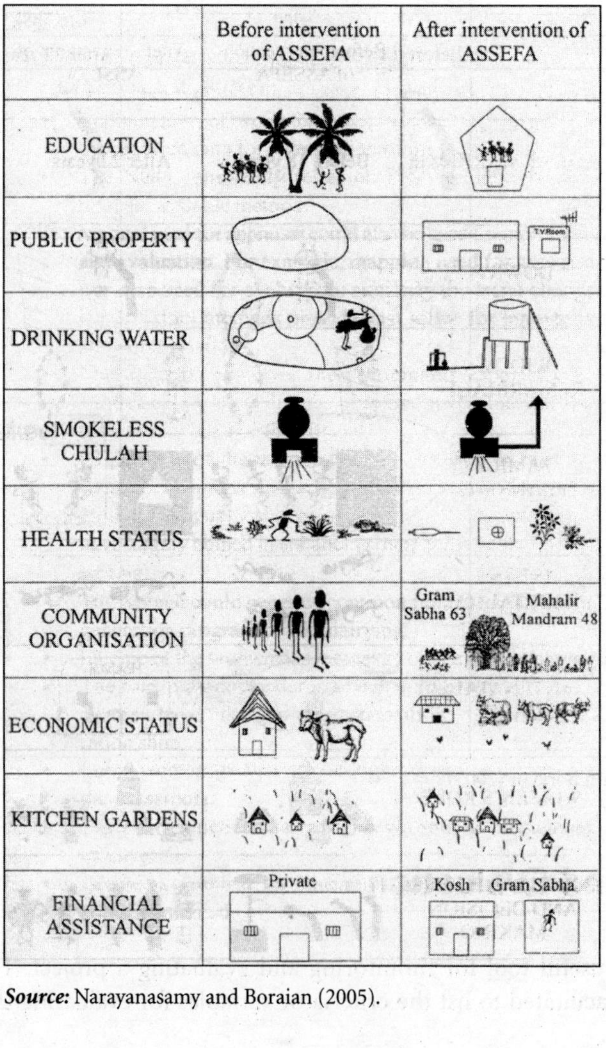

Source: Narayanasamy and Boraian (2005).

Impact Analysis

Trend analysis can be used to assess the impact of the activities carried out to raise the awareness level among the people. The PRA unit of Gandhigram Rural Institute (GRI) has carried out an evaluation study of a project titled Prevention of Female Infanticide in Usilampatti Block. The project-holders organised a series of activities like meetings, rallies, street plays, training programme and door-to-door campaign to bring about awareness on various issues related to female infanticide. Then the project-holders did not have the benchmark data to assess the impact of the activities carried out to generate awareness among the target group. Trend analysis was employed by comparing the awareness level before the intervention with the awareness level after the intervention.

The steps gone through are as follows:

- Select variables in consultation with the clients.
- Classify project villages into good, moderate and poor.
- Convene a meeting of the women in the village.
- Facilitate them to indicate the level of awareness among them. Seeds have been used to measure the level of awareness. Maximum of ten seeds were given to measure the level of awareness before the intervention. Supposing the participants have put only two out of ten seeds given, then it means the level of awareness is low. On the other hand, if they put seven out of ten seeds, the awareness level is high. Similarly, to measure the level of awareness for each variable under the 'after-intervention' category, ten seeds were given. The participants were facilitated to indicate the level of awareness using seeds. A comparison was made between 'before-interventions' and 'after-interventions'.

The exercise was carried out in all the villages and the results have been consolidated and presented in Table 10.5.

COMPLEMENTARITY WITH OTHER METHODS

The versatility of the method lies in its complementarity with other methods. The information generated out of the exercise would provide clues on the strengths of the village, and the opportunities available within the village. This in turn would provide a base for initiating SWOT analysis, if necessary. Similarly, the exercise would also help in identifying problems of the village. In other words, the information coming from the exercise would help to build a checklist for exercises like SWOT analysis and problem identification. Seasonal calendar helps triangulate the data and information generated from trend analysis, especially for the present situation. The timeline provides clues and signals for fixing the landmark years (sometimes two or three time frames) for trend analysis.

MERITS

- Trend analysis can be improvised and applied in several fields. It can help one to understand the past and provide clues to foresee the future. In other words, the data obtained under trend analysis can be used to forecast the future. It can enable to gauge the changes and the direction of the changes. It takes us to the past and relates the past to the present and then to the future. The discussion that follows a trend analysis provides an understanding of the dynamics of change.
- It is a visual exercise. It develops lively and active participation of all sections of the community irrespective of age. The old people always evince interest in narrating the past, while the younger ones are keen on listening about the events and incidents that occurred in the past.
- The outcome of the exercise can serve as a benchmark for assessing the effect of future programmes.

Table 10.5
Trend in Awareness Level

Variables	Good Villages		Moderate Villages		Poor Villages	
	Before	After	Before	After	Before	After
Awareness on personal hygiene	*****	*****	****	*****	**	*****
		*****		****		***
Awareness on nutrition and balanced diet	*****	*****	***	*****	*****	*****
		***		***		***
Awareness on immunisation	****	*****	***	*****	***	*****
		**		***		**
Awareness on AIDS	**	*****	****	*****	***	*****
		****		****		***
Awareness on family planning methods	*	*****	****	*****	***	*****
		*		***		***
Awareness on importance of female education	****	*****	*****	*****	*****	*****
		****		****		***
Awareness on physiological changes among adolescent girls	*	*****	**	*****	*	*****
		***		***		***
Awareness on demerits of early marriage	***	*****	*****	*****	*****	*****
		*****		***		****
Awareness on child-rearing practices	*	*****	****	*****	**	*****
		*		***		*

(Table 10.5 Contd.)

(*Table 10.5 Contd.*)

Variables	Good Villages		Moderate Villages		Poor Villages	
	Before	After	Before	After	Before	After
Awareness on antenatal and post-natal care	*	***** **	****	***** ***	**	***** *
Awareness on legal rights of women	*	***** **	***	***** **	*	*****
Awareness on government schemes	**	***** **	***	***** ***	**	***** *
Awareness on the advantages of savings scheme	*	***** **	****	***** ***	***	***** ***
Awareness on the need to maintain household accounts	*	***** **	****	***** ***	*	***** *
Awareness on leading a better life	***	***** ****	****	***** ****	***	***** **
Awareness on the evils of dowry system	***	***** ***	*****	***** ****	*****	***** ****
Prevention of female infanticide	****	***** ****	**	***** ****	***	***** ***

Source: PRA Unit, GRI (2001b).

LIMITATIONS

- Fixing the landmark or reference year is a little bit difficult. There may be a tendency to quickly fix the year in order to start the exercise. The year needs to be very carefully chosen to enable the participants to recall the past events without much confusion and difficulties.
- The information generated is mostly qualitative in nature. There may be a tendency on the part of the participants to 'over-play' about the past and 'downplay' about the present. Hence the facilitators have to 'cross-check' or triangulate by relating the information revealed from the exercise to the information generated from exercises like timeline, seasonal calendar, transect and mapping.
- There may be a tendency on the part of the facilitators to jump from topic to topic. This needs to be carefully avoided. All questions related to the selected topic must be exhausted with adequate probing. Sometimes the participants from the village are likely to hurry through the exercise, especially when the topics to be covered are many. One need not cover all the topics on the same day. The exercise needs to be done in a gradual manner.

SUMMARY

Trend analysis, a time-related method, is employed to explore temporal dimensions with a focus on change. The procedure for initiating the exercise starts with fixing a reference or a landmark year. The landmark years should be chosen in such a way that (*i*) the participants are able to capture the changes in all their details and diversity and (*ii*) the participants are able to relate to the years very easily.

The other steps to be followed include (*i*) preparation of checklist of questions for each topic; (*ii*) facilitating the participants to draw the matrix; (*iii*) ask the participants to enumerate the changes that occurred between the two reference periods under each variable; (*iv*) enable them to depict the changes in the matrix using symbols, seeds, stones, pebbles, flowers and other locally available material; (*v*) probe the reasons and causes for the changes; (*vi*) triangulate the information and (*vii*) share the outcome with the participants.

Trend analysis is being used in a wide spectrum of fields. A sample list includes the following: (*i*) changes in the socio-economic condition of the people, (*ii*) analysis of a problem, (*iii*) trends in the functioning of institutions, (*iv*) monitoring and evaluating a project and (*v*) gender analysis. It can complement and supplement other PRA methods such as SWOT analysis, seasonal calendar, timeline and focus group discussion.

Wider applicability, visual presentation and complementarity nature are some of the merits of the trend analysis method. The limitations are problem in fixing the benchmark year, tendency to 'downplay' or 'over-play' the past and present and the tendency to jump from topic to topic without adequate probe.

11

Seasonal Calendar

Seasons affect rural households. Seasonal variations have a great influence on the livelihood of the people. Certain months in a year bring in more work, more income and more food. These months of the season are also occasions for fun, festivals and ceremonies. People, by and large, are happy during such a time. On the other hand, certain months in a year have the opposite effect. People do not have work. Their income is less, resulting in less purchasing and in shortage of food, which are likely to result in malnutrition, loss in body weight, infant mortality, etc. This season is mostly a season of hunger and sickness. Poor households are normally exposed to shocks and risks which they may not be able to cope up with effectively. They are, thus, vulnerable to indebtedness and exploitation.

Any type of rural study has to necessarily take into account the seasonal variations in the activities and problems of the people. However, the conventional methods of research normally provide a snapshot view of the rural situation and condition and do not take a historical transect to understand the seasonal variations in the life of rural households. Robert Chambers observes, 'Poorest people are mostly seen particularly in those times when they are least deprived; and least seen when things are at their worst.' There are at least three important methods in the repertoire of participatory rural appraisal (PRA) which look at problems in a historical perspective. Timeline, for example, goes into memory lane as far as possible and attempts to sketch the trends and shocks which people have experienced over a long period of time. Trend analysis helps to understand the changes, both positive and negative, between two periods. A seasonal calendar peeps into the immediate past and helps to analyse the seasonal variations in rural households. Understanding the seasonal variations not only helps in positioning the problem of the poor with a proper perspective but also assists in designing an appropriate intervention strategy.

Seasonal calendar is a diagram drawn by people with locally available materials to provide a trend in the main activities, problems and opportunities of the community throughout the annual cycle. It can be drawn for major seasons, such as wet and dry season, or by months. A month-wise depiction of seasonal calendar helps to identify the months of great difficulty or vulnerability or other significant variables which have an impact on people's lives and livelihoods.

PURPOSE

A seasonal calendar can be used to study the following, among other things:

- Indigenous seasons
- Climate (rainfall and temperature)
- Crop sequences (from planting to harvesting)
- Crop pests and diseases
- Collection of wild fruits and herbs
- Livestock (births, weaning, sales, migration, fodder)
- Livestock diseases
- Income-generating activities
- Labour demand for men, women and children
- Employment in days for men, women and children
- Prices
- Marketing
- Human diseases
- Social events
- Types and quantity of cooking and heating fuel
- Migration
- Income and expenditure
- Savings
- Debt
- Quantity or type of food consumed
- Months of great strain and stress
- Months of happiness

PARTICIPANTS

As stated earlier, the type of participants depends upon the nature of the seasonal calendars that we propose to facilitate. A seasonal calendar on major activities, problems and opportunities of landless labourers in a village has to necessarily ensure participation of the landless labourers. They should be chosen from various age groups, sex and communities. This would make the discussion more lively, more broad-based and comprehensive. The number of participants can vary from ten to fifteen.

PROCEDURE

- Convene the meeting with the key informants. Their selection depends on the topics that we have chosen for the study. If, for instance, the subject of discussion is about agriculture, the key informants would be farmers of different categories with gender balance. If the topic of the study were livelihood sources and the associated problems, the landless labourers would be the key informants.
- Facilitate the people to choose a place where all could assemble. Ensure that the chosen place is adequate and convenient to draw the calendar. Avoid the courtyard of an individual house where some people may hesitate to assemble due to interpersonal conflicts. The calendar can also be drawn on newsprint, but that restricts discussion, debate, analysis and sharing. Hence, choose the ground as the medium.
- Explain the purpose of the exercise and the procedure undertaken for the exercise.
- Facilitate them to fix the season. It may be a major season or month-wise annual season. Let it be of their choice. Let the season selected or chosen be one that is in the immediate past and not the current season.
- Ask them to draw the grids or matrix on the ground with locally available materials such as ash, soil of different colours or *rangoli* powder or a piece of chalk and facilitate them to depict the season in columns. There would be thirteen columns—twelve for months and one for the variables that we propose to analyse. The number of rows depends on the number of variables.
- Ask when their year starts. The people are more familiar with indigenous or local months and seasons. Let them choose the month. If the participants are illiterate, ask them to present the months or major decisions by visual. For example, the month of Chittirai in the Tamil calendar is known for starting 'first plough' in the land after the harvest. Hence, the participants in the villages symbolically represent Chittirai with a picture of the plough. Likewise, each month has its own significance, which can be symbolically represented. This would enable the rural people to easily identify the months and take part in the exercise.
- Ask them to repeat the months by showing the symbols in order to confirm whether the participants are able to identify the months easily with the help of symbols.
- Start asking questions using the checklist. For important aspects such as crops, labour, income, expenditure, debt and migration, ask the participants to show duration or amounts by months or other time units using seeds, leaves, flowers, fruits, stick, twigs, pebbles, stones, etc., on the floor or ground.
- Select each topic and proceed gradually. Do not rush; do not dominate; do not try to impose your calendar on them; do not assume. Allow them to discuss and debate. When they are ready with the answers, ask them to depict them on the respective rows against the respective months, preferably in visuals. Remember that information got from the exercise would be mostly qualitative in nature. Do not insist on exact value or quantity. However, ensure that you are collecting facts. The seasonal calendar also provides a scope for gathering quantitative information.
- Interview the diagram; probe further and learn more about their activities, season-wise variations in their activities and how their livelihood opportunities are affected by seasons. Facilitate them to ponder over the conditions in which they live, the problems they have, the opportunities available to overcome the problems, etc.

- Ask the participants whether they would like to add more on the calendar. If they want to, allow them to do so.
- Triangulate the calendar with another set of participants, if possible.
- Copy the calendar drawn on the floor by the people; you can seek the help of local youth in copying the calendar. Write down the name of the village, date and the names of the participants from the village on the newsprint.
- Do not forget to thank the participants in their own language. Close the session in a most informal fashion.

Dos

- Decide the theme for the seasonal calendar.
- Decide the season in consultation with the people. Let it be their 'season'.

Don'ts

- Do not impose your choice of seasonal calendar on the participants.
- Do not use materials that restrict the participation of the people.

APPLICATION

Seasonal calendar has a wide application. It is being applied in agriculture, watershed management, forestry including social and community forestry, coastal resources and fisheries, livestock and animal husbandry, irrigation, livelihood analysis, participatory poverty assessment, health, food security and nutrition assessment and monitoring, sexual and reproductive health, adult literacy, education and participatory monitoring and evaluation. We would present a few applications with illustrations.

Agriculture

Seasonal calendar is highly suitable in understanding season-wise agricultural operations carried out in the field, cost of operation, income from each crop and various other pertinent variables. Carefully done, the exercise would help in assessing the cost of cultivation of each crop, the sale proceeds from each crop and the net income. This would also help in assessing the credit requirements, especially the extent of the loan required for each crop. The outsiders can have a better understanding of various types of crops cultivated (month-wise) in wet, dry and garden lands, the employment potentials in agricultural operations and other related issues (see Table 11.1). Properly facilitated, the data can be graphically represented by participants on the ground (see Figures 11.1 and 11.2).

Figure 11.1
Rainfall: Kasturinaickenpatti (Ref. Year, 1992–1993)

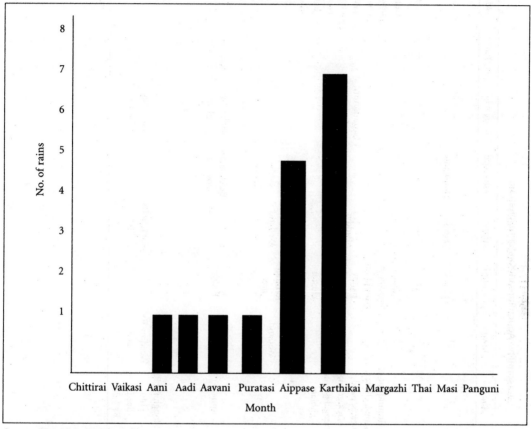

Source: PRA Unit, GRI (1993b).

Livelihood Sources

A seasonal calendar can be used to appraise the livelihood sources of different occupational groups. Such an appraisal helps to analyse the wide spectrum of livelihood options, the sources that fetch more employment and more income and the least lucrative source. However, we need to be careful in facilitating the exercise. Livelihood sources and income are likely to vary even within the same occupational groups. Hence, it is advisable to prepare a separate seasonal calendar for each category within an occupational group. We can take a clue from the outcome of the wealth-ranking exercise that provides the classification of a community based on wealth or well-being status. Based on that, we can attempt the exercise for different groups.

Table 11.1
Seasonality: Agriculture in Kasturinaickenpatti

Particulars	Chittirai	Vaikasi	Aani	Aadi	Aavani	Puratasi	Aippase	Karthikai	Margazhi	Thai	Masi	Panguni
Rainfall (no. of times)	–	–	–	–	1	1 Heavy	5 Heavy	6 Moderate	–	–	–	–
Ploughing (no.)	1	1	1	1	1	1	–	–	–	–	–	–
Sowing	Banana	Flowers, tomato, lady's finger, cholam	Brinjal, cholam, paddy, flowers, tomato	Groundnut, samai, cluster beans, paddy, black gram, bengal gram, cholam	–	Cholam, horse gram, groundnut, paddy bengal gram, cluster beans	Paddy	–	Groundnut, tomato	–	Cotton, flowers, tomato, paddy, groundnut, brinjal, lady's finger	–
Weeding		Garden land	–	–	Wetland	Rainfed area	Wetland	Wet & garden land	–			
Harvesting				Tomato	–	Paddy	–	Black gram, cowpea	Black gram, cholam	Paddy, banana	Paddy	
Expenditure												
Groundnut	Ploughing Rs 140	Ploughing Rs 140	Ploughing Rs 140	Ploughing Rs 140 Seeds Rs 1,000	Weeding Rs 200	–	Weeding Rs 200	–	Harvesting Rs 100	–	–	–

(Table 11.1 Contd.)

(Table 11.1 Contd.)

Particulars	Chittirai	Vaikasi	Aani	Aadi	Aavani	Puratasi	Aippase	Karthikai	Margazhi	Thai	Masi	Panguni
Cholam, Cl. beans, black gram	Ploughing Rs 140	Ploughing Rs 140	Ploughing Rs 140	Seeds Rs 100	Weeding Rs 200	Weeding Rs 200	–	–	Harvesting Rs 100			
Income												
Groundnut									Rs 4,500			
Cholam									Rs 2,700			
Black gram									Rs 1,500			
Cluster beans									Rs 1,000			
Employment (no. of days)	7	–	–	20	7	30	30	30	30	30	10	–
Water level in the well (in ft)	5	4	4	4	10	20	40	40	40	20	10	15

Source: PRA Unit, GRI (1993b).

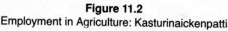

Figure 11.2
Employment in Agriculture: Kasturinaickenpatti

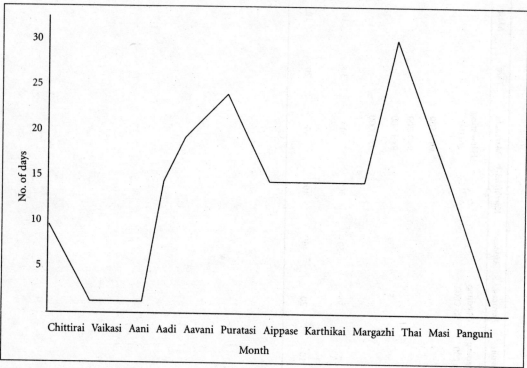

Source: PRA Unit, GRI (1993b).

The M.S. Swaminathan Research Foundation (MSSRF) in their study 'Joint Mangrove Management in Tamil Nadu' has used the seasonal calendar to assess the livelihood sources of the fishermen community. They have prepared seasonal calendars for five different groups within the same community, namely, (*i*) medium-rich group of men; (*ii*) medium-rich group of women; (*iii*) poor group of men; (*iv*) poor group of women and (*v*) poorest group of women.

The analysis of the outcome of the seasonal calendar indicated that the earning opportunities for the medium-rich group of men is on 240 days in a year; of these days, fishing alone (in sea, pits and puddles of mangroves) account for 215 days. The medium-rich group of women had 60 income-earning days, mostly through agricultural labour. Men from poor group are employed for 205 days in a year. Fishing accounts for 105 days; agricultural labour accounts for 75 days; and fishing for wage for canal fisher accounts for 25 days. Livelihood source for women from poor groups is agricultural labour (95 days) and work in salt pan (50 days). The sources of livelihood for the poorest women are collection and sale of deadwood from mangroves for about 60 days and work in the salt pan for about 50 days. Thus, a group-wise analysis of the seasonal calendar of livelihood sources indicates the diverse and varied nature of livelihood opportunities (see Figures 11.3–11.7).

Figure 11.3
Seasonal Livelihood Activities of Men Belonging to Medium-rich Families

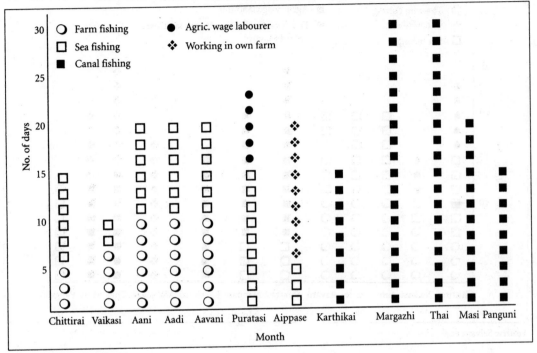

Source: Selvam et al. (2003).

Figure 11.4
Seasonal Livelihood Activities of Women Belonging to Medium-rich Families

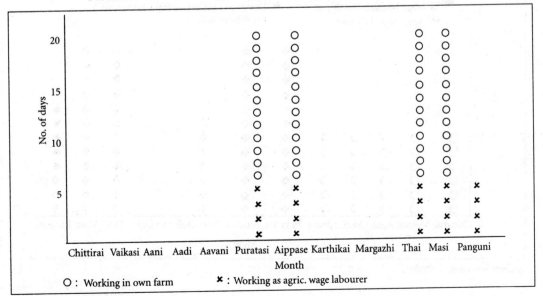

Source: Selvam et al. (2003).

Figure 11.5
Seasonal Livelihood Activities of Men Belonging to Poor Families

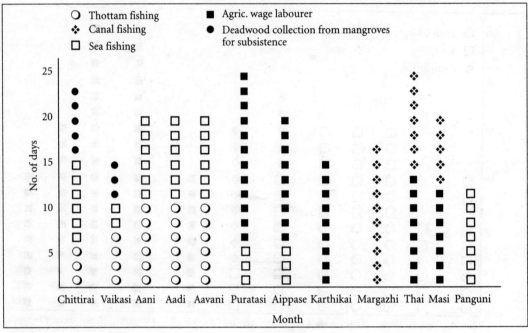

Source: Selvam et al. (2003).

Figure 11.6
Seasonal Livelihood Activities of Women Belonging to Poor Families

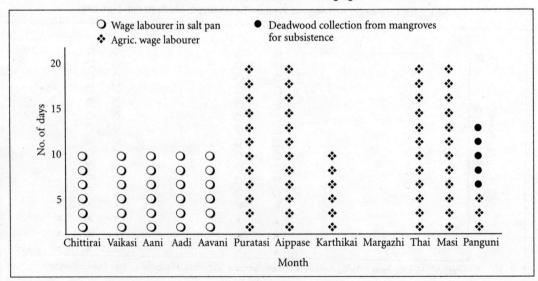

Source: Selvam et al. (2003).

Figure 11.7
Seasonal Livelihood Activities of Women Belonging to the Poorest Families

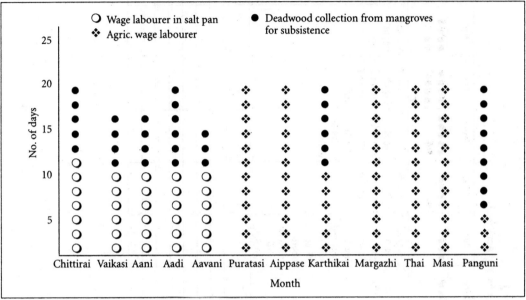

Source: Selvam et al. (2003).

Planning of Activities

A seasonal calendar can be used as a planning tool. An appraisal of the situation in a village by an NGO revealed that (*i*) topsoil has been depleted over a period of twenty years resulting in decline in soil depth; (*ii*) tree coverage in the forest has gone down; (*iii*) flooding has increased and (*iv*) extent of land available for agriculture has also gone down. Seized by the problem, the people along with the NGO prepared a soil conservation plan. The seasonal calendar helped them to decide the timing of activities such as land cleaning, bunding, diversion drain, construction of check dam and pitting and planting (see Table 11.2).

Health

This technique is widely used in health-related issues. It helps to know the illness by type and prevalence of disease-prone periods, water supply, access to facilities, births and deaths, stress and happiness, etc. (see Table 11.3). It is particularly useful for creating awareness among the members of the community and health workers on disease trends and times of stress. It helps in planning the timing of the intervention in conjunction with the variations of

Table 11.2
Seasonal Calendar: Planning of Activities

Details \ Month	Jan.	Feb.	Mar.	Apr.	May	Jun.	Jul.	Aug.	Sept.	Oct.	Nov.	Dec.
Rainfall	–	–	•	••	••	••••	•••	•••••••	•••••••	•••••••	••••••	••••
Agricultural operations	Harvesting of tablab and red gram	Threshing of ragi	Threshing of ragi	Ploughing	Sowing of gingelly	Sowing of groundnut	Harvesting of gingelly Sowing of ragi and samai Weeding operations in groundnut field	Weeding operations in ragi field	Harvesting of groundnut Sowing of horse gram	Harvesting of groundnut and ragi	Harvesting of ragi	Harvesting of sorghum and niger
Labour availability in persons	30	20	25	40	40	20	10	20	–	–	–	
Soil conservation activities proposed												
Land clearing	✓	✓										
Bunding	✓	✓										
Diversion drain		✓	✓									
Check dam		✓	✓									
Pitting				✓								
Planting					✓							

Source: Narayanasamy and Boraian (2005).

Table 11.3

Seasonal Health Calendar: Seasonality with Scoring

Month / Diseases	Jan.	Feb.	Mar.	Apr.	May	Jun.	Jul.	Aug.	Sep.	Oct.	Nov.	Dec.
Fever				●●●●	●	●					● ●●●●●●●●●	●●●●
Cold and whooping cough	●●●●										●●●●●●●●●●●●	●●●
Headache	●●●●●			●●●●●●		●	●●	●●	●●●●●	●●●●●●	●●●●●●	●●●●●●
Diarrhoea				●●●●●●●●●	●●	●	●		●	●●●●●●●●●●●●●●	●●●●●●●●●●●●	
Measles				●●●●●●	●●●●●●	●●●●						
Jaundice	●●●●	●●●●		●●●●●●●								
Vomiting	●	●●●		●	●●●●●●				●●●●●●	●●●●●●		
Scabies		●	●●	●●●●●●●●●	●●●●●●		●	●	●●●	●●●		
Tetanus									●	●●●●●●	●●●●●●	●●●●●

Source: Devavaram et al. (1991).

Note: Seasonal health calendar of nine diseases, Udayanampatti village; villagers used stickers to depict frequency of disease.

- water supply;
- disease;
- type and availability of food;
- income;
- migration; and
- how busy or free people are.

It can also help health workers to monitor the ongoing activities as well as serious problems, if any.

Food Calendar

A seasonal calendar can be used to assess the availability of food over a period of one year. This would help to ascertain months of abundance, months of scarcity, months of quality nutritive food and months of nutritional deficiencies (see Figure 11.8). This may be followed by a discussion on the coping-up strategies of people at times of scarcity of food.

COMPLEMENTARITY WITH OTHER METHODS

Seasonal calendar can be very effectively used with other methods for better understanding of a situation or condition. It can precede or succeed some of the methods of PRA. For instance, to understand the livelihood sources of different economic groups, wealth ranking precedes and seasonal calendar succeeds. Drawing of seasonal calendar may lead to livelihood analysis and further on to focus group discussion. In the case of forest-related issues and problems, a seasonal calendar along with social mapping, resource mapping and transect can be used to assess the biotic pressure on the forest. After estimating the extent of collection of various minor forest produce, mobility map can be used to ascertain the market sources for minor forest produce. This can be followed by a Venn diagram to assess the effectiveness of the market sources. To appraise and analyse agriculture-related issues, the use of transect, resource map, social map and seasonal calendar in a sequence would provide a comprehensive picture. It can also supplement a diet survey. While seasonal calendar provides a month-wise dietary pattern over a period of one year, the diet survey provides a diet pattern for a particular week. The seasonal calendar would help in undertaking a diet survey in different seasons as diet pattern of rural households does vary across the seasons.

A seasonal calendar may also complement the exercises 'access and control' by analysing the season-wise access and control of certain common property resources in a village.

Figure 11.8

Food Calendar: Nlaphwane Village, Botswana

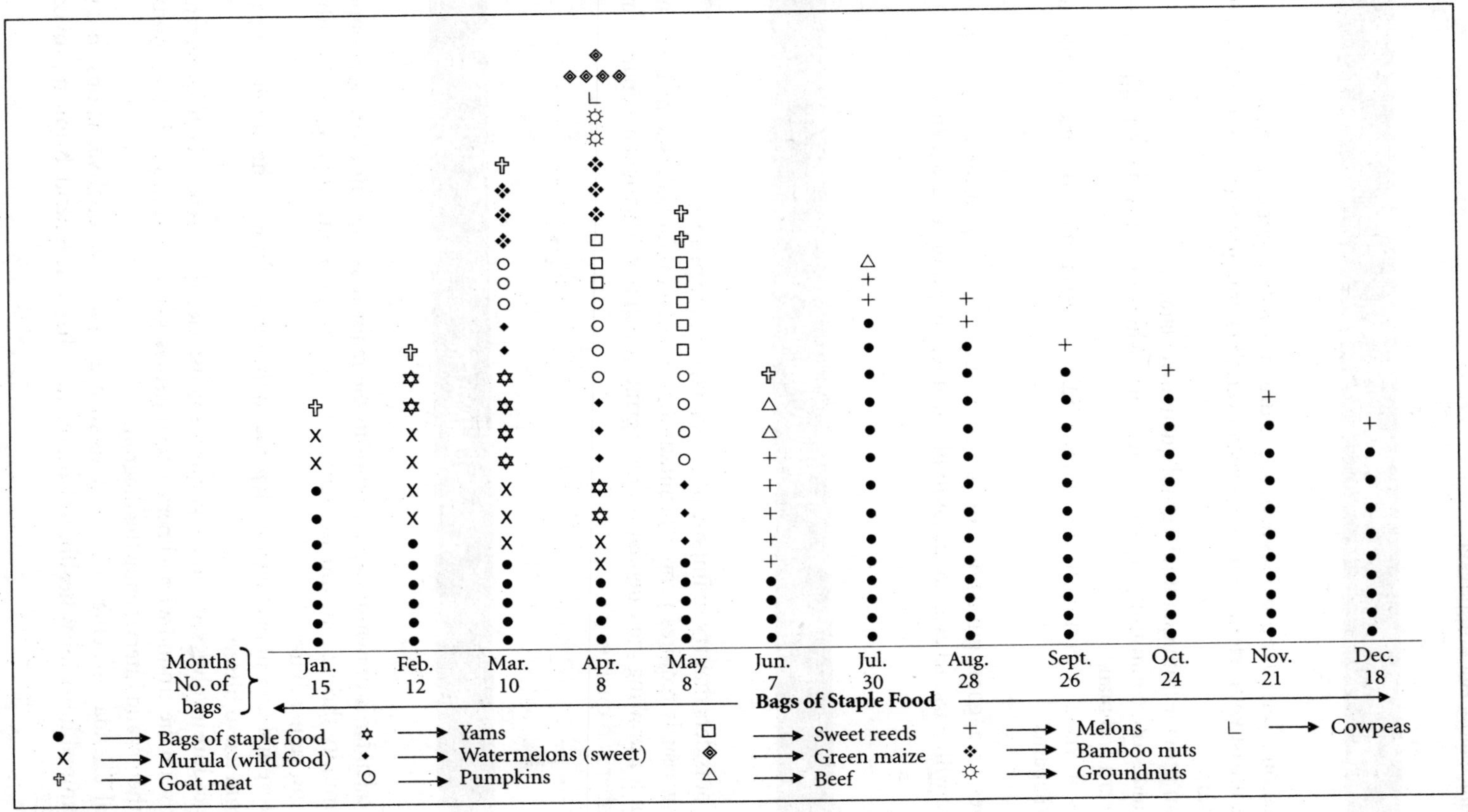

Source: Mukherjee (1994a).

MERITS

- A seasonal calendar provides a vivid picture of what has gone on in the community in the recent past with reference to the selected variables and gets them connected to the current scenario.
- It can provide both quantitative and qualitative data.
- It guides the community to travel back for a while and provides an opportunity to look forward and plan.
- It is a visual exercise. It therefore kindles a great deal of interaction among the participants.

It serves as a good guidepost for assessing the timing of development intervention in conjunction with seasonal availability of food, income, migration, disease, etc.

LIMITATIONS

- The outsiders may try to impose their calendar on the people.
- Using visuals requires proper facilitation and patience. Outsiders sometimes may try to go in for drawing the calendar on newsprint, which restricts the participation in terms of number and quality.

SUMMARY

A seasonal calendar is drawn to depict trends in the main activities, problems and opportunities of the community throughout the annual duration. It helps in identifying the months of great difficulties and vulnerability.

The nature and type of participants depend on the theme chosen. The number of participants may vary from ten to fifteen.

The procedure involves selection of key informants; selection of a barrier-free place; facilitation of the exercise on the ground with a liberal use of visuals; gathering and sharing of information on the chosen theme; and interviewing the diagram.

Seasonal calendar is being extensively used in assessing seasonal variations in agriculture, livelihood, animal husbandry, health, nutrition, etc. It has vast potentials for improvisation and can be effectively employed either to supplement or complement other methods of PRA. It can supplement the conventional methods too.

The merits are that it can be used as a planning tool, it is visual and ensures active participation. The limitations include tendencies to impose the choice of calendar on the participants and to draw the calendar on newsprint, which restricts participation.

12

Daily Schedule

We have seen time-related or temporal participatory rural appraisal (PRA) methods such as timeline, trend change and seasonal diagrams. Timeline is a method used to find out the important events and incidents that have happened in a community or a village and the shocks and trends experienced by the people over a long period. Trend analysis seeks to analyse changes between two periods. Seasonal calendar looks into the immediate past and attempts to analyse the seasonal variations.

Daily schedule, yet another member in the family of temporal methods, looks into the daily activities of the individuals in a community or members of the family. Individuals perform various tasks in a day. The nature, type and duration of work are not the same among the various categories of people. They vary across genders, age groups and occupational groups. An analysis of the daily schedule with reference to gender, age group and occupational group and seasons would reveal the activity pattern, discrimination in work, productive or unproductive use of time and work exploitation. It helps to know when people are free and when they are preoccupied.

MEANING

Daily schedule is employed to study labour patterns and other activities. It helps to know the various types of work done by an individual or a group in a day, and the distribution of workload throughout the day. It is temporal analysis on a daily basis. It also helps in comparing the daily schedule of different individuals or groups. The daily schedule is also known as daily activity schedule, daily activity profile, daily routine and 24-hour clock chart.

PURPOSE

Daily schedule may be used to

- document activities, *per se*;
- know the timing of activities;
- ascertain the periods in which more than one activity is carried out concurrently;
- describe new activities and their implications for time use;
- find out suitable time for meeting and training sessions;
- compare differences between schedules.

PARTICIPANTS

This exercise can be done either with individuals or with groups. When the exercise is practiced with a group of men or women, or children or a particular occupation group or age group, the group should be small. It should also be homogeneous in nature. A small and homogeneous group helps to arrive at a consensus. The number of participants in a group exercise may vary from three to six.

In case of comparison of workload between men and women (gender sensitisation exercise), men and women groups can meet separately and then join to share the outcome of the exercise.

PROCEDURE

There are five different approaches to facilitate the exercise (Jones 1996):

(*i*) Draw a day's timeline covering 24 hours' period (see Figure 12.1). The day is then subdivided, depending on the participants' perception of the day, by

- hours;
- morning, afternoon and evening;
- times when activity changes.

Along this timeline, different daily activities are placed. A number of different notations can be used, such as

- writing activities against time blocks;

- symbolising activities in time blocks;
- blocking time and coding it with keys; and
- graphing activities.

Figure 12.1
Days Timeline Covering 24 Hours

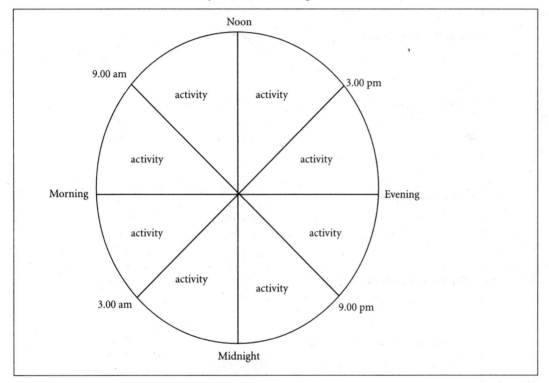

(*ii*) The second approach is based on symbols and relative estimation of time (see Figure 12.2). Symbols may be real objects, or they may be drawings. The symbols or drawings are placed along the line in the order in which the activities are undertaken each day. Seeds, pebbles, flowers or similar objects are then used to indicate the proportion of time spent on each activity at that stage in the day. Either free scoring or fixed scoring may be used. Alternatively, the total time spent each day for an activity can be estimated using seeds/pebbles, flowers, etc., by grouping together all those times when an activity such as cooking occurs, instead of attempting a chronological order.

(*iii*) The third approach involves construction of a matrix of activities (see Figure 12.3). Under this method, different activities are listed on one side of the matrix. The time blocks are indicated along the top. A comprehensive picture can be built up by filling in the matrix with symbols or scoring the relative amount taken by that activity. This

Figure 12.2
Daily Schedule Based on Relative Estimation of Time

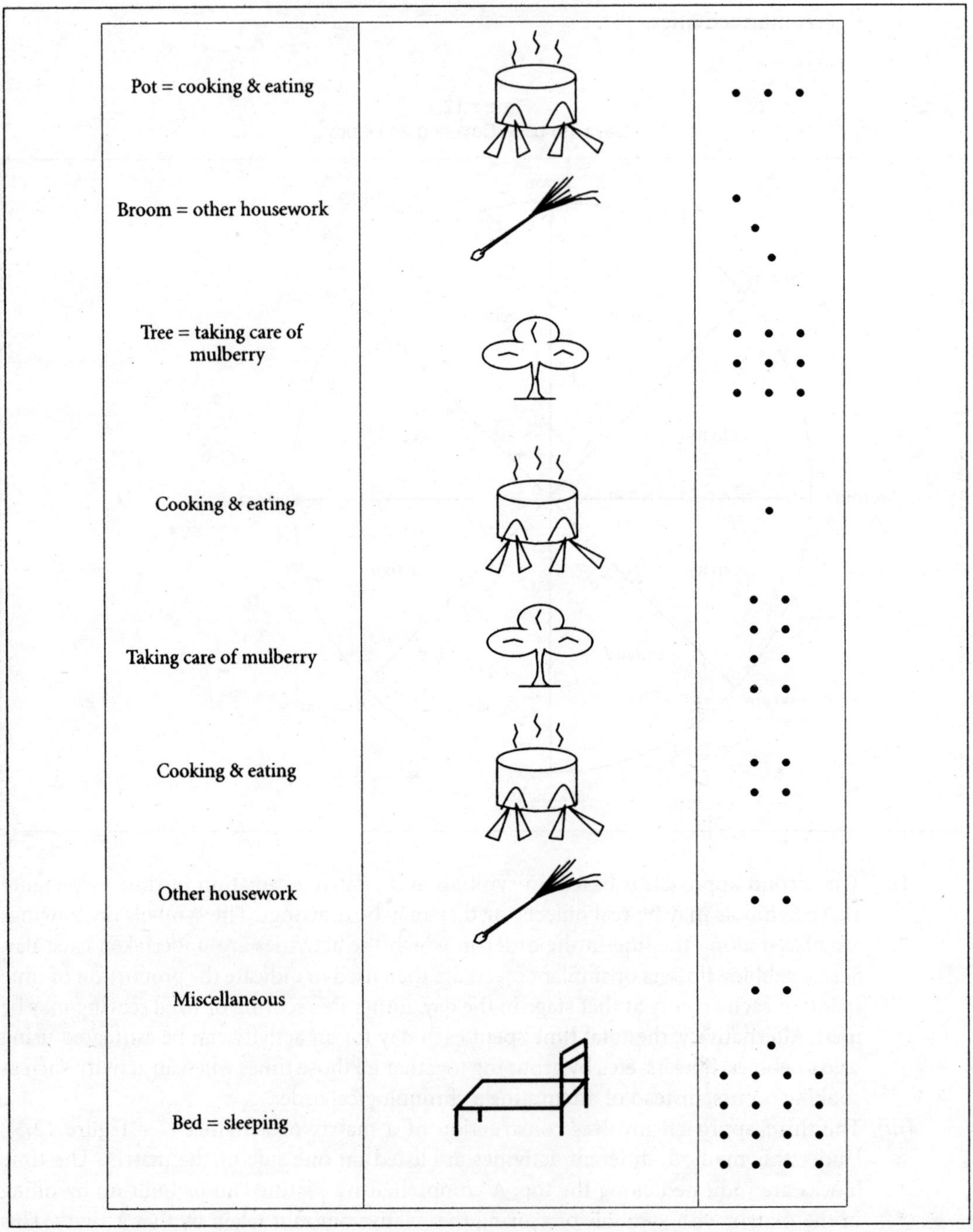

Pot = cooking & eating

Broom = other housework

Tree = taking care of
mulberry

Cooking & eating

Taking care of mulberry

Cooking & eating

Other housework

Miscellaneous

Bed = sleeping

Source: Jones (1996).

Figure 12.3
Daily Schedule Based on Matrix of Activities

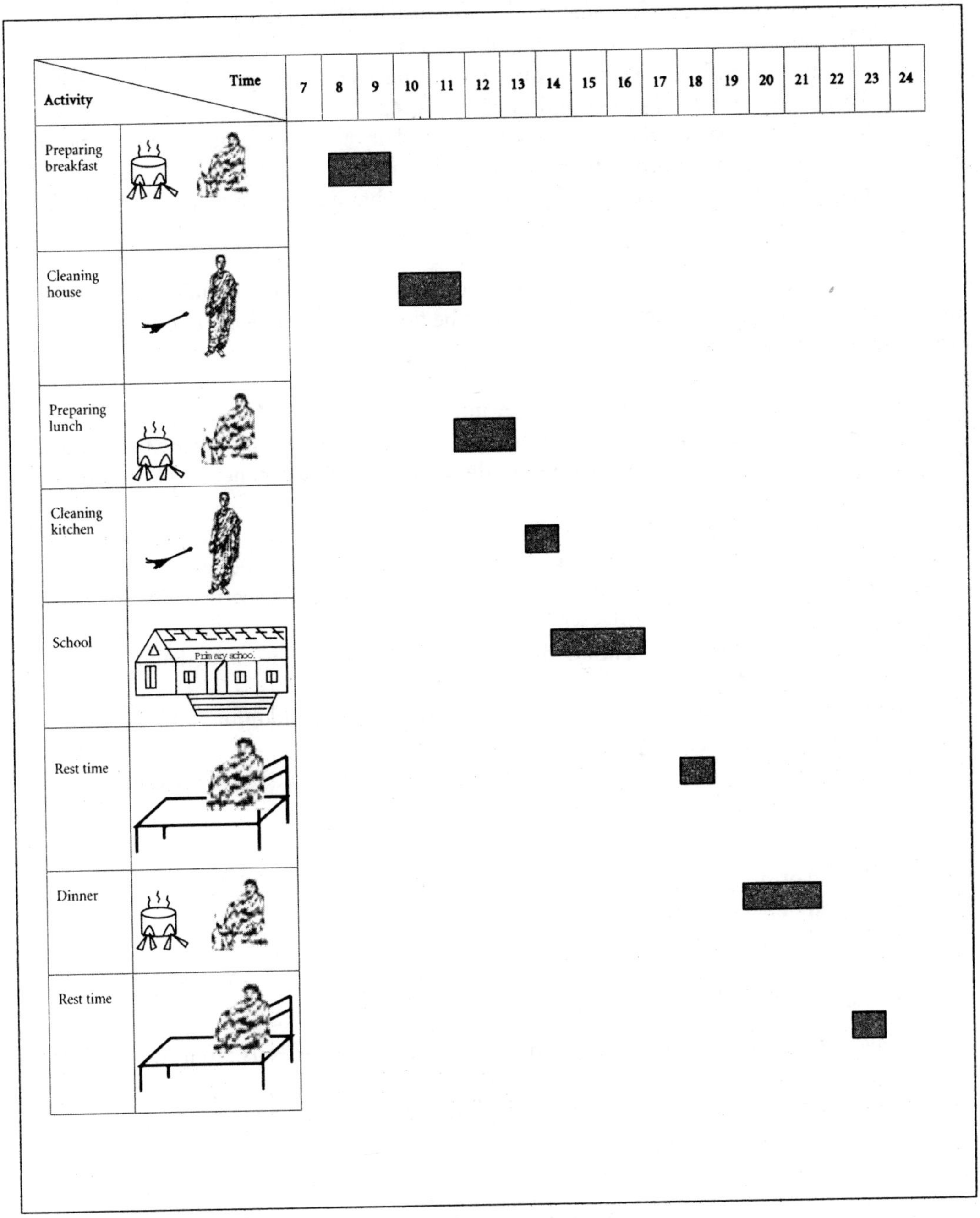

approach enables the expression of times when more than one activity is taking place simultaneously, as well as noting which one is dominating at any particular time. This can be very important in understanding the distribution of daily workload.

(*iv*) The fourth approach is card sorting. It can be used for charting daily workloads. Each activity is identified on a separate card, and arranged either by timing or by responsibility. This approach promotes a great deal of discussion.

(*v*) The fifth approach is the circular depiction of daily activity schedule. This can be done by asking a group of men or women to plot what work/activities they do from the time they get up till they go to bed. The information obtained can be plotted into a 24-hour wheel (clock), either on ground or on chart paper.

All these five approaches have been developed over a period of time through flexible use and improvisation of various methods. Whatever might be the approach in depicting the exercise, the procedure that one needs to follow is as follows:

- Choose and convene a meeting of the key informants.
- Explain the objective and purpose of the exercise to the participants. Ensure that the group is homogeneous as far as possible. Keep the number of participants small, varying from three to six.
- Initiate a discussion and ask them what they do on a normal day. Facilitate them to limit works/tasks/activities they perform from the time they get up till they go to sleep.
- Ask one of the participants to write down the activities listed. If the participants are illiterate, ask them to depict the activities with symbols.
- Ask the participants to mention the duration of each activity and depict it with an appropriate symbol.
- Facilitate the participants to complete the daily schedule with additions and deletions.
- Interview the diagram on a daily basis or schedule.
- Discuss the daily routine with the participants. The key points for discussion can be as follows:

  - Workload
  - Period of stress
  - Period of happiness
  - Period of free time
  - Liking or disliking for the activity
  - Their views and opinions on their utilisation of time

- Repeat the discussion on the diagram with another homogeneous group for verification and triangulation.
- Note down all the salient points that emerge during the discussion.
- Copy the output with all details.
- Thank the participants.

Dos

- Be clear about the objective and context of the daily activity schedule.
- Involve people from different age groups.
- Use symbols and visuals for better understanding and discussion.

Don'ts

- Do not overlook the discussion that follows the exercise.

APPLICATION

Daily schedules are being used to focus on women's activities and gender differences in the workload. Comparison can be made not only of the variations in individuals' workload overtime, but also between men and women, or that with women from different socio-cultural and economic backgrounds. Seasonal variations are most notable in relation to agricultural activities. Daily schedule in different seasons can be attempted (see Table 12.1).

Table 12.1
Daily Routine of a Woman: During Sowing Season

3.30 a.m.	Waking up and cleaning oven
3.45 a.m.	Preparing coffee
4.15 a.m.	Cleaning the farmyard and sprinkling it with cow dung water
4.45 a.m.	Cleaning the cattle yard
5.15 a.m.	Preparing food
6.05 a.m.	Leaving for field with food
	Field activity (sowing)
8.15 a.m.	Taking breakfast in the field
8.30 a.m.	Sowing
1.00 p.m.	Taking lunch and resting in the field
1.30 p.m.	Sowing
4.30 p.m.	Returning from field
4.45 p.m.	Taking care of animals
5.15 p.m.	Drawing water from the public well (no private wells; grown-up children help)
6.00 p.m.	Preparation of food (grown-up children help)
7.00 p.m.	Dinner
7.30 p.m.	Making arrangement for next day's field work
8.30 p.m.	Going to sleep

Within one gender only, the differences are quite notable between the young and old, the rural and urban, the professional and domestic. A daily schedule would help reveal the differences in use of time by women of different age groups and occupational groups.

Significant differences in perception can be found through an examination of women's ideas on men's time allocation, compared with men's, and men's ideas on women's time allocation, compared with women's. These illustrate the importance of involving all sections of population, especially those with whom it is intended to work in the end. We would present now a few areas where time analysis is extensively used.

Gender Analysis

Gender analysis is the systematic effort to document and understand the roles of women and men within the given context. An important tool that is being used in gender analysis, especially the gender division of work, is the daily activity schedule. The daily activity schedule is also called as 24-hour clock, listing three different types of work identified under the gender paradigm:

- Productive work
- Reproductive work
- Community work

Productive work, mostly, refers to wage work, which can be directly related to production, such as ploughing, sowing, irrigation, weeding, harvesting and any other type of farm or non-farm work. The reproductive work may not be directly linked to production, but it has an indirect impact on production. The reproduction work includes cooking, cleaning vessels, washing clothes, taking care of the children and the aged, tending animals and gathering of firewood for cooking. Community works involve cleaning streets, drainage, temple premises, participation in community festivals and ceremonies, etc. All these types of work entail some kinds of responsibilities and are related to their ascribed gender roles and expectations.

The procedure for doing the exercise is as follows:

- Mobilise the men and women from the village to carry out the exercise. After a brief discussion about the purpose of the exercise, ask the men and women to sit separately. Choose a place where the exercise can be conducted with the active participation of all.
- As men and women sit in two different groups, ask them to plot what work/activities they do from the time they get up till they go to bed. Plot this information into the 24-hour wheel either on the ground or on a chart paper. If men and women express that they are doing multiple works in a particular period, record that in the 24-hour wheel. If they find any work strenuous or difficult, flag those issues separately with different colours (see Figure 12.4).

Figure 12.4
A 24-Hour Wheel

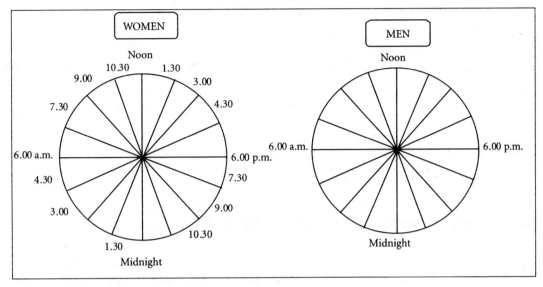

- This exercise would take about an hour. Do not bother about the nature of work while charting on the wheel. After the wheel is complete, ask the men and women participants to present their chart to each other. During this, they may challenge each other and make modifications.
- Again, divide the group into men and women. Facilitate the transfer of information. Plot productive, reproductive and social activities framework in the 24 hours wheel. Ensure that the participants develop a clear understanding on the definition of productive, reproductive and social activities. As a facilitator, you may read out one activity after another from the activity wheel and allow the participants to make decisions on the category of work. You may find that the participants are making the right decision in classifying the activities (see Table 12.2).
- After transferring the information to the framework, initiate the discussion on

  - who does how much work (use three different domains);
  - who takes how much of rest and leisure;
  - who participates in different social activities;
  - what promotes and hinders men and women to participate in different activities.

Table 12.2
Daily Schedule Framework

Activity	Men		Women	
	Type of work	*Issues*	*Type of work*	*Issues*
Productive				
Reproductive				
Community				

Such an analysis would help the participants in understanding the extent of work put in and the indispensable role played by the women in the family. It also largely sensitises about gender issues and creates awareness among the men to share the burden of work shouldered by the women.

Analysis of Issues Related to Child Labour

Daily routine diagram can help in assessing the workload of child labour in factory, hotel or farm-related work. Three cases are presented here. The first speaks of the daily routine of a boy (less than fourteen years of age) working in a vermicelli factory (see Table 12.3). The other two cases deal with a boy and a girl who tend buffaloes (see Tables 12.4 and 12.5). The daily routine diagrams have clearly revealed that the hours of work for the boy working in the vermicelli factory add up to around eleven a day. There seems to be virtually no scope for mental or physical development of working children like him. A girl below the age of fourteen shoulders the responsibility of a 35-year-old woman. The boys in some households have to cook food before they leave for their regular work.

Table 12.3
Daily Routine of Arumugam—A Boy Working in a Vermicelli Factory

6.00 a.m.	Rising, brushing and bathing
6.45 a.m.	Breakfast
7.00 a.m.	Combing hair and dressing up
7.15 a.m.	Starts for the vermicelli factory, carrying his midday meals. Walks fast with his other friends working in the factory so as to reach the factory before 8 a.m.
8.00 a.m.	Starts his work in the factory
12.30 p.m.	Lunch break
1.00 p.m.	Work resumes
7.00 p.m.	Comes out of the factory with Rs 1.50 (daily *bata*), buys groundnuts or some biscuits for 50 paise and walks slowly towards home, playing with his friends
8.00 p.m.	Reaches home, washes himself, has his dinner
9.00 p.m.	Sleeps or sometimes attends to the school of child labour run by Peace Trust and goes to sleep at 10 p.m.

Source: Narayanasamy et al. (1996).

Table 12.4
Daily Routine of Manikandan—A Boy Tending Buffaloes

6.30 a.m.	Gets up
6.35 a.m.	Readies the oven to cook. Cooks rice to be used for the whole day. By then, his mother prepares some gravy.
7.30 a.m.	His mother takes breakfast. Gives this boy some coin (25 or 50 paise) and she goes out for agriculture operation like weeding, transplanting and harvesting for wage.
7.45 a.m.	He has his breakfast and cleans the vessels
8.00 a.m.	Takes the buffalo to the field for grazing. He plays with other shepherds while the buffalo is grazing.
12.00 noon	Brings the buffalo back home. Feeds it some fodder. Then washes his hands and legs.
12.30 p.m.	He takes his lunch
12.45 p.m.	Goes roaming about in the village and plays with his friends (or sleeps)
3.00 p.m.	His mother is back after work and does some domestic chores. The boy takes the buffalo again for grazing, and plays.
6.00 p.m.	Brings the buffalo back home, cleans the buffalo yard and gives some fodder
6.30 p.m.	He has his dinner
8.15 p.m.	Sleeps

Source: Narayanasamy et al. (1996).

Table 12.5
Daily Routine of Chinnapappa—A Girl Tending Buffaloes

6.00 a.m.	Gets up. Fetches water from a place 2 km away. She goes three times and brings six pots of water. Cleans vessels. Cooks rice/maize. Prepares some gravy. Cleans her teeth.
7.30 a.m.	Takes breakfast and cleans the vessels used for cooking and breakfast
9.00 a.m.	Goes to field with the buffalo. She plays with her friends while the buffalo is grazing.
3.00 p.m.	Brings the buffalo back home. She takes her lunch. Sweeps the house. Fetches water sometimes, if necessary; or if called by her friends.
4.00 p.m.	Does some domestic chores
5.00 p.m.	Cooks food for the night or heats up the food cooked in the morning
6.30 p.m.	Cleans the buffalo yard, gives some fodder
7.15 p.m.	Washes herself
7.30 p.m.	Takes dinner
8.30 pm	Sleeps

Source: Narayanasamy et al. (1996).

Comparison of Workload of Fisherwoman and Fisherman

The M.S. Swaminathan Research Foundation (MSSRF) has undertaken an extensive study on the status of mangroves in Tamil Nadu. They have used daily schedule to understand the activities of fishermen and fisherwomen. The exercise has been carried out in various settings and among various categories of fishermen and fisherwomen. The exercise conducted in one of the settings (MGR Nagar) revealed that a fisherwoman normally wakes up at 4.00 a.m. and is busy with household activities until 8.00 a.m. She accompanies her male partner for fishing around 8.00 a.m., without taking any food. She returns with her partner at 3.00 p.m. Then, she spends around 30 minutes in selling the fish caught during the day. She takes food, bath, collects firewood, purchases rice and vegetables for the day from 3.30 to 5.00 p.m. She prepares dinner between 5.00 and 8.00 p.m. and serves it to all the family members between 8.00 and 9.00 p.m. She too takes the dinner, cleans vessels and comes out of kitchen around 9.00 p.m. She gossips with other women between 9.00 and 9.30 p.m. She sleeps from 9.30 p.m. to 4.00 a.m. (see Figure 12.5). The daily routine of a fisherman indicates that he works from 8.00 a.m. to 3.00 pm. Later, he has a lot of time for fun and recreation (see Figure 12.6).

Figure 12.5
Daily Schedule of a Fisherwoman

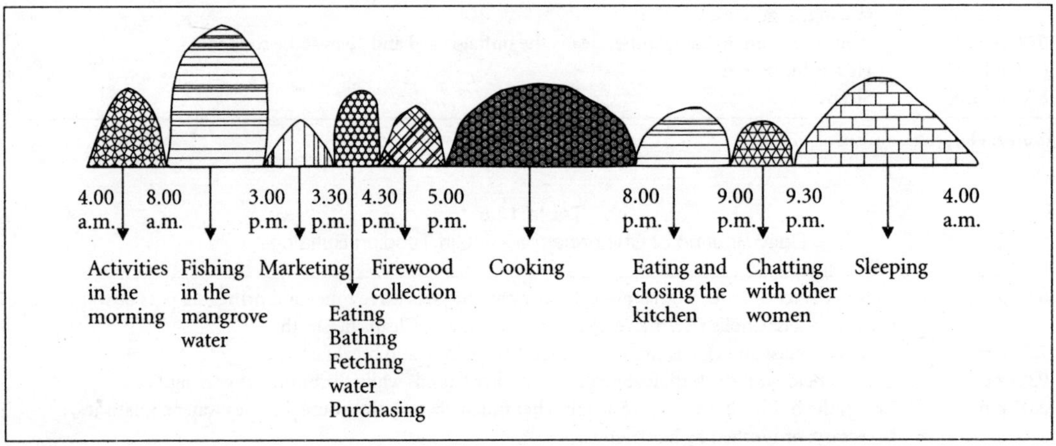

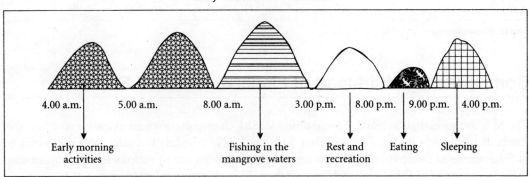

Source: Selvam et al. (2003).

Figure 12.6
Daily Routine of a Fisherman

Source: Selvam et al. (2003).

Differences in Workload across the Seasons

The daily routine can be used to ascertain the differences in workload of various groups of people across the season. For instance, the workload of landless agricultural labourers (men and women) can be ascertained during busy hours like sowing and harvesting and during summer when there is no work. Similarly, the workload of a farm woman and man can be ascertained during busy and lean seasons. Such a type of analysis may help in designing a suitable gainful income generation activity during the lean season. A diagram depicting the daily schedule of a woman during the busy season and lean season is depicted in Figure 12.7. The woman works for eighteen hours a day during the busy season. She sleeps for hardly six hours. During the lean season (summer), she is comparatively freer. She has a lot of free time at her disposal. This is all the more so in the case of women in dry-land agricultural region. This time can be meaningfully utilised for starting non-farm income generation activities through vocational training.

Figure 12.7
Daily Routine of a Farm Woman during Season and Non-season

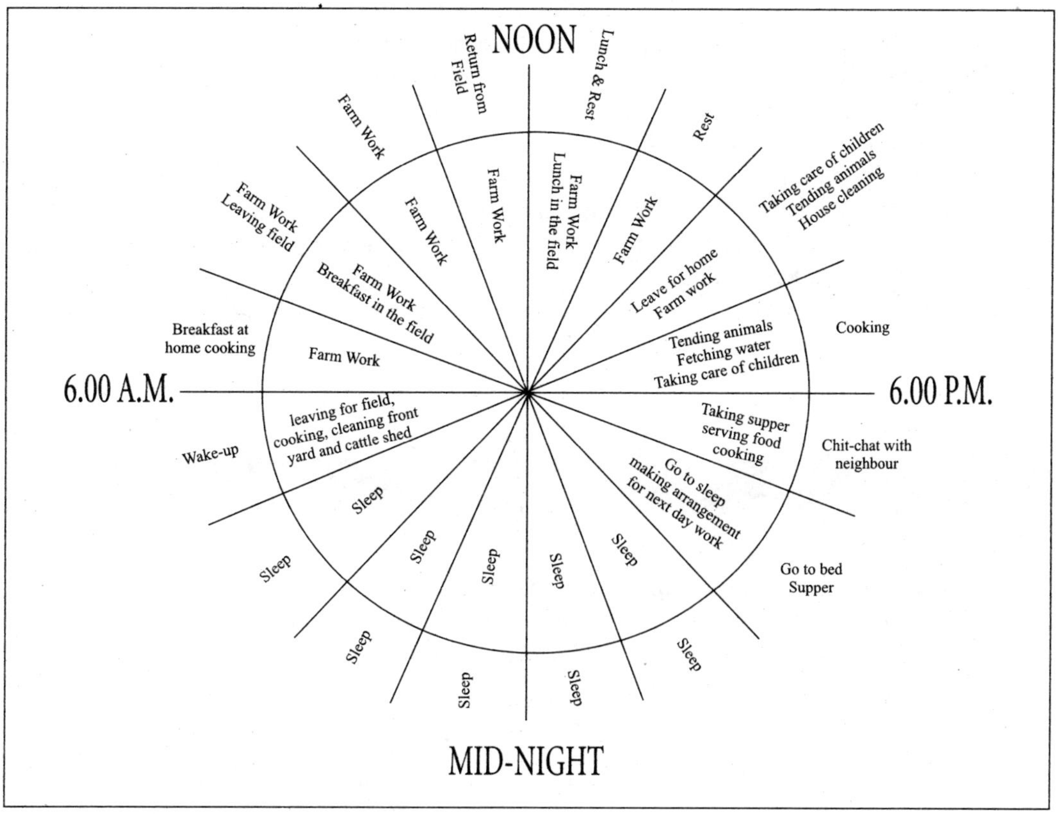

Note: Inner circle: season; outer circle: non-season.

COMPLEMENTARITY WITH OTHER METHODS

A transect walk both in the village and in the farms would provide a rough idea about the various activities undertaken by men, women and children. Daily routine or schedule may be initiated after transect. A semi-structured interview based on direct observation of activities may also lead to daily routine. Seasonal calendar provides a clear picture of seasonal variations in the activities of various seasons in the community. Based on the seasonal calendar, a series of season-wise daily schedules may be prepared. This would give an excellent idea about stress period and lean period in the life of men and women. Such daily schedules would complement and supplement the seasonal calendar.

MERITS

- It is a simple, strong and versatile method. It is non-threatening.
- It provides an understanding of how daily schedule differs among men and women and among different age groups.
- It can be used as a gender sensitisation tool.
- It can help in proper time management.
- It has the potential of relative measure and avoiding dependency literacy.
- It can be conducted among groups of small sizes, which in turn may be compared for analysis and understanding.
- The use of symbols and visuals makes the exercise interesting, and fun for even children and non-literate.

LIMITATIONS

- The exercise may become routine, as it is easy and simple to use.
- The discussion during the exercise would later provide valuable insights. The facilitators sometimes have the tendency to overlook the discussion.

SUMMARY

Daily routine or schedule is a tool for temporal analysis of labour patterns and other activities on a daily basis. The method is used to document the activities and the timing of activities and to compare the differences between schedules. This can be done with an individual or a group. It is preferable to have a small homogeneous group.

There are five different ways of doing the exercise:

- Drawing a daily timeline covering the 24 hours' period
- Using symbols and scores for ascertaining the activities and time estimation for each activity
- Constructing a matrix of activities, especially where more than one activity is taking place simultaneously
- Using the card ranking method
- Circular depiction of the daily schedule

This method is also employed to focus on women's activities and differences in the workload of men and women. Seasonal variations in workload can also be ascertained and studied.

The method has the potential of supplementing and complementing PRA and other conventional methods. A village transect and observation can lead to daily schedule. Similarly, based on the seasonal calendar, a series of season-wise daily routines may be prepared for different groups.

The merits of the method include the following: it is simple to use; it is a gender sensitisation tool; it helps the participants in proper time management. The limitations are that it is likely to become routine and the facilitators tend to ignore discussion on the output.

13

Wealth or Well-being Ranking

Inequality of wealth can be seen invariably in every human community. It is the most important characteristic that differentiates people within a community. Development initiatives and efforts should be able to recognise this difference, identify the asset-less and resourceless and mainstream them into the development process. Participatory rural appraisal (PRA) listens to the resourceless and aims to get them onto the bandwagon of development. Conventional approaches and methods of identifying the poor with their inherent biases could not do justice in this regard. Identification of the poor and vulnerable sections of the community under the conventional methods of research is a laborious task. Conventional methods use income as the 'proxy' indicator of poverty, which has serious limitations. The villagers' perception of poverty goes beyond the income indicator. The people who suffer from poverty (incidentally, they are the best poverty analysts) invariably consider factors such as size and quality of land, food security, the dependence on common property resources and the number of non-earning dependants. Further, it is very difficult to gather data on income from rural households, as rural livelihoods are diverse and complex in nature. Any attempt to impute the economic activities may suffer from estimation biases and therefore would fail to reflect the correct picture. Furthermore, the nature, causes and conditions of poverty vary from village to village. A single criterion, such as income, may not exhibit the varying nature of poverty.

The limitations and shortcomings of the conventional methods of identifying the poor led to the discovery of wealth or well-being ranking. It is a people-centric method based on locally evolved criteria. Wealth ranking, it is said, marked a breakthrough in participatory appraisal.

Wealth is defined in terms of access to or control over important economic resources; it is often observed through higher levels of income and expenditure. Nevertheless, these are the indicators of wealth rather than themselves constituting wealth. The definition of wealth in one village may not hold good for another village. This is because the nature of economic resources varies from community to community.

Sometimes wealth and well-being are interchangeably used. They are not the same. They are different. Wealth ranking involves generating a range of local criteria for wealth. It implies a materialistic focus on assets. These criteria mostly relate to ownership or access to tangible assets or resources. They do not touch upon intangible, social and other subjective or culturally constructed experiences of well-being. The term well-being is a much broader description of the quality of life. It is the more inclusive or invasive version of wealth ranking. It is concerned not only with economic security and physical health but also with the subjective status of mind and social relationships (World Bank, 1999) (see Tables 13.1 and 13.2).

Table 13.1
Well-being Categories and Criteria for Identifying Them

Category	Criteria
Happy	• Have surplus food • Have savings • Not affected by shocks • Have power
Doing well	• Have surplus food • Can withstand shock
Pulling along	• Enough food • Can send some children to school • Have to borrow at times
Facing difficult times	• Lack of resources • Children do not go to school • Not able to borrow from anyone • Have to go without food a few times • Drunken husband, beat-up wife
Miserable	• Female-headed households • Children do not go to school • Handicapped • Lack of proper shelters • Have to go without food for days • Depend on charity

Source: World Bank (1999).

Table 13.2
Wealth Ranking: Category and Criteria

Pile Category	Criteria
I	• Mostly landowners • Houses are made of permanent material • Own a huge number of livestock • Mostly receive remittance from children working in Manila and abroad
II	• Mostly tenants • Tenants, at the same time landowners of small land parcels • Mostly own a large number of livestock • Mostly receive remittance from children working in Manila
III	• Tenants of small land parcels • Hired labourers • Don't have livestock • Old folk depend on children's support

IV	• Majority not cultivating any land parcels
	• No livestock
	• Depend mainly on any of the following sources of income:
	  ♦ Fishing
	  ♦ Tube gathering
	  ♦ Gathering and selling firewood
	  ♦ Working as hired labour/maid

Source: Banlina and Tung (1992).

PARTICIPANTS

The number of participants for this exercise depends on the method that one adopts. The number in the case of card-sorting method varies from two to five. However, strictly speaking, the participants do not work as a group. Each informant sorts the pile and leaves. Under the second method, in which one uses a combination of social mapping, semi-structured interviewing (for establishing criteria and collection of data based on the criteria) and card sorting, the number of participants may vary from six to ten. The key informants under this method work as a group. The number of participants with regard to wealth ranking through social mapping can be ten or more. Here again, the key informants work in groups.

Working with groups, especially with a mixed one, is better for various obvious reasons. First, it is quick; second, reliability is much greater; third, the group exhibits a broader perspective; fourth, the problem of 'don't know' or/and 'no response' is reduced or eliminated.

However, while working in groups, we need to be more cautious because groups, which are too large, tend to be dominated by outspoken individuals. Further, the wealthier class may hijack both the ranking process and the decision over criteria. Hence, we need to keep the number of members at an optimum level.

PROCEDURE

There are two ways or tools for ranking the households based on wealth:

- Wealth ranking by card sorting;
- Wealth criteria–based card sorting.

Wealth Ranking by Card Sorting

Barbara E. Grandin (1998) developed this method. She has vividly described the procedure for wealth ranking in her famous manual *Wealth Ranking in Smallholder Communities: A Field Manual.* It is a method to understand relative wealth within a specific area. It helps to learn how rich and poor households in an area differ from each other and about the local criteria of well-being. It is particularly useful to identify different socio-economic groups and to investigate the impact of an intervention on these different groups. Wealth ranking, she suggests, can be done well with up to 100 households.

Wealth ranking is a community-based activity. The households ranked should be members of the same community—a village, a neighbourhood, a ward or a group. They are people who live near each other, attend each other's ceremonies, etc.

The procedure as suggested by her consists of seven stages. They are described in the following manner:

• **Stage I, General background activities:** The first step is to define the community and its members. This can be done with the help of a local informant. The unit chosen will depend on the number of households it contains. A unit with 100 or less is desirable as the informants need to know the people well. It should be neither too big nor too small. Too small a size will result in sampling bias. Too big a size will make the exercise cumbersome.

Having defined the community, the next step is to discuss and arrive at the local concept of wealth. It is important to determine the best indigenous concept in order to ensure the comparability of the data obtained from various informants.

The next step is to define the household. A household is one where a group of people live together and eat from the same pot. Sometimes two or three families may live under the same roof but not eat from the same pot. Each family is then a household. Local informants will be able to provide such information provided they are properly facilitated.

• **Stage II, Community-specific background activities:** The first step under this phase is to obtain a list of households. The list may be obtained through a census, health records or a school. The list so obtained needs to be checked to ensure that it is complete. Then it should be written down and a code number should be assigned to each household. Write the names of each household on an index card. The size of the card may be 3 inch x 5 inch. Each card should be given a number for easy reference. The next step is to find several reliable local informants. The informants chosen should be long-standing members of the community who are knowledgeable and honest. They should represent a cross section of the community. We may then choose a quiet place to interview, discuss and finalise ranks of the households based on wealth.

• **Stage III, Introduction to the informants:** This is an important stage where we need to make the informant quite clear about the exercise. The local informants should understand the value of knowing about the different problems of rich and poor. We also need to discuss and finalise the local word or phrase for well-being, the unit being ranked to check and the name on each card, and ensure that it stands for the whole household, not just for the individual.

• **Stage IV, Actual card sorting:** Explain the procedure to the informant. Make sure that he/she understands the procedure fully. He should know that he has to put the cards into piles (or rows), each of which is a different level of well-being. He should also know that he can make as many piles as possible and change the number of piles or the location of a card during the exercise. If the informant is literate, he can read the cards himself; otherwise, the facilitator can read the names.

The cards should be shuffled before they are given to the informant so that they are in a random order.

Ask the informant to take each card and place it before him, creating a series of piles, each of which is to represent households of similar wealth status. Each informant should decide the number of piles as long as there are at least three. The informant at any point can increase the number of piles by simply inserting a card between the existing files. Answer any question as the informant sorts the cards.

Once the informant has finished sorting all the cards into piles, the next step is to review each pile. Explain to the informant that you want to double-check the households that he has grouped together. Read out each card in the different piles to check if the cards have been grouped correctly. Start with the file of the richest or poorest and continue with the pile/row next to it. Allow the informant to make changes if he wishes so. Write down the household numbers pile-wise on a recording sheet.

• **Stage V, Follow-up discussion with the informant:** The informant, in the process of sorting the cards and verifying the groupings, will be constantly thinking about wealth differences in his community. Now it is the right time to discuss in detail the nature of differences between people of different wealth ranks. Do not ask about specific households as this might be sensitive information.

The informant still has the piles of cards in front of him. It will be easy for the informant to explain more fully what makes people in one group different from people in the other group. It is easier to begin with the richest group. Point to the pile and ask what these groups have in common that makes them rich. Repeat this for each file.

Record the information obtained, both the actual ranking and any comments as individuals or groups. Thank the informant.

• **Stage VI:** Repeat the above (introduction, card sorting and follow-up discussion) with three or more informants.

• **Stage VII, Computing and grouping:** Calculate the score for each household for each informant. The simplest and easiest way in which the individual informants score can be computed into an average score for each household is to give each household a score for each informant which is as follows:

$$\text{The score} = \frac{\text{Pile number of household in which household is located}}{\text{Total number of piles made by that informant}}$$

If there are three piles, the richest pile gets a weight of $1/3 = 0.33$. The middle gets $2/3 = 0.66$. The poorest gets $3/3 = 1$. If there are five piles, proceed in the same way except now the denominator in the fraction is 5. The richest pile gets a weight of $1/5 = 0.20$; the second gets $2/5 = 0.40$; the third gets $3/5 = 0.60$; the fourth gets $4/5 = 0.80$; and the poorest gets $5/5 = 1$. Under this system, the poorest gets the highest number (see Table 13.3).

Table 13.3
Record of Information from the Informants' Piles

Informant	Pile No.	Cards	Weight
I	1	2, 5, 8, 13, 18, 23, 27	1/4 = 0.25
	2	1, 4, 7, 14, 17, 20, 21, 26	2/4 = 0.50
	3	6, 9, 10, 15, 19, 22, 24, 28, 30	3/4 = 0.75
	4	3, 11, 12, 16, 25, 29	4/4 = 1.00
II	1	2, 8, 13, 23, 27, 1, 7	1/3 = 0.33
	2	5, 18, 20, 21, 17, 10, 15, 19, 22, 28, 12, 16, 25	2/3 = 0.67
	3	14, 30, 26, 6, 9, 24, 3, 11, 29, 4	3/3 = 1.00
III	1	2, 8, 27, 18, 13	1/5 = 0.20
	2	5, 23, 1, 4, 7, 6, 9, 10	2/5 = 0.40
	3	14, 17, 20, 15, 19, 22	3/5 = 0.60
	4	21, 26, 24, 28, 30	4/5 = 0.80
	5	3, 11, 12, 16, 25, 29	5/5 = 1.00

Write down the household numbers in a line; write the score for each household given by each informant (see Table 13.4). Do not include any households that were ranked by less than two informants. Calculate the average score for each household.

Table 13.4
Calculation of Average Score

Card No.	Score From			Total Score	Average Score
	Informant I	Informant II	Informant III		
1	0.50	0.33	0.40	1.23	0.41
2	0.25	0.33	0.20	0.78	0.26
3	1.00	1.00	1.00	3.00	1.00
4	0.50	(1.00)	(0.40)	1.90	0.63
5	0.25	0.67	0.40	1.32	0.44
6	0.75	(1.00)	(0.40)	2.15	0.72
7	0.50	0.33	0.40	1.23	0.41
8	0.25	0.33	0.20	0.78	0.26
9	0.75	(1.00)	(0.40)	2.15	0.72
10	0.75	0.67	0.40	1.82	0.61
11	1.00	1.00	1.00	3.00	1.00
12	1.00	0.67	1.00	2.67	0.89
13	0.25	0.33	0.20	0.78	0.26
14	(0.50)	(1.00)	0.60	2.10	0.70
15	0.75	0.67	0.60	2.02	0.67
16	1.00	0.67	1.00	2.67	0.89
17	0.50	0.67	0.60	1.77	0.59
18	0.25	(0.67)	(0.20)	1.12	0.37
19	0.75	0.67	0.60	2.02	0.67
20	0.50	0.67	0.60	1.77	0.59
21	0.50	0.67	0.80	1.97	0.66
22	0.75	0.67	0.60	2.02	0.67
23	0.25	0.33	0.40	0.98	0.33
24	0.75	1.00	0.80	2.55	0.85
25	1.00	0.67	1.00	2.67	0.89
26	(0.50)	(1.00)	0.80	2.30	0.77
27	0.25	0.33	0.20	0.78	0.26
28	0.75	0.67	0.80	2.22	0.74
29	1.00	1.00	1.00	3.00	1.00
30	0.75	1.00	0.80	2.55	0.85

$$\text{Average score} = \frac{\text{Total of its score}}{\text{Number of scores}}$$

Find any unreliable scores, where one informant gave a low score and another gave a much higher score. As they are unreliable, they should be treated with care and should be investigated further to understand why they have such different scores.

Write the average score for each household in large numbers on the index cards used for the exercise. Put the index cards in order from the lowest to the highest average score (rich to poor). Copy on a sheet of paper in the following order: the average score and the household number.

Divide this list of households, ranked according to relative well-being into groups. This can be done by looking for a large gap in the average score (which implies a big jump in difference of well-being) and making that as the dividing point between two categories of well-being (see Table 13.5).

Table 13.5
Classification of Cards According to Wealth

Category	Average Score	Card No.	Remarks
POOREST	1.00	30	
	1.00	11	
	1.00	29	
	0.89	12	
	0.89	16	
	0.89	25	
	0.85	24	
	0.85	30	
	0.77	26	?
	0.74	28	
	0.72	6	?
	0.72	9	?
	0.70	14	?
	0.67	15	
	0.67	19	
	0.67	22	
	0.66	21	
	0.63	4	?
	0.61	10	
	0.59	17	
	0.59	20	
	0.44	5	
	0.41	1	
	0.41	7	
RICHEST	0.37	18	?
	0.33	23	
	0.26	2	
	0.26	8	
	0.26	13	
	0.26	27	

Note: ? = Score with discrepancies; one informant has given a low score; another a high score.

Merits of the method

- This method helps in quickly clustering and ranking households so that researchers or development workers are able to understand better the realities of different groups.

- The respondents or participants are asked only to group people and not to provide any sensitive information. Hence, there will not be any hesitation on behalf of the participants to take part.
- The level of agreement among the informants in wealth ranking is quite high. Hence, only three to five informants are necessary for the exercise.

Limitations of the method

- The method is extractive in nature. Once the information is collected from the respondents or participants, the scoring, ranking and grouping are done by the facilitators or the researchers. The respondents may not know the final output of the exercise if the principle of 'sharing' is not followed.
- The participants who carry out the ranking may not know all the households. Hence, there is a possibility for gaps between the wealth ranks of individual households.
- The final division of the households into wealth groups is a subjective choice of the researcher.
- It relies on all people knowing each other, so this is not workable in a large community.
- Comparisons between different villages are not possible.
- Development workers or researchers tend to adopt only the mechanics of the technique to produce a list of average ranking scores, without making use of its real potential that lies beyond the numbers.

Precautions to be taken

- Mean ranks should not be used.
- If the data is incomplete, values must be imputed before obtaining average marks.
- Split the population into groups with equal number of households.
- Obtain ranks from as many people as possible so that peculiar extreme scores do not have a great influence on the final groupings.

Wealth Criteria–based Card Sorting

Under the card-sorting method, the questions on wealth status in terms of assets possessed are not asked. Cards without any information on the status of wealth are piled by the participants based on their personal knowledge. Under the recorded wealth criteria–based card-sorting method, the wealth or assets possessed by the household are recorded first on a card before sorting them out (Sarch 1992). The procedure is explained here.

• **Step 1, Preparation of list of households:** Facilitate the participants to draw the social map. Let it be a base map with the number of houses (type-wise) and with number of families or households in each house, because in certain houses there might be more than one family. Copy the map on newsprint. Ask the participants to give numbers to each of the households on the map and to note down the name of the head of the household. Check the exact number of houses and households as this would be the base for further facilitation of wealth ranking.

Prepare index cards and note down the household number and the name of the head of the household for each of the households as given in social map. Do not omit any households. The number of cards should be in accordance to the number of households in the village.

• **Step 2, Fixing criteria for wealth ranking:** To start with, ask the participants how the households in their community can be classified based on the wealth status. Ask them not to compare themselves with households in the neighbouring villages or nearby towns and cities. Allow them to use the local language to name each class. Sometimes they may say they do not have rich households in their village. Classification is likely to vary. We have come across different classifications. A few of these include:

- ♦ Rich, middle and poor
- ♦ Rich, middle, poor and poorest
- ♦ Middle, poor and poorest
- ♦ Poor, very poor and poorest

Go by their classification and ask them to list the criteria based on which the households have been classified. A question can be raised at this stage: what is the basis on which you have classified the household as poor, rich, etc.? Spend enough time in eliciting criteria from the respondents. If possible, facilitate the participants to use visuals for each of the criteria elicited. This would help in gathering information on the wealth status of each household. Ask one of the participants to read or explain the criteria developed. This would help in fine-tuning the criteria developed. Note down the criteria developed on newsprint (see Table 13.6).

• **Step 3, Collection of information:** Keep the index card with the household number and name of the head of the household before the participants. Keep the social map too in front of them. Based on the criteria developed, ask questions on the possession of assets for each household.

Note down the details on the backside of the card. Use only one card per household (see Figure 13.1).

Repeat the procedure for all the households.

• **Step 4, Sorting and grouping the cards:** On the completion of gathering information for all households, shuffle the cards and read out the information recorded on the backside of the card. Do not read the name or the household number. Now ask the informants to place the cards in appropriate columns drawn on the floor (see Figure 13.2).

Table 13.6
Criteria for Wealth Ranking

Poorest	• Eat only two times a day • Landless destitute widows • Aged people without food security • Lack of livelihood security during non-agricultural season • Landless labourers • Non-recipient of any entitled government schemes • May own one or two goats or sheep • Physically weak • Disabled
Poor	• May not own land; the entire family may earn wages through farm work • Work on some kind of non-farm micro-enterprise • May own less than an acre of rain-fed land, but may not cultivate continuously due to water scarcity and remain daily wage earners • May own less than 1 acre, sow intermittently but do not employ labourers; the entire family involves in the cultivation operation • May own one or two cattle
Middle	• May own land between 1 and 3 acres with assured water for irrigation • They work on the field and also employ labourers • Possess some livestock • May borrow money for farm operations but do not remain indebted for quite long
Rich	• Own above 3 acres of land and energised motor pump sets • May not always work on the field • Sow every year • Lease in additional lands often • Possess milch animals • Own plough bullocks • Employ one or two farm labourers permanently • May be in a position to lend money locally, or run a business in the nearby town or have one of the family members on a salaried job

Source: PRA Unit, GRI (1998b).
Note: These criteria were developed in four remote villages of Vedasandur Block for a study called Hunger Free Area Programme sponsored by the government of Tamil Nadu. They are relevant only to those four villages.

Figure 13.1
Sample Index Card

P. 1	P. 2
HH No. : 1 Head of the HH : R. Palani	• Tiled house • 0.5 acres of dry land • Two goats • Agricultural labour • Non-earning dependants : 2

Figure 13.2
Well-being Category

Pile – 1	Pile – 2	Pile – 3
 😊 Rich	 😐 Middle	 ☹️ Poor

Repeat the procedure for all the cards. Once all the cards are sorted out, read the number and name of the head of the household under each category. Allow them to make changes in the pile. But do ask them why they would want to make the changes. Triangulate the information by repeating the exercise with another set of key informants.

• **Step 5, Superimposing the category on the map:** Households classified based on the wealth status may be marked on the social map. The poor households may be marked with red circles around the houses, the middle-income ones with a yellow circles and rich with green circles. Alternatively, *bindis* of different colours can be used.

• **Step 6, Share the information with wider audience:** The outcome of the exercise may be shared with a wider audience if the participants agree to this. Sharing would facilitate triangulation of the classification of the houses and the results become more authentic and reliable.

Merits of the method

- The objectivity of the outcome is likely to be more for three reasons. First, information for ranking is collected based on the criteria developed in consultation with the people. Second, ranking is done based on the information recorded on the card and by masking the name of the head of the household. Third, it is a group exercise.
- All the households without any omission would get classified since social mapping is used as the base.
- The exercise is done by the people; the outsiders' role is that of being facilitators. Participants know the outcome of the exercise as they do it. There is a greater transparency and participants exactly know the status of various households in the village.
- A good amount of quantitative and qualitative information about each household is available which can be made use of for further investigation, analysis and action.
- It is a visual exercise and therefore ensures active participation.

Limitations of the method

- The method helps in arriving at three or four broad categories of wealth and the households that fall under each category. However, it has failed to rank the households under each category.
- Collection of information, even if it is minimal, for each household is a laborious task. Participants are likely to get bored after going through a few households. Sometimes, it may turn out to be a mechanical process.
- It is time-consuming.

Precautions to be taken

- It is advisable to carry out this exercise in a small community with the number of households not exceeding 100.
- The entire process mapping, criteria development, information gathering, card sorting and grouping need not be done on the same day. The entire exercise can be spread over a period of two or three days, mostly in the evenings.
- The criteria developed need to be sharper and more focused.

APPLICATION

Wealth ranking is a path-breaking method in PRA. It is being applied in various fields. A few applications of wealth ranking are given here:

- Wealth ranking helps in assessing whether the various programmes meant for the poor, implemented and operated by different development agencies, including the government, have reached them or not.
- It helps in explaining the conditions of poverty and ranking households on that basis.
- It facilitates to structure the research process. Wealth ranking, for example, would help to identify the poor. This, in turn, would facilitate one to investigate and analyse the various issues related to the poor. It may be, for instance, the livelihood opportunities, options and strategies of the poor and their coping strategies in times of crisis or lack of security with regard to their livelihood. For assessing the nutritional status, the exercise can be a starting point. It can help in fixing the sample for a nutritional survey.
- Wealth ranking would enable us to hear genuinely different voices, the voices that speak from and about realities other than those configured by development discourse and institutions.

- This can be applied in water and sanitation projects. The classification can be used to identify groups with which to hold a focus group discussion, for mapping the access of the poor for water supply and sanitation facilities, functions and jobs, and to identify their differential rates of participation in community decision making, management of services, benefits, etc. It can also be used as a perspective against which to assess the financial data and community contributions, tariffs for services, the extent of subsidies, etc.
- It can help to target the poor sections of society. Development workers can focus on efforts where the need was greatest and prevent better-off families from capturing resources.

COMPLEMENTARITY WITH OTHER METHODS

Normally, social mapping is used as the starting point for wealth ranking or well-being ranking. The outcome of wealth ranking can be superimposed on social map for a better clarity and understanding. Wealth ranking can help in fixing upon the key informants for a focused group discussion. It can also help in fixing upon the key informants to Venn diagram and mobility map exercises. For instance, a Venn diagram with different wealth groups or classes would help us to know to what extent the poor have been able to make use of the services of different institutions compared to the rich and middle classes. Wealth ranking can also help in carrying out livelihood analysis by selecting the poorest of the poor and the richest.

SUMMARY

Wealth ranking, a people-centric method for classifying the households in a community into different classes based on locally evolved criteria, has been claimed as a 'breakthrough' in PRA. Wealth is an access to or control over important economic resources. Of late, wealth and well-being are used interchangeably. However, there are certain differences among the two. Wealth has a materialistic focus on assets, whereas well-being is more inclusive; it describes the quality of life.

There are two prominent methods of wealth or well-being ranking. They are (*i*) wealth ranking by card sorting and (*ii*) wealth criteria–based card sorting and mapping.

Barbara E. Grandin has developed the 'card sorting' method. The steps to be followed in the method are the following: Discuss and decide the local concept of wealth; define households in the local language; obtain names of households and write the names and the numbers for each household on the index card; choose informants; ask the informants to sort the cards one after the other into different piles (poorest, poor, middle, rich) based on the criteria; repeat the exercise with three to five participants; and compute the average score and group them. The merits of this method are that the work is done quite quickly, and it can be done with just three to five participants. The limitations of this method are that it is extractive in nature; it is not workable in large communities.

The second method is the 'improvisation of card sorting' method. The steps involved are: preparation of a list of households using the social map; establishing the criteria for wealth ranking; preparation of index cards; collection of information based on the criteria; sorting and grouping the cards; superimposing the category on the map; and sharing the outcome with a wider audience. The merits of this method are the following: (*i*) it is more objective; (*ii*) use of visuals; and (*iii*) all the households get classified without any omission. The demerits are the following: (*i*) failure to rank households under each category; (*ii*) collection of information is laborious and mechanical; and (*iii*) it is time-consuming.

The number of participants for this exercise depends upon the type of methods we adopt. Card-sorting method requires three to five participants. It is mostly done as an individual exercise. The other method is visual and group exercise. The number of participants can be more.

'Wealth rank' can be used to identify the target group of a project or scheme, to select the sample for a study, and to identify the focus group. This method can be used in effective combination with other methods.

14

Pair-wise Ranking

INTRODUCTION

A significant aspect of participatory bottom-up planning is ascertaining the priorities of the people and integrating such priorities in the development plan. People during the course of interaction in participatory rural appraisal (PRA) may reveal a wide range of problems and express several needs. These problems and needs should be prioritised so that decision can be taken on which are the most important problems to be solved and which are the most important needs to be fulfilled. Pair-wise ranking, a ranking method in PRA, helps to prioritise the problems and needs of the people. It is a tool that can uncover the most important problems of the community. It is a structured method for ranking a list of items in priority order.

MEANING

Pair-wise ranking compares pairs of elements, such as the preference for needs, problems, food items, trees, credit sources and recreational activities. It normally leads to analysis of the decision-making rationale. It can also portray the relevance and appropriateness of interventions through an increased understanding of priorities. The technique can be used among different groups on a specific topic or theme across the group which would help to compare preferences and priorities of different people.

PARTICIPANTS

This method can be practised either in a mixed group or specific groups formed on the basis of well-being category, gender, age, occupation, etc. A larger mixed group is likely to promote more discussion. However, the needs and priorities of the poor and the voiceless may get sidelined. For instance, while assessing the needs and priorities of the community in a large mixed group, the needs of the elite and those who are dominant in the community would naturally get highlighted. On the other hand, a large mixed group based on a certain homogeneous character is better as each individual will have an equal voice in discussion, debate and decision; and each voice will be heard and respected. The large mixed group is good, but such an ideal situation does not prevail in all the communities. Hence, it would be advisable to go in for specific groups based on certain homogeneous characters such as gender, caste, class, occupation and age. The outcome of the exercise of each of these groups may be shared in a plenary for further discussion which would assist in arriving at a consensus. The number of participants depends on the nature of topic or theme. It can vary from six to ten. There is nothing wrong if the number exceeds ten.

PROCEDURE

- Decide the items to be ranked; it may be trees, problems, needs, food item, method of teaching, etc.
- Ask the participants to list any problems, using the brainstorming technique.
- Choose the most important problems with the help of participants. You may even go in for NSL (Now, Soon, Later) chart for classifying the problems.
- Having chosen the problems, facilitate the people to draw the matrix on the ground.
- Enter or visually represent each problem in the rows and columns. Use visuals as this would generate more participation and greater discussion.
- Facilitate the participants to compare the first problem in the row with various problems listed in the column one by one. Ask them to enter their preferences in the respective grids.
- Move on to the second problem in the row; keep that as a constant and compare it with the third and subsequent problems and enter the preference in the relevant grid. One should remember that one has already compared the first against the second.
- Then move on to the third problem in the row and keep that as a constant; compare that with the fourth and subsequent problems in the respective grids.
- Repeat the steps cited until all the problems are compared pair-wise.
- Ask the participants to count the number of times each problem was selected; place it in column 'Score' (Table 14.1).
- Now ask the participants to rank the problems based on the number of times the problem was selected (see Table 14.1).
- Ask for reasons for the preference. The exercise should not be a mere comparison of pairs. It should go into the reasons for preference.

Dos

- Ensure that the items to be prioritised are small in number.
- Be sensitive to the representativeness of the participants' responses.
- Make decisions in a consensus-oriented manner.

Don'ts

- Do not attempt to rank a longer list of items as it would make the process too tedious as the number of comparisons would be vast.
- Do not interfere or interrupt while the participants are trying to arrive at a consensus.

Table 14.1
Pair-wise Ranking: An Illustration

Item	A	B	C	D	E	F	G	Score	Rank
A	–	B	C	A	E	F	A	2	V
B	–	–	C	B	E	F	B	3	IV
C	–	–	–	C	C	C	C	6	I
D	–	–	–	–	E	F	D	1	VI
E	–	–	–	–	–	F	E	4	III
F	–	–	–	–	–	–	F	5	II
G	–	–	–	–	–	–	–	0	VII

APPLICATION

The method was originally applied mostly in agriculture and forestry. The areas explored in these fields include crop and variety preferences, tree species preferences, problems in agriculture and problems in forestry. Subsequently, the technique has been employed in almost all fields. Some of the fields where this technique is commonly used are

- sources of credit;
- sources of income;
- disease;
- expenditure;
- needs of children;
- problems;
- potentials;

- sources of drinking water;
- teaching methods; and
- recreation.

The method is also used in urban areas, especially in slums. Further, the method is helpful in ascertaining the importance of different criteria. By comparing the criteria directly, the relative importance of different criteria can be discussed, and therefore the scoring from the matrix is fully understood.

We will now see a few applications of pair-wise ranking with illustrations from the field.

Preference for Sources of Credit

Pair-wise ranking can be employed with ease to ascertain the preference of credit sources. The villagers mostly prefer informal sources, even though the cost of loan is exorbitant. Why do they prefer such agencies? Pair-wise ranking can help not only in identifying the preferences of the people but also in unearthing the causes for preference or non-preference.

While conducting a study on credit delivery in practice, we employed pair-wise ranking to ascertain the preferences of the people in a village. The sources of credit in pairs are compared and a more favoured preference is marked. A different pair is presented and the comparisons are made till all the pairs are compared. The reasons for the choice or the preference are enquired into. Pair-wise ranking provides a very clear picture about the agencies preferred by the people in the area without any ambiguity (see Table 14.2).

Table 14.2
Pair-wise Ranking: Sources of Credit

Source of credit	SBI	CB	COOPs	Ts & CAs	LSs & Rs	PMLs	Total score	Rank
State Bank of India	–	SBI	SBI	Ts & CAs	LSs & Rs	SBI	3	III
Canara Bank	–	–	CB	Ts & CAs	LSs & Rs	PMLs	1	V
Cooperative banks	–	–	–	Ts & CAs	LSs & Rs	PMLs	0	VII
Traders and Commission Agents	–	–	–	–	LSs & Rs	Ts & CAs	4	II
Local Sources and Relatives	–	–	–	–	–	LSs & Rs	5	I
Professional Money Lenders	–	–	–	–	–	–	2	IV

Source: Narayanasamy et al. (1998).

While carrying out pair-wise ranking, the participants were asked, 'What are the causes for preferences or non-preferences?' The participants listed the positive and negative features of the organisations. Thus, it may help in knowing the reasons for preferences.

Teaching Practices in Schools

Pair-wise ranking can be adopted to ascertain the preference of teachers and pupils on teaching and learning methods. Abigail Mulhall and Peter Taylor in their study, *Using Participatory Research Methods to Explore Learning Environment of Rural Primary School Pupils*, have used pair-wise ranking to assess the school teaching practices in four countries of Asia and Africa. The process involved ranking of ten methods of teaching and learning against each other by preference. A matrix was pre-drawn with all the teaching methods appearing in the row and column headings in the same order. Two separate groups were formed—one group consisting of teachers and another consisting of students. Each group was asked to complete the matrix. The groups completed it by having a dialogue among themselves on finding a better method in teaching and learning, by pairing the various methods of teaching and learning. The number of times each method was selected was counted and placed in the total column. The methods were then ranked according to the total number of times they were selected (see Table 14.3). The teachers considered this exercise as a form of in-service training. The researchers concluded that the use of participatory approaches made the research fun, both for the researcher and the interviewees.

Table 14.3
Pair-wise Matrix Ranking of Teaching Methods: Pupils' Response

Teaching Method	A	B	C	D	E	F	G	H	I	J	Total Score	Rank
A. Teacher explains, asks questions and gives examples	–	A	A	A	A	A	G	A	I	J	6	III
B. Pupils ask questions and give examples	–	–	C	D	E	B	G	B	I	J	2	VI
C. Teacher reads from textbooks	–	–	–	D	E	C	G	C	I	J	3	V
D. Pupils read from textbooks	–	–	–	–	E	D	G	D	I	J	4	IV
E. Pupils write	–	–	–	–	–	E	E	E	I	J	6	III
F. Teacher punishes pupils	–	–	–	–	–	–	G	H	I	J	0	VIII
G. Pupils repeat or recite	–	–	–	–	–	–	–	G	I	G	7	II
H. Pupils teach others	–	–	–	–	–	–	–	–	I	J	1	VII
I. Teacher demonstrates	–	–	–	–	–	–	–	–	–	I	9	I
J. Pupils learn by doing	–	–	–	–	–	–	–	–	–	–	7	II

Source: Mulhall and Taylor (1998).

Disease Problem Ranking

Alice Welbourn, in her note on the use of disease problem ranking with relation to socio-economic well-being, has vividly illustrated the disease problem ranking by using the pair-wise ranking method. The process is described in the following steps:

- Selection of two groups of women, namely, better off and worse off based on the 'well-being ranking' exercise
- Convening the meeting of the groups separately
- Asking the groups to list the diseases affecting them and rank such diseases using the pair-wise ranking method

The exercise revealed that while the better-off women mentioned four illnesses, with measles considered as the worst problem, the worse-off women interviewed in the same village mentioned six illnesses. These included eye infection, which was also considered as their worst problem. Better-off women had not mentioned an eye problem at all. The diagrams produced by women in the village contained no writing initially and were entirely understandable to all concerned (see Figures 14.1 and 14.2).

Figure 14.1
Disease Ranking: Better-off Women

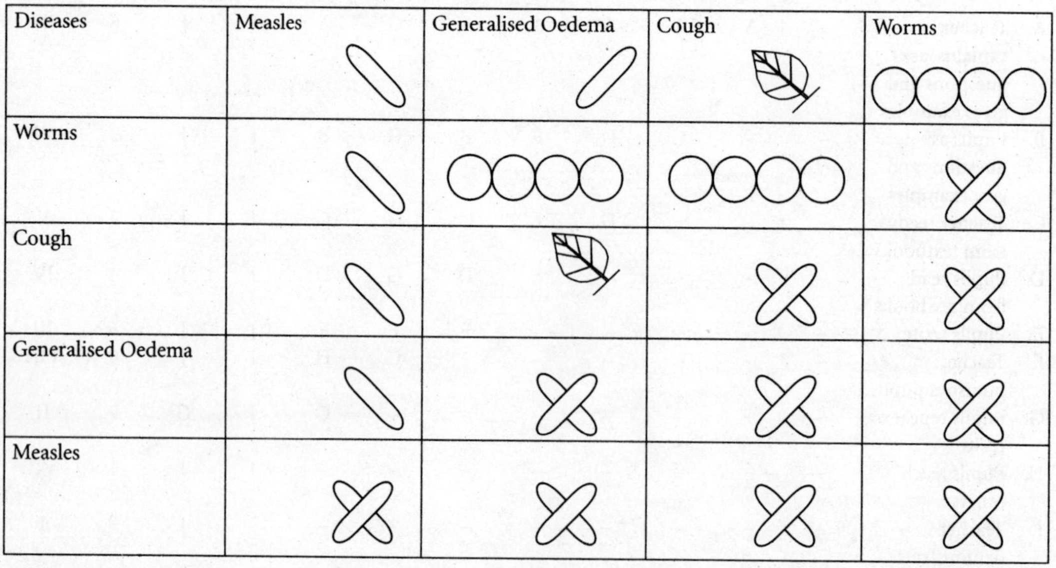

Source: Welbourn (1992a).
Note: Measles—3, Worms—2, Cough—1, Generalised oedema—0.

Figure 14.2
Disease Ranking: Poor Women

Sickness	Measles ◈	Abnormal Pains ○○	Heart Complaints ◉	Malnutrition ☠	Whooping Cough ✳	Eye Infection ★
◈	★	★	★	★	★	⊠
○○	◈	○○	◉	☠	⊠	⊠
◉	◈	○○	◉	⊠	⊠	⊠
☠	◈	○○	⊠	⊠	⊠	⊠
✳	◈	⊠	⊠	⊠	⊠	⊠
★	⊠	⊠	⊠	⊠	⊠	⊠

Source: Welbourn (1992a).
Note: Eye infection—5, Measles—4, Abnormal pains—3, Heart complaints—2, Malnutrition—1.

COMPLEMENTARITY WITH OTHER METHODS

The method can be used as a precursor to a more detailed matrix ranking and to obtain more details about specific themes arising out of group discussion. For instance, it may help in harvesting the criteria for preferences, which then can be further ranked using either pair-wise ranking or other ranking methods, such as 100-seed scoring technique.

Pair-wise ranking succeeded by wealth ranking exercise would help in organising the exercise with various homogeneous smaller groups, such as well-off and poor. This would facilitate better interaction, avoid biases and would give a better insight on the problem and priorities of different sections of the community.

Sometimes transect can precede pair-wise ranking. Transect, along with direct observation and semi-structured interview with the participating villagers and chance encounters, would give a clear idea about the problems related to resources. Pair-wise ranking can be done to identify the most important problem related to resources. Further exercises can be planned to study the problem in depth.

For institutional analysis, pair-wise ranking can succeed Venn diagram. Pair-wise ranking can supplement logical framework analysis (LFA). The first step in LFA is problem tree analysis or cause and effect analysis. Pair-wise ranking can assist in identifying the most important problems in the community, based on which the cause and effect analysis can be done.

MERITS

- Pair-wise ranking provides an excellent starting point for interviewing the diagram. It also leads to further discussion and exploration of various issues related to the ranked issue or problem.
- It is quite friendly with other methods of PRA and it can be used in combination with other methods such as transect, resource mapping, social mapping, Venn diagram, wealth ranking, cause and effect diagram and focused group discussion.
- It can supplement and complement the questionnaire survey.
- It can be visually presented on the ground. As a result, it can assist in greater participation and access.
- It stimulates discussion among the participants and elicits detailed knowledge and understanding.
- It provides great scope for using the ground as the medium. Hence, locally available materials, which are people-friendly as well, can be used for ranking and analysis.

LIMITATIONS

- Pair-wise ranking by simply comparing the pairs without discussion would be tedious and sometimes boring.
- If the number of items to be ranked is more than ten, it is likely to result in boredom for both the villagers and outsiders. Hence, it is better to limit the number of items to less than ten in order to reduce the risk of boredom.
- Facilitators have a tendency to draw the grid on a sheet of paper, which invariably makes the facilitator fill the grids. This is more extractive in nature; as a result, the participants are likely to lose interest.
- Rankings are subjective choices and are open to influence by the interview environment and context. Hence the technique of ranking among alternatives must be used with caution.

SUMMARY

Pair-wise ranking is a valuable method for comparing pairs of elements such as problems, potentials and needs. The method can be practised in large mixed groups or small specific groups. Small groups based on gender, age and well-being would be ideal as it would avoid biases as well as register the voice of all.

The process of this method involves listing the problems or needs or potentials; one then has to choose the most important problem and draw a matrix on the ground by visually representing or depicting the problems on the row heading and column heading; then compare each pair and enter the preferred item in the relevant grid; count the number of times each problem was selected; rank the problem based on the number of times the problem was selected by asking the reasons for their preferences.

Originally applied in the field of agriculture and forestry, this method is now being used in several fields. The method can be very effectively used in combination with various PRA methods such as transect, resource mapping, Venn diagram, wealth ranking and others. It also assists in LFA by identifying the most important problem, which in turn would help in carrying out the problem tree analysis.

The merits of this method are that (*i*) it is an excellent starting point for interviewing the diagram and (*ii*) it can effectively supplement greater participation. The limitations are that (*i*) it is tedious and boring if done without discussion; (*ii*) comparison of more than ten items would be tedious and at times boring; and (*iii*) ranking is based on subjective choices and is likely to be influenced by the interview environment and context.

15

Matrix Ranking and Scoring

A village or a community may have several problems. However, the degree of intensity may vary among the problems. Some problems may be serious and may require immediate attention while some other problems may be less serious and may be attended to later. It is also not possible to address all the problems at a given time. Similarly, a village or a community may have several needs. Some of these needs may be 'immediately felt' needs, which need to be fulfilled soon. Some needs may be fulfilled after some time. A development researcher or worker should understand the problems and needs of a village or a community and should ascertain the problems and needs in the order of urgency. This is essential for better programme planning and realisation of the objectives of the plan. The ranking and scoring exercise helps to prioritise the problems and needs.

Ranking and scoring exercises are used to analyse, prioritise and present information. These exercises can be powerful modes of representing quite complex information in a way that is clear to both the participatory rural appraisal (PRA) team and the local participants. Ranking exercises allow sets of data to be compared, discussed, adjusted and looked at from different points of view in a way that is very difficult in a simple discussion with no visual reference. Results of ranking exercises can be used as a direct representation of the analyses carried out and provide an easy-to-understand record of discussion held with the local people on different topics.

Matrix ranking and scoring exercise is one of the commonly practiced tools in almost all contexts under PRA. It is a tool that can be used to stimulate discussions among people whenever any choices are to be made. It helps to make the decision-making process transparent. It helps to achieve a better clarity on the existing perceptions about the advantages and disadvantages of various possible solutions. It also aids in identifying key constraints and opportunities and to discuss the selection of criteria. It not only provokes a discussion of the criteria for selection, but also attempts to develop an understanding of the basis for making choices and decisions (Jones 1996). It is also possible to use the technique as a planning tool. There are different types of matrix ranking and scoring. However, they can be grouped together under three heads as they involve more or less similar approaches and the distinction between them is often thin:

- Matrix ranking
- Matrix scoring
- Other forms of matrices

Ranking means placing or putting something in order (Theis and Grady 1991). Scoring relates to the weight or prominence people give to different items. Matrix ranking involves listing the elements down one side and the criteria on which they are judged, gained from formal discussion or pair-wise ranking across the top. Each element is then considered in terms of each criterion. For instance, tree species could be discussed in terms of fodder, fuel, food, cost, medicine and shade. For each criterion, the tree species are ranked in the order of preference, in much the same way as a simple ranking, but repeated for each criterion. In the case of matrix scoring, not only the preferences are found, but the relative weight given to each preference is also indicated. Hence, a more detailed analysis is available through awarding each element a number of counters depending on the preferences.

PURPOSE

The main purpose of the method of creating a matrix is to discover the individual's or group's relative prioritisation of components on a single issue. It can be part of the analytical process, including values placed on the non-tangible as well as physical things. It provides an opportunity for people to identify and express priorities and options for action. It also helps in targeting and allocation of resources for the priorities identified by the people. It facilitates the people to analyse their problems in a systematic way and in several incidents; they come to be aware of their problems and priorities through a systematic analysis.

PARTICIPANTS

This is most often a group exercise. Experiences in the field indicate that a large number of participants take part in the exercise. It is always better to have a mixed group of men and women from different sections of the community in order to ensure objectivity in the outcome. In case it is difficult to ensure the participation of all the sections of the community, the exercise can be conducted in small groups of different sections of the community and the outcome of the exercises can be presented and shared in a larger gathering for consolidation. This would also speed up the process. Women sometimes may be reluctant to voice their opinion in large gatherings. It would be appropriate if the exercise is conducted separately for women. It is better to avoid drawing matrices on the paper as it would restrict the participation of many and the discussion would be confined to a few. On the other hand, drawing matrices on the ground with locally available materials would ensure larger participation, transparency and triangulation.

PROCEDURE (MATRIX RANKING)

- Convene a meeting of people comprising men and women from different sections of the community.
- Explain the purpose of the exercise. It is important that the ranking system being used is clear to the facilitator and participants.
- Choose the theme for discussion. It depends on the purpose of the appraisal. If the purpose is to assess the preference of trees, then tree species would be the subject for discussion. If the purpose is to ascertain fuel preference, fuel types would be the subject for discussion.
- Ask them to list the items—trees or fuel types. Facilitate them to choose the most important item. The number of items may vary from three to eight.
- The next step is to facilitate the participants to list the criteria. This is an important stage. Spend adequate time with the participants without rushing, as it would provide very useful information about the criteria or factors based on which the participants choose an item (Chambers 1988).
- Elicit criteria from the participants by asking questions like, what is good about each item? What else? Continue asking till all the possible criteria are elicited. Similarly, ask, what is bad about each item? Continue asking until no more replies come from the respondents.
- List all the criteria; convert the negative criteria into positive ones by using the opposite of the negative criteria.
- Draw up a matrix with the items across the top and criteria down the side. It can be visually represented.
- Ask which item is best in terms of the criteria. The questions which need to be posed at this stage are:

  ◆ Which is the best, the next best?
  ◆ Which is the worst?
  ◆ Of the remaining, which is better?

- Record the ranking directly onto the matrix.
- Force a final choice with a question on the lines of 'if you could have only one of these, which would you choose? Which next?' (see Table 15.1).

Table 15.1
Matrix Ranking of Rice Varieties

Criterion \ Rice Variety	Rasi	IR 50	IR 36	Hiramoti	Masuri	Nagrasal
Resistance to pests	1	6	5	4	3	2
Drought resistance	1	3	4	2	5	6
Length of straw for thatching	4	6	5	3	2	1
Market price	4	3	3	4	1	2
Suitability for light soil	1	2	1	2	–	–
Eating quality	4	2	2	3	5	1
Suitability for kharif and rabi	1	1	1	–	–	–
Recovery of aged seedlings	4	4	4	3	2	1

Source: Jones (1996).

Notes: (i) 1 = Best; 6 = Worst.
   (ii) Ranking is done based on the number of items chosen for ranking. There are six varieties. Hence, rank varies from 1 to 6.

Procedure for Matrix Scoring

- Decide what should be ranked.
- Find the key informants who are knowledgeable and willing to participate and discuss.
- Facilitate them to decide which item is going to be ranked.
- For each item ask what is good about it, what else, what else, then what is bad, what next, what next, and so on.
- List the criteria that have been identified. Make the negative criteria into positive.

Ask the key informants to give scores. Scoring is of two types, namely, (*i*) free scoring and (*ii*) closed scoring. Free scoring enables the participants to score each element against each criterion, with no limit placed on the score. There is complete freedom of expression. Closed scoring can be done in three ways. First, each box (element for that criterion) can be scored against, say between 0 and 5. This is repeated over the whole matrix. Second, a fixed number of points can be awarded for each criterion (row or column) and these are distributed between the elements in that row or column in relation to their perceived importance. Third, a fixed number of points is allowed for the entire matrix, and these points must be distributed between both elements and criteria as participants decide. It is debatable whether a better comparative analysis can be achieved through closed or free scoring. Free scoring has the advantage that elements and criteria which are particularly important can be expressed as such, whereas those with little importance will be scored appropriately. Closed scoring has the benefit of being restricted, and thus potentially more comparable between rows and columns. However, this type of comparison is nearly always invalid due to variation in the relative importance of criteria (Jones 1996).

- You can choose either free scoring or closed scoring. It depends on the purpose. Make clear to participants the methods of scoring. Suppose, you opt for a fixed scoring on a 1–5 scale.

Consider each criterion against the item and facilitate the participants to give a score to each of the items in such a way that the item scoring high for that particular criterion gets high scores and others get low scores depending on the magnitude in the range 5 (highest) and 1 (lowest). Ask the participants to record the score in the relevant cell using locally available materials such as seeds, pebbles, flowers and charcoal.

- Move on to the next item or object and keep repeating till all the objects and criteria are covered (see Table 15.2).

Table 15.2
Matrix Scoring of Cotton Varieties

Variety / Criterion	Cotton Varieties		
	Karunganni	Lakshmi	LRA 5166
Duration	X X X X X X X	X X X X X	X X X X
Bolls/plants	X X X X X X X X X X X X X X X X X X X X X X X X X X X X X X X X X X X	X X X X X X X X X X	X X X X X X X X X X X X X X X X X X X X X
Boll weight	X X X	X X X X X	X X X X X X X X X
Pest resistance	X X X X X	X	X X
Response to manuring	X X	X X X	X X X X X
Ease of boll picking	X	X X X	X X X X X
Possibility of inter-cropping	X	X	X X X
Pesticide use	–	X	X X X
Yield	X	X X	X X X X
Net return	X	X X X	X X X X
Overall rating	3	2	1

Source: Vijayraghavan et al. (1992).
Notes: (i) Free scoring has been adopted.
  (ii) Low score means worst; high score means best.

- While deciding on scoring, the participants normally discuss, debate and decide. Listen to what they discuss, as it would provide a great deal of valuable information.
- On completion of the matrix scoring, ask participants to explain the matrix in detail. Ask them to draw inferences from the matrix.
- Interview the matrix.
- Copy the matrix on a sheet of paper with all the details.

Direct Ranking (Preference)

The procedure is comparatively simple:

- Choose a set of problems or preferences to be prioritised. These could be, for example, general problems of the community, preferences for tree species or sources of credit.
- Draw a matrix on the ground and write the items to be prioritised in the rows. Write the name of the key informants in the column.
- Ask the key informant to give his/her favoured item in the set in the order of priority.
- Repeat these for several key informants.
- Record the responses of each key informant in the matrix against his name.
- Calculate the total scores and assign the rank.
- The item with the highest score would get the first rank and item with the lowest score would get the lowest rank (see Table 15.3).

Table 15.3
Direct Ranking: Problems' Prioritisation by Scheduled Castes

Problem	Phool Das	Bhadu Das	Shiv Das	Ram Lal	Chachru	Kamal Das	Ratan Das	Baldev	Bhagwan Das	Total	Rank
Lack of non-farm livelihood opportunities	9	9	9	9	–	10	10	10	10	76	II
Soil erosion	8	8	10	8	–	9	8	8	7	66	III
Lack of raw material for blacksmiths/ carpenters	6	–	7	–	10	2	5	5	5	40	X
Lack of training in rearing of sheep/goats and other livestock	9	10	8	10	9	10	10	7	8	81	I
Lack of training in piggery/ poultry	10	–	9	7	–	8	8	8	7	57	VII
Discrimination against SCs	10	7	8	6	–	8	6	7	8	60	V
Uncultivable land	9	6	7	5	–	7	10	10	10	64	IV
Problem of a knitting centre	8	–	9	–	–	6	8	8	7	46	IX
Lack of electricity	8	5	6	4	–	5	10	10	10	58	VI
Non-availability of horticultural plants	9	–	8	3	–	6	5	8	8	47	VIII

Other Matrices

Matrices can be used to identify and rank the priorities or the problems in a group using a simple set of criteria. It helps to gain a historical perspective on the problems. It also helps to assess the impact of such problem from the point of view of those involved. The procedure to be followed is given here:

- Brainstorm a list of problems that are on the agenda of the groups involved or drawn from problems already identified in a participatory way.
- Write each problem on a separate card.
- Develop criteria with the group for categorising each of the problems. The problems may be categorised as 'most serious', 'serious' and 'less serious'. The criteria should include the number of people affected, severity of the consequences, frequency, etc. Write the list of criteria on a flip chart or paper.
- Referring to these criteria, ask the participants to sort the problem cards into three categories. With the codes ('MS' for most serious, 'S' for the serious and 'LS' for the less serious) scribbled on the back of each card, arrange them into three different groups.
- Decide together on the period over which you will measure changes—whether, for example, it is for two years, five years or ten years. Ask the participants to think whether during this time period, each problem has become 'worse', 'remained the same' or has become 'better'. Sort the cards into three groups. Write codes on the back of each card according to the change in category: 'W' for worse, 'S' for same and 'B' for better.
- Make a matrix. Label the rows as 'becoming worse', 'remaining the same' and 'becoming better'. Label the columns as 'most serious', 'serious' and 'less serious' (see Table 15.4).
- Interview the matrix and probe further by asking the following questions:

  - Why are certain problems getting worse?
  - Why are some problems improving?
  - What role does the government play on this?
  - What other powerful actors have influenced the changes?
  - What roles have citizens and organisations played in these changes?
  - Are the most serious problems getting better or worse?
  - What can the people and the government do to change this?

Table 15.4
Matrix of Problem Classification

	Most Serious	Serious	Less Serious
Becoming worse	• Female infanticide • Child labour • Child marriage	• Malnutrition • Hunger	• Problem of the aged
Remaining the same	• Domestic violence	• Unemployment • Corruption	• No training opportunities
Becoming better	• Untouchability	• Sanitation • Literacy	• Lack of transport

- Record answers to the questions as it would provide a valuable insight while formulating a plan to solve the problems.
- Copy the matrix on a sheet of paper with all the details, including those of the participants.

Hundred-seeds Scoring Technique

This is a sort of 'closed' scoring method. It can be used to prioritise the problems or preferences or rank the criteria. It can be done either in groups or among individuals. The procedure is as follows:

- Decide upon the theme.
- Ask the participants to list the problems or items to be prioritised.
- Write the problems on cards, use one card for each problem. It would be better to present it visually, especially in a gathering of a large number of illiterates.
- Arrange the cards vertically.
- Distribute 100 seeds, beans or pebbles to the participants.
- Explain how to distribute these 100 seeds to various problems identified. The most serious problem would get more seeds, the next serious problem would get less seeds and the least serious problem would get the least number of seeds.
- Now hand over the stick to the participants. Let them discuss, decide and distribute the seeds.
- Observe how they distribute. Listen to what do they discuss before they decide.
- Interview the diagram or table.
- Copy the output with all details.

Dos

- Be clear about the method of ranking or scoring.
- Ensure that the participants agree upon the criteria for ranking.
- Interview the matrix and probe further.

Don'ts

- Do not mix positive and negative criteria.
- Do not impose your criteria on people.

Matrix ranking and scoring have been extensively used under PRA in almost all the contexts. Areas of application of matrix include the following:

- Water preference ranking of different sources, for domestic or irrigation
- Fuel types, preference and problems and comparison of urban and rural
- Food type, preference for sources, access, problems, preference for use
- Income generation, preference for activity and problem
- Educational issues, literacy
- Project preferences, priorities, interventions
- Institutions, service provision
- Livestock preferences, fodder types, diseases, etc.
- Agriculture, soil types, production problems, species, variety, trial performance, pest damage, etc.
- Forestry, species, preference, advantages, disadvantages, utility, varieties, forest products, medicines, utility management system, inventory, etc.
- Local problems and opportunities
- Healthcare providers and diseases
- Types of illness vs access and utilisation
- Scoring characteristics of health providers
- Scoring characteristics or effectiveness of types of treatment by type of illness
- Characteristics of diseases
- Gender issues

We now present certain applications in detail with illustrations for better understanding.

Institutional Analysis

Matrix scoring enables to attempt institutional analysis based on multiple indicators. The procedure is as follows:

- Ask participants to list different institutions in the community.
- Place them along the first column of the matrix.
- Ask the group to discuss the basis on which they differentiate among these institutions. Ask the following questions:

  - How do you rate the effectiveness of these institutions?
  - What factors do you consider to judge effectiveness?

- Facilitate the people to generate their own criteria.

- Ask the group to give scores for all the institutions in the list against each of the selected criteria.
- Calculate the total score for each institution.
- Rank the institution based on the score (see Table 15.5).
- On completion of the exercise, ask why one institution is perceived to be more important than others. This may lead to other criteria that are not listed in the matrix.

Table 15.5
Matrix Scoring and Ranking of Institutions

Criterion / Institution	Effective Service (50)	Easy Accessibility (50)	Trust (50)	Friendly Approach (50)	Timely Help (50)	Total Score (250)	Rank
SHG	45	50	45	50	40	230	1
Cooperative bank	30	25	40	20	40	155	5
Commercial bank	35	20	40	15	35	145	7
Moneylender	25	40	15	25	45	150	6
Panchayat	35	35	30	45	15	160	4
School	20	30	30	10	30	120	8
Pre-school	35	40	45	35	40	195	2
Health centre	15	20	25	30	10	100	9
Village headman	35	30	30	35	40	170	3

Source: World Bank (1999).
Notes: (i) Each criteria is scored against 50.
(ii) Higher the score, better the performance of the institution.

Reproductive Health

Matrix scoring techniques can be used in reproductive health programmes. For instance, the sources of information regarding reproductive health and the preference for the sources based on the criteria can be ascertained using 'matrix scoring technique'. It can be employed among different age groups. An illustration from Nigeria where matrix scoring was employed in a school to ascertain the sources of information and reasons for preferences is given in Table 15.6. The steps followed were (i) selection of participants; (ii) identification of sources of information; (iii) evolving the criteria for preference of sources; (iv) giving the score for each source against the criteria evolved; and (v) summation of score and ranking.

Analysis of Access and Control over Resources

Common property resources in a village are of several uses to the people. They provide livelihood opportunities to many poor households. However, all of them do not have access and control over resources. There are certain restrictions on making use of common property resources based on caste and gender. In other words, certain caste groups do not have access and control over common property resources. In order to assess the extent of access and control over resources for different caste groups in a village, matrix scoring technique can be used. The steps are: (*i*) identification of common property resources; (*ii*) listing the various caste groups; and (*iii*) ascertaining the extent of access to resources and extent of control. It would be better if the exercise is conducted after establishing a rapport with the people (see Table 15.7).

Table 15.6
Matrix Scoring with Secondary School Girls at Nurudeen Grammar School, Ogbomoso

Factor \ Source	Female Teachers	Male Teachers	Mother	Father	Doctor	Friend
Knowledge	✿✿✿	✿	✿✿	✿	✿✿✿✿✿ ✿	✿
Familiarity	✿✿✿	✿	✿✿✿✿✿ ✿	✿✿	✿	✿
Secrecy	✿	✿✿	✿✿✿✿✿	✿✿	✿✿✿	✿✿
Friendliness	✿	✿	✿✿✿✿✿	✿✿✿✿✿		✿✿✿
Proximity	✿✿✿✿	✿	✿✿✿✿✿	✿✿✿		✿✿
Total	12	6	23	13	10	9

Source: Ishola et al. (2003).

Table 15.7
Access and Control over Common Resources

Resource \ Community	Thevar Community	Other Caste Groups (Carpenter, Dhobi, Barber)	Scheduled Caste
Pond	Δ	Δ Δ Δ	Δ
Tank	Δ	Δ	
Tamarind trees	Δ	Δ Δ Δ	Δ
Well	Δ	Δ Δ Δ	
Temple	Δ	Δ Δ Δ	
Temple (SC)			Δ
Well (SC)			Δ
Borewell	Δ	Δ Δ Δ	
Borewell (SC)			Δ
Nullah	Δ	Δ Δ Δ	
Nullah (SC)			Δ
Cremation ground	Δ	Δ Δ Δ	
Cremation ground (SC)			Δ

Source: PRA Unit, GRI (1995d).

Decision-making Matrix

A perception of who makes decisions in the family can help to examine decision-making patterns in the family and help to ascertain gender relations and equality in a community. The decision-making matrix can be attempted on (*i*) decision making over assets; (*ii*) responsibility for family needs; (*iii*) decision making about child-bearing; and (*iv*) decision making about short-term and long-term household development works in the family.

We would briefly state the procedure for decision-making matrix in the household development case. (*i*) Ask the group to list the different types of short-term and long-term decisions they take regarding household development work. Use objects or drawings to visually represent these items and place them along the vertical axis of the matrix. (*ii*) Make one column for men and another column for women, again using visual representations. (*iii*) Briefly discuss the meaning of the term 'decision making'. Come to a common understanding with regard to the concept. You may also ask the participants to draw on personal experiences to illustrate their definition. (*iv*) Give the group ten beans or seeds or small stones for each category, and ask participants to indicate who makes decisions about each development work. They can use the beans or seeds to show the degree of participation in making decision. For instance, if the women make decisions regarding selection of crops to be grown, the participants can put all the ten beans or seeds against the picture of women in the 'selection of crops to be grown' row. If men and women have equal voice in decision making, participants can put five beans against men and five against women (see Table 15.8).

Table 15.8
Direct Matrix Ranking of Criteria for Vegetables

Criterion \ Vegetable	Pepper	Cabbage	Eggplant	Cauliflower	Tomato	Onion
Continuous production	3	5	1	6	2	4
Production time	–	–	2	–	1	4
	(4.5)	(4.5)		(4.5)		
Production/duration	–	–	1	–	1	4
	(4.5)	(4.5)		(4.5)		
Ease of marketing	4	5	3	6	1	2
Consumption by farmer	4	5	3	6	2	1
Ease of transport	4	1	5	1	1	6
		(2)		(2)	(2)	
Pest resistance	1	6	2	5	4	3
Nursery size	3	3	1	3	2	3
	(4.5)	(4.5)		(4.5)		(4.5)
Transplant labour	5	2	1	2	2	6
		(3)		(3)	(3)	
Harvest labour	3	1	3	1	3	6
	(4)	(1.5)	(4)	(1.5)	(4)	
Original score	27	28	24	30	20	32
Current score	42.5	41	25	43	23	42.5

Source: Fielding et al. (1998).
Notes: No score given by farmer.
Values in brackets show rankings that should be used where there are equal preferences.

COMPLEMENTARITY WITH OTHER METHODS

Matrix ranking and scoring can be effectively used in combination with other methods. In some cases, matrix ranking can either precede or succeed other methods. For instance, 'transect walk' through the fields and observation of various crops and irrigation sources can lead to preference ranking of crops or irrigation sources. Alternatively, a transect can follow on from ranking in order to verify the different species on land-use practices. Problem prioritisation using matrix ranking or scoring may lead to the practice of a series of PRA tools like social mapping to analyse the problems in depth. Alternatively, social maps help in the identification of various problems, which may lead to the prioritisation of problems. Ranking exercise can supplement or complement the survey method. For instance, nutrition survey can be complemented or supplemented by preference ranking and scoring and decision-making matrix.

MERITS

- The matrix ranking and scoring and other forms of matrices are, by and large, easy to understand and practice. After the facilitator's input in the initial stage, the participants slowly take over. It is thus self-sustaining.
- It has wide applications. It can be practised in almost all the contexts.
- The exercise provides a vast scope for using locally available materials and thus the participation of even the illiterates can be ensured.
- It can be conducted among different types of participants. For instance, it can be conducted separately among men and women, among different caste groups, among different wealth groups and results be compared. Such an analysis provides a broad perspective of the issue being studied.
- It has a good scope for improvisation in terms of material, purpose and further analysis. Matrix categories can be broken down into details. For example, a matrix for analysis of sources of fuel may compare different types, including firewood. A second matrix could examine different species used for fuel purposes.
- The method can also act as a strong stimulant for discussion.
- The method also helps in triangulation of information. Ranking and scoring exercises are rarely carried out in isolation, so the information received from other related exercises can be used for triangulation.

LIMITATIONS

Matrix ranking and scoring do suffer from certain limitations. They are listed as follows:

- Problems of comparability may arise if items compared are from complementary niches, not competitive ones. Different cereals may be chosen at different times not because they have a better taste or high nutritional value, but because they are available at different times. Two crops may grow on different soil types and the choice of planting is determined not by market factors or preference but by practicality. It is therefore important that the matrix is not used in isolation and these factors are fully discussed.
- The facilitators do not always know what to do when the participants cannot decide which of the two items they prefer.
- Scores from columns or rows are often summed. This may be misleading unless the significance of different criteria is clearly understood.
- Some facilitators may be wary of placing analytical emphasis on matrices. If some of the criteria are missed out, the matrix may not help in effective planning.
- Facilitators may sometimes choose the literate people in the community and ask them to write the names of the elements and the criteria into the matrix. Of course, they do follow the principle of handing over the stick but to the educated section of the population only.
- Facilitators have a tendency to push their own criteria onto the participating villagers. It would be appropriate if such criteria were indicated separately.

PRECAUTIONS

The technique of matrix ranking among other alternatives must be used with caution (Ashby 1990). The limitations in matrix ranking and scoring can be overcome if facilitators are cautious in doing ranking exercises. The facilitators have to keep in mind the following points to overcome the limitations:

- The facilitator has to prepare an exhaustive list of criteria. Carrying out preference ranking based on an incomplete list of criteria will give faulty information (Fielding et al. 1998).
- When equal preference occurs, an average score must be given, of the score which would have been allocated to those items if they had not been considered equal. When a person gives two items the same preference, the average rank for the two items must be given. Thus, if a farmer considers two crops as equally best, they do not get a rank of 1 each, instead they get $(1+2)/2$ or 1.5 each (Fielding et al. 1998) (see Table 15.8).
- Negative and positive criteria should never be mixed. The negative ones should be converted into positive ones, or vice versa, before starting the analysis.

- Facilitators and participants should be quite clear on what method of ranking or scoring is being used. This would make the practice of exercise smooth, and confusions, if any, can be avoided.
- The participants should agree upon the criteria, which should be clear and unambiguous.
- The items ranked must be considered carefully. Are the criteria irrelevant? Should the poorest score have been given to that item? Finding an answer to these questions would help solve the problem.
- The facilitators should adapt the exercise to the requirements of the study and the environment. He/she should also make sure to get the perspective of the people on any ranking process he or she undertakes.

·Summary

Matrix ranking and scoring are employed in varied contexts. It is employed to ascertain the preference, tasks, priorities and choice of the people and reason behind preferences. Ranking is putting something in order while scoring is related to the weight given to different items.

The exercise can be conducted in groups or among individuals. Groups would be better as it would provide the preference and choices of the community, and the criteria for the choices would also be broad-based.

The procedure for drawing a matrix ranking is simple. However, the facilitator has to ensure that the criteria for ranking and scoring are evolved internally. While scoring, the participant may resort to either 'free scoring' or 'closed scoring'. Depending on the situation, the type of scoring can be decided.

The matrix ranking and scoring are now being widely employed. They are being used in almost all fields, such as institutional analysis, leadership assessment, reproductive health, methods of learning and teaching, access and control over resources, decision making and evaluation of projects.

The merits of these methods are that they (*i*) are simple to practise and easy to understand, (*ii*) can serve as stimulant for discussion and (*iii*) can be used as appraisal, planning and evaluation tools.

The limitations are that (*i*) the facilitator is likely to impose his/her own criteria and (*ii*) no further probe might be carried out after the matrix is drawn.

16
Force Field Analysis

'Force field analysis' (FFA), a technique developed by sociologist Kurt Lewin, is employed to identify and analyse the forces affecting a problem situation so as to bring about a change (Lewin 1951). According to him, whenever there is a need or proposal for changes, there are some forces of resistance. They are also known as restraining, inhibiting, discouraging or hindering forces. They are negative, emotional, illogical, unconscious, social and psychological in nature. Similarly, there may be in a given situation certain adoptive forces which are supportive to change. They are referred to as driving or inducing or encouraging or helping forces. These forces, by and large, are positive, reasonable, logical, conscious and economic in nature.

In the first step, both these kinds of forces are identified and isolated. In the second step, a measure or value is assigned to each of these forces. Positive values are assigned to the forces that support the change and negative values to the forces that resist or retard the change. In the third step, the value of the forces for the changes, the value of the forces against the changes and the resultant forces 'for' or 'against' the changes is computed (see Figure 16.1 and Table 16.1).

The above analysis of forces and their qualitative presentation is somewhat notional and is bound to include a certain measure of value judgement.

Let us consider the example of a self-help group (SHG). There is a certain climate in the group, a certain level of positive or negative interaction of feeling safe or unsafe in expressing feelings or talking about concerns of respect or disrespect in communication among members of the group. We may really want to change that level. We may desire to create a climate that is more positive, more respectful, more open and more trusting. The logical reasons for this are the driving forces that act to raise the level. Such forces may be in the form of homogeneity among members, a desire to work together, a desire to promote economic well-being, a desire to get connected to external environment, etc.

Figure 16.1
Force Field Analysis

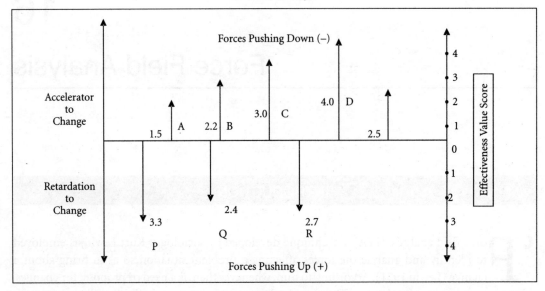

Source: Banerjee (1981).

Table 16.1
Table of Forces

Forces against changes	A	B	C	D	E	Total
Values (−)	1.5	2.2	3.0	4.0	2.5	13.2
Forces for changes	P	Q	R			
Values (+)	3.3	2.4	2.7			8.4
Resultant forces against change (−)						4.8

Source: Banerjee (1981).

Further, increasing the driving forces is just not enough since our efforts are opposed by restricting forces. For instance, members of the group may not be open-minded and may exhibit casteism; a few may even tend to dominate. Increasing the driving forces may bring results for just a while. But as long as the restraining forces are there, it becomes increasingly harder to bring the changes. Hence, in order to reach the desired level, it would be advisable to increase the helping forces and simultaneously weaken the hindering forces.

PROCEDURE

FFA is used in PRA with the main aim of setting the goals based on the analysis of the current situation. This technique, therefore, should be used with the groups that have already been facilitated to analyse their situation. The steps to be followed in practising this technique in the field are as follows:

- Select a group of people who work in more or less a similar situation and share a common problem. The size of the group should be small varying from three to five. If the group is larger, we may divide them into smaller groups and ask them to work separately. The outcome can be shared among the groups in a plenary session.
- Create an atmosphere in which the participants freely interact. Unfreeze them. Loosen them up.
- Explain the purpose of the exercise. Make sure that the participants are fully aware of the purpose and the method of carrying out the exercise.
- Ask people to define the present situation and problem, and the major goal or the change they want. Facilitate them to write one summary statement about the present situation and goal. The goal or change should as far as possible be in quantitative terms.
- Ask the group to write or diagram the present situation and the goal either on the ground or on the paper. Ask the participants to concentrate on the problem situation written or depicted. Ask them to visualise the problem situation in a state of temporary equilibrium by two sets of opposing forces, namely, driving forces and restraining forces. Use the exhibit to explain the concept (see Figure 16.2).

Figure 16.2
Force Field Analysis: An Illustration

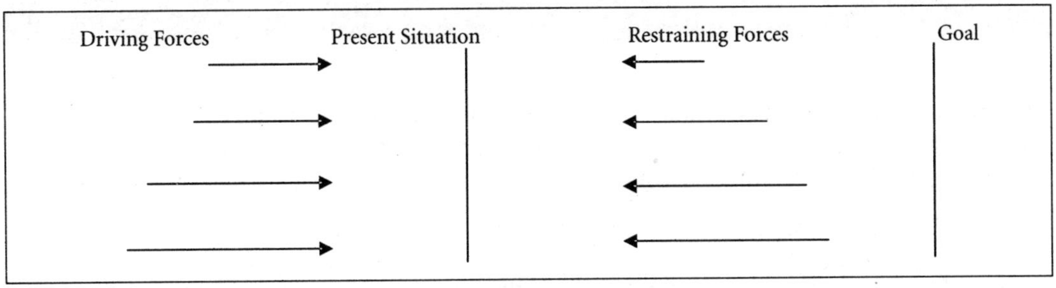

Source: Hope and Timmel (1992).

- Ask the participants to list the helping forces on the left side. The participants may be facilitated to write each helping force on a small card and to draw shorter or longer arrows to indicate the strength of the forces which are pushing the present situation towards the goal. Facilitate the participants to list the hindering or restraining forces which prevent change or reduce its power. Ask the participants to write down each of the restraining forces on a card. Again use longer or shorter arrows to indicate the strength of the forces.

- Explain that one can gradually move towards the goal either by strengthening the helping forces or by weakening the hindering forces. Create new insights that actually transform these restraining forces into driving ones. Sometimes pressure from helping forces may result in development of resistance in restraining forces. In such cases it is better to start by reducing restraining forces. This is possible to a certain extent by involving them in the problem, immersing them in it and making them feel it as their problem. They would then tend to become an important part of the solution.
- Facilitate the group to choose any one of the helping forces they could strengthen or one of the hindering forces, which they could reduce or weaken. Taking this force as the new situation, ask them to identify their goal in regard to working with this force.
- Facilitate the participants using brainstorming technique to have a detailed analysis and key probe. Use smaller cards to write down possible interventions for each of the driving or restraining forces so as to increase or reduce their magnitude, respectively.
- Draw a new diagram, again listing the helping and hindering forces related to their new sub-goal. This process can be repeated two or three times.
- On completion of the exercise, ask the participants to copy the diagram onto newsprint (paper) with details of the date, location, participants from the village, facilitators and legends containing the details of the scoring system and the symbols used (see Figure 16.3).
- The procedure outlined is only indicative and suggestive and not exhaustive and prescriptive. Always follow the golden rule, 'Use your own best judgment in all circumstances'.

ASSIGNMENT OF WEIGHTS TO FORCES

The strength of the forces is indicated by the size of the arrow. The longer the arrow, the greater is the effect of the force; the shorter the arrow, the lesser the effect of the force. We may also think of assigning weight to the forces depending on the nature and type of participants. We discuss a few of the techniques here.

- Hundred-seed scoring technique: Under this method, ask the participants to list as many driving forces and restraining forces as possible. Ask them to write each 'force' on a card. Give them 100 seeds and ask them to distribute the seeds among various driving forces based on effect of each force on the present situation and the desired goals. A driving force which has a greater effect on the 'situation' and 'goal' would be assigned greater number of seeds and the force which has lesser effect on the 'situation' and 'goal' would be assigned

Figure 16.3
Force Field Analysis: Ariankundru Village

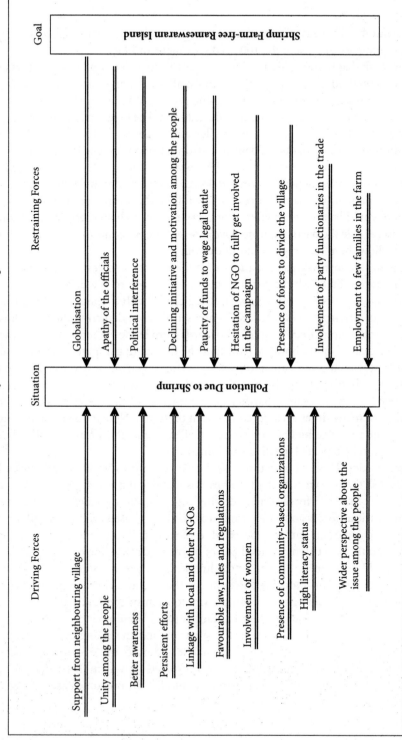

Source: Narayanasamy and Manivel (2002).

lesser number of seeds. The participants are to be adequately explained about the purpose of assigning 'weight' using the 100-seed scoring technique.

- Using Venn diagram to assign weight: Under this method, similar to what was stated in the previous method, ask the participants to list all the driving forces that help in realising the goal, and restraining forces that hinder the process of realising the goal. Ask them to write each force on a card. Keep circles of different sizes. The bigger circle represents greater effect on present situation or goal. The smaller circle represents less effect on goal or present situation. Ask participants to identify a strong driving force and facilitate them to put its card in a bigger circle. The process can be repeated till all the identified driving forces are put into various circles, depending on the degree of effect of each driving force on the desired situation or goal. The same process can be followed for ranking the restraining forces. The ground would be the best medium for carrying out such an exercise. After completing the exercise, enable the participants to have a look at the outcome of the exercise and if they feel like it, allow them to carry out modifications.

- Pair-wise ranking: Ask participants to list the driving and restraining forces. Take up the driving forces first. Ask the participants to write each of the driving forces in two cards. Draw a grid or matrix on the ground using chalks with as many rows and columns as the number of driving forces listed. Keep one set of cards depicting the problems in the grid from top to bottom. Keep another set of cards from left to right on the top in the same order as in the case of top to bottom. Now take the first card; compare with the other forces one by one listed on the new card and ask them to say which one is stronger. Record the progress in the matrix by putting the 'force' symbol, abbreviations or serial number of the force preference in the relevant cell. After the completion of the exercise, ask the participants to count how many times each 'force' has been preferred. Note it down against the item at the end of the row. The higher the frequency of the force, the stronger is the force. The same exercise can be repeated for the restraining forces.

- Direct ranking: Under this method, ask the participants to list all the 'driving and restraining forces'. Ask them to write each of the forces under driving or restraining forces in a card. Use different colours for forces under 'driving' and 'restraining' categories. Ask participants to discuss various forces and assign ranks to each force, based on the strength of the force.

- Scoring: The participants may be asked to identify the inducing and inhibiting forces. The forces should be written on small pieces of cards. Draw a line on the ground with a piece of chalk. Place a sheet of paper on the line with the present status of the situation written on it. Place cards on inducing forces above the line and cards on inhibiting forces below the line. Ask participants to assign a score to each of the forces by placing seeds on the cards. The maximum score is ten for each force. The number of seeds denotes the extent of the effect of the given force on the situation and the change. After the completion of exercise, facilitate the participants to analyse the outcome. Scoring with seeds helps the illiterate and unlettered participants to get involved actively in the exercise. It also provides space for flexibility, and the participants can modify the outcome based on this analysis and reflection.

APPLICATION

FFA has wide applications. It is used in diverse contexts ranging from organisational change to development. Following are the steps to be taken: (*i*) identify the forces responsible for the present status of any aspect, (*ii*) analyse how the situation has been changed and (*iii*) arrive at a plan for change. We now discuss a few areas of application of FFA.

Family Level

FFA can be used to assess the encouraging and discouraging factors of a family living in poverty to come out of that state. A detailed analysis of the forces that encourage a poor family to come out of poverty and the factors that discourage the family to extricate itself from poverty would help in designing an appropriate strategy for poverty alleviation.

CBO Level

FFA can be applied in CBOs for organisational change and development. It would help the CBOs in assessing their present condition or situation, their future role and goals, the factors that would help them in achieving the goals, the factors that would restrain them in achieving the goal and steps to be taken to overcome the restraining forces. It would also serve as a guidepost and enable them to ascertain what they should start doing and what they should stop doing for reaching the desired destination.

Village Level

The method along with other PRA methods can be effectively used to prepare a micro-plan for a village. An important step in the preparation of a micro-plan is ascertaining the vision of the community. In any micro-plan prepared, the activities envisaged should reflect the vision of the community, which would help to set the major goal. The goal should be realistic, should emerge from the people and should be attainable within a reasonable period of time.

The preparation of a micro-plan involves an appraisal of the existing situation or condition, identification of problems and priorities, setting the goal, designing of activities, choosing appropriate strategies, etc. Appraisal and analysis using a battery of PRA methods would help in ascertaining the existing situation. Using FFA, the participants can fix the major goal. It is not an easy task. FFA needs to be conducted among different age groups, social groups, sexes, occupational groups and economic groups to gauge the aspirations of different sections of the community and to meaningfully formulate the goal. It is a tedious task, but has to be done very systematically so as to ensure the integration of the aspiration of different categories of people into the goal. It stimulates a process of intense communication in the group and helps them to work out a strategy involving one or more sub-goals which will be a concrete step towards the major goal (see Figure 16.4).

Figure 16.4
Force Field Analysis: Adidravidar Colony

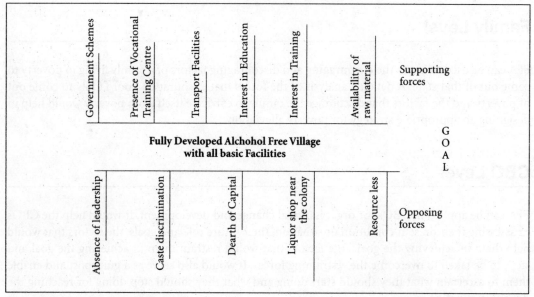

Source: Narayanasamy and Manivel (2002).

Institutional Level

The technique can also be used to analyse the current situation of the formal institutions, such as school, cooperatives, panchayat, health centre and other institutions. Such an analysis would enable them to know their present conditions, the changes that they want to introduce, and the helping and hindering forces in moving towards the change. It would open up new avenues for organisational change and development.

Individual Level

The technique could be applied at the individual level too. For instance, the performance of the students could be analysed using this technique. The students in a rural school may be categorised as highly performing students, moderately performing students and poorly performing students, based on their performance in the tests. FFA can be applied within each category of students to assess the present situation, the inducing forces in reaching the desired level and the inhibiting forces that affect the realisation of desired level. This could help the teachers to design an appropriate strategy, especially for the 'poor' and 'moderately' performing students, in order to achieve desired results.

Monitoring and Evaluation

FFA can also be used as a monitoring and evaluation tool. Analysis and presentation of data and information on the present situation, desired situation and driving and restraining forces provide a sort of benchmark. In other words, they would serve as baseline information. Once the activities are initiated towards achieving the goal or desired situation, the outcome of the activities carried out can be compared with baseline data and information. This would help in ascertaining the deviations, if any, between the planned outcome and actual outcome. Periodic monitoring would help in narrowing down the deviations and achieving the desired situation or goal.

COMPLEMENTARITY WITH OTHER METHODS

PRA methods provide scope for improvisation and complementarity. FFA complements other PRA methods and vice versa. For instance, a transect-based resource map may reveal a problem situation like soil erosion, declining groundwater and reduction in common property resources (CPRs). FFA may be used further to facilitate the participants in discussing the causes of problems, arriving at a solution and identifying driving and restraining forces in realising the solution. Here, FFA complements other PRA methods. To rank the forces, as described earlier, the scoring and ranking method can be used. Other PRA methods complement the FFA.

MERITS

FFA has been added in the menu of methods of PRA only recently, though it has wider applications. Richard Montgomery reported the first instance of application of FFA in PRA in 1995. Somesh Kumar (1999) has extensively used this technique in various locations for varied purposes. The author of this book has used this technique for a project called Preparation of Micro-plan for Mandapam Block in Rameswaram (2003). The merits of the method may be briefly stated as follows:

- The participants in the exercise are motivated to think about the present situation in which they live, the changes they want, the forces—both inducing and inhibiting—that help or retard in achieving the change. This adds tremendous lucidity to the field of change and the issues at stake. It facilitates the people to develop vision and goal.
- The exercise is visual in nature. It allows the use of symbols and visual depiction. The present situation and the forces are quantified and presented for analysis. The visual nature of the exercise enables even the illiterate participants to contribute. Further, the diagram depicted on newsprint or ground provides a vast scope for further discussion, analysis and decision. It also helps in modifying the forces based on further analysis.
- Assigning measures of value (positive and negative) to these forces throws light on the mechanics of effective change, the steps required and their priorities.
- It is a simple exercise. It is also easy to practice. Locally available materials can be used. Flexible use of materials, such as cards, seeds and pebbles, permits to make modifications, additions and deletions without extra efforts. This, in turn, improves the quality of output and discussion.
- It provides a clear signal for the participants and the facilitators on what to do next in order to bring about a desirable change in the situation. It makes them think ahead, plan and act.

LIMITATIONS

- The method is likely to become facilitator-driven if adequate precautions are not taken. Precautions to be taken would include explaining the exercise, facilitating them to carry out the exercise and a liberal use of visuals.
- The facilitators may sometimes skip the discussion and rush to complete the exercise. The focus here is on the output and not on the process. As a result, the facilitators are likely to lose a lot of valuable information. The output in such a case may not truly reflect the voice of the participants.
- It is little bit difficult to practise this exercise among the illiterate participants. Hence, it is advisable to use symbols and visuals among such participants.

The limitations cited are not with the method but with the facilitators. These limitations could be easily overcome if the facilitators follow the basic tenets of PRA, which include: (*i*) do not rush; (*ii*) do not dominate; (*iii*) do not lecture; (*iv*) listen and learn; and (*v*) hand over the stick.

SUMMARY

FFA is a planning exercise mostly employed to locate and analyse the inducing and inhibiting forces affecting a problem situation, to bring about a positive change. The steps to be followed in the exercise are: (*i*) ask the participants to define the present situation and the major goals in quantifiable terms; (*ii*) enable them to identify the driving and restraining forces; (*iii*) facilitate these to ascertain the extent of effect of each force on the present situation and the desired situation; (*iv*) enable the participants to assign weight to each force based on the extent of its effect or influence on the present and desired situation; (*v*) guide the participants to think about the possible interventions that would weaken the restraining forces and strengthen the inducing forces; (*vi*) repeat the exercise for addition and deletion, if any; and (*vii*) share the outcome of the exercise with a wider audience for validation.

FFA has been improvised and applied in several contexts. The prominent areas of application include micro-plan, education, self-analysis, monitoring and evaluation.

FFA is complementary in nature. It can effectively complement PRA methods like 'transect', 'resource map' and 'social map'. Similarly, PRA methods like 'ranking' and 'scoring' can complement FFA.

The merits of FFA are that (*i*) it facilitates the people to develop vision and goal; (*ii*) it is simple and easy to practise; (*iii*) the visual nature of the exercise enables active participation of the people; and (*iv*) it also enables participants to think ahead, plan and act. A significant limitation of the method is that it is likely to become facilitator-driven, with focus on the output rather than on the process.

17

SWOT Analysis

INTRODUCTION

Participatory rural appraisal (PRA) methods are used to appraise and analyse the existing situations and conditions in rural areas and to plan and initiate action to improve the conditions of the people. Closely associated with the development of rural life is the functioning of various institutions and organisations (formal and informal) in various walks of life, namely, economic, social, political, educational, cultural, etc. The functioning and growth of institutions and organisations are subject to the influence of internal and external factors. For instance, the functioning of a village cooperative, a rural economic organisation, is influenced by internal and external factors. Similarly, the functioning and growth of a self-help group (SHG), a socio-economic organisation, is very much influenced by external and internal forces. Any development activity in the rural areas should, therefore, involve a careful study of various organisations in terms of their strengths, weaknesses, opportunities and threats (SWOT).

Further, such organisations in rural areas with an aim of promoting the overall socio-economic and political interests of the members need to have a long-term strategic plan. There are tools in PRA which help formulate plans. In the last chapter, we discussed force field analysis (FFA), which has been used to assess the supporting and opposing forces affecting a problem situation so as to bring about a change. SWOT is one such technique. It has been borrowed from management discipline. It has been used as a strategic planning tool. It identifies and evaluates the internal and external factors that are favourable or unfavourable to achieve the given objectives.

MEANING

SWOT analysis is a management technique. The technique is credited to Albert Humphrey who led a research project at Stanford University in the 1960s and 1970s using data from Fortune 500 companies. It is a strategic planning tool used to evaluate the strengths, weaknesses, opportunities and threats in a project or a business venture. It involves specifying the objectives of the business venture or project and identifying the internal and external factors that are favourable and unfavourable to achieving that objective. It is used to develop a plan that takes into consideration many different internal and external factors and maximises the potential of the strengths and opportunities, while minimising the impact of weaknesses and threats.

The first letter in SWOT stands for strengths. Strengths describe the positive attributes— tangible and intangible. Strengths arise from the resources and competencies available to an organisation. They include positive attributes of the people in an organisation, including their knowledge, background, education, credentials, contacts, reputations or the skills they bring to the job. They also include tangible assets, such as capital, equipments, credit, clients, information and processing systems and other valuable resources within the organisation.

'W' in SWOT stands for weaknesses. They are the attributes of the organisation that are harmful to achieving the objective. It is the limitation or deficiency in one or more resources or competencies. Weaknesses might include a lack of expertise, limited resources, a lack of access to skills or technology. These are features that are under your control, but for a variety of reasons they are in need of improvement to effectively accomplish the objective.

'O' in SWOT stands for opportunities. They are the external conditions that are helpful in achieving the objective. An opportunity is a major situation in an organisation's environment. Opportunities are everywhere. They are the external attractive forces that represent the reasons for the organisation to exist and prosper.

'T' stands for threats. Threats are the external conditions that are harmful to achieving the objective. A threat is a major unfavourable situation in an organisation's environment. Threats are key impediments to the organisation's current or desired position. The better one is able to identify the potential threats, the more likely one can position oneself to proactively plan for and respond to them.

SWOT is not only used in management field but also in development fields. Even individuals can make use of this tool for taking decisions that affect their lives.

PARTICIPANTS

The participants who undertake this exercise should be those who have a better understanding about their living conditions and their organisations (society, association, group, etc.) and their knowledge on the environment in which the organisations/institutions are functioning. An appropriate mix of all age groups and the participation of men and women makes the exercise rewarding. The type of participants to be involved depends on the context, the situation and type of organisation to be appraised and assessed using SWOT. For instance, an analysis of the functioning of a farmers' association using SWOT requires the participation of members and office-bearers and other stakeholders associated with the organisation. Similarly, an analysis of the working and future plan for a SHG does warrant the participation of members, office-bearers and the promoters of the group and other relevant stakeholders. The number of participants for this exercise may vary from eight to twelve. However, they should be key informants who have actively participated in the activities of the association or organisation and also have a fairly good knowledge on its external environment.

PROCEDURE

- Decide on the institution or organisation, the project that you would like to appraise using SWOT analysis.
- Determine the participants who would be able to effectively participate in the exercise and contribute to the conduct and completion of the exercise.
- Convene a meeting of the participants in a place chosen by them.
- Spend enough time to explain the purpose and the need for carrying out the exercise.
- Explain in detail the technique of SWOT and each term included in SWOT in the local language. Make sure that the participants fully understand the concept of strengths, weaknesses, opportunities and threats.
- Facilitate them to draw the matrix on the ground for carrying out SWOT analysis. The matrix consists of four quadrants. Use a quadrant for analysing strengths, another for weaknesses, the third for opportunities and the fourth for threats (see Table 17.1). Keep enough flash cards to record the strengths, weaknesses, opportunities and threats.

Table 17.1
SWOT Framework

	Positive	Negative
	Strengths	*Weaknesses*
Internal	What do you do well? What unique resources can you draw on? What do others see as your strengths?	What could you improve? Where do you have fewer resources than others? What are others likely to see as your weaknesses?
	Opportunities	*Threats*
External	What good opportunities are open to you? What trends could you take advantage of? How can you turn your strengths into opportunities?	What obstacles do you face? What trends could harm you? What threats do your weaknesses expose you to?

- Ask participants to list out the strengths. Allow them to debate, discuss each strength and come out with the strengths of the organisation. The questions that may be asked to elicit the strengths of the organisation are:

  - What do we do exceptionally well?
  - What advantages do we have?
  - What valuable assets and resources do we have?
  - What do people/stakeholders identify as their strengths?

While appraising the strengths of an organisation/institution, consider from an internal perspective and also from the point of view of outsiders, and be realistic. In looking at the strengths of an organisation, think about the positive factors and forces in relation to the other organisations of a similar nature around. Ask the participants to write in a separate flash card and place it in the appropriate quadrant.

- Ask the participants to list the weaknesses. The possible questions that could be raised to assess the weaknesses are:

  - What could you improve?
  - What should you avoid?
  - What are we criticised for?
  - Where are we vulnerable?

Ask them to consider the weaknesses from an internal and external basis. Ask them to write each weakness in a separate flash card and put it in the relevant quadrant.

- Facilitate the participants to discuss and list the opportunities available for the organisation. The questions that could be raised are:

  - What opportunities do we know about, but have not been able to address?
  - Are there emerging trends on which we can capitalise?

Useful opportunities can come from such things as

- changes in technology and market, both on a broad and narrow scale;
- changes in government policy related to the field;
- changes in social patterns, population profiles, lifestyle changes, etc.; and
- trends in local events.

Encourage them to come out with changes by giving suitable examples and illustrations. Facilitate them to draw opportunities for the organisation from the changes that are happening. Ask the participants to write each opportunity in a separate flash card and put them in a respective quadrant.

- Ask the participants to discuss the threats to the organisation. The questions which are relevant to bring out the threats are:

- What external roadblocks exist that block your progress?
- Are any of your weaknesses likely to make you critically vulnerable?
- Does changing technology threaten your position?

Ask them to have an open and expansive perspective while scanning the threats. Facilitate them to read out the threats once again and finalise them.

- After listing the strengths, weaknesses, opportunities and threats, encourage them to rearrange, rephrase and reword the points if they wish so. Flash cards used will help the participants to revisit, rephrase and rearrange.
- Facilitate the participants to review the SWOT matrix with a view to create an action plan to address each of the four areas. Remind them that

  - strengths need to be maintained and built upon;
  - weaknesses need to be remedied or stopped;
  - opportunities need to be prioritised and optimised;
  - threats need to be countered or minimised.

Dos

- Create an atmosphere in which everyone is free to express his or her own views.
- Encourage the participants to be open in expressing their views.
- Encourage discussions on each and every issue before coming to any conclusion.
- Facilitate the participants to follow logic in their discussion. For example, help them to discuss the internal factors/forces which are positive in nature that can be followed by negative factors/forces.
- Ask the participants to explain sufficiently if there is any problem in understanding the views.

Don'ts

- Don't ask vague questions.
- Don't discourage the participants if you do not understand their views.

APPLICATION

SWOT is a popular tool in profit-seeking organisations. It is now increasingly used in non-profit organisations and government units and by individuals. PRA has included this technique in its menu. Following are the main applications:

- SWOT can be used as a simple icebreaker, helping people get together and 'kick off' strategy formulation. This can be practised in SHGs and activity/programme-specific groups (such as eco-development committee, water and sanitation committee, water-users' association and health committee; see Table 17.2).
- SWOT can be used to analyse the strengths, weaknesses, opportunities and threats of local-level institutions, such as cooperatives, schools, NGOs and community-based organisations (CBOs).
- SWOT analysis may be used in any decision-making situation when a designed end state (objective) has been defined. For example, when the ultimate objective of an SHG is defined, SWOT analysis can be employed to assess the factors that would help realise the objective and the factors that would stand in the way of realising the objectives.
- It can be applied at the individual level too. For instance, it can be applied for understanding strengths and weaknesses of various types of leaders and the opportunities they have and the threats they face. Such an analysis would help the leaders to take best advantage of their talents, abilities and opportunities for the betterment of the organisation or the community they lead.

Table 17.2
SWOT of the SHGs

Strengths	Weaknesses
• Homogeneous membership • Accommodative nature of the members • The spirit of cooperation among the members • Attitude of sharing knowledge and information • Optional savings • Regular meeting of the SHGs • Amicable settlement of issues • Selection of right beneficiaries • Repayment ethics among the members • Financial strength • Good maintenance of accounts	• Poor attendance at times • Over-dependence on project staff • Problem in convening weekly meeting • Need to repeatedly remind the members of the meeting • Tendency to migrate often • Traces of lack of confidence • Tendency to withdraw savings • Illiteracy • Prime motive is availing of loan and project services
Opportunities	Threats
• Good link with banks • Links with women's development corporation • Continued support to the women's development corporation • More number of educated adolescent girls • Potential for more enrolment • Possibilities for extension of production loans • Formation of a federation of SHGs • Growth of SHGs in the surrounding areas • Bank's readiness to provide loans to SHGs for income-generation activities • Strong and active animators • Consistent guidance from the project staff	• Lack of cooperation from men • Corrupt officials • Misguidance from other SHG promoters/NGOs

Source: Narayanasamy and Manivel. (2004).

- SWOT can be used to assess the strengths, opportunities and constraints for initiating micro-enterprises by SHGs. Such an analysis would help in deciding whether the enterprise could be initiated. OUTREACH, an NGO based in Bangalore, has used SWOT analysis among members of the SHGs, to find out the feasibility of promoting an agro-service centre in a village (see Table 17.3).

Table 17.3
SWOT Analysis on Proposed Agro-service Centre

Strengths	*Weaknesses*
• Availability/supply of agricultural inputs on time • Generation of profit for the *sangam* • Development of business skills among the members • Possibility of forming different committees like purchase committee • Creation of good name and goodwill for the *sangam* • Membership with IFAD • Membership in cluster-level association	• Lack of administrative ability among the members • No knowledge in maintenance of accounts • Paucity of working capital • Lack of entrepreneurial skills • Insisting on credit transactions by the members • Failure on the part of the members to make use of the services
Opportunities	*Threats*
• Firming up the linkages with the government departments (agricultural department, etc.) • Timely supply of required inputs to farmers • Reduction in unnecessary expenditure to farmers • Provision of service to farmers in adjoining villages • Ineffective functioning of cooperative agro-service centre • Training in account keeping to members • Problems related to obtaining licence, payment of tax may be solved as the *sangam* is the member of IFAD • Motivating other members of the *sangam* for purchase of inputs from the centre through cluster-level association	• Obtaining licence • Non-cooperation from the people • Natural calamities like excessive/inadequate rainfall • Insistence on credit transaction by the public • Competition from private traders

Source: Narayanasamy and Boraian (2005).

COMPLEMENTARITY WITH OTHER METHODS

SWOT may be used at the end of the appraisal of a situation or condition. Exercises like social mapping, resource mapping, seasonal calendar, Venn diagram, trend analysis and mobility map will provide a fair idea about strengths and opportunities of a given situation or condition and weaknesses and threats of/to a given situation or condition. The inferences drawn and the learning experienced from such exercises are likely to support and supplement the practice of SWOT. This is so because participants of the exercise, both insiders and outsiders, will have a fair idea about the internal as well as external environment. Introduction of SWOT analysis at this stage will enable the facilitator and other members of the team to effectively facilitate the exercise by drawing inferences from various exercises. The participants from inside, that is, the villagers, will have a good knowledge on the strengths, weaknesses, opportunities and threats of/to a given situation or condition. This would help them to carry out the exercise with ease and confidence. Thus, many popular PRA exercises are likely to supplement and complement SWOT analysis.

SWOT and FFA can complement each other as both these are planning tools and deal with the forces that support or retard the realisation of a goal, objective or vision. However, SWOT is more comprehensive in nature as it classifies the factors and forces into internal positive and negative forces and external positive and negative forces. The SWOT analysis is much deeper. The data and information gathered through FFA can also be used to cross-check the information gathered through SWOT.

MERITS

- SWOT is a simple and powerful tool for analysing the strengths, weaknesses, opportunities and threats and to formulate a strategic plan.
- SWOT helps an organisation to see itself for better and for worse.
- Organisations, whether profit-seeking or non-profit-seeking, are insular and inward-looking. SWOT analysis is a means by which an organisation can understand better what it does very well and where its shortcomings are.

LIMITATIONS

- Opportunities external to the organisation/group are often confused with strengths internal to the organisation. They should be kept separate.
- Sometimes SWOT analysis is confused with possible strategies. SWOT is a description of conditions while possible strategies define actions. This error is made with reference to opportunity analysis. To avoid this error, it may be useful to think of opportunities as 'auspicious conditions'.
- SWOT should not exist in the abstract. It can exist only with reference to an objective. If the desired end state is not openly defined and agreed upon, participants may have different end states in mind and the results will be ineffective.

- As it is a simple tool, users of the tool may have a tendency to use it without a great deal of thought. The results under such circumstances are likely to become useless.

SUMMARY

SWOT analysis is a simple but powerful framework for analysing the strengths, weaknesses, opportunities and threats that the organisations are facing.

It is a strategic planning tool. It is used to evaluate the strengths, weaknesses, opportunities and threats in a given situation or condition or those of an organisation. Strengths in SWOT analysis describe tangible and intangible positive attributes like resources and competency available in an organisation. Weaknesses are those attributes of the organisation that are harmful to achieving the objectives. Opportunities are the external conditions. They help in realising the objective of the organisation. Threats are external conditions that stand in the way of achieving the objectives.

The participants for the exercise should be carefully chosen. It depends on the purpose of the exercise. It would be better if the participants are those who have a fairly good knowledge on the environment—both internal and external.

The procedure to be followed is as follows. Facilitate the participants to draw the matrix on the ground. Ask them to list the strengths, weaknesses, opportunities and threats, to record them in flash cards and to place them in respective quadrants. Facilitate them to revisit the matrix and reword, rephrase and rearrange if necessary. Ask them to formulate an action plan based on the analysis. Create an atmosphere where everyone present can meaningfully participate. Ensure that a logical sequence is followed throughout the exercise.

The technique can be applied both at the organisational and at the individual level. All organisations (profit and non-profit) can use the technique. The applications include assessing the strengths, weaknesses, opportunities and threats and strategic planning. All the popular tools in PRA will supplement and support SWOT analysis. FFA can be used as a complementary tool. The merits of the tool are that (*i*) it is simple and powerful and (*ii*) it helps the organisation to evaluate itself. The limitations are that (*i*) opportunities are often confused with strengths; (*ii*) they are also confused with strategies; and (*iii*) the effective practice and the ultimate outcome depend on clear statement of an end state objective.

18
Pie Diagram

A diagram is any simple schematic device which presents information in a readily understandable form. Diagrams are basic to participatory rural appraisal (PRA). They are extensively used in PRA. The reasons are quite obvious. Diagrams can capture and present information in a more precise, clear and succinct way than words. Diagrams are shared information. They can be checked, discussed and amended. They help develop consensus and aid communication between different people and disciplines. The people who are involved in diagramming must continually be asking questions during the process. These questions are mostly open-ended in nature than in a formal survey. This is likely to create a lively discussion. The diagram helps in the development of interview. 'Interviewing the diagram' is often emphasised in PRA. Rural people can easily understand and contribute to the diagram (Pretty 1989b). There are many types of useful diagrams in PRA like maps, transects, seasonal calendars and Venn diagrams. A pie diagram is one such diagram used in PRA.

MEANING

A pie diagram or pie chart uses pictures to compare the sizes, amounts, quantities or proportions of various items or grouping of items. Pie charts make it easier to understand the data because they present data as a picture, allowing the results to stand out. They can generate discussions and information about the proportion of a population or of items, such as land area or income. Pie diagram in other disciplines, as Somesh Kumar (2003) has observed, is used as a tool to present information in a visual form based on factual data. Pie diagram in PRA is employed more as a method to help the local people to arrive at the constituents of a whole and also their proportions. It is not just a presentation tool. Pie diagram in PRA deals with both factual and perceptual data.

PARTICIPANTS

The number and type of participants to be involved in the exercise depend on the context. Supposing, the pie diagram is about farm-related aspects; men and women from the farming community can be involved as participants. In case the discussion is about general aspects of village life (e.g., proportion of people involved in different occupations), mixed groups can be considered. Supposing, the pie diagram is at the household level; either individuals or members of the same household can be involved. A homogeneous group of participants can also be involved to look at specific issues. For example, to examine the influence of factors such as age, sex, occupation on education or expenditure, homogeneous groups based on age, sex, etc., can be involved. The number of participants in the case of a group exercise may vary from four to ten.

PROCEDURE

- Decide on the type of data or information to be depicted through a pie diagram.
- Decide on the type of participants required to carry out the exercise.
- Convene a meeting of the participants and explain the purpose of the exercise and the mode of doing the exercise.
- Facilitate the participants to draw the circle or pie. Ask them to divide the circle or pie into segments which are proportional in size to the importance of that particular element (see Figure 18.1). Remember that the output is a divided circle in all cases. However, the methods used to achieve this may vary. Some of the options are as follows:

  - You may carry out a discussion over proportions and agree upon them before the lines are marked on the chart or ground.
  - You may ask the participants to choose movable lines, such as sticks or pens, for analysis and the subsequent discussion may centre on changing these lines.
  - You may facilitate the participants to create a circle of beans which can be divided and re-divided.
  - You may use movable counters to indicate relative proportions during the initial discussion.

- Make participants (who are not familiar with concepts of proportions or percentage) understand the concept by introducing simple techniques. Let us suppose that we like to discuss the expenditure pattern of a poor family. You may use 100 seeds and ask the participants, 'Out of 100 seeds how many seeds are spent on food, how many seeds are spent on educating the children, how many seeds are spent on recreation, …..'. Alternatively, you may use 100 paise and ask 'Out of 100 paise how many paise are spent on food ….'

Figure 18.1
A Simple Pie Chart

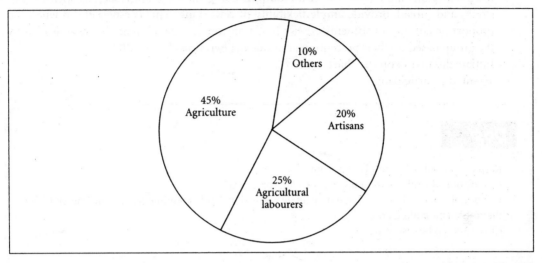

- You may also facilitate the respondents to draw pictures on the slices of a pie, indicating what each slice in the pie represents (see Figure 18.2). This would help the illiterate people to participate in the discussion.

Figure 18.2
Pie Diagram with Pictures

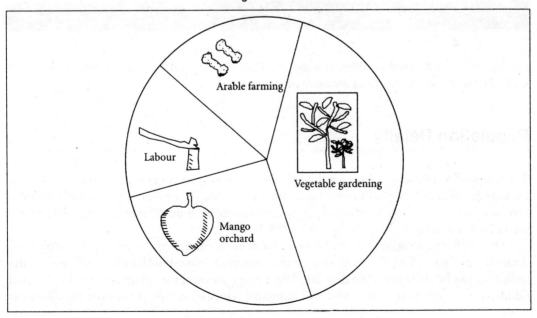

- Ask participants to rework on the pie by dividing and subdividing a number of times until the participants are satisfied with the output. Using movable lines, such as sticks, seeds, stones and thread, provide ample flexibility of reworking. This is especially so when the proportions of the constituents are not based on concrete data but are being arrived at by the group based on their perception after due deliberation (Kumar 2003).
- Initiate discussion on the chart.
- Thank the participants.

Dos

- Keep the procedure as simple as possible.
- Include only the information necessary to interpret the chart.
- Use flexible materials as they would facilitate corrections and amendments both during and after the construction of diagram.
- Charts should be easy to read.

Don'ts

- Do not use too many notations on the chart.
- Do not draw wide-reaching conclusions from the data if they are not justified by the chart.

APPLICATION

Pie diagrams can be used in different contexts. They can be used both at community level and individual level. The applications are quite extensive.

Population Details

The composition of the population with respect to various aspects can be meaningfully examined. For example, it can be used to examine the livelihood sources. The proportion of people engaged in various activities and the proportion of people earning income from different sources and activities can be analysed using pie diagram (see Figure 18.3).

The caste-wise distribution of the households in a village can be attempted using a pie diagram (see Figure 18.4). The economic composition of the household based on well-being status indicators can be shown in a pie diagram. The literacy status in the village can also be depicted. Gender-wise, religion-wise, caste-wise and economic status-wise, literacy status of the village can be shown separately and critical comparison and analysis can be attempted. The pie diagram can also be used to examine the use of health care facilities by people in a village. The alternative treatments available, the proportion of households using such facilities, mode of transport, etc., can be analysed through a pie diagram.

Figure 18.3
Income Generation in Amemo

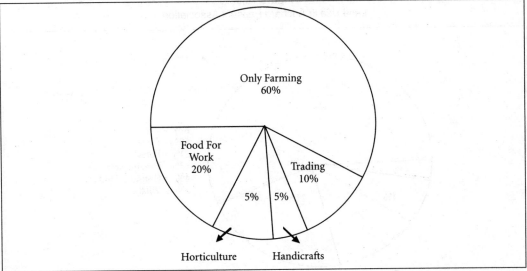

Source: Guijt and Scoones (1991).

Figure 18.4
Pie Chart Showing Distribution of Castes in Dobang Kunda (Old Women)

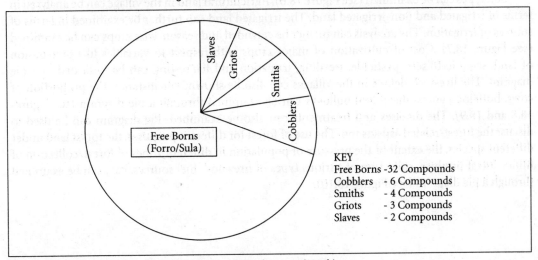

Source: International Institute for Environment and Development (1992b).

Agriculture and Natural Resources

Pie diagrams are extensively used to discuss the issues related to agriculture and natural resources. The land-use pattern in a village can be shown, indicating the lands fully utilised, underutilised, not utilised, etc. (see Figure 18.5).

Figure 18.5
Land Use in Ancharo Peasant Association

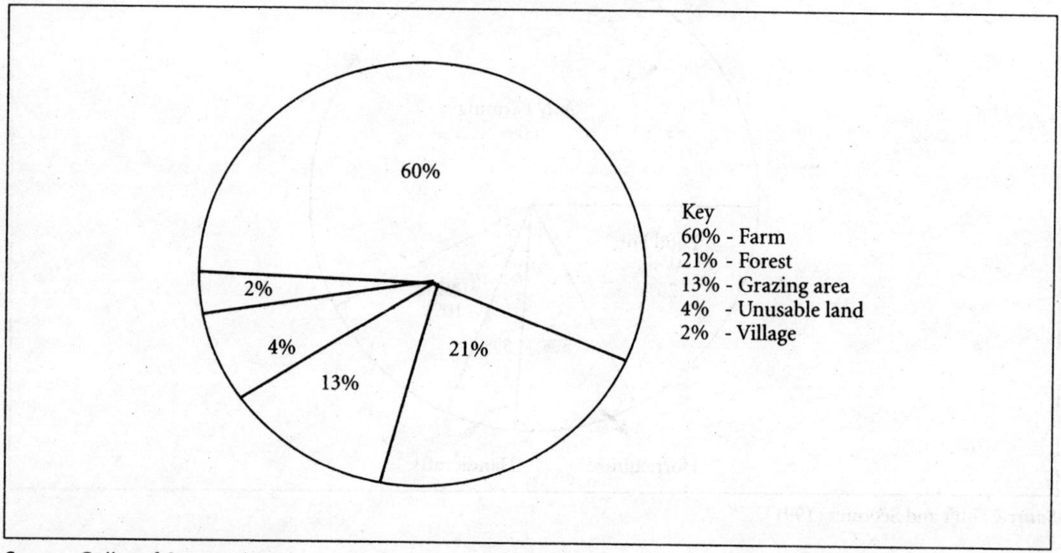

Key
60% - Farm
21% - Forest
13% - Grazing area
4% - Unusable land
2% - Village

Source: Guijt and Scoones (1991).

Soil types can be examined (see Figure 18.6). Agricultural land in the village can be analysed in terms of irrigated and non-irrigated land. The irrigated land can further be examined in terms of sources of irrigation. The analysis can further be extended and season-wise crops can be examined (see Figure 18.7). Cost of cultivation of major crops with respect to variables like preparation of land, seed, fertilisers, pesticide, weeding, irrigation and harvesting can be indicated in a pie diagram. The livestock details in the villages can also be shown. For instance, the proportion of cows, buffaloes, goats, sheep and bullocks can be examined through a pie diagram (see Figures 18.8 and 18.9). The diseases and treatments can also be examined. Pie diagram can be used to discuss the forest-related aspects too. The use of forest for different purposes, the forest land under different species, the extent of the pressure of population in different zones of forest, collection of minor forest produce, collection of various types of firewood, fuel sources, etc., can be examined through a pie diagram (see Figure 18.10).

Figure 18.6
Major Soil Types in Amemo

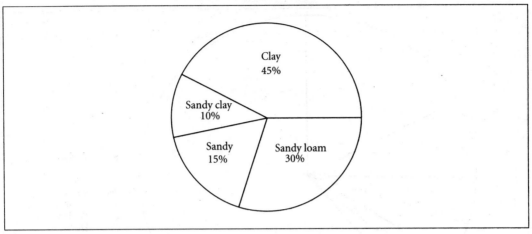

Source: Guijt and Scoones (1991).

Figure 18.7
Crop Choice for Meher Season, 1983

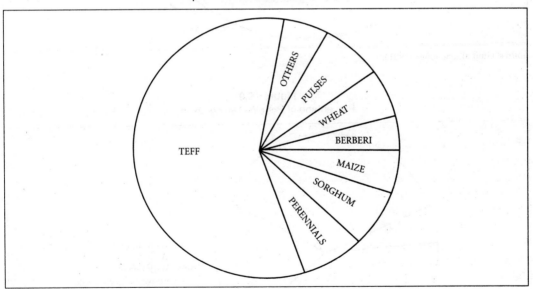

Source: Guijt and Scoones (1991).

Figure 18.8
Presence of Animals in Amemo Peasant Association

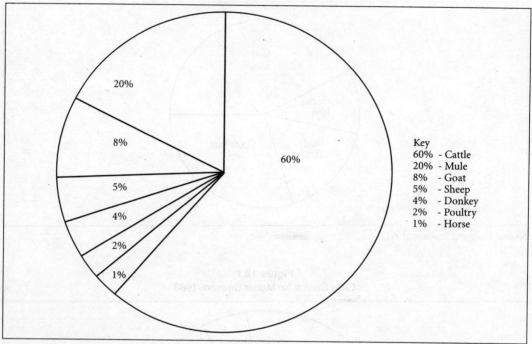

Key
60% - Cattle
20% - Mule
8% - Goat
5% - Sheep
4% - Donkey
2% - Poultry
1% - Horse

Source: Guijt and Scoones (1991).

Figure 18.9
Percentage of People Owning Oxen

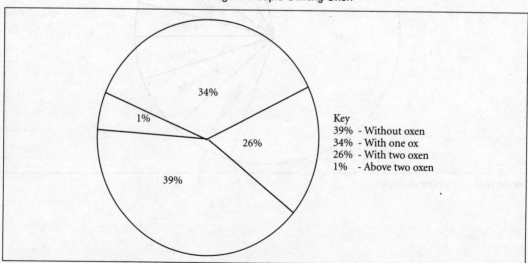

Key
39% - Without oxen
34% - With one ox
26% - With two oxen
1% - Above two oxen

Source: Guijt and Scoones (1991).

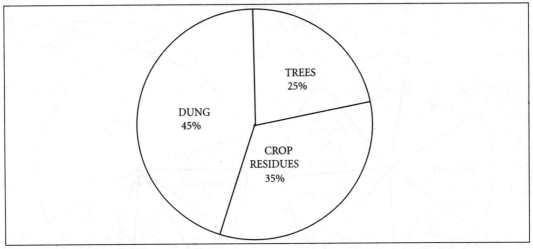

Figure 18.10
Fuel Sources in Amemo Peasant Association (1983 E.C.)

Source: Guijt and Scoones (1991).

Individual Level

Pie charts can be developed at individual level. Some indicative items of application are as follows:

- Household income;
- Household expenditure (see Figure 18.11);
- Livelihood sources;
- Plot-level agricultural analysis;
- Crop-wise cost of cultivation (see Figure 18.12);
- Sources of debt;
- Perception of a problem: specific issue, health care, organisation, etc. (see Figure 18.13).

Comparative Analysis

Pie diagram has also been used to compare various variables/aspects related to agriculture, natural resources, population, etc. A few such applications are listed here:

- Comparison of land use, employment, etc., between two periods
- Comparison of income and expenditure between rich and poor households

Figure 18.11
Pie Charts of Income and Expenditure: Four Old Men

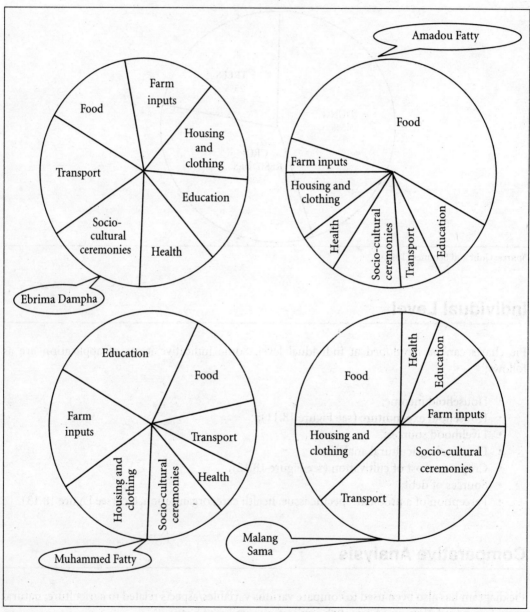

Source: IIED (1992).

Figure 18.12
Preparation of Expenditure on Inputs for Cotton and Maize

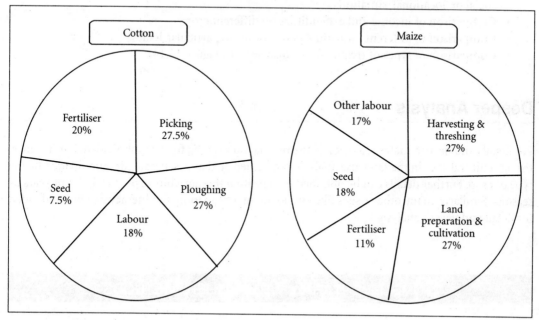

Source: Guijt and Scoones (1991).
Note: Information is from one old and one young farmer. Both are comparatively wealthy.

Figure 18.13
Farmers' Perceptions of the Relative Impact of Organisations Concerned with Development
in Abela Sipa Peasant Association

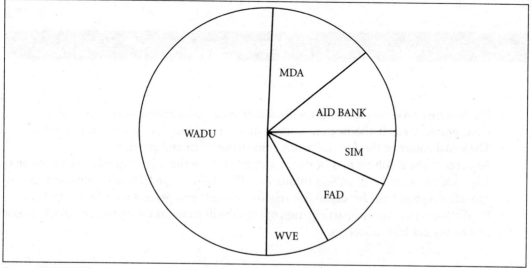

Source: IIED (1991).

- Comparison of income and expenditure between households in different employment, social or 'locational' situations
- Comparison of income and expenditure on different crops
- Comparison of different individual perceptions on particular issues
- Comparison of types of treatment for diseases (see Figure 18.14)

Deeper Analysis

For details and deeper analysis, a piece of the pie diagram can be further subdivided. For instance, the agricultural slice in the land-use analysis can be depicted as a 'separate pie' and divided by the type of crop. Further details can be obtained by repeating this agriculture pie for different years or seasons. Similarly, many other issues like employment, occupation and literacy can be subdivided for detail and deeper analysis.

COMPLEMENTARITY WITH OTHER METHODS

The pie diagram can be effectively used for visually presenting the data and information gathered through PRA methods like social mapping, resource mapping and participatory census. This, in turn, helps even the illiterate participants to analyse the data and information in a more meaningful way. Pie diagram may also lead to focus group discussion on issues that require further insight.

MERITS

- Pie diagram provides a clear basis for discussing and understanding distribution of an aspect, issue, problem, etc. It also helps in understanding the dynamics within a community.
- The visual nature of the exercise makes comparison clear and easier.
- Sometimes, the absolutes may be difficult to calculate or the subject may be such a one that respondents might be unwilling to quantify. Pie diagram can help solve this problem by providing a good basis for discussing relative amounts and percentages (Jones 1996).
- Pie diagrams facilitate the participation of even the illiterate, as the method employs visuals and locally available materials.

Figure 18.14

Most Frequent Types of Treatment for Serious Childhood Diseases

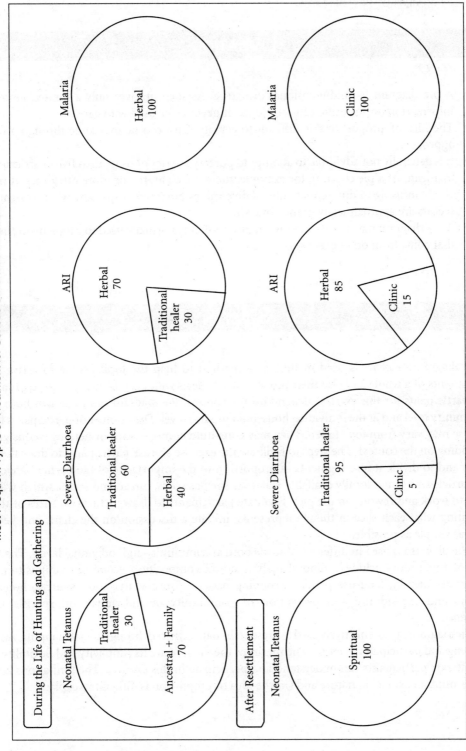

Source: Marindo-Ranganai (1995).

LIMITATIONS

- A pie diagram is unidimensional in nature. As such, it gives only a limited amount of information on a specific subject. Hence, it needs to be used with care.
- The idea of 'proportions' is difficult to explain. This can be overcome through a flexible approach.
- It is generally not advisable to attempt to portray a series of more than five or six categories by means of a pie chart. If, for example, there are eight, ten or more categories, it may be very confusing to differentiate the relative values portrayed, especially when several small sectors are approximately of the same size.
- A pie diagram may not be used as a major tool. It is normally used to supplement the ideas that come from other exercises.

SUMMARY

A pie diagram or chart is used in PRA as a method to help the local people to arrive at the constituents of a whole and also their proportions. It deals with both factual and perceptual data. The participants for this exercise depend on the context. Pie diagram can be drawn both at the community level and at the individual household or farm level. The number of participants for the exercise may vary from four to ten. They may constitute homogeneous or heterogeneous groups, depending on the context. The steps to facilitate the exercise are: ask participants to draw the circle or pie and to divide it into segments in proportion to the importance of the particular element; ask participants to use locally available materials such as seeds, thread and sticks, which will help them to work and rework on the pies. Facilitate participants to draw pictures on slices of the pie, indicating what each slice in the pie represents; initiate a discussion on the chart; and keep the chart as simple as possible.

Pie diagram is used in different contexts both at community and individual levels. The broad areas of application include livelihood analysis, ethnic composition, economic composition, land ownership, literacy, land-use pattern, cropping pattern, forestry, irrigation sources, household income and expenditure and perception of community or individuals on specific issues/problems.

Pie diagram can be effectively used to present the data gathered through social mapping, resource mapping and participatory census. The merits of the method are its simplicity and flexibility. Even the illiterate participants can understand and participate in this exercise. The limitations are that (*i*) it is unidimensional in nature and (*ii*) the idea of proportion is difficult to explain.

19

Body Mapping

INTRODUCTION

Maps and models are used extensively in participatory rural appraisal (PRA) to study the physical and social structure and features of a village, locate the various natural and physical resources and study the ecological environment of a village. They serve as a guide to understand the people's perception of the spaces in which they live and work. The technique of mapping is also used as a 'health data gathering tool' that illustrates all or part of the human body in a visual form. The technique is known as body mapping. People have certain perceptions about their body. They have their own classification and visual description of it. Further, different cultures have different ideas of bodily functions and on how medical interventions work within the body. It may be difficult to explore the issues related to the body verbally because community members may be unfamiliar with anatomical vocabulary and the words may have different meanings in different cultural contexts. As a result, the health workers and extension personnel find it difficult to pass on the messages relevant to health, diseases, birth control and pregnancy to the community. It was felt that visual body mapping, drawn by local people, may, to a greater extent, help overcome these problems. The outcome was the emergence and the use of body map in PRA. It is mostly used to study health- and gender-related issues.

MEANING

Body mapping is a visual method of describing the location of body organs and to describe bodily functions. The maps may consist of one large drawing, or of several smaller drawings to illustrate a process or practice. Body maps are diagrams, which represent part or all of a body drawn by women/men on paper or on the ground to examine their knowledge about reproduction and their interpretations of non-indigenous contraception (Cornwall 1992). It provides a shared point of reference for the researcher and the community members.

PURPOSE

Body mapping has been mostly practised among women. It is becoming popular among gender trainees and women activists. Body mapping can be used to explore the following issues:

- The reproductive system
- Behaviour that has positive or negative effects on the body
- Nutritional status and ill-effects of malnutrition
- How specific diseases affect body parts
- How alcohol affects the body
- How malaria makes a person sick
- How worms make a person sick
- How HIV/AIDS make a person sick

PARTICIPANTS

Some of the subjects explained in body mapping can be embarrassing. It may restrict the participation of mixed groups. Hence, the facilitator needs to decide the subjects that he/she is going to discuss through body mapping. Women in certain culture may be hesitant to discuss issues related to body in the presence of men. Hence, it would be desirable that an exclusive women's group is formed to discuss such issues. It makes sense to divide participants by gender or age group depending on the subject and situation. The size of the group from the village may be small. The number of participants may vary from six to ten.

PROCEDURE

The procedure that can be followed to facilitate body mapping is outlined here:

- Select the theme or subject of body mapping, for example, reproductive system or diseases. Decide the data and information to be gathered through the exercise.
- Select the key informants. If the exercise on body mapping is related to women, select a group of women who are willing to participate and ask them to draw the map. You may include local birth attendants, village health nurses, traditional healers (women), local therapists (women) because the presence of such local women in a sensitive exercise like body mapping would help in establishing rapport and cooperation in carrying out the exercise. Ensure that the group is not too big.

- Introduce the exercise to the participants. Kick off informally by asking the women about how do they gain knowledge about their bodies. What are the sources? Which families have adopted family planning methods? Once you feel that the participants are at ease and are likely to get going, facilitate them to draw the map.
- Ask them to draw the map on the ground. The materials that could be used include charcoal, *rangoli* powder and chalk piece. The participants may start with the profile of the body and then move on to draw the organs of the body. Remember the purpose of the exercise and accordingly facilitate them to draw the parts of the body about which you would like to have the discussion. Supposing, the topic of interest is conception or birth control, ask them to draw body parts and organs related to the topic. You may also facilitate the participants to draw the map on a big chart paper. However, ground is a better medium. Use 'your best judgement' in selecting the medium.
- Allow the participants to draw the map at their own pace. Do not rush. Do not interfere, do not take lead. Be an effective facilitator. Intervene when it is essential.
- On completion of the map, start the discussion. Encourage the participants to explain the map in detail. You may ask certain key questions now. The questions now may be related to who has control over their bodies. In addition, how their own control over their body can be enhanced may also be asked now.
- The participants may have questions to ask. Encourage them to ask questions. Spend enough time in answering questions and clearing their doubts.
- Ask participants to consolidate the inferences drawn from the body map and explain the same. Participants may share the map and findings with persons who are knowledgeable about the issues and feedback, if any, may be incorporated.
- Copy the diagram on a chart paper with all details, such as names of the participants, the names of the members of PRA team, the place and the date.
- Thank the participants for their contribution.

Dos

- Spend enough time in understanding local culture and ideas and in establishing a rapport with the women's group.
- Instil confidence in them.
- Encourage them to participate freely.
- Be culturally sensitive.
- Let women facilitators deal with women-related issues.
- If needed, carry out the exercise in a 'one-to-one situation'.

Don'ts

- Do not underestimate the participants' knowledge.
- Do not compel women to share any information.

APPLICATION

Body maps are mostly applied for understanding of health-related issues, including reproductive health and gender issues. Some of the areas of applications include the following:

- The application in the health field include mapping of stages of foetal growth, generating themes for discussion from antenatal care to sources of nutrition during pregnancy; clarifications of what patients anticipate when undergoing surgery or expectations of voluntary surgical procedures, such as vasectomy and tubal ligation; and perceptions of cancers, heart disease, intestinal stomach disorders, etc. (Cornwall 1992).
- It may be used to understand the extent to which the women have control over their bodies, sexuality and fertility. The exercise can be followed by a discussion on (*i*) the extent to which their husbands/partners meet their sexual needs, and more generally the extent to which women have control over their bodies, sexuality and fertility; (*ii*) the coping strategies used by single women (widows, destitute women), who have opted or are forced to remain single, to deal with their sexuality; (*iii*) why is that widowers are allowed to remarry and lead a normal sex life, while widows cannot (Murthy 1995).
- The exercise can be used in fertility awareness education. The exercise may help in familiarising women with their menstrual cycles. It encourages women to identify their fertile and non-fertile periods, and become less dependent on contraceptives. It may enable women to identify their gynaecological disorders.
- Body mapping can be used to ascertain issues related to contraceptive methods. What are the reasons for accepting or not accepting the various contraceptive methods? What are the anxieties they have regarding these methods? These questions can be analytically discussed through body-mapping technique.
- Body mapping can be used to analyse issues related to gender discrimination. For example, body mapping can be employed to show how restrictions are imposed on the girl child (see Figure 19.1).
- Attempts have also been made to apply body mapping as a potential HIV/AIDS educational tool. It was found that creation of body maps increased the biomedical understanding of HIV/AIDS and, to some extent, the health-enhancing behaviour. Apart from gaining factual knowledge about their health, the body map can also help in initiating conversation on personal, emotional, cultural and socio-economic challenges of being HIV-positive.

COMPLEMENTARITY WITH OTHER METHODS

Body mapping is mostly used for sharing health-related issues and in gender sensitisation research and training. This is a sensitive exercise. Hence, this cannot be initiated without building an adequate rapport with the people. It is, therefore, better to start with rapport-building exercises like 'do it yourself' before starting the exercise. It can be preceded by PRA techniques like mapping, with particular reference to health, timeline with reference to health, ranking exercise, etc. These exercises would not only provide information on health-related aspects but would also help build up rapport with the community.

Figure 19.1
A Girl's Childhood

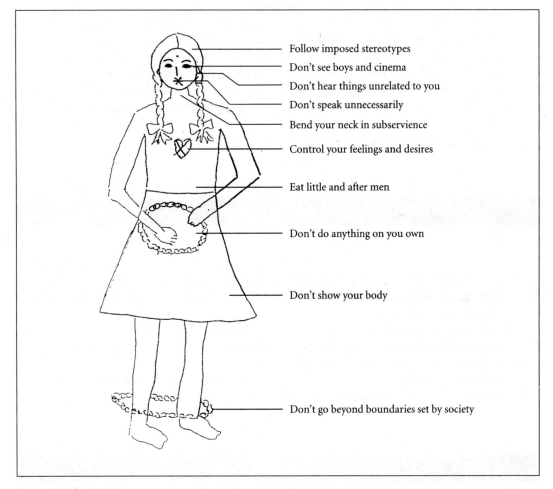

Source: Murthy (1995).

Body map can be succeeded by PRA exercises like access and control and decision-making matrix. These exercises are likely to enhance the understanding of health and health-related issues. They are also likely to complement and supplement the inferences from body mapping.

MERITS

- It facilitates communication. It is a device, used as part of an approach, which aims to find ways of improving access to appropriate information (Cornwall 1992).
- It may help gain an insight into the local perceptions of health-related issues. It provides a great deal of opportunity for the outsiders to know the local names and concepts about the part of the body and their functions. This, is turn, would help the health communication projects to meet the expectations of their target audience.
- It can also serve as a bridge between local knowledge and Western science. Body mapping may help unearth the differences between local perceptions and scientific views of the human body and thereby helps in bridging the gaps and in arriving at a common level of understanding. As Andrea Cornwall has rightly said, 'It is not a replacement of western medical ideas with local ideas but a building process, where possible, using local knowledge and idioms as building blocks from which to construct versions which make sense in local terms.'
- It has been very useful in introducing sensitive topics.

LIMITATIONS

- It is a sensitive exercise. The facilitator needs to be careful in using this. As stated earlier, the exercise can be conducted with the community only after establishing adequate rapport with the community.
- The exercise cannot be conducted in a mixed group of men and women as women will not be willing to be part of the exercise in the presence of men. The facilitator needs to be very cautious while conducting this exercise.
- While facilitating the exercise among women, the team from outside cannot be a mixed group. It has to be necessarily a group of women.

SUMMARY

Body mapping is a visual exercise that describes and locates the body organs and bodily functions. Practised mostly among women, the exercise serves various purposes like understanding reproductive system, contraception, nutrition and diseases. Being a sensitive exercise, the facilitator has to be very careful in choosing the participants. It is better to avoid a mixed group of men and women. If the subject matter is women-related issues, involve only women. The procedure among other things involves a selection of theme or topic, choosing the right type of participants, establishing a good rapport with the participants, introducing the exercise, interviewing the diagram and sharing the information with others. The fields of application include health-related issues, reproductive health system, contraception, gender sensitisation and communication strategy. The method can complement other PRA methods like access and control and decision-making matrix. The merits are that (*i*) it facilitates communication, (*ii*) it helps gain insight into the local perception of health, (*iii*) it builds the bridge between local knowledge and Western science and (*iv*) it helps introducing sensitive topics. The limitations are that (*i*) it cannot be practised in mixed groups and (*ii*) it is a sensitive exercise.

20

Interviewing and Dialogue

INTRODUCTION

Interviewing and dialogue skills are quite essential in any kind of work. This is all the more important in rural development work where the outside professionals' level of information and understanding about the rural situation are limited. Interview, in true sense, means dialogue. Dialogue is based on people sharing their own perceptions of a problem, offering their opinions and ideas and having the opportunity to make decisions or recommendations. A good and lively dialogue can be initiated through good interviewing. This helps us to gain more accurate insights into rural situations, problems, customs, practices, systems, values and the way the rural people think, act and perceive things. This is especially critical while designing rural development programmes meant for these people. Good interviewing and dialogue facilitates an information flow that is true, authentic and relevant (Mascarenhas 1996).

Participatory rural appraisal (PRA), with its intense faith in human beings, their power to make and remake, their power to create and recreate, makes use of interviewing and dialogue quite extensively to interact with people. We will discuss in this chapter three types of interviewing and dialogue techniques followed in PRA, namely, (*i*) semi-structured interview; (*ii*) focus group discussion; and (*iii*) direct observation. We have included direct observation as a method of interviewing and dialogue, because direct observation is considered in PRA as an intensive process of observation followed by interviewing and dialogue between the outsiders and insiders. Jules N. Pretty (1995) has classified direct observation as an interviewing and dialogue method.

SEMI-STRUCTURED INTERVIEWING

Introduction

Interviewing is one of the major methods of data collection. It is defined as 'a two-way systematic conversation between an investigator and an informant, initiated for obtaining information relevant to a specific study'. It involves not only conversation but also learning from the respondent's gestures, facial expressions and pauses and his environment. It is useful for collecting a wide range of data from factual demographic data to highly personal and intimate information relating to a person's opinions, attitudes, values, beliefs, past experiences and future intentions. Interviewing is often superior to other data-gathering methods. People are usually more willing to talk than to write. Once a rapport is established, even confidential information may be obtained. It permits probing into the context and reasons for answers to questions.

Types of Interviews

Interviews may be broadly classified into (*i*) structured or directive interview; (*ii*) unstructured or non-directive interview; and (*iii*) semi-structured interview (SSI) (see Table 20.1).

Structured interview is an interview made with a detailed standardised schedule. The same questions are put to all the respondents and in the same order. Each question is asked in the same way in each interview, promoting measurement reliability. This type of interview is used for large-scale formalised surveys (Krishnaswami 2002).

Unstructured interview is the least structured one. The interviewer encourages the respondent to talk freely about a given topic with minimum of prompting or guidance. Under this type, a detailed pre-planned schedule is not used. An interview guide is used. The interviewer avoids channelling the direction of the interview. Instead, he develops a very permissive atmosphere. The questions are not standardised and not framed in a particular way.

SSI is a focused interview. The interviewer under this type attempts to focus the discussion on the actual effects of a given experience to which the respondents have been exposed. This type of interview is free from inflexibility of formal methods, yet gives the interview a set form and ensures adequate coverage of all topics.

Table 20.1
Structured, Semi-structured, Unstructured Interviews: A Comparison

Structured	Semi-structured	Unstructured
Useful when research questions are very precise and quantified answers are needed	Useful where some quantitative and some qualitative information is needed	Useful to help set the research focus or explore new or sensitive topics in depth
Questions must be asked in a standard way	Questions may be asked in different ways but some questions can be standard	More like a conversation, no standard questions, just topic areas
All questions must be asked	Question can be left out and others added	Follow or ask the respondents to establish what is important to discuss
Most questions have preset answers to choose between	Include a mix of questions—some open and some closed	Avoid questions which can have responses as a simple 'Yes' or 'No'
Results are easy to analyse	Analysis is fairly straightforward	Analysis requires time and skill
Follow many of the same rules as questionnaire		Follow many of the rules as focus groups

Source: Laws et al. (2003).

Semi-structured Interview Technique under PRA

Participatory methods have contributed to adjust the interview to make it more conversational, while still controlled and structured. This is referred to as semi-structured interview (SSI). Under this, only some of the questions and topics are predetermined. Many questions are formulated during the interview. Questions may be asked according to a flexible checklist or guide and not from a formal questionnaire (Mikkelsen 2005). In short, it is a guided conversation, where only some of the questions are predetermined and new questions or insights arise as a result of discussion and visualised analysis. SSI technique is extensively used in PRA. It complements and supplements many of the methods used under PRA.

SSIs are held with the following:

- Individuals for representative Information: Interview a number of individuals on the same topic.
- Key informants for specialised information: Key informants have special knowledge, which others do not have. For example, the midwives in a rural setting may have special knowledge on delivery and birth complications.
- Groups for general community-level information.
- Focus groups to discuss a specific problem in detail and in depth.

Group interviews can take a number of different forms, depending principally upon the objectives and the mix of interviews. They may be casual or formal and pre-arranged to groups. Formal groups include community groups, such as a self-help group (SHG), or health groups involving selected mix according to age or wealth. The purpose of the interview may be to explore and analyse a topic, focus on problems and opportunities jointly faced by the group or discuss important conflicts between and within groups.

SSI Guidelines

- Begin with the appropriate traditional greeting and some small talk.
- Begin the questioning by referring to someone or something visible. Ask questions in a logical order. Make sure to start with an interesting but straightforward question to which everyone will have some answer.
- Conduct the interview in an informal fashion and mix questions with the discussion.
- Keep an appropriate level of eye contact, and note any non-verbal signals which might help in understanding what has been said.
- Encourage the members of the group to tell their story the way they want; only later on, check through your questions to make sure that their account contains the information you need.
- Ask sensitive questions only after building sufficient rapport with the people and only when the members of the group are at ease with you.

- Look for apparent inconsistencies in what people are saying and probe further to unearth the thinking behind them.
- Judge the response. The responses from the participants may be in the form of a fact, opinion, rumour or lie. The interviewers need to be careful in judging the response. Facts alone need to be carefully found out, as responses are likely to come from different corners of the group.
- Avoid leading and vague questions.
- Keep a discrete eye on the time. Ensure that an individual interview does not exceed forty-five minutes. Ensure also that the group interview takes no longer than two hours.
- Ask members of the group on how they felt about the process and if there is anything else they would like to say.
- Ask participants to summarise the outcome of the interview and ask them to show the information.
- Give sincere thanks to all the participants for the support and for the time they have spent with you.
- Ensure that the content writer has been able to record the outcome of the interview.

Guidelines for Asking Questions

- Begin with a simple question. Always start the interview with simple questions. Difficult and sensitive questions may be put near the end of the interview so that if the respondents decide not to answer these, you do not lose his/her willingness to answer other questions.
- Avoid certain questions. While conducting SSI techniques, questions should be properly worded and asked. Questions should be simple and to the point. The following questions should be avoided:

  - **Leading questions:** A leading question is one that is worded in a way as to influence the respondent to give a certain answer. It does not elicit an accurate answer or correct viewpoint of the respondent(s). For example, 'Are you for giving too much power to the local government?'
  - **Loaded questions:** A loaded question is one that contains words, which are emotionally coloured, and suggests an automatic feeling of approval or disapproval. Using words like 'terrorism', 'bureaucracy', 'greedy' and 'oppressed' may seem to imply a judgement. Such words can cause bias in the answers. Respondents may be reluctant or nervous to give answers (Mikkelsen 2005).
  - **Ambiguous and vague questions:** An ambiguous question is one that does not have a clear meaning. It may mean different things to different people. For example, 'Do people raise small animals?', 'What do you think about the education you have received?'
  - **Multiple questions:** They contain two or more different ideas or references. For example, 'Do you favour or oppose the idea of increased job security and productivity-linked wage system for women?'

- **Hypothetical questions:** They are questions based on a situation that is not real but might happen. For example,' If you had been able to complete the vocational training in a trade, what would you be doing today?'
- **Offensive or insensitive questions:** They are questions that are rude and insulting in nature. They are likely to upset the people. For example, 'Why do you not think it is important to pay for noon meals at school?'

- Do not assume 'answerability'. An important bias that affects interviewing is the assumption of answerability. The interviewers expect that answers to their questions should automatically come from the respondents. It should be noted that answers to the question hinge on people's idea of knowledge. We need to realise that one cannot know everything. The respondents may not know, cannot remember, cannot express the answer well in words, have no strong opinion or are unfamiliar with answering questions. Even if they know a little, it cannot be uttered in a moment. Therefore, answers and answerability are not expected to come quickly and are not always assumed knowable and speakable. The implication is that if the interviewer wants to learn, he or she has to stay around watching and living (Mitchell and Slim 1991).
- Resist 'nutshelling' pressure. Interviews often aim to contract issues and simplify them rather than to explore complexity. The interviewers want the respondents to put the issues in a nutshell. Of course, brevity is a virtue. But short, quick answers often give a veneer of simplicity, which glosses over a great deal of complexity. The interviewers should not be alarmed if the respondents seem to be 'talking around'. In fact, they should be prepared to follow the course of conversation and resist the temptations to make the respondents 'nutshell' issues (Mitchell and Slim 1991).

SSI: Errors and Limitations

Interviewers along with team members are likely to commit certain errors and mistakes while interviewing. The common errors are enumerated as follows:

- Failure to listen closely;
- Repeating questions;
- Helping the respondents by suggesting answers while they are temporarily lost;
- Asking vague questions;
- Asking insensitive questions;
- Failure to probe further;
- Failure to cross-check and triangulate the information;
- Failure to judge the responses—believing everything;
- Allowing interviewing to go on too long;
- Over-generalisation of inferences;

- Relying too much on what the well-off, the better-educated, the old and the men have to say;
- Ignoring anything that does not fit into the ideas and perceptions of the interviewer; and
- Giving too much weight to answers that contain quantitative data and information.

Summary

Interview is a two-way systematic conversation between the interviewer and respondents. Its aim is to obtain information relevant to a study. Interview may be broadly classified into three categories, namely, structured, unstructured and semi-structured interview. In PRA, the SSI technique is extensively used. It is a guided interview where only primary questions are predetermined. Many questions will come up only during the interview. SSI is held with individuals, key informants, group and focus groups. SSI is based on certain guidelines, which provide a congenial atmosphere for the interviewer and the respondents to gather and share information. The interviewer has to avoid questions, such as leading questions, insensitive questions, vague questions, multiple questions and hypothetical questions. He should also avoid interview biases like expecting the respondents to answer all the questions and to answer the questions in a nutshell.

Focus Group Discussion

Introduction

Focus groups are basically group interviews. A moderator guides the interview while a small group discusses the topics that the interviewer raises. What the participants in the group say during their discussions is the essential data in focus groups. Typically, there are six to eight participants who come from similar backgrounds, and the moderator is a well-trained development professional who raises his questions from a predetermined set of discussion topics (Morgan 1998), otherwise known as a focus group discussion (FGD) checklist.

The hallmark of focus groups is their explicit use of group interaction to produce information and insights. There is progressive recognition to the use of focus groups in social research. Their use in applied/action research outside academic settings is very extensive. Focus group interviews are much used where the qualitative data is highly usable. Focus group discussions generally generate a lot of qualitative data. The data, information and insights developed are useful to explain and understand certain empirical phenomena. The information generated through FGD is often used to supplement, complement or strengthen the argument made using quantitative data. Focus group as an interview technique has become improvised as professionals from several disciplines started using it for varied purposes. In action research, often enough, FGDs have become the sole method to collect data.

The Basic Tenet of Focus Groups

The basic tenet of focus group is listening and learning. David L. Morgan (1998) points out to a three-part process of communication in an FGD: (*i*) the research team members decide what they need to hear from the participants; (*ii*) the focus groups create a conversation among the participants around these chosen topics; and (*iii*) members of the research team summarise what they have learned from the participants. This is what Chambers (2006) calls 'handing over the stick and reversal of learning'. An FGD moderator should, first of all, be prepared to listen and learn. This should be an active process of interaction, clarification, debriefing and assimilation. Three basic defining features of focus groups are: they are a research method for collecting qualitative data, their focused efforts are aimed at data gathering and they generate data through group discussions. There are certain principles that govern this discussion process, such as mutuality of trust, being open and purposive, willing to listen and learn, on-the-spot analysis, probing, cross-checking, validating the data gathered, and so on.

The features expressed above are unique to focus groups and they cannot be associated with the questionnaire survey approach. In survey, there are well-defined sampling procedures that rely on statistical formulae. In focus groups, the research team uses its judgement to select 'purposive samples' of participants who meet the needs of a particular project. Surveys use a fixed set of questions, with exactly the same set of predetermined response options. Focus groups allow considerable flexibility in how questions are asked from group to group. The analysis of focus groups, however, involves a more subjective process of listening to and making sense of what was said in the groups. The basic point is that focus groups and surveys use very different approaches in meeting the more general goal of gathering information. Depending upon the context and requirements of the report, the researchers need to determine which method they would go for.

Basic Uses of Focus Groups

Focus groups, at the outset, came for use in market research. Of late, depending upon the ingenuity of the social researcher/development practitioner, it is used in several different fields. Where qualitative insights are very much essential to understand reality, especially from the experiences of people undergoing a problem/experiencing a phenomenon, focus groups get significance. Morgan (1997) offers three basic uses for focus groups in current social science research. First, they are used as a 'self-contained' method in studies in which they serve as the principal source of data. Second, they are used as a 'supplementary' source of data in studies that rely on some other primary method such as a survey. Third, they are used in 'multi-method' studies that combine two or more means of gathering data in which no one primary method determines the use of the others.

In self-contained uses, focus groups serve as the primary means of collecting qualitative data. In supplementary uses of focus groups, the group discussions often serve as a source of preliminary data in a primarily quantitative study. For example, the data can be used to generate survey questionnaire or to develop the components of action programmes/project interventions. It can also serve as follow-up data to assist the primary method. For example, a poorly understood survey's results can be explained clearly using the focus group results. In multi-method studies, focus groups are used so as not to miss some qualitative dimension that might not get covered in other methods. Used in a self-contained fashion, focus groups can form the basis for a complete study. That approach to the use of focus groups, and focus group results are expanding can be realised from studies that come to the forefront year after year. The uses of focus groups, especially among those who believe in action research, are very much broad-based. They use it as a technique of data collection very frequently. The advantages they explain are many, including time and utility of the data gathered.

Another important area of use of focus groups is evaluation studies, where the evaluation team can use the focus group to assess the impact of a given project among the clients or beneficiaries of the project in question. However, like in any other research, it is the rigour of enquiry, credibility of the results and relevance of the findings to the requirements that usually determine the quality of the focus group research (Steele et al. 1999) .

Where to Use and Where Not to Use Focus Group Discussions

- Appropriate uses:
  - ◆ When there is a gap between those who serve and those who need to be served, in other words, between providers of the service and recipients of the service, focus groups are appropriate.
  - ◆ When investigating complex behaviour and motivations, focus groups can be handy.
  - ◆ When the research problem requires to be understood, demand diversity of analysis and focus group can be used.
  - ◆ When gathering data is not sufficient and getting closer to people is required, focus groups can be used.
  - ◆ When quantitative data is not sufficient to draw conclusions and arrive at findings, FGDs can be useful.
- Inappropriate uses:
  - ◆ If the FGD carried out would not lead to useful social action, avoid doing FGDs. Asking them to tell about their problems may imply that you are going to do something about solving those problems.

- Avoid focus groups if the participants are not comfortable with each other.
- Where the topic of discussion or the problem discussed is not relevant to the clients' groups, FGD results may not be insightful.
- Where the requirement is more statistical data to be able to understand the problem in hand, FGD would not help.

Steps in Conducting Focus Group Discussion

- Planning: As focus groups are usually semi-structured, allowing discussions to develop while being moderated, careful planning is very significant. The complexity that might arise due to being optimally prepared could be faced without much difficulty if we have our focus group plan properly prepared. During the planning stage, care needs to be taken of conceptualising the study, developing discussion topics, determining the time required, the composition of the interviewers' team, the type of informants we need to form as focus groups, the place of holding the FGD, logistical arrangements, etc. Talent also makes a big difference in the planning process. Experience can greatly affect planning, especially in writing the questions and selecting the participants.

  Among the resources that are necessary for good planning, talent is perhaps the most important. The research team should foresee crucial issues at the beginning of the study. They should write questions that fit the study and select participants who can address these topics. Novice focus group researchers may produce long lists of questions that cover far more topics than the group discussion can handle, or they may have questions that make perfect sense to them but are going to require a great deal of translation before the participants will be interested in them. These issues must be dealt with during the planning process, or the price you pay later will be quite high.

- Enlisting or selection of the group itself: This is the second most important step in conducting focus groups. A typical focus group has seven to eight participants. Having the right kind of informants in the focus group will determine the quality of discussion and the results of the research. Enlisting participation from a group of informants who do not know or know little about the topic being discussed would not yield the desired results. It is always good to make the recruitment face to face instead of arranging by phone or through a third person who may not moderate the focus group. You need to have enough number of right informants to conduct the focus group. They should be aware of the topic to be discussed in-group. If the informants recruited were people who experience or have experienced the phenomenon to be discussed, the results would be enriching knowledge. The findings and suggestions would be realistic and practicable.

  A test for finding out if the group is focused and has relevance to the issues/topic being discussed is the 'activeness and free flow' of the discussion. A topic irrelevant to the group would get revealed in the discussion by making the job of the moderator very difficult. The moderator would find it very hard to take the discussion to the desired end/length.

- Moderating the focus group: Moderating the focus group is a skill that can be developed with every successive focus group. Talented focus group moderators know how to clarify the problem, categorise questions, phrase questions, sequence questions, probe answers and the entire route of questioning. The moderator needs to have a good idea of what should be the opening, introductory, transition, key and ending questions. He should start very informally with traditional greetings, start the topic with very general and known questions, and proceed to unknown and specific questions. A typical FGD can take place between one-and-a-half hours and two hours, depending upon the issue to be understood and the interest of the informants.

  As a principle, closed-ended questions should be avoided, and open-ended questions should be fully made use of. The helpers, such as what, why, how, when and where, should be very liberally used in order to cross-check the validity of the data being collected. There should be consistency in the questions. While answering the questions, the group should be able to appreciate the focus and also that it serves the purpose of the research, instead of answering questions at random with no focus in search. One of the important aspects of moderating is recording the discussion. Recording can be done in several ways: complete shorthand note taking, taking longhand notes and recording in memory, mechanical tape recording, and so on. A different person, familiar with the topic being discussed, should be assigned the role of note taking or recording the discussion.

- Analysing and reporting: This is a challenge for many researchers and even for talented development practitioners. There are several talented moderators of focus groups who do not know how to analyse and report the focus group results. The descriptive nature of information generated makes the analysis difficult. This is also a reason why, often, the results of focus groups are criticised of subjectivity and researchers' bias. Familiarity with the critical ingredients of qualitative analysis will be of immense help in analysing the qualitative data and reporting the results of focus groups. There are some specific skills required for analysing and reporting the focus group results. By the time the focus group or a series of FGDs comes to an end, the major findings would float on the surface of the minds of the researchers' team.

  The data and information could be in the form of notes, recorded cassette/CD or charts. Whatever be the form, these require to be transcribed in the first place to have the entire length of discussion ready in hand. No matter whether they are on a tape recorder or a notebook, they should be typed out on a computer with crude segmentation and category systems. Identifying themes, sub-themes, patterns and semantic relations can take place gradually in the subsequent stages. If the data is amenable, construction of diagrams, tables, matrices and graphs can also be attempted. We can corroborate and validate the results by presenting the results to the same focus groups, where the data sets were collated. They may validate it or would want revision of some of the ideas that the researchers' team did not understand properly or misunderstood. Then it becomes the report of the focus group.

Analysing and reporting are not as simple as it is presented here. It requires several skills during the process of analysis. The use of words, the context, internal consistency among themselves, frequency of comments made of certain things, extensiveness of the comments, specificity of responses, and what was not said and why (interpreting non-verbal signals) could be some of the items to consider while analysing and reporting FGDs (Brueger 1998). Finally, the report may be prepared taking into consideration the purpose the report is supposed to serve, and the type of readers it is meant for.

Summary

FGD and research reports based on focus groups have come to be widely used, especially after participatory approach to community development became a popular method of project intervention. There are a great many uses for focus groups, in combination with other methods or even as an independent method of qualitative data collection. We have come a long way since focus groups were used only as a preliminary, exploratory research. Exploration, certainly, is the strength of qualitative research in general and focus groups in particular, so we should neither downplay this key contribution nor allow ourselves to be limited by it. The aspects of purposive sampling and possibility for bias while making notes, transcribing or interpreting the results should be carefully avoided so as to get reality in the interest of the cause we are working for.

DIRECT OBSERVATION

Introduction

Observation is viewing or seeing. We observe something or the other while we are awake. Many such observations are casual in nature. They have no specific purpose. But then, observation as a method of data collection is different from casual viewing. Observation is defined as 'a systematic viewing of specific phenomenon in its proper setting for the specific purpose of gathering data for a particular study'. Observation as a method includes both 'seeing' and 'hearing'. It is accompanied by perceiving as well (Krishnaswami 2002). Observation is a classical method of scientific enquiry. The body of knowledge of various natural and physical sciences has been built upon centuries of systematic observation. It also plays a major role in formulating and testing hypothesis in social sciences. Behavioural scientists observe interactions in small groups; anthropologists observe simple societies and small communities; political scientists observe the behaviour of political leaders and political institutions. In a sense, all branches of social sciences begin and end with observation (Webb and Webb 1932).

Characteristics of Observation

Observation as a method of data collection has certain characteristics. First, it entails both physical and mental activity. Second, it is selective. A researcher does not observe anything and everything, but selects the range of things to be observed on the basis of the nature, scope and objectives of his/her study. Third, it is purposive and not casual. Fourth, it captures the natural social context in which a person's behaviour occurs. Fifth, it grasps the significant events and occurrences that affect social relations of the participants.

Types of Observations

Observation may be classified in different ways. With reference to the investigator's role, it may be classified into (*i*) participant observation and (*ii*) non-participant observation. In terms of mode of observation, it may be classified into (*iii*) direct observation and (*iv*) indirect observation. With reference to the rigour of the system adopted, observation is classified into (*v*) controlled observation and (*vi*) uncontrolled observation.

'Participant observation' is a method where the observer is a part of the phenomenon or group which is observed and he/she acts as both an observer and a participant. Under 'non-participant observation', the observer stands apart and does not participate in the phenomenon observed. 'Direct observation' means observation of an event personally by the observer when it takes place. 'Indirect observation' does not involve the physical presence of the observer, and the recording is done by mechanical, photographic or electronic devices. 'Controlled observation' involves standardisation of observational techniques and exercises of maximum control over extrinsic and intrinsic variables by adopting experimental design and systematically recording observation. 'Uncontrolled observation' does not involve control over extrinsic and intrinsic variables.

Application

It is a widely adopted method in PRA. It is used in combination with other methods. This method is flexible and allows the observer to see and record subtle aspects of events and behaviour as they occur. He/she is also free to shift places and change the focus of observation. Direct observation is useful when the information we want is about observable things and when we need to cross-check people's account of what happens (Laws et al. 2003).

Procedure

The quality of direct observation can be ensured through the adoption of step-by-step procedure. The steps that can be adopted are briefly stated here:

- Determine the focus of the observation. The direct observation has to be selective due to time and resource constraints.
- Establish the objective of direct observation and information required.
- Timing of the observation has to be decided in consultation with the people. Time is critical in direct observation. Wrong timings can distort the findings.
- Establishing rapport with the people, community or organisation to be observed is important before embarking on direct observation.
- Make sure that those being observed are aware of the reasons for your study and they do not see you in negative terms.
- Allow sufficient time for observation. Brief visits can be deceptive, partly because people tend to behave differently in the presence of observers.
- Note down any events that you do not understand and try to clarify them with the participants from the community.
- Write down your first impression about your observation before the analysis stage later on.
- Analyse, summarise and report in relation to the objectives set out at the start of the exercise.
- Check for reliability and validity. Direct observation techniques are susceptible to errors and bias that can affect reliability and validity. These can be minimised by recording observation promptly, seeking clarification on the spot, using a multi-disciplinary team, etc.

Merits

- Direct observation allows the observer to view what the users actually do in the context. It allows the observer to focus attention on specific areas of interest.
- An event, institution, facility or process can be studied in its natural setting, thereby providing a richer understanding of the subject.
- It directly records what people do as distinct from what they say they do.
- It can generate a large amount of data in a short time.
- It can generate data which may provide the basis for further discussion with those observed.

Limitations

- Direct observation is susceptible to observer bias. The very act of observation can affect the behaviour being studied.
- It focuses on observable behaviour and therefore it is not possible to understand the motives of the people through this method.
- At times, it has the danger of leading to oversimplification or distortion of the meaning of the situation.
- Observation may not be of use in studying past events or activities.

Summary

Observation is a systematic 'seeing' or viewing of a specific phenomenon in its natural setting. The main characteristics of observation can be summarised as follows: (*i*) it is a physical and mental activity; (*ii*) it is selective; (*iii*) it is purposive; and (*iv*) it captures important events and occurrence that affect the social relations of the participant. Observations are of different types. They are participant and non-participant observation; direct and indirect observation and controlled and uncontrolled observation. Direct observation is a widely used method in PRA. It is a flexible method. The quality of data gathered through direct observation depends on the adoption of a systematic procedure. The merits of direct observation are its directness, flexibility and richness of insights generated. The limitations are that (*i*) it is susceptible to bias; (*ii*) it has the danger of leading to oversimplification; (*iii*) it is not possible to understand the motives of the people; and (*iv*) it is not of use in studying past events.

21

Members of PRA Team: Roles and Responsibilities

Participatory rural appraisal (PRA) is basically a teamwork. The team comprises insiders and outsiders. The team is multidisciplinary in character, essential for understanding and studying a problem, situation or condition from varied angles and dimensions. The team from outside interacts with the team from inside and vice versa. They jointly learn. Individual interaction has limited scope in PRA and seldom resorted to. Further, a structured questionnaire or schedule is seldom used. Semi-structured interview (SSI) technique using a checklist is invariably adopted in the process of learning. SSI has its own limitations and shortcomings. The members of the team as individuals and as a team are likely to commit errors which ultimately undermine the outcome of PRA. Furthermore, PRA strongly believes in methodological pluralism. Two or more methods can be simultaneously used. For instance, study of the physical and social structure of a village demands use of methods like transect, direct observation, mapping and interviewing. It is, therefore, essential that PRA exercises in the field are carried out with great care and diligence. This is possible to a greater extent when each member of the team knows what is expected of him/her, what he/she is supposed to do and not to do.

ROLES

The roles of the members of PRA team are clearly defined. They fall under five categories:

- Facilitator;
- Interviewer;
- Content writer;

- Process observer; and
- Gatekeeper.

The roles and responsibilities of each member of the team are very significant for the quality and validity of the data and information (both quantitative and qualitative), which in turn depend on the effective performance of each player in the team.

We will now see the roles and responsibilities of members of the PRA team.

Facilitator

Facilitation is the fundamental function of PRA. It is the key of PRA. It unlocks the human potential of individuals, thus increasing their capacity to think, to relate, to act and to reflect from a foundation of communication competencies. Tim Kennedy defines facilitation as 'the process of change which takes place while organizing and mobilizing the competencies of the community members' (White 1991). Shirley A. White says 'effective facilitation is an act that engages the creative forces within persons which energizes thinking and doing'. It is based on the premise that all people have a right to voice their views and become partners in the development process. It is communication that enables people to express themselves to collaborate, to become effective participants and act on their own behalf. The process of facilitation commences where the community members are present and normally leads to empowerment and mutual respect, ensuring sustainable development. The outcome of the facilitation process is strengthening of knowledge and decision-making abilities, enabling co-equal, collaborative relationship which transform an individual from a position of powerless and voiceless existence to the point where they become active communicators. The person who performs the function of facilitation is known as a facilitator. Robert Chambers defines a facilitator as 'a person who enables others to express themselves'.

The characteristics of a facilitator

The outcome of PRA largely depends on a skilful facilitator. The facilitator therefore needs to possess certain competencies. A few such competencies may be inherent in the facilitator while others need to develop them through experience. Essential competencies required of a facilitator are stated here (White 1991):

- He/she must be socially committed. He has to get in tune with the local population and needs to spend a lot of time in the field. He must learn as much as possible about the history and culture of the place where he would be working.
- He/she must be sensitive. He/she has to identify himself/herself with the local situation and the life of the local people with their specific culture, values and life.
- He/she should get a good orientation and historical perspective as early as possible conveying the political and development environment.

- He/she has to respect, understand and preserve the diversity of the individual and the community.
- He/she must possess certain basic qualities such as open-mindedness, honesty, integrity and intellectual curiosity.
- He/she should have the courage of conviction and take the risks that are necessary to empower the people.
- He/she must be able to cope up with conflicts, hostility, rejection, avoidance, deception, suspicion, envy and erratic behaviour.
- He/she has to recognise the importance of individuals in relation to collective well-being.
- He/she must be competent, confident and conscious, and most of all an unbiased communicator.
- He/she must avoid criticising participants or debating their positions, making procedural decision for the groups without asking for their preferences, pressurising them into making a decision and talking excessively.
- He/she should be empathetic in personal interactions.
- He/she should be democratic in his communication and relationships.
- He/she must be knowledgeable about the participatory process.

Above all, it is a combination of many factors, though the most important ones are those that come from within, that is, through the spirit, attitudes and values of the individual in his or her commitment to the people.

Role

The facilitator is sort of a leader of the PRA team. He/she is the linker, the motivator and the synergiser. His/her responsibilities include the following:

- He/she has to convene a meeting of the people at a place which is convenient for them. He has to put the people together in order to make things happen, to catalyse thinking, motivation, interaction, action, research and reflection.
- He/she has to create and maintain an environment for dialogue, learning and transformation. He/she has to see that the environment is supportive, creative, consensual and facilitative.
- He/she has to explain the purpose of the exercise and make the ways and means of carrying out the exercise clear to the participants. In other words, he/she has to see that the methods to be practised are mutually understood.
- He/she has to set the agenda for discussion based on PRA exercise.
- He/she has to ensure that the discussion or reflection is focused.
- He/she has to see that he/she, along with the team members, listens effectively, clarifies the doubts of the insiders and summarises the outcome.
- He/she has to watch out for and deal with intense emotion, if any, of the insiders.
- He/she has to enforce strict adherence of ground rules by the team members.

- He/she has to launch into a partnership with the people, which transforms the way they look at themselves and feel about themselves, the way they relate to their neighbours and friends and the way they view their community.
- Once the climate for dialogue and interaction is set, he/she may hand over the stick to the interviewers. However, he/she has to see the process of interaction without continued interruption and domination from outside.
- He/she has to ensure that the process of interaction commences and ends naturally; he/she along with the team members keeps a positive and optimistic perspective throughout the exercise.
- He/she has to speak the people's language. He/she has to walk the path of opportunities with them so that they can reach a higher ground.

Stages of facilitation for capacity development

The facilitator cannot immediately acquire all the competencies required of him for the exercise. He/she has to go through five stages of facilitation development (Gubbels and Koss 2000). He/she would be able to lead the PRA team once he/she reaches the final stage of facilitation. The various stages of facilitation that require different types of support are embryonic, emerging, growing, well-developed and mature (see Table 21.1).

Table 21.1
Stages of Facilitation

Roles and Responsibilities	Facilitation Development Stages				
	Embryonic	Emerging	Growing	Well-developed	Mature
Team leader Trains and mentors					Able to lead and train new facilitators
Facilitator Leads and supports				Able to plan, adapt and create some leadership	
Team member Facilitates and plans			Able to adapt some planning & exercise creation		
Beginner Facilitates with support		Able to facilitate with support, little adaptation			
Participant Exposure to methods	Able to participate in exercises				

Source: Gubbels and Koss (2000).

- Embryonic: An individual is exposed to PRA for the first time at this stage. He/she is just a participant. He/she is able to participate and observe the PRA exercise.
- Emerging: Having learnt about PRA methods as a participant, an individual may be able to facilitate PRA exercise in the field with support and guidance from an experienced person.
- Growing: The facilitator at this stage becomes a member of the PRA team. He/she takes on more responsibilities for planning, practising and evaluating PRA exercise in the field. As a member of the team, he/she becomes more familiar and comfortable with adapting and creating exercises and continues to develop his/her facilitation skills through a regular feedback session.
- Well-developed: A facilitator at this stage has enough experience with PRA methods to take on more of a leadership role within a PRA team. Facilitators at this stage can also innovate on new tools and techniques or improvise the existing methods.
- Mature: A mature facilitator is able to help others develop their facilitation skills. He or she can serve as a team leader and can mentor the less experienced facilitators during participatory workshops. At this stage, a facilitator is very comfortable in organising the PRA exercise tailored to specific situations, designing exercises and coordinating the process from preparation to action planning.

Developing facilitation skills at any stage is an ongoing, hands-on process that requires the ability to be self-critical and to accept feedback from others. Good facilitators are not those people who know how to facilitate, but they are the ones who have the courage to continuously try out new ideas and welcome both positive and critical feedback.

Interviewer

An interview is a conversation or dialogue between two or more people. The interviewer is the one who asks questions. The interviewee or the respondent is the one who answers the question. PRA uses individual as well as group interviews. In an individual interview the information is of a specific, sensitive, confidential or personal nature. Group interview is broader in nature and may be based on specific topics. The information sought is not of a personal or confidential nature. Whatever may be the type of interview, the quality, validity and authenticity of the information largely depend on the way in which the interview is conducted by the interviewer and the qualities of the interviewer.

Guidelines

The interviewer has to follow certain guidelines. They are briefly stated here:

- The interviewer along with the team members has to choose a setting with little or no disturbance. He/she has to ensure that the respondents are comfortable.

- He/she should then explain the purpose of the interview. An interview should have a clear purpose and focus.
- He/she should prepare a checklist or primary questions.
- He/she should ask questions that encourage description, discussion and depth. He/she should ask questions that encourage respondents to explain and elaborate. The questions that begin with 'how' are particularly effective. Beware of questions that begin with 'why', especially at the beginning of the interview, because this discourages elaboration. The following is an example:

  - **Discourages elaboration:** Did you register for the programme to increase your knowledge in the field?
  - **Encourages elaboration:** Please tell me how you got interested in this programme.

- He/she should organise the interview. He/she should organise the topics and know the issues he/she wants to cover in advance. He/she has to group similar topics and questions together to improve the flow of the interview and provide structure. It is a good practice to begin the interviews with general questions because they are easy to answer and can help break the ice.
- He/she should schedule an ample time for the interview.
- He/she has to pay attention to the non-verbal behaviour, especially the signs of the respondents being comfortable or uncomfortable. Non-verbal behaviour helps you decide when to pursue more information, when to pack off, when to offer reassurance and when to change topics.
- He/she should be prepared to ask follow-up questions, such as 'Could you tell us something more about that?' or 'What do you mean by that?', while allowing the interviewee ample time to think about and respond to questions. Silence can encourage an interviewee to expand on an answer. But then, extended silences can become awkward, particularly with people he/she is meeting for the first time.
- After the interview, he/she should write notes about how he/she thought about the way in which the interview went, other feelings and impression about the respondents, etc., and share them with members of the PRA team.

Qualities of the interviewer

Kvale (1996) has outlined the qualities of a skilled interviewer:

- He/she should be knowledgeable. He/she should become thoroughly familiar with the focus of the interview.
- He/she should be clear. He/she should ask simple, easy, short questions without using jargon.
- He/she should be gentle. He/she should allow the respondents to finish. He should give them time to think. He should tolerate pauses.

- He/she should be sensitive. He/she should listen attentively to what is being said and how it is said. He/she should be empathetic.
- He/she should be open and flexible. He/she should respond to what is important to the respondents.
- He/she should be critical. He/she should be prepared to politely challenge what is being said. In other words, he/she should be in a position to question inconsistencies, if any, in replies of the respondents.
- He/she should remember and integrate. He/she should relate what is being said to what has previously been said.
- He/she should be able to interpret. He/she should clarify and extend meanings of the respondents' statement without changing their meanings.

Dos

- Show interest and enthusiasm in learning from the people.
- Be sensitive to the moods of the respondents and build on it.
- Be alert—look for information and leads, seize upon them and follow.
- Create an atmosphere of confidence, trust and enjoyment.
- Remember that everyone has something to say. Involve the silent ones, especially the women.
- Listen carefully and facilitate an information flow.
- Allow 'cross-checking' of information among the participants.
- Check alienation from your group. Involve yourself in what is going on.

Don'ts

- Don't feel superior to participants.
- Don't hesitate to clear your doubts.
- Don't take the participants for granted.
- Don't monopolise the interview.
- Don't follow a single track of pursuing something that is of interest only to you.
- Don't misinterpret the information.

Content Writer

We use a combination of methods in PRA. Data and information (quantitative and qualitative) flow from people, places and process. They are analysed on the spot, mostly by the people facilitated by the team from outside. The analysed data and information and the inferences drawn along with the visuals and diagrams are to be meticulously recorded and documented for action. The content writer is responsible for this important task.

Tasks

The content writer has to keep the checklist of topics and questions prepared by the team for interaction with the people and use that checklist as the basis for recording the transactions.

Most of the PRA exercises are visual in nature. The visuals in the form of maps, seasonal calendars, Venn diagrams, trend analysis, matrices, etc., drawn by the people on the ground have to be redrawn by the content writer on a newsprint or paper with utmost care, without omitting any details. The legends used should be carefully noted down.

The visuals presented can be part of SSIs or conversations introduced as a means for the local people to express, share and analyse their knowledge. It is known as 'interviewing the map', 'interviewing the diagram' and 'interviewing the matrix'. It means using visuals as a medium for further discussion and analysis. For example, on the completion of a participatory social map, the interviewer can ask people to locate highly vulnerable people on the map and further ask them about the nature of vulnerability, their livelihood opportunities and options and their coping strategies. During interviewing the diagram a great deal of information is likely to flow in. The content writer has to record all such information.

He/she has to keenly observe and listen to the proceedings and wait for the final confirmed responses to emerge and record such responses.

He/she has to ensure that he/she has recorded only cross-checked, triangulated and valid information and data.

On completion of the exercise, he/she has to share recorded data and information with the people gathered. This would be a sort of recheck on the data collected. It also fulfils the requirement of the culture of sharing.

He/she has to also present the data and information to the members of the PRA team and seek clarification on commission and omission of information and data.

The process determines the quality of the data and information. Hence, the content writer has to sit with the process observer and ensure that the recorded data and information satisfy the tests of trustworthiness.

He/she has to note down the place, date, objectives and participants of the exercise. Due acknowledgement should be given to inside participants by recording their names on newsprint or paper. A copy of visuals along with the data and information should be given to the participating group from the village or location where the exercise was done.

Process Observer

Process observation is a method of documenting, reflecting on and evaluating the implementation of PRA. It is a critical component in PRA because it (*i*) provides immediate feedback; (*ii*) maintains the quality of PRA work; (*iii*) enables the practitioners to adhere to the principles and values of PRA; (*iv*) builds confidence among members of the PRA team; (*v*) helps improve the existing methods and promotes methodological innovation; and (*vi*) helps to explain the accuracy, reliability and replicability of the information gathered and shared. Good practice and principles, such as openness, flexibility, adaptability and improvisation of methods, depend on critical reflection by members of the PRA team. The quality of PRA and the credibility can be improved if the process is observed, reflected upon, and learning experience feedback is put into practice.

Tasks

The process observer in the PRA team has to observe and take down notes on events, incidents and transactions that occur in the course of gathering and sharing information. Based on this, he/she prepares a report that is shared among the team members during in-house session for reflection, reaction and action.

Guidelines

The process observer has to look at the process from three angles (Narayanasamy and Ramesh 1996):

(*i*) Atmosphere-based
(*ii*) Team-based
(*iii*) People-based

(*i*) Atmosphere-based

- Is the atmosphere for information gathering informal, free, congenial, conducive and non-threatening?
- Is the location a common place where all sections of the community, including the women, could assemble?
- Is there any place-specific barrier to assembling and discussing?
- How are the seating positions placed?
- Who seems to occupy the superior place?
- Does the seating position provide scope and opportunity to establish eye contact with the participants?

(*ii*) Team-based

- Is there role reversal? Do the outsiders act and behave as learners?
- Is there any role confusion and role change among the team members?
- Do the members of the PRA team play their assigned roles correctly and effectively?
- Is there any rushing?
- Is the learning process gradual and progressive?
- Is there coherence and cogency between successive questions?
- Are the questions jumbled, leading to confusion and ambiguity among the participants?
- Does the interviewer establish eye contact with every participant?

- Does he focus only on a few active participants or lead informants?
- Is there adequate probing and cross-checking of information?
- Are the six helpers in PRA, namely, what, when, where, who, why and how, adequately and appropriately used?
- Are the information generated triangulated, cross-checked and substantiated?
- Is the facilitator sensitive to the needs of the group?
- Is the discussion too lengthy or too short?
- Is 'shoulder tapping' done whenever necessary?
- Are the team members sensitively reminding each other of the need to take a listening attitude?
- Are 'chance encounters' made use of or ignored?
- Are there any language barriers?
- Does the team share the information with the people?
- Is there a natural starting and a natural ending of the PRA exercise?

(iii) People-based

- What is the ratio of mix of participants?
- Is there fair representation of young and old, men and women, rich and poor?
- Are there any dominants from inside?
- Which local people appear to be excluded from the process?
- Do the participants from inside do, say, show, map the diagram with natural involvement, enthusiasm and willingness?
- Is there any reluctance on part of the participants in carrying out the PRA exercise?
- Are locally available materials used in the exercises?
- Is sufficient time given to the participants to discuss, debate and arrive at a conclusion?

A few more tips for the process observer

Effective PRA normally leads to or results in a 'change' of the people. The change is normally in the form of better knowledge and awareness of the conditions in which they live. This change does not occur immediately. It occurs as the groups pass through different stages of development. The process observer should have a 'third eye' and a 'second hand' to observe and note the changes in the knowledge and behaviour of the participants towards themselves and the outsiders in successive visits and interactions.

There are five stages through which a well-facilitated group passes, namely, rapport-building, confidence-gaining, self-appreciation, capacity-building and empowerment, and action. The process observer has to note and record the 'changes' in the participants in each of the stages. The guiding questions to note the change in each stage are presented here.

- Rapport-building
  - Is there transparency in the relationship between the participants from inside and the outside team?
- Confidence-gaining
  - Has the participating group gained adequate confidence on the motives and purposes expressed by the outside team?
  - Have the outsiders enabled the participating group to gain confidence in their own analysis and interpretation of the situation and events?
- Self-appreciation
  - Has the process of PRA paved the way for self-appreciation by the participating group of their own analysis and interpretation of situation and events?
- Capacity-building and empowerment
  - Does the process enable capacity-building and empowerment?
  - Is it superficial?
  - Has the stick been handed over?
  - Do people effectively handle the stick?
  - Has the dependency syndrome started waning?
- Action
  - Does the PRA process tend to initiate action or merely enable the outsiders to deliver a fine speech, roll up the information charts drawn by the villagers and quickly leave once and for all?
  - Has the outside team raised the expectations and exceeded the scope of PRA, or have they empowered the people to facilitate their own change?

The guidelines cited would largely help us wherever we have failed to adhere to the basic tenets of PRA. A continuous and critical reflection on the process would enable us to handle the PRA methods with ease, confidence and ingenuity and enable us to carry out feedback analysis in practice. This would enhance the quality of PRA. Process observation, therefore, is an important component of PRA. However, it is a difficult task. The person who observes the process has an all-absorbing role to play. He/she must be an intense, patient listener and a keen observer of PRA methodologies and principles.

Gatekeeper

PRA is conducted in different settings like fields, open grounds, school, community buildings, public places and temples, where people can gather, interact and discuss. The purpose of convening a meeting at such places is to ensure the participation of all sections of the community. Such places also provide the right type of ambience for the group to carry out the exercise.

Such places have their merits and limitations. The merits are that (*i*) visuals, drawings and diagrams can be effectively facilitated as such places provide space required for the exercises; (*ii*) they provide an enabling environment for all people to participate; and (*iii*) all sections of the community irrespective of age, sex and caste can be involved. The limitations are that (*i*) the process is likely to get disturbed if there are saboteurs in the village and (*ii*) it is difficult to close the group as participants are likely to leave or go out in the middle of the exercise.

The task of the gatekeeper is to help the PRA team to overcome these limitations. He/she has to clearly tackle and manage the saboteurs, such as drunkards, hypercritics and development brokers, in a setting.

Children normally get involved in PRA exercises. They help a great deal by collecting the locally available material for carrying out an exercise. They do act as participants. However, they disturb the process occasionally. It is the task of the facilitator to see that they are engaged; otherwise simple, small games may be organised for them. He/she may involve them in singing songs or in sports or may tell them stories. This would not only keep children away from the place of exercise but also build up a better rapport between the team and the community.

The gatekeeper should help the facilitator to 'close' the group as early as possible and help him/her to complete the exercise without any disturbance from within and outside.

SUMMARY

PRA is a teamwork. The members of the team define and specify roles, such as facilitator, interviewer, content writer, process observer and gatekeeper. Each member of the team has to effectively perform the role assigned to him/her to maintain the trustworthiness and validity of the outcome in the form of data and information.

The facilitator is the leader, thinker, organiser and synergiser of the team. His/her primary responsibility is to enable others to explore themselves. He/she must have a thorough understanding of the people with whom he/she works. He/she must possess basic qualities, such as open-mindedness, honesty, integrity and intellectual curiosity. He/she must have the right attitude and behaviour. His/her primary role is to see that the process of PRA begins and ends well with all concerned taking active participation. He/she should create a convivial atmosphere, so that everybody enjoys participation. The facilitator, in order to become quite competent in performing his/her role, has to go through five stages of facilitation, which include embryonic, emerging, growing, well-developed and mature.

The interviewer's role is quite significant in PRA. The interviewer, by and large, uses the SSI technique where some of the topics and questions are predetermined and new questions come up in the course of interaction. He/she has to be very careful and intelligent in asking questions. He/she has to avoid leading, vague and ambiguous questions. He/she should provide many opportunities for the group to discuss debate and come out with answers. He/she should be capable of judging the response. He/she should develop the qualities of a skilled interviewer.

The task of the content writer is to record the outcome of the PRA exercise. He/she has to redraw the visuals, diagram and maps that were drawn on the ground by the people. He/she has to ensure that information and data gathered are cross-checked and validated. He/she has to further ensure that all the participants are properly acknowledged.

Process observation is a critical component in PRA as a process observer helps in locating the errors and mistakes committed in the field and also by overcoming such errors in future. The process observer should observe the process from three different angles, namely, atmosphere-based, team-based and people-based. His/her report on the entire process helps the team to reflect on what went right and what went wrong in the course of carrying out the PRA exercise.

The role of the gatekeeper is to ensure a smooth start and a smooth end of the PRA exercise by effectively tackling the saboteurs.

All five players of the PRA team have to stick to the assigned role. They should not change their roles as this may create confusion and disturb the process.

22

Application of PRA Methodology: A Few Illustrations

We have discussed the various methods of participatory rural appraisal (PRA), their applications, strengths and weaknesses. The PRA methods, as we have seen, help in collecting both qualitative and quantitative information which is by and large triangulated in the process of gathering information itself. The methods can be practised with a cross section of a wide variety of audience as they are flexible, interactive, semi-structured, visual and user-friendly. The strength of PRA lies in its methodological pluralism. It has several methods in its menu. These methods should not be viewed in isolation. It is the combination of flexible and innovative use of these methods that enrich both the process and the outcome of the appraisal. Hence, the researchers and field workers interested in employing PRA tools should adequately prepare themselves before using these methods in the field. They need to know the major themes or issues and sub-themes, the data required to have better insight into the various sub-themes and issues and the methods that can be used to collect the data and information. We present a few broad themes and issues and the PRA methods that can be used to appraise and analyse the themes and issues:

- Participatory poverty assessment
- Sustainable livelihood analysis
- Analysis of hunger
- Vulnerability analysis
- Institutional analysis
- Participatory evaluation

The framework suggested for each theme and issue is neither rigid nor a blueprint. It is only indicative. While practising the framework in the field, the PRA team can feel free to use its own judgement. It can be innovative in using the methods. It can improvise the methods depending on the local situation and condition. However, the basic principles of PRA should be kept in mind while employing the framework.

PARTICIPATORY POVERTY ASSESSMENT

The World Bank in the year 1999 undertook a global research on 'Consultations with the poor' (World Bank, 1999). The purpose of the study was to enable a wide range of poor people in diverse countries and conditions to share their views in such a way that they can inform and contribute to the concept and content of the World Development Report 2000–01. It was also expected to provide a micro-level perspective of the poor people's own experience of poverty and responses to it, illuminating the nature of risk and vulnerability.

There were four main themes for the analysis of the study:

- Exploring well-being
- Priorities of the poor
- Institutional analysis
- Gender relations

The checklist of issues and the methods of PRA proposed for the study are presented in Table 22.1.

Table 22.1
Participatory Poverty Assessment (PPA)

Theme	Data Requirements	Methods	Remarks
Physical and demographic features	Location of the village or settlement Physical structure of the village or settlement Infrastructure of various types Houses: types Number of families: caste-wise female-headed households Population: sex-wise, age-wise, literacy status-wise Disabled persons Destitutes Totally resourceless households	Village transect Direct observation Social mapping Semi-structured interview (SSI)	Start with village transect. This would help in having a rough mental map of the physical structure of the village. This can be followed by social map Observe and ask questions using the SSI technique

(Table 22.1 Contd.)

(Table 22.1 Contd.)

Theme	Data Requirements	Methods	Remarks
Well-being/ill-being analysis	Local definition of well-being, ill-being, deprivation and poverty Listing of criteria based on which households are placed in different well-being groups/categories Listing of different well-being groups/categories of households as identified by the local people Characteristics of households in each of these categories Preparation of households in each category	Well-being analysis listing and scoring SSI	Social map is the basis for carrying out well-being analysis. Hence start with social mapping with a list of households and heads of households. Employ well-being analysis to identify the various categories of households and superimpose them on social map
People's perception about security, risk, vulnerability, opportunities, social exclusion and crime and conflict	People's definition of security and risk Households with and without security; how are they differentiated? The factors that make household insecure or at greater risk Trends in security/risk with reasons Main kinds of shocks that people have faced Coping strategies/mechanisms adopted to overcome the sudden shocks to sources of livelihoods Opportunities for socio-economic mobility: increase and decrease with reasons Groups which have made use of opportunities Groups which could not make use of opportunities: reasons Possibilities for moving out of poverty: requirements needed for people to move out of poverty Households/groups excluded from active participation in community life or decision making with reasons Impact of such exclusion Power relation between the excluded and the included Social cohesion or unity as perceived by the people Trends in social unity, crime and conflict	Timeline Trend analysis Seasonal calendar Causal: impact assessment Scoring Case studies In-depth interview with individual households Focus group discussion (FGD)	Keep the social map and well-being analysis as the basis for discussion Employ timeline, trend analysis and seasonal calendar for studying the short-term and long-term trends Conduct an in-depth interview with one poor man and one poor woman who have fallen into poverty; and one poor man and one poor woman who have moved out of poverty Conduct cause and effect diagram on the causes and effects of poverty Based on the above exercises, go in for FGD with key informants

(Table 22.1 Contd.)

(Table 22.1 Contd.)

Theme	Data Requirements	Methods	Remarks
	Tensions or conflicts between groups in the community: reasons and impact Coping strategies of the households with decline in well-being Changes in the number and types of well-being categories Changes in the criteria for determining categories Causes for changes Typology of deprivation: sudden, seasonal, cyclic, chronic Foreseeable changes in the future		
Problems and priorities	Problems faced by the different groups within the community and prioritisation of such problems Differences in problems and priorities with reference to age, gender, social hierarchy and economic well-being Problems faced by the poor Changes in the problems over a period People's vision for the future Problems that can be solved by people themselves Problems that can be solved only with external support	FGD Listing Scoring Ranking Trend analysis Malady remedy analysis	Brainstorm with different groups of people to list the problems Use open or closed scoring method to assign scores to problems Rank the problems Use trend analysis to find out changes in the problems
Institutional analysis	The most important formal, informal, government, non-government and market institution within and outside the community Importance attached to each institution Impact of such institutions on men and women: positive and negative Gender differences Rating of these institutions by the people in terms of trust and confidence that they place on them Effectiveness of these institutions and factors behind the judging of effectiveness	Mobility map Venn diagram Listing and scoring Ranking FGD Case study	Start with mobility map to ascertain the various institutions within and outside the community Categorise them Use Venn diagram and scoring and ranking techniques to find out the effectiveness of these institutions Go in for FGD to understand the various issues related to the functioning of the institutions Select one or two institutions and sketch the profile of the institutions using case study method

(Table 22.1 Contd.)

(Table 22.1 Contd.)

Theme	Data Requirements	Methods	Remarks
	Profile of some institutions in some depth Support of the institutions during times of crises, such as loss of property, job or livelihoods, poor crops, disease, environmental crisis Availability of informal safety nets Informal social networks		
Gender relations	Conditions of women over a period of time Changes in women's and men's responsibilities within the households and reasons Changes in women's and men's responsibilities in the community and reasons Women's and men's role in the decision-making process within the household and reasons Women's and men's role in the decision-making process within the community and reasons Changes in violence against women within the household and in the community with reasons Gender relation among different sections of the community The socio-economic conditions of women over a period of time	Activity schedule Access and control over resources Decision-making matrix Trend analysis FGD	Employ daily routine or activity schedule for men and women separately Facilitate the exercise on access and control over resources for men and women Practise the decision-making matrix among men and women separately The outcome of the exercise would provide an understanding of the gender relations in the households and the community Use trend analysis for ascertaining changes in the conditions of women Use FGD for an in-depth analysis

Source: World Bank (1999).

SUSTAINABLE LIVELIHOOD ANALYSIS

The Department for International Development (UK) has developed a framework known as 'sustainable livelihood framework', which presents a comprehensive analysis of the main factors that affect people's livelihoods, and the typical relationship between these. The framework can be meaningfully used to assess the contribution of the existing activities for livelihood sustainability and to plan new development activities for sustainable livelihood.

The core issues presented in the framework are:

- livelihood assets, which include human capital, social capital, physical capital, natural capital and financial capital, having a strong influence on the livelihood of the people;
- structures and processes which represent organisations, institutions, policies and legislation that shape livelihood;
- livelihood strategies which denote the range and combination of activities and choices that people make in order to achieve their livelihood goals;
- vulnerability context which speaks about shocks (drought, flood, storm, civil conflicts and epidemics), trends, seasonal shifts in prices, employment opportunities, food availability which affects people's livelihoods;
- livelihood outcomes which are the achievement or outputs of livelihood strategies.

The framework is quite comprehensive and provides a vivid picture of appraising the various issues. The framework does suggest various PRA and other conventional methods that are to be judiciously used to appraise and analyse various issues connected with sustainable livelihood. We present in Table 22.2 the issues related to sustainable livelihood, the data requirements and the methods that can be used to appraise the various issues.

Table 22.2
Sustainable Livelihood Analysis

Issue	Data Requirements	Methods	Remarks
Human capital	Complexity of the local environment Sources of information that are valuable to the livelihood of people Groups which do not have access to the sources of information The effect of exclusion on the nature of information available Existence of tradition of local innovations Sources of technology—internal or external or both Type of information which the people feel they lack Awareness of their rights Awareness of the policies, legislations and regulations that impact their livelihoods Life expectancy at birth Infant mortality rate Enrolment in primary school Completion rate in primary school Literacy rate Public expenditure per capita Physicians per thousand population Primary school student–teacher ratio Education, health and sanitation facilities	Review of secondary data Social mapping Timeline Trend change Mobility map Venn diagram Scoring and ranking	Secondary sources often provide a good overview of human capital issues. Hence, it is always desirable to review the existing secondary sources. Data gap, if any, in human capital can be collected by employing participatory methods Start with social map This can be followed by a series of PRA exercises like timeline, trend change, mobility map, Venn diagram and scoring and ranking to understand the various issues related to human capital

(Table 22.2 Contd.)

(*Table 22.2 Contd.*)

Issue	Data Requirements	Methods	Remarks
Social capital	Number of formal and informal groups Membership in such groups Composition of membership Nature and quality of groups Relationship among the members of the groups People's coping strategies at times of crisis and the extent to which they have relied on social resources to see them through Institutional linkages Degree of participatory decision making Extent of trust in the group Extent of reliance on networks of support Household income from remittances Household expenditure for gifts and transfers Old age dependency	Social map Timeline Matrix/preference ranking Venn diagrams	Social maps can help identify and locate the institutions and social relations to which people have access Timeline can be used to track broad changes in social capital and to examine why some associational links and institutions are more resilient than others to shocks and stresses Matrix/preference ranking can show the relation priority that people attribute to given social networks as well as help to understand the significance of these for particular aspects of livelihoods Venn diagrams provide an additional means for establishing the role, responsibilities and expectations that people have concerning various formal and informal institutions

Natural capital	Quantity/quality of natural resources, such as
	    land;
	    water;
	    forests;
	    mineral;
	    marine/wild;
	    common property resources;
	Various groups and their access to various types of natural resources
	Nature of access rights (i.e., private ownership, rental, common ownership, highly contested access). How secure are they? Encroachment
	Conflict over resources
	Productivity of resources and related issues, such as salinity to soil structure and fertility, value of different trees
	Trend in productivity and related issues
	Existing knowledge which can help increase the productivity of resources
	Spatial variability in the quality of resources
	The effect of externalities on the resources
	Versatility of the resource: can it be used for multiple purposes?
		Transect
		Direct observation
		Mapping
		Ranking and scoring
		Timeline
		Trend change
		Seasonal calendar
		Access and control over resources
		Venn diagram
		Mobility map
		Focus group discussion (FGD)
			The distribution of community and privately owned natural assets can be ascertained through transect-based social and resource mapping
			The quality of the resources may be known by direct observation and interaction
			The importance of resources can be ascertained by using scoring and ranking methods
			Historical changes in productivity and issues related to natural resources can be found out by using timeline, trend change and seasonal calendar
			Conflict over natural resources may be understood by access and control over resources and timeline
			Property rights regimes and the rules of access to customary and communal lands can be studied using FGD and Venn diagram

(*Table 22.2 Contd.*)

(*Table 22.2 Contd.*)

Issue	Data Requirements	Methods	Remarks
Physical capital	Items that enhance income (e.g., bicycle, agricultural implements, security mechanism) Home quality and facilities Pipe water, electricity, waste disposal and other services Personal consumption items such as radio, television, grinder, mixer, gas stove Transport Energy Access to information communications	Mapping Direct observation Access and control Short survey Ranking and scoring Causal diagram	The existence and quality of the physical assets can be studied through social map, direct observation and inventory techniques Mapping, causal diagram, Venn diagram, ranking and scoring techniques can be used to research the people's perception of infrastructure provisions, accessibility and cost by different groups
Financial capital	Financial service organisations: formal and informal The type of services provided by such agencies and conditions Access to such organisations Factors which prevent from gaining access The current level of sources and loans Where do people keep or invest their savings? Flow of remittance income Mode of transmission of remittance income Reliability of remittance Seasonal variations in remittances Who controls remittance income when it arrives? How is it used? Is it reinvested?	Preference ranking and matrix scoring Seasonal calendar Venn diagram Mobility map Semi-structured interview (SSI) FGD	Preference ranking and matrix can be used to compare the different credit sources or savings Mobility map can be used to understand location of sources of credit Venn diagram can be employed to find out the effectiveness of services rendered by the credit providers Seasonal calendar can help reveal within-year variations in savings and borrowings patterns SSI and FGD can help develop an understanding of the wider financial environment. Assessment of financial matter is a delicate issue. Making an accurate and thorough assessment of these issues requires a great deal of skill, use of a variety of methods and extensive triangulation
Policy, institutions and process	Social relations: the way in which aspects such as gender, ethnicity, culture, history and religious and kinship affect the livelihoods of different groups within a community Social and political organisation: decision-making process, civic bodies, social rules and norms, democracy, leadership power and authority	Venn diagram SWOT analysis Key informants' interview Case studies Secondary data review	Social relations and process relate closely to social capital. Many of the methods discussed in that context are equally valid here. SWOT analysis can be used to analyse the performance of organisations

(*Table 22.2 Contd.*)

(Table 22.2 Contd.)

Issue	Data Requirements	Methods	Remarks
	Governance: the form and quality of government system (structure, power, effectiveness, efficiency, rights and representation) Service delivery: the behaviour, effectiveness and responsiveness of state and private service delivery agencies Policy and policy process: the effect on livelihood of key polices and the way in which the policy is determined		Secondary sources may be resorted to for analysing policy and policy changes. To know the effect of policy, structured interview with key informants using checklist may be resorted to
Livelihood strategies	What does the livelihood portfolio of different social groups look like? How and why this is changing over time? How long-term is people's outlook? Are they investing in assets for the future? If so, which type of asset is a priority? How positive are the choices that people are making? Which combination of activities appears to be working best? Is there any discernible pattern of activities adopted by those who have managed to escape from poverty? Which livelihood objectives are not achievable through current livelihood strategies?	Group discussion Key informants' interviews Seasonal calendar Preference ranking Wealth ranking	Group discussions can describe evolving patterns of activity in a community and reasons for changes Key informants' interview may help reveal patterns of activity or strategies adopted by those who have managed to escape from poverty Seasonal calendar can capture the peaks and troughs in time allocation to different activities Preference ranking reveals people's criteria for decision making about their strategies Wealth ranking can produce an initial division of households ensuring discussions; may shed light on the different strategies followed by a given wealth group
Vulnerability context	Events and trends that cause stress The existence of trends and sudden changes in such trends Historical occurrences of flood, drought, epidemics, local environmental trends and cyclones Level of food stores across the year, rainfall, crop-planting and harvesting schedules, food prices, changes in health status Trends in rainfall, temperature, producers' and consumers' prices across the year, population density degradation, mortality, morbidity	Key informants' discussion Timeline Seasonal calendar Preference ranking Review of secondary data	There are two core considerations: (i) the extent to which different groups are exposed to particular trends/ shocks/seasonality; and (ii) the seasonality of their livelihoods to these factors. A combination of methods cited would help analyse the vulnerability of the poor.

(Table 22.2 Contd.)

(*Table 22.2 Contd.*)

Issue	Data Requirements	Methods	Remarks
Livelihood outcome	More income Increased well-being Reduced vulnerability Improved food security More sustainable use of natural resource base	Wealth ranking Matrix scoring Force field analysis	Force field analysis can be used to ascertain the vision of the community Wealth ranking can be employed to ascertain the improved well-being Matrix ranking would help identify sustainable use of natural resources

Source: http://www.livelihoods.org/info/guidance_sheets_pdfs/section2.pdf.

ANALYSIS OF HUNGER

Hunger is the starkest form of human deprivation. It is an inability to secure food needed to support a healthy life. More pervasive in impact are malnutrition and under-nutrition. Although acute hunger or famine receives more attention, it should be remembered that the great majority of hunger deaths comes not from starvation but from nutrition-related sicknesses and diseases.

Availability of food is a necessary condition to end hunger. But it is not a sufficient condition to ensure security of food for all. Nutrition security requires physical and economic access to a balanced diet and a conducive environment for its effective biological utilisation. Freedom from hunger is the first step in the alteration of poverty and is a prerequisite for active participation of the people in the economic activity. Hunger depletes strength and reduces the immune competence of the people and makes them vulnerable to infectious diseases, aggravating further the problems of hunger. Non-food factors play an important role in determining both access and effective biological utilisation. This is why food security involves attention to sustainable livelihoods, safe drinking water, environmental sanitation, primary health care and primary education. Any analysis on hunger should take care of all these factors. PRA methods along with the conventional methods of appraisal can be meaningfully employed to assess hunger and hunger-related issues. The Gandhigram Rural Institute (GRI) undertook a study called Hunger-Free Area Programme on the advice of the M.S. Swaminathan Research Foundation (MSSRF), Chennai, funded by Government of Tamil Nadu (PRA Unit, GRI 1997). The framework followed for the study is presented in Table 22.3.

Table 22.3
Assessment of Hunger (Absolute and Silent) at the Micro-level

Theme	Data Requirements	Methods/Tools	Remarks
Identification of hunger families and related issues	Mapped description of the houses Age, caste, sex, education, type of houses, occupation, land, livestock, possession of ration cards Availing of benefits under different schemes implemented by development agency Availability of community infrastructure such as link road, overhead tank, primary school, fair price shop, mini-health centre, cooperative institutions, banks, *balwadis*, noon-meal centre, community hall, community television, veterinary hospital, hand pumps, wells	Village transect Social map Direct observation Semi-structured interview (SSI)	Transect-based social map would help in gathering basic data about the village in which appraisal on hunger is to be initiated Cards can also be issued along with social map to gather information on households
Targeting the poor	Classification of households based on wealth and well-being Evolving criteria for classifying the households based on well-being Identification of families which eat only once or twice a day	Well-being analysis Focus group discussion (FGD)	Social map and cards prepared can be used for this exercise
Livelihood sources and opportunities of the hunger families	Sources of income: main and supplementary Existing livelihood opportunities Spending patterns Food habits, frequency, items, adequacy, etc. Debts: sources, interest, repayment behaviour Alcoholics, if any: frequency Livestock, if any Savings Starvation, if any Ailments: health problems Coping strategies in times of food scarcity Possibilities for generating additional livelihood opportunities	Livelihood analysis Individual in-depth interview	One or two poorest of the poor households may be obtained from wealth-ranking exercise Livelihood analysis can be attempted by using in-depth interview technique Similarly, livelihood analysis may be attempted for a rich family. This would provide a comparative picture and would help know the problems of the hunger families from a comparative perspective.

(Table 22.3 Contd.)

(*Table 22.3 Contd.*)

Theme	Data Requirements	Methods/Tools	Remarks
The cyclical and seasonal nature of hunger	Season-wise crops grown Employment opportunities: farm and non-farm gender-wise Income Expenditure Debt Savings Food scarcity Fodder scarcity Migration Diseases Festivals	Seasonal calendar FGD	Seasonal calendar provides a broad picture about the main activities, problems and opportunities throughout the annual cycle. It helps to identify the months of greatest difficulties and vulnerability or some other significant variability having an impact on people's lives and livelihoods
Availability of facilities and services	Visit to various places, institutions of different types with details such as frequency of visit, distance between the village and the place of visit, purpose of visit, preference and access	Mobility map FGD	This is drawn to know whether the facilities are available within a reasonable distance. For example, location of ration shop under the public distribution system (PDS) within such reach would help the poor households to avail the rice and other needs quickly and without foregoing the wage work

Effectiveness of institutions	Different types of institutions, such as
	  credit institutions;
	  health institutions;
	  educational institutions;
	  agricultural institutions;
	  welfare institutions;
	  community-based organisations;
	  panchayats;
	  other formal and informal institutions
	Importance attached to such institutions
	Effectiveness of such institutions
		Venn diagram
		FGD
			Mobility map would provide information on institutions
			The effectiveness of the institutions in terms of accessibility and quality of services provided can be found out by using Venn diagram
			FGD can help to have a detailed analysis of the institutions

(*Table 22.3 Contd.*)

(*Table 22.3 Contd.*)

Theme	Data Requirements	Methods/Tools	Remarks
Allocation and reach of the various schemes	Various schemes of the government meant for different categories of the people Reach of the government schemes Gap between availability and reach Causes for the gap	Secondary data review Social map Gap analysis	Actual allocation can be obtained from records Reach of the schemes can be ascertained through social map Gap analysis can be used to find out the gaps and causes
Assessment and prioritisation of possible options for development activities	Schemes available but not utilised Schemes available but not adequate Schemes available but of poor quality Schemes available, but do not match with needs Schemes not wanted by the people Missing elements in the existing schemes What should we stop doing? What should we continue doing? What should we start doing? Options for new development interventions Operational strategies suggested by the people Facilities and infrastructure available and to be created	Innovation assessment Matrix ranking FGD	Various schemes as obtained in the previous exercises can be listed They can be classified and ranked using matrix ranking technique FGD can be used to ascertain the innovation suggested by the people
Nutritional status	Dietary habit of the poor households Height and weight of the children Signs and symptoms that are generally attributed to deficiency diseases	Diet survey Anthropometric measurements Clinical assessment	Study the dietary habit of each of the families for a period of one week using direct observation and recall method Take the weight and height of the children and compute body mass index Go in for clinical assessment to identify the signs and symptoms that are attributed to deficiency diseases

Source: PRA Unit, GRI (1997).

VULNERABILITY ANALYSIS

Vulnerability is defined as an exposure to risks, which the people are not able to cope up with. In other words, the people, especially the poor, the marginalised, the deprived, the powerless, do not have the wherewithal to effectively face the risks to which they are exposed. Vulnerability analysis assumes importance in the context of sustainable livelihood analysis and poverty assessment. Rapid assessment of vulnerability can be attempted using participatory methodology. The methodology that can be adopted to analyse the vulnerability is shown in Table 22.4.

Table 22.4
Vulnerability Analysis

Stages	Data Requirements	Methods	Remarks
Identification of vulnerable groups	Landless Pregnant mothers in poor families Female-headed households Migrants Aged Children of migrant workers Widows Family with alcoholics Households with large number of non-earning members Families which work in hazardous industry Families with differently abled children	Transect Social mapping SSI FGD	Checklist is essential for effective field work

Focusing	Socially excluded
	People with high risk
	Totally resourceless
	People living in very poor environment and unhygienic conditions
		Well-being/ill-being ranking
		Livelihood analysis
		In-depth interview with
		  one poor woman
		  one poor man
		  one family with no food security
			Social map is the basis

Identification of causes	Immediate causes and the causes behind each of the immediate causes The effects and impacts	Cause and effect diagram or problem tree	

(Table 22.4 Contd.)

(*Table 22.4 Contd.*)

Stages	Data Requirements	Methods	Remarks

Trends in vulnerability	Employment
	Wages
	Livelihood opportunities
	Prices
	Education
	Social status
	Cultural practices
	Status of women
	Status of aged
	Status of girl children
	Coping strategies
	Safety nets
	Access to resources or capital
	Access to various forms of
	    natural resources
	Governance
		Historical transect (timeline)
		Trend analysis
		Seasonal analysis
			Provides a historical background
			Helps to know the long-term trend
			    and short-term trend

Institutional analysis	Educational institutions
	Health institutions
	Political institutions
	Parastatal organisations
	Leaders: formal and informal
	Government departments
		Mobility map
		Venn diagram
			To ascertain the location and
			    distance for availing services
			To ascertain the effectiveness or
			    otherwise of the institutions
			    and the reasons thereof

Resource analysis	Common property resources
	    (CPRs), such as:
	        ponds
	        grazing land
	        promboke land
	        irrigation tanks
	        community buildings
	        trees/forests
	        other CPRs
		Resource mapping
		Access and control
			CPRs provide livelihood
			    opportunities to vulnerable.
			    Do poor have access and
			    control over CPRs?

Gender analysis	Status of women in society	Activity schedule Access and control Decision-making matrix	Help assess the status of women
Future vision	Goal settings	Force field analysis	Where are they? Where do they want to be? Supporting and opposing forces

INSTITUTIONAL ANALYSIS

PRA tools can be effectively used to assess the functioning of any formal or informal grass-roots-level organisation. The PRA unit of GRI undertook a study, using participatory methods, to find out the causes for the dormancy of a milk producers' cooperative society and to ascertain the feasibility of reviving the society. After reviewing the secondary sources of data, a menu of PRA methods was used to analyse the various issues related to the dormancy of the society. The methodology adopted is given in Table 22.5.

Table 22.5
Rise and Fall of an Institution: An Appraisal

Issue/Problem	Sub-topic/Checklist	PRA Tools and Methods	Remarks
Milk production and productivity	Number of households in the village Number of landless, marginal, small and large farmers in the village Number of households that own milch animals: cows, buffaloes Number of dry animals Number of milch animal owners who were the members of milk producers' cooperative society Quantity of milk produced: cow milk, buffalo milk Present arrangements for disposal of milk by the members of the society	Review of secondary sources Mapping	Study the records maintained at the society Collect the relevant data Facilitate members to draw the social map which can be used for collecting the data on milk production
Historical profile of the dairy cooperative society	Year of establishment of the society Reasons for starting the society Who took the initiative? Who was the first president of the society and subsequent presidents? What was the arrangement for marketing of milk prior to the establishment of the society? Boom period Recession period Remarkable milestones in the functioning of the society Supersession of board Year of closure Period of private dealers' entry in production- and marketing-related activities	Secondary data review Timeline	Key information can be gathered through the review of records and registers maintained at the society Such information can be supplemented by the information from the timeline exercise

(Table 22.5 Contd.)

(*Table 22.5 Contd.*)

Issue/Problem	Sub-topic/Checklist	PRA Tools and Methods	Remarks
Change in the production and marketing of milk	Price of the cow, buffaloes at different periods of time Nature and extent of milk business prior to the establishment of the society Nature and extent of business after the establishment of the society Nature and extent of milk business during the period of special officer Nature and extent of milk business after the closure of the society Problems related to production and marketing of milk at different periods Price of fodder, milk at different periods Opinion of people about the functioning of the society at different periods of time Positive aspects in the functioning of the society at different periods of time	Trend change Focus group discussion (FGD)	Timeline would help in fixing the different periods to be compared. Allow them to fix the time period Using the FGD method, probe into the reasons for the changes
Season-wise problems and prospects	Seasonal variations in milk production; milk productivity; fodder availability; price of the fodder; price of the milk; receiving sale proceeds from the society/milk union Seasons of prompt payment for milk Seasons of irregular payment	Seasonal calendar Semi-structured interview (SSI) technique	While timeline and trend change provide long-term trends, the seasonal calendar indicates trends in the immediate past After drawing the calendar, a detailed discussion can be held using the SSI technique Interview the calendar
Persons behind the rise and fall of the society	Who are responsible for starting the society? Who took initiative to promote the functioning of the society? Leadership qualities found among the various office-bearers of the society Where exactly things went wrong and why?	FGD SSI technique Case study Leadership assessment	SSI technique may be followed Interview may be held with key persons associated with the society, members of SHGs, a few private milk traders, small and large milk producers FGD can be held with a cross section of all stakeholders Leadership assessment can be done with a few key informants

(*Table 22.5 Contd.*)

(Table 22.5 Contd.)

Issue/Problem	Sub-topic/Checklist	PRA Tools and Methods	Remarks
Circumstance that led to the closure and its effect	Why was the society closed? Reasons behind the closure Impact of closure on the production and marketing of milk Opinion of the people on the closure Advent of private milk traders and their impact on production and marketing	Causes and effect diagram SSI technique	SSI technique has to be followed after facilitating cause and effect diagram to analyse the impact in detail
Revival of society or otherwise	Presentation of information gathered on various issues pertaining to the closure of the society Summarise the findings to facilitate interaction Facilitating the people to crystallise their ideas Enabling the people to do their own analysis and arrive at decisions	Analysis group discussion SWOT analysis	Present all outcomes of the PRA exercises and facilitate the people to analyse and arrive at decisions
Decision on the sources of marketing	Listing the criteria that people consider preferable in various sources of marketing Individual preference in selling milk Compare the preference of individual in establishing milk marketing society	Matrix scoring Preference ranking	Elicit the criteria for marketing of milk List the various sources of marketing Prepare a matrix to know the preference

Source: Narayanasamy et al. (1998).

PARTICIPATORY EVALUATION

Monitoring and evaluation are integral parts of the project cycle. Several methods, approaches, tools and techniques have been developed and adopted to evaluate projects and programmes. The methods so developed do suffer from certain limitations: (*i*) mono-method bias that arises from relying on a single data collection method; (*ii*) tendency to ignore many valuable qualitative methods; (*iii*) failure to analyse the process of change; (*iv*) long delays in the presentation of results and reports; (*v*) exclusion of primary stakeholders in the evaluation process; and (*vi*) expensive. Many of these problems or limitations can be overcome by following participatory monitoring and evaluation (PM&E) methods which tend to see evaluation as a process. Under this approach, the primary stakeholders of the project decide the focus of the valuation. The primary stakeholders tend to develop an increased awareness and understanding of the factors affecting their situation and thereby increase their control over the development process.

The steps involved in participatory monitoring and evaluation (PM&E) are

- review objectives and activities;
- review reasons for evaluation;
- why are we doing evaluation;
- what do we want to know;

- develop evaluation questions;
- decide who will do the evaluation;
- identify the direct and indirect indicators;
- identify the information sources for evaluation questions;
- determine the skills and labour that are required to obtain information;
- determine when information gathering and analysis can be done;
- determine who will gather information;
- analyse and present the results.

Participatory monitoring and evaluation are being attempted to monitor and evaluate people based and people-centred projects. A participatory methodology developed for a watershed project is presented in Table 22.6.

Table 22.6
Participatory Monitoring and Evaluation

Activities	Indicators	Methods	Remarks
Shelterbelt development and maintenance	Shelterbelt development and maintenance Number of farmers who have given consent for establishing shelterbelts Reasons, if any, for opposing Extent of land in which shelterbelts are established Survival rate of different tree species Farmers' opinion/satisfaction over the species of trees planted in the shelterbelts Cost of shelterbelt maintenance (cost of watering, watch and ward) Willingness of the farmers to take over the maintenance of shelterbelts Number of farmers accepting/refusing the responsibility with reasons Number of workers who have migrated Number of farmers trained in nursery production Number of farmers producing seedlings and the net income from the activity Number of farmers who continue production of nurseries after the contact period Number of local males and females hired for project work Number of man-days of employment generated Number of landless and marginal farmers employed Increase in wage rate	Transect Direct observation Social map Resource map Focus group discussion (FGD) Scoring technique Case study Secondary data review Trend change Timeline	The first step is to go in for extensive transect and observe the various works executed under the project Facilitate the participants to draw the resource map and social map. This would provide the basis for further discussion based on FGD Scoring technique can be used to assess the survival rate of trees Case study can be used to assess the cost of establishing shelterbelt

(Table 22.6 Contd.)

(*Table 22.6 Contd.*)

Activities	Indicators	Methods	Remarks
Inter-belt development and maintenance	Extent of land brought under cultivation between shelterbelts The type of farmers benefited Nature and variety of crops cultivated in the inter-belt Extent of fallow and unused land brought under cultivation Production of agricultural, horticultural and agro-forestry produce Distribution of subsidy-adequacy and timeliness Improvement in household-level income	Transect Direct observation Resource map Social map FGD Case study Secondary data review Trend change	It can be done along with first activity. The same procedure can be followed
Moisture conservation and waterways' protection	Number of check dams constructed Number of waterways repaired Number of percolation ponds dug People's involvement Maintenance of tanks, ponds and ooranies Length and quality of vegetative bunds Area with strip and contour ploughing	Transect Direct observation Resource map FGD	It can be done along with the first and second activities listed above. The same procedure can be followed
Borewells	Number of borewells sunk Quality of water and yields Number of borewells under working condition Number of borewell committees and its composition Number of men and women trained in borewell maintenance Maintenance of borewells	Transect Resource map Matrix scoring FGD	Criteria for active borewells can be evolved and scoring technique can be used to assess the functioning of borewells

Farmers' association	Number of associations formed
	Number of active associations
	Composition of farmers' association
	Number of meetings convened
	Nature of issues discussed:
	    issues repeatedly occurring;
	    issues leading to quick consensus;
	    issues leading to discussions;
	    issues leading to deadlock
	Periodicity of the meetings
	Activities undertaken:
	    initiated;
	    prospects for successful completion
		Secondary data review
		Social mapping
		Scoring and ranking
		FGD
		Case studies
		Sustainability analysis
			To start with various kinds of books as maintained by the association, maybe thoroughly study them, to have a better understanding of the functioning of the association
			Case studies can be built up on one well-functioning association and on one poorly performing association

(*Table 22.6 Contd.*)

(*Table 22.6 Contd.*)

Activities	Indicators	Methods	Remarks
	Participation in the project activities		Social mapping can be used
	Number of members openly supporting		to assess the background
	Number of members openly opposing		of the members
	Quicker participation		FGD with the members of
	Savings		the association would let
	Periodicity of savings		us know the problems
	Method of savings		and prospects of the
	Type of credit		association
	Rate of interest		Sustainability analysis using
	Repayment of loan by members		scoring and ranking
	Maintenance of records and account books		techniques would help assess the sustainability
	Audit of accounts		of associations
	Linkage with bank and outside agencies		
	Community development works undertaken		

SUMMARY

Participatory approaches and methods have been increasingly used in several fields of rural development. They are also being used in the urban area in a limited context. The PRA team that intends to study an issue, a situation or a problem needs to prepare a basic framework of methodology to be adopted in the field. The framework should contain the answers to the following questions:

- What are the major themes or issues for appraisal?
- What are the sub-themes or issues that need to be probed?
- What are the data or information requirements in order to have an insight into each sub-theme or issue?
- What are the methods to be adopted to collect the required data and information?
- How are the methods going to be sequenced?

An illustrative methodology on selected major themes in areas such as livelihood analysis, poverty assessment, vulnerability analysis, hunger analysis, institutional analysis, participatory monitoring and evaluation has been presented. The methodology suggested is tentative and flexible. The PRA team while practising the methodology in the field can adapt the methodology depending on the local situation and condition. However, they should keep in mind and strictly follow the basic tenets of PRA.

Glossary

Access	An opportunity in practice to use a resource, store or service or to obtain information on material, technology, employment, food or income.
Accountability	The state of being accountable; liability to be called on to render an account; the responsibility to someone or for some activity.
Action research	Can be described as a family of research methodologies that pursue action (or change) and research (or understanding) at the same time. It is 'learning by doing'.
Appropriate imprecision	Implies not measuring what need not be measured or more accurately than needed.
Capability	The quality of being capable; the ability to do something.
Carrying capacity	The population that can be supported indefinitely by an ecosystem without destroying the ecosystem.
Case study	An in-depth and a comprehensive study of a person, a social group, an episode, a process, a situation, a programme, a community, an institution or any other social unit.
Chain of interviews	An interview which may result in a series of interviews with different persons on the same subject.
Chance encounters	Encounters with those in a community who are met during the transects. They know something of a situation or condition, for example, woodcutters, minor forest produce collectors in forest.
Civil society	An intermediate realm situated between the state and the household, populated by organised groups or associations which are separate from the state; enjoy some autonomy in relation with state; and are formed voluntarily by members of the society to protect or extend their interests, values or identities.
Client	The receiver or beneficiary of an output of a process, either internal or external to a hospital or an organisational unit. A client could be a person, a department, clinic, etc.
Community	A social group of any size whose members reside in a specific locality, share the same government regime and often have a common cultural and historical heritage.

Complex	That which has many parts, categories, linkages and relationships (*i*) within a system and/or (*ii*) between it and its parts and the surrounding environment.
Consensus	General agreement reached within a group.
Constraint	Forces that hinder reaching an outcome or the solution to a problem.
Criteria	Standards against which something can be judged or assessed.
Data	Highly specific quantitative measurements, usually numeric, which can be compared to standards or norms directly or can be combined with other measurements to produce new information for comparison with standards or norms.
Data collection	Gathering facts on how a process works and/or how a process is working from the customer's point of view. All data collection is driven by knowledge of the process and guided by statistical principles.
Deprivation	Lacking what is needed for well-being. Deprivation has dimensions which are physical, social, economic, political and psychological/spiritual. It includes forms of disadvantage such as social inferiority, physical weakness, isolation, poverty, vulnerability, powerlessness and humiliation.
Development	To make something better than it was. It means 'to improve'.
Diagram	A simple schematic device which presents information in a readily understandable form.
Direct observation	A technique which relies on directly observing the field objects, events, processes, relationships or people and recording this mentally and in note or diagrammatic form.
Diverse	Having variety, differences, with many different things and/or forms of the same type of thing.
Emic	Expressing the views, concepts, categories and values of insiders.
Empowerment	A process where people can make a choice and take actions on their own behalf with self-confidence, from a position of economic, political and social strength.
Epistemology	The theory of knowledge, especially with regard to its methods, validity and scope. Epistemology is the investigation of what distinguishes justified belief from opinion.
Etic	Expressing the views, concepts, categories and values of outsiders.
Evaluation	A process that attempts to determine, as systematically and objectively as possible, the relevance, effectiveness and impact of activities in light of the objectives.
Flowchart	A graphical representation of the flow of a process.
Gender	The social descriptions, roles and responsibilities attached to women and men.
Hamlet	A cluster of houses, which is not recognised as an administration unit.
Ill-being	The experience of a bad quality of life.

Impacts	The long-term socio-economic results or changes that usually happen beyond the life of the project and are attributable to the achievement of outcomes.
Indicator	A way to measure, indicate or point out with more or less exactness. It is something that is a sign, symptom or index of. It is something used to show virtually the condition of a system. An indicator provides, wherever possible, a clearly defined unit of measurement and a target detailing the quantity, quality and timing.
Information	Quantitative data and/or qualitative facts organised in such a way as to allow rational judgements to be made in light of a desired set of goals.
Input	The resources necessary to carry out a process.
Intervention	Any programme or project or other planned effort designed to produce change in a target population.
Key informants	Persons in a community who are aware of the various aspects related to the life and conditions of the village and who are willing to share such information with outsiders.
Key probe	An in-depth analysis of a problem, issue, situation, condition, etc.
Livelihood	A means of living, and the capabilities, assets and activities required for it.
Logical framework analysis	An analytical presentational and management tool, which can help planners and managers to plan, monitor and evaluate development projects or programme intervention.
Matrix methods	A consensus development technique. A group of people who are familiar with the problem at hand are asked individually to array a list of potential responses to a problem into a preferred order based on a specified set of criteria for the solution. Through various scoring techniques, individual preferences are combined to form a group preference.
Methods	A systematic procedure, technique or mode of inquiry employed by a particular discipline.
Monitoring	The continuous or periodic surveillance over the implementation of an activity, to ensure that the input delivery, work schedules, targeted outputs and other required actions are proceeding according to plan.
Non-governmental organisation	A self-governing body of the people who have joined together voluntarily to study or act for the betterment of the community.
Norm	A level of performance that is deemed acceptable.
Objective	The operational articulation of the purpose and aims of an activity, representing the desired state, which the activity is expected to achieve.
Optimal ignorance	Implies knowing what is not worth knowing.
Outcomes	The specific measurable institutional or community-level results that will be produced by the end date of a project such as new programmes or processes that will be sustained after the life of the project. Outcomes are the logical results of project outputs.

Outputs	The immediate measurable results necessary to produce the outcomes. Outputs are direct consequences of the implemented activities.
Participation	The voluntary involvement of people in a self-determined change; people's involvement in decision-making process about what to be done and by whom.
Participatory deliberation	An approach to making or informing decisions which is participatory (in that it includes all those with an interest, especially often-excluded groups) and deliberative (in that it prioritises an effective communication between different perspectives and rests on qualitative judgement rather than quantitative analysis).
Participatory micro-planning	It is a methodology that allows individuals to perform the task of situation analysis, comprehend the complexity of problems, strategise and solve effectively personal and collective problems.
Pluralistic	This refers to a situation in which many diverse viewpoints and interests are afforded equal status and attention, without attempts to reduce them to a single 'consensus' or 'majority' view.
Policy appraisal	A general term for the business of assessing different policy options in advance of a policy decision and which includes qualitative deliberation as well as quantitative assessment or analysis. Contrasts with 'evaluation', which tends to come after the decision.
Poor	It has its common and wide meaning. This goes beyond its use as the adjective for poverty to include the broader sense of being deprived, in a bad condition and lacking basic needs.
Poverty	A condition in the lack of physical necessities, assets and income. It includes, but is more than, income poverty. Poverty can be distinguished from other dimensions of deprivation.
Power	Can be defined as the degree of control over material, human intellectual and financial resources exercised by the different sections of the community.
Problem	Existence of a gap between a desired condition (or level of condition) and the condition that actually exists.
Problem statement	A concise description of a process in need of improvement, its boundaries, the general area of concern where quality improvement should begin and why work on the improvement is a priority.
Process	The way individuals or organisations interact, learn, assess information, gauge opportunities and solve problems and make decisions to reach their goals. A process is integrated, multi-faceted and systemic.
Programme	An organised set of activities, projects, process or services directed towards the attainment of specific objectives. The time period of a programme is generally long-term, of ten years and above.

Project	An undertaking that is designed to achieve certain specific objectives with a given budget and within a specific period.
Project goal	Refers to wider and higher-level objectives and to which the project is designed to contribute. It is a statement of intention to be achieved or reached.
Quality	The degree to which the actual performance or achievement corresponds to the set standards.
Ranking	To determine the relative position of a problem, a cause or a solution based on criteria.
Secondary data	Data acquired by other people at an earlier time and which is relevant to the area and/or subject of study and is available in published or unpublished form.
Self-help group (SHG)	A formalised group of twenty to twenty-five people voluntarily formed on the basis of affinity who meet regularly for the purpose of achieving a common objective through mutual support. They contribute to their common saving fund, lend credit to the members and plan development activities in order to develop skills, knowledge and confidence.
Social audit	A local public review of the quality of government decision making.
Stakeholders	Individuals or organisations directly or indirectly affected by the implementation and results of social and development programmes facilitated or promoted or implemented.
Sustainability	Development that meets the needs of the present without compromising the ability of future generation to meet their own needs.
System	A set of interrelationship between organisation and actors in a process for common purpose.
Tool	A tangible device used to help accomplish the purpose of a technique.
Triangulation	Triangulation is a form of cross-checking for validating the data and information collected.
Trustworthiness	The quality of deserving to be believed: how believable a representation of reality deserves to be.
Village	A cluster of communities comprising a group of houses and associated buildings larger than a hamlet.
Vulnerability	Exposure and defencelessness. It has two sides: the external side of exposure to shocks, stress and risk; and the internal side of defencelessness, meaning a lack of means to cope without incurring damaging loss.
Watershed	A geographical unit encompassing the land that lies within a drainage basin, from the ridge line of the catchment area to the drainage point or outlet.
Well-being	The experience of a good quality of life.

Bibliography

Absalom, Elkanah, Robert Chambers, Sheelu Francis, Bara Gueye, Irene Guijt, Sam Joseph, Deb Johnson, Charity Kabutha, Mahmuda Rahman Khan, Robert Leurs, Jimmy Mascarenhas, Pat Norrish, Michel Pimbert, Jules Pretty, Mallika Samaranayake, Ian Scoones, Meera Kaul Shah, Parmesh Shah, Devika Tamang, John Thompson, Ginni Tym and Alice Welbourn. 1995. 'Sharing our Concerns and Looking to the Future', *PLA Notes*, 22: 5–10 (Feb.).

Adnan, S. and A. Barret. 1992. *People's Participation, NGOs and the Flood Action Plan*. Dhaka: Research and Advisory Services.

Ahmad, Bashir, Nazia Tabassum and Parsa Arbab Gill. 2003. 'Diagnosing Priorities for Rural Women's Welfare through Participatory Approaches in Punjab, Pakistan', *PLA Notes*, 46: 73–76 (Feb.).

Alcorn, Janis B. 2000. 'Key to Unleash Mapping's Good Magic', *PLA Notes*, 39: 10–13 (Oct.).

Anbalagan, K., G. Karthikeyan and N. Narayanasamy. 1997. 'Assessing Pollution from Tannery Effluents in a South Indian Village', *PLA Notes*, 30: 3–6 (Oct.).

Appleton, Judith. 1990. 'Nutrition and RRA', *RRA Notes*, 8: 6–9 (Jan.).

Ardon, Patricia. 2002. 'Participation for Whom?', *PLA Notes*, 43: 29–30 (Feb.).

Arnstein, Sherry. 1969. 'A Ladder of Citizen Participation in the USA', *Journal of the American Institute of Planners*, 35 (4): 216–25.

Ashby, J.A. 1990. *Evaluation Technology with Farmers: A Handbook*. Cali. Colombia: CIAT.

Atkinson, S. 1992. 'Interviews with Key Informants and Household Surveys: Central Ethiopia', *Disaster*, 16 (3): 255–58.

Banerjee, Shyamal. 1981. *Principles and Practice of Management*, p. 175. New Delhi: Oxford & IBH Publishing Co.

Banlina, F.T. and L.Y. Tung. 1992. 'Farmi's Experiences of Wealth Ranking in the Philippines; Different Farmers Have Different Needs', *RRA Notes*, 15: 48–50 (May).

Beebe, J. 1987 'Rapid Appraisal: The Evolution of the Concept and the Definition of Issues in KKU'. *Proceedings of the International Conference on Rapid Rural Appraisal Systems Research and Farming Systems Research Project*, University of Kohn Kaen, Kohn Kaen, Thailand.

Bhattacharjee, Paranita. 2001. 'Social Mapping at Thenganayakanahalli Village', *PLA Notes*, 41: 33–35 (Aug.).

Biggs, S. 1989. 'Resource-Poor Farmers' Participation in Research: A Synthesis of Experience from Nine National Agricultural Research System OFCUE', Comparative Study Paper 3. The Hague: International Service for National Agricultural Research.

Brueger, Richard A. 1998. *Analyzing and Reporting Focus Group Results.* New Delhi: Sage Publications.

Busch, R. 1983. *Two Ears of Corn: A Guide to People Centred Agricultural Improvement.* World Neighbours: Oklahoma City.

Chambers, Robert. 1981. 'Rapid Rural Appraisal—Rationale', Discussion Paper 155. Brighton, UK: Institute of Development Studies.

———. 1983. *Rural Development: Putting the Last First.* London: Longman.

———. 1988. 'Direct Matrix Ranking in Kenya and West Bengal', *RRA Notes,* 1: 13–18 (Jun.).

———. 1992. 'Rural Appraisal: Rapid, Relaxed and Participatory', Discussion Paper 311. Brighton: Institute of Development Studies.

———. 1994a. 'Participatory Rural Appraisal: Analysis of Experience', *World Development,* 22 (9): 1253–68.

———. 1994b. 'Twenty-one Ways of Forming Groups', *RRA Notes,* 19: 100–104 (Feb.).

———. 1994c. 'Participatory Rural Appraisal: Challenges, Potentials and Paradigm', *World Development,* 22 (10): 1437–54.

———. 1995. 'Making the Best of Going to Scale', *PLA Notes,* 24: 57–61 (Oct.).

———. 1997. *Whose Reality Counts: Putting the First Last.* London: Intermediate Technology Publications.

———. 2003. 'Participation and Numbers', *PLA Notes,* 47: 6–12 (Aug.).

———. 2004. 'Reflections and Directions: A Personal Note', *PLA Notes,* 50: 23–34 (Oct.).

———. 2006. 'Rural Appraisal: Participatory and Relaxed'. London: Institute of Development Studies, University of Sussex.

Chambers, Robert, Arnold Pacey and Lori Ann Thrupp (eds). 1990. *Farmer First: Farmer Innovation and Agricultural Research.* London: Intermediate Technology Publications.

Cohen, John M. and T. Norman Uphoff. 1977. 'Rural Development: Participatory Concept and Measures for Project Design', *Rural Development Monograph No. 2.* Ithaca, NY: Center for International Studies, Cornell University.

Conway, Gordon R. 1989. 'Notes from the Field', *RRA Notes,* 1: 3 (Jun.).

Conway, Gordon R., Jennifer A. McCracken and Jules N. Pretty. 1989. *Training Notes for Agro Eco System Analysis and Rapid Rural Appraisal.* London: IIED.

Cornwall, Andrea. 1992. 'Body Mapping in Health RRA/PRA', *RRA Notes* 16: 69–76 (Jul.).

Cornwall, Andrea and Gerett Pratt. 2003. 'The Trouble with PRA: Reflections and Dilemmas of Quality', *RRA Notes,* 47: 38–44 (Aug.).

Cornwall, Andrea and Irene Guijt. 2004. 'Shifting Perceptions, Changing Practices in PRA: From Infinite Innovation to the Quest for Quality', *PLA Notes* 50: 160–67 (Oct.).

Cornwall, Andrea and Rachel Jewkes. 1995. 'What is Participatory Research?' *Social Science and Medicine,* 41 (12): 1667–76.

DANIDA 1995. 'Methods for Evaluation of Poverty Oriented Aid Interventions', Report of seminar organised by the Ministry of Foreign Affairs and DANIDA, 5–6 July 1995, Copenhagen. Copenhagen: DANIDA.

Datta, Dipankar and Iqbal Hussain. 2003. 'Targeting the Extreme Poor: Field Experience from Dimla, Bangadesh', *PLA Notes*, 47: 55–60 (Aug.).

Davis, Robert. 1997. 'Combining Rapid Appraisal with Quantitative Methods: An Example from Mauritonia', *PLA Notes*, 28: 33–36 (Oct.).

Dayal, Rekha, Christine Van Wijk and Nilanjand Mukherjee. 2000. 'Methodology for Participatory Assessment', *Water and Sanitation Programme*. Washington, DC: World Bank.

Dessalegn, Debebe. 1990. 'The Role of Community Participation in RRA Methods in Ethiopia', *RRA Notes*, 8: 15–18 (Jan.).

Devavaram John, Nalini, J. Vimalanathan, Abdul Sukkar, Krishnan, A.P. Mayandi and Karunanidhi. 1991. 'PRA for Rural Resource Management', *RRA Notes*, 13: 102–11 (Aug.).

Dunn, Tony. 1993. 'Learning to Use RRA and PRA to Improve the Activities of Two Land Care Groups in Australia', *RRA Notes* 18: 21–32 (Jun.).

Dunn, Tony and Allan McMillan. 1991. 'Action Research: The Application of RRA to Learn about Issues of Concern in Land Care Areas near Wagga, NSW', Paper presented at the conference on Agriculture, Education and Information Transfer, Murrumbigee College of Agriculture, NSW, 30 Sept.–2 Oct.

Dwaraki B.R. and N. Narayanasamy. 1994. 'PRA for a Vibrant Cooperative Sector', *Development in Practice*, 4 (1): 63–66.

Ejigu, Jonfa, Haile Mariam Tebeje, Tadesse Dessalegn, Hailu Halala and Andrea Cornwall. 1991. 'Participatory Modelling in North Omo, Ethiopia: Investigating the Perceptions of Different Groups through Models', *RRA Notes*, 14: 24–25 (Dec.).

FAO. 1997. *Participation in Practice: Lessons from the FAO's People's Participation Programme*. Rome: FAO.

Farnworth, Cathy Rozel. 1998. 'Musings on the Use of Chapatti Diagram', *PLA Notes*, 31: 9–12 (Feb.).

Fielding, William J., Janet Riley and Ben A. Oyejola. 1998. 'Ranks Are Statistics: Some Advice for their Interpretations', *PLA Notes*, 33: 35–39 (Oct.).

Firdaus, Ali A. 2005. 'People's Participation: A Framework', *Asia-Pacific Business Review*, 1(1): 1–7 (Jan.–Jun.).

Friedmann, John. 1996. *Empowerment: The Politics of Alternative Development*. Oxford: Blackwell.

Gill, G. 1991. 'But How Does It Compare with Real Data', *RRA Notes*, 14: 5–13 (Dec.).

Gill, Gerard J. 1993. 'Are Some "Participatory" Techniques Culturally Biased? (or, Are We Hooked on Mom's Apple Pie?)', *RRA Notes*, 18: 12–14 (Jun.).

Grandin, Barbara E. 1998. *Wealth Ranking in Smallholder Communities: A Field Manual*. Nottingham: Intermediate Technology Publications.

Grosvenor, Ruth Alsop. 1989. 'Wealth Ranking in a Caste Area of India', *RRA Notes*, 4: 5–12 (Feb.).

Groverman, Verona. 1990. 'Wealth Ranking in Swaziland: A Method to Identify the Poorest', *RRA Notes*, 9: 6–11 (Aug.).

Gubbels, Peter and Catheryn Koss. 2000. *From the Roots Up: Strengthening Organisational Capacity through Guided Self-Assessment*. Oklahoma: World Neighbour.

Guijt, Irene. 1992a. 'A User's Note: Wealth Ranking by Cards', *RRA Notes*, 15: 65–69 (May).

———. 1992b. 'The Elusive Poor: A Wealth of Ways to Find Them', *RRA Notes*, 15: 7–13 (May).

Guijt, Irene, Mae Arevelo and Kiko Saladoves. 1998. 'Tracking Change Together', *PLA Notes*, 31: 28–36 (Feb.).

Guijt, Irene and Ian Scoones (eds). 1991. *Rapid Rural Appraisal for Local Level Planning, Wallo Province, Ethiopia*. London: IIED.

Guijt, Irene and Jules N. Pretty. 1992. *Participatory Rural Appraisal for Farmer Participatory Research in Panjab (Pakistan)* (Training workshop report, Sept.). London: IIED.

Hanson, Lori and Cindy Hanson. 2001. 'Transforming Participatory Facilitation: Reflections from Practice', *PLA Notes*, 41: 29–32 (Aug.).

Hardcastle, James, Barney Long, Le Van Lanh, Giacomo Rambaldi and Do Quo Son. 2004. 'The Use of Participatory Three Dimensional Modeling in Community Based Planning in Quang Nam Province, Vietnam', *PLA Notes*, 49: 70–76 (Apr.).

Hari, M. John. 1992. 'In True Partnership with People: Participatory Action Research and the Poor', *SEARCH News*, VII, (1) (Jan.–Mar.).

Heller, Frank, Eugene Pusic, George Strauss and Bernhard Wilpert. 1998. *Organizational Participation: Myth and Reality*. London: Oxford University Press.

Hobbs, Andrew and Mary Simasiku. 2000. 'Participatory Learning and Action Requires Good Facilitators—Who Aren't Always Around', *PLA Notes*, 37: 63–66 (Feb.).

Hope, Anne and Sally Timmel. 1992. *Training for Transformation. Book 2: A Handbook for Community Workers*. Gweru, Zimbabwe: Mambo Press.

Huub, Gaymans and Yani Maskoen. 1993. 'Community Self Survey', *RRA Notes*, 18: 15–20 (Jun.).

IIED. 1991. 'Farmer Participatory Research in North Ethiopia', *Report of Training Course in Rapid Rural Appraisal for Local Level Planning*. London: IIED.

———. 1992. *From Input to Impact: Participatory Rural Appraisal for Action Aid, The Gambia*. London: IIED.

———. 1994. *Whose Eden? An Overview of Community Approaches to Wildlife Management*. London: IIED and ODA.

Inglis, Andy. 1991. 'Harvesting Local Forest Knowledge: A Comparison of PRA with Conventional Surveys', *RRA Notes*, 12: 32–40 (Jul.).

Institute of Development Studies. 1995. *PRA Methods Pack*. Brighton, UK: University of Sussex.

Ishola, Gbenga, Wumi Adekunle, Temple Jagha, Bola Abedimeji, Yemi Olawale and Lucy Eniola. 2003. 'Using PLA in Understanding and Planning an Adolescent Life Planning and Reproductive Health Programme in Nigeria', *PLA Notes*, 46: 62–66 (Feb.).

Jones, Carolyn. 1996. *PRA Methods Pack*. Brighton, UK: Institute of Development Studies.

Kaplan, Allan. 1999. 'The Development of Capacity', *NGLS Development Dossier*. Geneva: UN Non-governmental Liaison Service.

Kersten, Stephany. 1996. 'Matrix Ranking: A Means to Discussion', *PLA Notes*, 26: 21–25 (Jun.).

Krishnaswami, O. R. 2002. *Methodology of Research in Social Sciences*. Mumbai: Himalaya Publishing House.

Kumar, Alok. 1992. 'Trends in Health Care, *RRA Notes*, 16: 48–50 (Jul.).

Kumar, Somesh (ed.). 1996. *ABC of PRA: Attitude and Behaviour Change.* A report on the proceedings of South–South Workshop on Attitudes and Behaviour in PRA. Patna: Action Aid India and PRAXIS.

———. 1998. '3D Venn Diagram in PRA: A Methodological Innovation', *PLA Notes*, 31: 76–77 (Feb.).

———. 1999. 'Force Field Analysis Applications in PRA', *PLA Notes*, 36: 17–23 (Oct.).

———. 2003. *Methods for Community Participation.* New Delhi: Vistaar Publications.

Kvale, S. 1996. *Interviews: An Introduction to Qualitative Research Interviewing.* Thousands Oaks, CA: Sage Publications.

Lammerink, Marc P. and Eveline Bolt. 2006. *Supporting Community Management: A Manual for Training in Community Management in the Water and Sanitation Sector.* Delft, The Netherlands: IRC.

Laws, Sophie, Caroline Harper and Rachel Marcus. 2003. *Research for Development: A Practical Guide.* New Delhi: Vistaar Publications.

Leay, Sarah. 2003. 'Are We Targeting the Poor: Lessons from Malawi', *PLA Notes*, 47: 19–24 (Aug.).

Leurs, Robert. 1998. 'Current Challenges Facing Participatory Rural Appraisal', *Public Administration and Development*, 16: 57–72.

Lewin, Kurt. 1951. *Field Theory in Social Science.* New York: Harper and Row.

Lightfoot, Clive, Dennis Garrity, V. P. Singh, R. K. Singh, Nancy Axinn, K.C. John, P. Mishra, Ahamed Salman and Robert Chambers. 1990. *Training Resource Book for Participatory Experimental Design.* Faizabad: Narendra Dev University of Agriculture and Technology.

Locke, Edwin. 1968. 'Toward a Theory of Task Motivation and Incentives', *Organizational Behavior and Human Performance*, 3: 157–89.

MANAGE. 1995. 'Farmer Participatory Research', *Extension Digest*, 3 (3).

Marindo-Ranganai, Ravai. 1995. 'Comparison Diagram for Demographic Data Collection: Examples from the Tembomvura, Zimbabwe', *RRA Notes*, 22: 53–61 (Feb.).

Mascarenhas, James. 1991. 'Participatory Learning Methods: Recent Experience from MYRADA and South India', *RRA Notes*, 13: 49–57 (Aug.).

———. 1992. 'Transects in PRA', *PRA-PALM Series.* Bangalore: MYRADA.

———. 1996. 'Interviewing in PRA'. *PRA-PALM Series.* Bangalore: MYRADA.

Mascarenhas, James and P.D. Prem Kumar. 1991. 'Participatory Mapping and Modelling: User's Notes', *RRA Notes*, 12: 9–20 (Jul.).

Mascarenhas, James, Parmesh Shah, Sam Joseph, Ravi Jayakaran, John Devavaram, Vidya Ramachandran, Aloysius Fernandez, Robert Chambers and Jules Pretty (eds). 1991. *Participatory Rural Appraisal: Proceedings of the 1991 Bangalore PRA Trainers Workshop (RRA Notes*, 13: 10–48). Bangalore: MYRADA.

McCracken, J.A. 1988. *Participatory Rural Appraisal in Gujarat: A Trial Model for the Aga Khan Rural Support Programmme.* London: IIED.

McCracken, J.A., Jules N. Pretty and Gordon R. Conway. 1988. *An Introduction to Rapid Rural Appraisal for Agriculture Development.* London: IIED.

McGee, Rosemary. 1997. 'Ethnography and Rapid Appraisal in Doctoral Research on Poverty', *PLA Notes*, 28: 55–58 (Feb.).

Mearns, Robin. 1988. 'Direct Matrix Ranking (DMR) in Highland Papua New Guinea', *RRA Notes*, 3: 11–14 (Dec.).

Mearns, Robin, D. Shombodon, G. Narangerel, U. Turul, A. Enkhamgalan, B. Myagmarzhav, A. Bayanjargal and B. Bekhsuren. 1992. 'Direct and Indirect Uses of Wealth Ranking in Mongolia' *RRA Notes*, 15: 29–38 (May).

Meyer, Marian and Naresh Singh. 1997. 'Two Approaches to Evaluating the Outcome of Development Project', *Development in Practice*, 7 (1): 59–64 (Feb.).

Mikkelsen, Britha. 1995. *Methods for Development Work and Research: A Guide for Practitioners*. New Delhi: Sage Publications.

———. 2005. *Methods for Development Work and Research: A New Guide for Practitioners*. New Delhi: Sage Publications.

Mitchell, John and Hugo Slim. 1991. 'The Bias of Interviews', *RRA Notes*, 10: 20–22 (Feb.).

Montgomery, R. 1995. 'Force Field Analysis: Identifying Forces For and Against Change', *PLA Notes*, 23: 11–15 (Jun.).

Morgan, David L. 1997. *Focus Group as Qualitative Research*. New Delhi: Sage Publications.

———. 1998. *The Focus Group Guidebook*. New Delhi: Sage Publications.

Mosse, David. 1995. 'Authority, Gender and Knowledge: Theoretical Reflection on PRA', *Economic and Political Weekly*, 30 (11): 569–78 (18 Mar.).

Mosse, David and Mona Mehta. 1993. 'Genealogies as a Method of Social Mapping in PRA', *RRA Notes*, 18: 5–11 (Jun.).

Mukherjee, Amitava. 1995. *Participatory Rural Appraisal Methods and Application in Rural Planning*. New Delhi: Vikas Publishing.

Mukherjee, Neela. 1992. 'Villagers' Perception of Rural Poverty through the Mapping Methods of PRA', *RRA Notes*, 15: 21–26 (May).

———. 1994a. 'Livestock, Livelihood, and Drought: A PRA Exercise in Botswana', *RRA Notes*, 20: 127–30 (Apr.).

———. 1994b. *Participatory Rural Appraisal: Methodology and Applications*. New Delhi: Concept Publishing Company.

———. 1997. *Participatory Rural Appraisal and Questionnaire Survey*. New Delhi: Concept Publishing Company.

Mulhall, Abigail and Peter Taylor. 1998. 'Using Participatory Research Methods to Explore the Learning Environment of Rural Primary School Pupils', *PLA Notes*, 33: 11–16 (Oct.).

Murthy, Ranjani K. 1995. 'Gender and Participatory Approaches: Implications and Experiences', in Anna Robinson, *PRA and Gender (Abstracts)* (unpublished). Brighton, UK: Institute of Development Studies.

MYRADA. 2000. *A Manual for Capacity Building of Self-Help Groups*. Bangalore: MYRADA.

Narayanasamy, N. 1993. 'PRA Exercise in Indian Village: A Retrospective Evaluation of the Process', *RRA Notes*, 19: 19–23 (Dec.).

———. 2001. 'PLA Menu for the Study of Women Leadership at the Grassroot Level', *Quarterly Journal of the Institute for the Study of Developing Areas*, 11(2): 53–69 (Apr.–Jun.).

Narayanasamy, N. and M.P. Boraian. 1993. 'Community Participation in Small and Big Villages', *PLA Notes*, 18: 44–46 (Jun.).

Narayanasamy, N. and M.P. Boraian. 2005. *Participatory Rural Appraisal: The Experience of NGOs in South India.* New Delhi: Concept Publishing Company.

Narayanasamy, N., B.R. Dwaraki, B. Tamilmani and R. Ramesh. 1996. 'Whither Children's Hour?', *PLA Notes*, 25: 65–69 (Feb.).

Narayanasamy, N., B.R. Dwaraki, M.P. Boraian and R. Ramesh. 1998. *Analysing Community Problems: Tentacles of PRA Methodology.* Mumbai: Himalaya Publishing House.

Narayanasamy, N. and S. Manivel. 1997. 'The Need to Crosscheck the Results of Wealth Ranking', *PLA Notes*, 29: 89–91 (Jun.).

———. 2002. 'Micro Plan for Mandapam Block' (unpublished paper). Gandhigram: GRI.

———. 2004. 'SGSY Assisted SHG's in Theni District: An Evaluation' (unpublished paper). Gandhigram: GRI.

Narayanasamy, N. and R. Ramesh. 1996. 'Process Observation in PRA: Guidelines and Reflections', *PLA Notes*, 26: 56–58 (Jun.).

National Council of Applied Economic Research. 1992. *Evaluating the Impact of Commercialization of Rural Dairy Sector: An Application of RRA Technology.* New Delhi: National Council of Applied Economic Research.

Oakley, P. 1991. *Projects with People: The Practice of Participation in Rural Development.* Geneva: International Labour Office.

Paul, S. 1986. 'Community Participation in Development Projects: The World Bank Experience', World Bank Discussion Paper 6. Washington, DC: World Bank.

Potten, David. 1989. 'Monitoring and Evaluation—PBME and Rapid Rural Appraisal', *RRA Notes*, 7: 45–47 (Sept.).

PRA Unit, GRI. 1993a. 'PRA in Kathiranampatti Village' (unpublished paper), Gandhigram.

———. 1993b. 'PRA in Kasturinaickenpatti' (unpublished paper), Gandhigram.

———. 1995a. *PRA Retreat in a Rural Setting* (Workshop report), May. Gandhigram.

———. 1995b. 'Baseline Survey, DANIDA-aided Comprehensive Watershed Development Programme' (unpublished paper), Tirunelveli.

———. 1995c. 'PRA in a Harijan Colony' (unpublished paper), Gandhigram.

———. 1995d. 'PRA-based Baseline Survey for Comprehensive Watershed Development Programme' (unpublished paper), Gandhigram.

———. 1995e. 'PRA Training in a Village' (unpublished paper), Gandhigram.

———. 1996a. 'Priming PRA for Project Formulation' (unpublished paper), Gandhigram.

———. 1996b. 'PRA in a Scattered Village' (unpublished paper), Gandhigram.

———. 1997. 'Planning for Hunger Free Area Programme' (unpublished paper), Gandhigram.

———. 1998a. 'PRA for Assessing the Development of Women Leadership' (unpublished paper), Gandhigram.

———. 1998b. 'Hunger Free Area Programme' (unpublished paper), Gandhigram.

———. 2000. 'Status of Ooranis: PRA Based Analysis' (unpublished paper), Gandhigram.

———. 2001a. 'Decision Making and Effectiveness of Leaders' (unpublished paper), Gandhigram.

———. 2001b. 'Prevention of Female Infanticide in a Selected Block', (unpublished paper), p. 60, Gandhigram.

PRA Unit, GRI. 2002. 'Report of the Mid-term Evaluation of Integrated Tribal Development Programme' (unpublished report), Gandhigram (Feb.).

Pretty, Jules N. 1989a. 'Ranking—Wealth Ranking in Sudan', *RRA Notes,* 7: 25–28 (Sept.).

———. 1989b. 'Diagram', *RRA Notes,* 7: 4–5 (Sept.).

———. 1995. *Regenerating Agriculture: Policies and Practices for Sustainability and Self-reliance.* London: Earth Scan Publication.

Pretty, Jules N. and Ian Scoones (eds). 1989. *Rapid Rural Appraisal for Economics: Exploring Incentives for Trade Management in Sudan.* London: IIED.

Pretty, Jules N. and Irene Guijt (eds). 1992. *PRA for Farmers Participatory Research in Panjab (Pakistan),* Report of the training workshop organized by Pakistan–Swiss Potato Development Project, Gujranwala, Punjab Province, Pakistan (June). London: IIED.

Pretty, Jules N., Irene Guijt, Ian Scoones and John Thompson. 1995. *Participatory Learning and Action: A Trainer's Guide.* London: IIED.

Pretty, Jules N., S. Subramanian, N. Kempu Chetty, D. Ananthakrishnan, C. Jayanthi, S. Muralikrishnasamy and K. Renganayaki. 1992. 'Finding the Poorest in a Tamil Nadu Village: A Sequence of Mapping and Wealth Ranking', *RRA Notes,* 15 (May).

Rambaldi, G. and J. Callosa-Tarr. 2000. *Manual on Participatory 3-D Modeling for Natural Resource Management.* Quezon City, The Philippines: NIPAP, PAWB-DENR.

Ramesh, R., N. Narayanasamy and M.P. Boraian. 1997. 'Getting Fisherfolk off the Hook: An Exploratory PRA in South India', *PLA Notes,* 30: 54–58 (Oct.).

Rhoades, Robert E. 1987. 'Basic Field Techniques for Rapid Rural Appraisal', *Proceedings of the International Conference on Rapid Rural Appraisal,* Thailand.

Richards, Michael, Jonathan Davies and William Cavendish. 1999. 'Can PRA Methods Be Used to Collect Economic Data. A Non-timber Forest Product Case Study from Zimbabwe', *PLA Notes,* 36: 34–40 (Oct.).

Richards, Paul. 1995. 'Participatory Rural Appraisal: A Quick and Dirty Critique', *PLA Notes,* 24: 13–16.

Roos, Mattilda and Mampore Mahalle. 1998. 'Investigating Local Markets Using PRA', *PLA Notes,* 33: 45–53 (Oct.).

Sarch, Marie-Therese. 1992. 'Wealth Ranking in the Gambia: Which Households Participated in the FITT Programme', *PRA Notes,* 15: 14–20 (May).

Schreckenberg, Kathrin. 1995. 'The Respective Merits of PRA and Conventional Methods for Long-term Research', *PLA Notes* 24: 74–77 (Oct.).

Scoones, Ian. 1989. 'Preference and Direct Matrix Rankings, Sudan', *RRA Notes,* 7: 28–30 (Sept.).

———. 2005. 'PRA and Anthropology: Challenges and Dilemmas', *PLA Notes,* 24: 17–20 (Oct.).

Selvam, V., K.K. Ravichandran, V.M. Karunagaran, K.G. Mani and G. Evanjalin Jessie Beula. 2003. *Joint Mangrove Management in Tamil Nadu; Process, Experiences and Prospects*. Chennai: M.S. Swaminathan Research Foundation.

Sen, Siddhartha. 1993. 'Defining Non-profit Sector', Working Paper 12. Baltimore: The Johns Hopkins University, Institute for Policy Studies.

Shah, Paramesh, Girish Bharadwaj and Ranjit Ambastha. 1991. 'Farmers as Analysts and Facilitators to Participatory Rural Appraisal and Planning', *RRA Notes*, 13: 84–94 (Aug.).

Simanowitz, Anton. 1999. 'Pushing the Limits of Mapping and Wealth Ranking', *PLA Notes*, 34: 4–8 (Feb.).

Singh, Katar. 1995. *Rural Development: Principles, Policies and Management*. New Delhi: Sage Publications.

Steele, Stephen F., AnneMarie Scarisbrick-Hauser and William J. Hauser. 1999. *Solution Centered Sociology: Addressing Problems through Applied Sociology*. New Delhi: Sage Publications.

Theis, J. and H.M. Grady. 1991. *Participatory Rural Appraisal for Community Development*. London: IIED and SCF.

Torres, Victor Hugo. 1998. 'Institutional Issues for Monitoring Local Development in Ecuador', *PLA Notes*, 31: 50–56 (Feb.).

Uphoff, N. 1992. *Local Institutions and Participation for Sustainable Development*, Gatekeepers Series SA31. London: IIED.

VeneKlasen, Lisa and Valerie Miller. 2002a. *A New Weave of Power, People and Politics*. Oklahoma City: World Neighbors.

———. 2002b. 'Causes, Consequences, and Solutions', *PLA Notes*, 43: 18–19 (Feb.).

Veneracion, Cynthia C. (ed.). 1989. *A Decade of Process Documentation Research: Reflection and Synthesis*. Manila: Institute of Philippine Culture, Ateneo De Manila University.

Vijayraghavan, R., S.R. Subramanian, Jules N. Pretty and K.C John (eds). 1992. *Participatory Rural Appraisal for Agriculture Research at Aruppukottai (Tamilnadu)*, p. 84. Coimbatore (India) and London: Tamilnadu Agricultural University and IIED.

Webb, Sidney and Beatrice Webb. 1932. *Methods of Social Study*. London: Longmans Green.

Welbourn, Alice. 1981. 'RRA and the Analysis of Difference', *RRA Notes*, 14: 14–23 (Dec.).

———. 1992a. 'A Note on the Use of Disease Problem Ranking with Relation to Socio-economic Well-being: An Example from Sierra Leone', *RRA Notes*, 16: 86–87 (Jul.).

———. 1992b. 'Rapid Rural Appraisal—Gender and Health: Alternative Ways of Listing the Needs', *IDS Bulletin*, 23 (1): 8–18.

White, Sarah and Jethro Pettit. 2004. 'Participatory Methods and Measurement of Well-being', *PLA Notes*, 50: 88–96 (Oct.).

White, Shirley A. 1991. *The Art of Facilitating Participation*. New Delhi: Sage Publications.

Whiteside, Martin. 1997. 'Two Cheers for PRA', *PLA Notes*, 28: 71–73 (Feb.).

Wignaraja, P. 1991. 'Towards Praxis and Participatory Development', in P. Wignaraja (ed.), *Participatory Development*, p. 202. Karachi: Oxford University Press.

Willmer, Abigail and Jennifer Ketzis. 1998. 'Participatory Gender Resource Mapping: A Case Study in a Rural Community in Honduras', *PLA Notes*, 33: 17–22 (Oct.).

World Bank. 1996. *The World Bank Participation Source Book, Environmentally Sustainable Development*. Washington, DC: World Bank.

———. 1999. 'Consultations with the Poor: Methodology Guide for the 20 Country Study for the World Development Report 2000–01', a study commissioned by the Poverty Reduction and Economic Management Network. Washington, DC: World Bank.

World Bank Development Research Group. 2003. *Evaluating Community Driven Development: A Review of the Evidence*. Washington, DC: World Bank.

Index